QUEER MOBILIZATIONS

Edited by Manon Tremblay

QUEER MOBILIZATIONS

Social Movement Activism and Canadian Public Policy

UBCPress · Vancouver · Toronto

23 22 21 20 19 18 17 16 15   5 4 3 2 1

Printed in Canada on FSC-certified ancient-forest-free paper
(100% post-consumer recycled) that is processed chlorine- and acid-free.

ISBN 978-0-7748-2907-6 (bound). – ISBN 978-0-7748-2908-3 (pbk.). –
ISBN 978-0-7748-2909-9 (pdf). – ISBN 978-0-7748-2910-6 (epub)

Cataloguing-in-publication data for this book is available from Library and Archives Canada.

Canadä

UBC Press gratefully acknowledges the financial support for our publishing program of the Government of Canada (through the Canada Book Fund), the Canada Council for the Arts, and the British Columbia Arts Council.

This book has been published with the help of a grant from the Canadian Federation for the Humanities and Social Sciences, through the Awards to Scholarly Publications Program, using funds provided by the Social Sciences and Humanities Research Council of Canada.

A reasonable attempt has been made to secure permission to reproduce all material used. If there are errors or omissions they are wholly unintentional and the publisher would be grateful to learn of them.

Cover photos (left to right, from top): Cynthia Flood and daughters Isabel and Margaret, Vancouver, 1978?, courtesy of Don Hann; National Gay Conference, Winnipeg, 1974, courtesy of Canadian Lesbian and Gay Archives (CLGA), 1986-032/02P(09); Stop Police Violence, photo by Gerald Hannon, courtesy of CLGA, 1983-018/26P(04); York Gay Alliance at National Gay Conference, Ottawa, 1975, photo by Gerald Hannon, courtesy of CLGA, 1986-032/02P(40); Geoff Meggs, Mike Lombardi, and Ellen Woodsworth at Gay Pride Parade, Vancouver, 2009, photo by Tilo Driessen, courtesy of the City of Vancouver; National Gay Conference, Toronto, 1978, courtesy of CLGA, 1986-032/10P(38)

UBC Press
The University of British Columbia
2029 West Mall
Vancouver, BC, V6T 1Z2
www.ubcpress.ca

Contents

Foreword

Canada has a long and rich history of queer organizing, and much of it has, until now, been untold and undocumented. Quebec and especially Ontario are well represented, but about the west and the east, much less is known. This comprehensive study of queer mobilization fills this gap by providing an overview of political activism from one end of the nation to the other. Focusing principally on the organizational and activist work of Canadians who identified with the gay liberation and subsequently gay equality movements that launched in the 1960s, this collection offers a valuable tool for understanding the similarities and the differences between regional organizations and politics. Seeing Canada as a series of regions stitched together rather than as a unified whole is an approach to Canadian history established in the early 1970s. *Queer Mobilizations* reminds us that this is as relevant today as ever. Only by making a concerted effort, as Manon Tremblay has here, to draw out the histories of the people and places east, west, and north of Ontario and Quebec (we shall have to wait for the history of the North) do we have the opportunity to see this period in its fullness.

Activism in Canada has been deeply influenced by events in the United States. The non-violent equal rights strategies adopted by the African American civil rights movement in the 1950s and '60s, the radical activism of the Yippies, anti-Vietnam war activists, the Black Panthers, and the New Left student movements of the 1960s helped shape the way Canadians and others responded to similar concerns on their own soil. Political and social organizations were formed on university campuses and in major cities, alternatives to the "bar scene" were built, and political strategies to contest queer oppression in law and everyday life were vigorously pursued.

In Canada, as in the United States, sexism divided lesbian and gay communities. Driven away by their treatment as second-class citizens, women channelled much more of their energy into struggles against (and for) pornography, against violence against women, and for reproductive rights even as they struggled against homophobia in the women's movement. In Canada Indigenous people and people of a heritage other than French and English contested the "two founding nations" myth and began organizing against state and social marginalization and oppression. Works by anti-colonial writers like Franz Fanon and Pierre Vallières were required reading. A good deal of early women's and gay liberation writing addressed race-based oppression as an extension of gay and women's oppression. As these movements became more and more focused on formal strategies to challenge laws and practices that targeted them as a group, attention to what we now call "intersectionality" waned.

The failure to sustain a critique of race has been rightfully characterized as an extension of white privilege. This critique is about much more than including people of colour and Indigenous people in an organization, which is tokenism at its best. It is about recognizing that racism actually changes the way oppression exerts itself, and the need to develop theories that take this into account. For example, when white gay liberationists launched a critique of the nuclear family and the church as sources of oppression, they did not see that for many people of colour, these very institutions were their source of strength in resisting racism. When white feminists defined sexual violence against women as a feminist issue, African American and Canadian feminists explained that any discussion about sexual violence had to address the way men in their community were targeted as sexual predators. As readers dive into this collection to learn about the remarkable achievements of lesbian, gay, and queer activists during the past forty years, we must take care not to simply acknowledge this critique and move on with business as usual, but to keep it in the forefront of our minds as we proceed.

These pages document a time when a large number of people experienced becoming part of the lesbian, gay, and queer community as finding "home" and "family." The profound stigma attached to same-sex and queer desire and to gender non-conformity – let's not forget that many early participants in pride marches wore paper bags over their heads to hide their identities – made finding a place where you could "be yourself" a deeply liberating experience. Most lesbians, gays, trans* people, and queers were delighted to partake in the expansion of spaces to hang out, dance, share a few drinks, and meet new lovers. Others made the political battle against oppression a centrepiece of their lives. Their activism was, in many ways, their primary lover. It is a cliché, to be sure, but no less true that to them – those who are known to us and those whose actions are unrecorded – much is owed.

One thing I hope readers will gain from this book is a sense of just how essential grassroots activism is in creating a robust, dynamic, and progressive society. Shouting down the police and marching against unjust laws is one kind of activism, but there is so much more that it takes to create change. There are people who answer phones, people who support those struggling with familial, religious, and other conflicts, including depression. There are those who help others find housing and access services, and the artists who speak our truths and who challenge them at the same time, those who lay out and type up newsletters, and those who archive it all.

Although it is still the case that queer lives are stigmatized, we live in different times. We enjoy full legal rights, but more than that, everyday people are not as terrified or mystified by who we are, and we are less likely to be treated as monstrous or a threat to others. The public face of the lesbian, gay, and queer community has become moderate, even placid. Pride Day, organizers declare, is not about activism, it is about celebration. Rather than use our newly gained legitimacy to contest the multiple sites and forms of oppression that persist, we have used it to court corporate sponsors and political favour. We are now on the inside, not wanting, it seems, to look out.

This book can function as a road map, as a lesson plan in activism. History does not repeat itself, not exactly. Means of communication have changed, when and where people congregate are different. The way public officials respond, or don't respond, to its citizens has become hostile and militarized. New times require new measures. Nevertheless, we have a rich past we can draw upon for inspiration and insight into queer mobilizations.

– Elise Chenier, Director, Archives of Lesbian Oral
Testimony (ALOT) and Associate Professor,
Department of History, Simon Fraser University

Acknowledgments

The idea for this book emerged in the summer of 2011, when *The Lesbian and Gay Movement and the State* (Ashgate) was published; I felt that it was necessary to explore the hypothesis that the LGBTQ (lesbian, gay, bisexual, transsexual, transgender, and queer) movement was not simply a victim of governments in Canada but that it resisted their attempts to box it in – and may even have had some influence on them. I discussed this idea with Miriam Smith, who not only considered it sufficiently fertile to nourish a book project but also encouraged me to go ahead. For this I would like to express my heartfelt thanks: her confidence in this project gave me the confidence in my ability to bring it to fruition.

I would like to extend my gratitude to everyone who agreed to join me in the adventure of producing this book. This was quite a gesture of faith as this book brings forth my second life's work: having been associated with the subject of women in politics for almost a quarter-century (life goes by so fast!), I was not a known quantity to my colleagues working on the subject of LGBTQ activism. The contributors to this project showed their trust in me by working with someone with no record in the field – and this is not insignificant when one considers the overloaded schedule that every academic faces. What is more, they showed infinite patience by always responding quickly and courteously to my many editorial queries. Finally, I would like to thank them for staying on board, for this book has been a long – but incredibly fascinating – journey.

Elise Chenier did me the honour of writing the foreword for *Queer Mobilizations*. Elise is both a leading light in sexualities studies in Canada and a highly respected academic for her pioneering work at the Archives of Lesbian Oral Testimony. Her contribution to the book greatly enhances its value.

Submitting a manuscript for evaluation is a process that is usually both painful and gratifying. *Queer Mobilizations* has been no exception to this rule. Two readers evaluated the manuscript – twice. They produced substantial and detailed reports that resulted in significant improvements. I would like to thank them for taking their work very seriously: they devoted a good deal of time to reading the manuscript and preparing their reports. I hope that the finished product is up to their standards.

Käthe Roth also had a hand in the preparation of this project. I have been working with Käthe since 2008, when she translated my book *Quebec Women and Legislative Representation* (UBC Press). Translation is a difficult and delicate task; more than transferring words from one language to another, it involves rendering an idea, a vision of the world, and a personality. I have found in Käthe that rare translator who has brilliantly conveyed my strangest, most preposterous, and most rebellious thoughts.

UBC Press fulfills the highest criteria for scholarly publishing, and so in submitting my project to the press I had a feeling that I was not in for an easy time ... and that premonition was borne out. Nevertheless, I was able to complete the project thanks to the extraordinary support provided by the entire UBC Press team. Emily Andrew is a fabulous editor: enthusiastic about my project, she firmly steered it through the development process, and yet she was sensitive to my uncertainties and helped me see the light at the end of the tunnel. I am very grateful to production editor Ann Macklem for her professionalism, impressive efficiency, and infinite patience. I also thank Patricia Buchanan who has indexed the book; it is a challenging task that in this case has yielded an invaluable tool for the reader.

Finally, I dedicate this book to my parents. Thérèse and Isidore have been models of discipline and perseverance. They not only transmitted these values to me but also showed me how powerful they were when it came to successfully meeting a challenge. *Queer Mobilizations* is one result of this intergenerational communication, and it stands today as the embodiment of our shared pride.

QUEER MOBILIZATIONS

Introduction

MANON TREMBLAY

In January 2013, Kathleen Wynne was elected leader of the Ontario Liberal Party, thus becoming premier of Ontario. This victory made history in two ways: first, Wynne became the first female premier of Ontario; second, and more significant to this book, as a lesbian she was the first openly LGBTQ person in Canada to take the reins of a (federal or provincial) government,[1] and she was one of the first in the world to do so (along with Jóhanna Sigurðardóttir, prime minister of Iceland from 2009 to May 2013; Elio Di Rupo, prime minister of Belgium since December 2011; and Xavier Bettel, prime minister of Luxembourg since December 2013; on LGBTQ politicians in Canada, see Everitt and Camp 2014). It would be no exaggeration to say that queers in Canada have come a long way since the time when homosexuality was a criminal offence. That said, even though Wynne's acceding to the Ontario premiership is important – if only in terms of being a role model – it does not solve the numerous injustices to which LGBTQ people in Canada are subjected regarding, for instance, acts of indecency, age of consent, and state censorship practices. In other words, that a lesbian is a premier should not be the tree that hides the forest: non-heteronormative sexualities are always the target of regulation, not to mention repression, in Canada. In fact, there are always a wide range of ideological and practical mechanisms the deployment of which has the consequence of (over)valuing heterosexuality and making LGBTQ sexualities less desirable – unless they become respectable by homo-normalizing. Examples of such mechanisms are heteronormative hegemony (Ludwig 2011) and the public policy decision-making process.

The objective of *Queer Mobilizations: Social Movement Activism and Canadian Public Policy* is to explore the numerous and diverse relationships between LGBTQ activism and the federal, provincial, and local governments in Canada. More specifically, the authors herein explore how these governments regulate (and even repress) and influence LGBTQ movements, and how these movements have mobilized to shape public policy across political spectrums from the urban to the pan-Canadian level. In this introduction, I first situate this book at the theoretical level. To do this, I present several ideas taken from social movement theory, identity politics, and public policy analysis in order to provide a background against which to highlight the context of the mechanisms used to regulate and repress queer sexualities in Canada. These theoretical elements also provide a framework for appreciating each of the chapters in this collection. Second, I give a brief description – necessarily incomplete and biased – of queer activism in Canada in order to provide a historical background that is complemented and enriched by the following chapters. Third, I review the state of knowledge about LGBTQ activism in Canada, with the aim of shedding light on the contribution and originality of this book to this field of research. Finally, I outline the content of *Queer Mobilizations*.

Some Theoretical Elements

Queer Mobilizations is situated within the context of social movement theory (notably the notion of identity politics) and public policy analysis. To begin with, identity politics is a fairly controversial notion, with both defenders and critics. The former use identity as a discursive strategy for claiming liberal citizenship rights, in a fashion similar to cultural, ethnic, or racial minorities: how one is born cannot justify discrimination and second-class citizenship. The latter argue that it entails the dangers of essentialism and the consequent reification of fixed categories (such as heterosexuality versus homosexuality). The objective of this book is not to take a position in favour of either of these sides but, rather, to consider the notion of identity politics as having something to contribute to the study of LGBTQ activism and its interactions with governments in Canada, notably in bridging the two analytic axes at the heart of its raison d'être: (1) how the government regulates (or represses) queer activism and (2) how LGBTQ activism mobilizes to shape public decisions and policies.

Herein, I identify two main readings of identity politics that are interrelated and complementary. One might be called socio-psychological in that it refers to a process in which certain social characteristics are emphasized as signposts for collective action – for instance, the *Aboriginal* movement, the *black* movement, the *disabled* movement, the *women's* movement, the *youth* movement, and the *lesbian and gay* movement. These movements are based on the idea that certain social characteristics are not neutral (i.e., "natural") but, rather, are evidence (and the result) of historical and socio-political relations of appropriation and exploitation, even oppression – relations that cut across the lines between inclusion in and exclusion from civil, social, and political citizenship. To be lesbian or heterosexual cannot be reduced to a genetic lottery; performing a non-heteronormative sexuality brings into daily life a series of experiences that leaves no doubt with regard to the second-class citizenship of non-heterosexual individuals. For instance, being gay means being invisible in the public space (e.g., in the arts and the media, which depict mainly manifestations of heterosexuality); sometimes being rejected by one's family because of one's sexual orientation (what girl is rejected by her parents because she is heterosexual?); being the target of jeering and teasing, prejudice, intimidation, harassment, and even physical violence in school; and being subjected to discrimination, subtle or overt, on the job (e.g., when it comes to career progression) and in state-provided services (such as health care provision). Although the body is biological, it is also social in that the codes it carries and the way it is perceived orchestrate the relations within which it is inscribed; for example, gays are beaten because their ways of expressing themselves, or even moving, are suspect to their assaulters (what heterosexual man is assaulted because his way of speaking or walking is considered too masculine?). When social characteristics are the cause of inequality, injustice, marginalization, or oppression, they may inspire in the people who bear them a sense of belonging to a minority or of being a second-class citizen. This sense of being deprived is conducive to voicing grievances and claims, which are the raw materials for social movement activism (Gurney and Tierney 1982).

The other reading of identity politics is political. This reading conveys the idea that identity is a radical political act, and it is a major component of the LGBTQ movement: its collective identity and action processes; its aims, claims, tactics, and strategies; its resources and networks; and so on (see Melucci 1996). LGBTQ people express this aspect of identity in various ways. First, declaring one's queer identity publicly in an environment defined by the exclusion of that identity constitutes an act of confrontation. In effect, openly saying that one is LGBTQ in a society in which heterosexuality is the norm means not only exposing this exclusion but also revealing the completely artificial nature of a "heterosexually homogeneous" societal order. Second, publicly declaring one's non-heteronormative identity is an act of resistance against invisibility – and thus against denial of existence. This resistance becomes even more empowering (and provocative) when it is combined with pride in being lesbian, gay, bisexual, transsexual, transgender, or queer. Third, identity orients the exchanges between the LGBTQ movement and governments in Canada (similar to the orientation provided by language or region) by constituting, for example, an argument for claiming protection against discrimination or a canvas for formulating public policies. In these exchanges, such a declaration – that is, the act of naming and of naming oneself – is a radical political act. In effect – and fourth – the act of naming, and thus of defining, the other is political in nature, and it is an act that may make a difference between disgrace and pride. On the one hand, medicine and psychiatry have designated "homosexuality" as a disease, even a scourge; religions have called it a moral sin; and legislatures have declared it a crime. Although the label "queer" is largely accepted today, it remains painful to an older generation for which it was an insult. On the other hand, by insisting on being "out" and shouting "Gay is good" and "Out of the closet and into the street," the gay liberation movement has turned the insult on its head and reinterpreted it as pride. In this perspective – and fifth – naming oneself is a political act that activates a process of framing and public coming into existence. Indeed, the capacity to name oneself not only brings oneself into existence but also does so in the desired light. For example, homosexuality (or, at least, homoerotic acts) existed before the word "homosexual" was coined in the last third of the nineteenth century (Katz 1995, 83–112), but naming it brought it – for better or worse – into the world of social comprehension, of what exists. Nevertheless, many LGBTQ people reject the word "homosexual" not only because medicine and psychiatry have defined it as an illness or disease but also because it was created by those outside of the queer community. For example, many in that community prefer the names "lesbian," "gay," or "queer," which are considered more positive and empowering than "homosexual."

Naming oneself is a radical political act not only because it mobilizes a process of defining the LGBTQ movement in relation to society as a whole but also because it challenges the power relations within the LGBTQ movement itself. The evolution of labels to designate activism around sexual preferences and desires shows that words are not neutral but convey identities that reveal inclusions and exclusions (for a discussion, see Stein 2012, 5–9). Just as the word "homosexual" was not unanimously acceptable, so the word "homophile," used in the 1950s and 1960s, was not appealing to the more radical sexual activists, notably because it dwelt on the notion of love (*philia* in ancient Greek) rather than on the notion of sex. The term gradually fell from favour,

Manon Tremblay

and it died away in the 1970s with the advent of the gay liberation movement, which insisted not only on liberating sexualities (and not only same-sex sex) from their normative straitjackets but also on reinterpreting gender and sexual identities and acts of resistance in a positive light. However, the gay liberation movement provided little visibility to lesbians, who were present in large numbers and active in its ranks; this explains, at least in part (along with the activism of lesbian feminists), the adoption of the label "lesbian and gay movement" in the 1980s. In the 1990s it became common to speak of the "LGBT movement" and the "queer movement," among other descriptors, to convey a concern with inclusion and the unity of non-heteronormative sexualities and identities. Yet, as a number of authors in this book show, it is possible that this unity exists only on the discursive level and that, in fact, there are tensions among "L," "G," "B," "T," and "Q" people. Despite this, but keeping this comment in mind, in the introduction and conclusion of *Queer Mobilizations* I use the initialism "LGBTQ."[2]

In sum, albeit controversial, the notion of identity politics should not be discarded as it offers tools for studying LGBTQ activism and its interactions with governments in Canada – at least when interpreted through a socio-psychological reading (which refers to a sense of belonging to a minority and being a second-class citizen as a consequence of a negatively charged identity marker) and a political reading (which refers to the idea that identity is a radical political act that constitutes a major component of LGBTQ activism). In this regard, identity politics conveys the political nature of relations between the LGBTQ movement and governments in Canada: for one thing, it challenges *politics* through the identity-based power relations that the LGBTQ movement bears and embodies; for another thing, it challenges *policy* in that it forms a communication vector between the movement and governments in Canada, notably via public policies.

Although today lesbians and gays enjoy "virtual equality" (Vaid 1995) with heterosexuals,[3] non-heteronormative sex is regulated, or even repressed, by various ideological and practical mechanisms based on the premise that heterosexuality is the norm and that LGBTQ desires and sexualities are acceptable only when they ape heterosexual ones. One of these mechanisms is heteronormative hegemony (Ludwig 2011); another is the process of making public policy decisions.

It was in the late 1960s, during the turbulence of the sexual revolution, that the conjuncture allowed for a challenging of what Gary Kinsman (1996, 39–40) then described as heterosexual hegemony. This notion brings to mind the writings of feminist lesbian authors such as Charlotte Bunch ([1976] 2010), who argue that, in male-supremacist societies, heterosexuality is a political institution; Adrienne Rich (1980), who develops the idea of "compulsory heterosexuality"; and Monique Wittig (1989), in whose view heterosexuality, more than an institution, is a political regime. Heterosexual hegemony is now better known as heterosexism,[4] which Knegt (2011, 8) defines as "the social system that favours opposite-sex sexuality and relationships, including the presumption that everyone is heterosexual or that heterosexual attraction and relationships are 'normal' and therefore superior." As a hegemonic mechanism, heterosexuality is subtly forced on people not by state coercion and violence but by consent and adherence to the values underlying civil society institutions and promoted by the state – values allegedly embodied in such institutions as the family, the school system, the labour and leisure markets, the media, and the consumer regime. Its strength lies in its invisibility as it is cloaked in the idea of being simply "common sense" (Ludwig 2011, 55), as being a fact stemming from nature. Thus, heterosexual hegemony is naturalized through sex and gender roles, which are portrayed as opposed and mutually exclusive, and it is imposed on people by what can be called "daily habitus," public discourses, and state policies. As revealed by the authors in this book, in both the past and the present queer activists – especially liberationist ones – have challenged the heterosexist fabric of Canadian society and sought to broaden the range of possibilities with regard to sexualities. And this is precisely the objective of *Queer Mobilizations:* to explore the power relations between LGBTQ movements and governments in Canada on the terrain of regulation of non-heteronormative sexualities.

The process of public decision making is another mechanism used to regulate and repress queer sexualities. Many of the authors in this book choose to explore this process via a liberal pluralist approach, while others have adopted more critical perspectives. Although the liberal pluralist approach is not faultless – far from it! – it has been, and still is, one of the mainstream approaches used for studying states, governments, and public policies in Canada as well as their outcomes and their impacts on political actors and civil society. Of course, other approaches can be used to study the interrelations between governments and LGBTQ activism in Canada, notably critical approaches such as neo-Marxism, postcolonialism, and 1970s liberationist analysis. For instance, the postcolonialist approach suggests that Canada is a colonial settler state project, based on the colonization of Indigenous peoples; the subordination of Québécoises and Québécois, Acadians, and the waves of non-white immigrants and migrant workers brought into the country; and other factors. Nevertheless, those who prefer these critical approaches will not be totally

Manon Tremblay

unsatisfied with *Queer Mobilizations* since they are manifested (albeit timidly) in some chapters; indeed, I would posit that some of the authors have, at least in part, made use of these critical approaches by examining certain minority groups in Canada, such as Aboriginals, Quebec francophones, and trans activists. That said, there are three reasons that the liberal pluralist approach serves as the underlying theme of this book.

The first reason is that the liberal pluralist approach is based on the assumption that Canada is a pluralist political society in the sense that its operating economy feeds on the setting in confrontation of a plurality of actors that are profoundly unequal with regard to their respective capital resources. Some of these actors are political-institutional bodies such as parliaments, governments, the courts, and the police, and others are societal bodies such as social movements, community milieus, and alternative media. The LGBTQ movement and governments in Canada are part of, and contribute to, this dynamic. The second reason is that the liberal pluralist approach dissects what *is* rather than pleading in favour of what could – or should – be. The objective of liberal pluralism certainly is not to challenge formal government institutions or the rules and practices of the political game (although some might see this as problematic); rather, it is to understand not only their basic principles, structures, standard operating procedures, strategies for enduring or transforming in space and time, limitations, and outcomes (especially in civil society) but also any reforms that might be made. The last reason that the liberal pluralist approach is preferred is that it is easily combined with the institutionalist perspective. In the view of March and Olsen (2006, 3),

> an institution is a relatively enduring collection of rules and organized practices, embedded in structures of meaning and resources that are relatively invariant in the face of turnover of individuals and relatively resilient to the idiosyncratic preferences and expectations of individuals and changing external circumstances ... There are constitutive rules and practices prescribing appropriate behavior for specific actors in specific situations. There are structures of meaning, embedded in identities and belongings: common purposes and accounts that give direction and meaning to behavior, and explain, justify, and legitimate behavioral codes. There are structures of resources that create capabilities for acting. Institutions empower and constrain actors differently and make them more or less capable of acting according to prescriptive rules of appropriateness. Institutions are also reinforced by third parties in enforcing rules and sanctioning non-compliance.

According to this reading, the LGBTQ movement and governments in Canada are institutions in that they have identities, structures, rules, and resources that are relatively stable and stand up to particular situations and in that they deploy actors whose practices are coded and whose actions are more or less successful. Each of the numerous case studies cited by the authors in this book offers a field of analysis for decoding and revealing LGBTQ activism and governments as institutions of Canadian political society.

This short discussion of the ideological and practical mechanisms designed to regulate and repress non-heteronormative sexualities cannot conclude without addressing the question of policing. In fact, one may conceptualize policing mechanisms on a range from the more subtle to the more overt. As mentioned above, heteronormative hegemony is a subtle yet powerful mechanism in promoting the heterosexual lifestyle. Higgins (2011) notes that (homo) normalization has replaced police repression as a means of regulating and repressing queer sexualities. Governments have at their disposal an arsenal of means to subtly control non-heteronormative sex. For example, the federal government can count on statutes dealing with citizenship and immigration; provincial governments may frame LGBTQ activism via health care, social services, and education policies; and municipalities may use regulations to keep the peace and order and ensure good government, health, and general well-being – the last manifested in regulations on public posting and public manifestations such as parades.

Policing LGBTQ communities is an overt yet unstable means of regulating and repressing queer sexualities. Indeed, although police violence was commonly used from the 1970s to the late 1990s (including raids on bars, saunas, and other LGBTQ social sites), today these acts have little legitimacy. This type of policing of non-heteronormative sexualities certainly has not disappeared, however, as evidenced in the recent police raids on men's bathhouses in Calgary and Hamilton (Knegt 2011, 57). In fact, many of the traditional mechanisms are still in place, including section 210 of the Criminal Code on bawdy houses, censorship of LGBTQ art, and attacks on particular queer sexual practices. Policing is also chameleon-like in that it adapts to the situations in which it is deployed, perhaps to be in tune with community standards of tolerance – for example, depending on whether it occurs in a large city, a small town, or a rural area. Nevertheless, police zeal in this area has been tempered by at least two factors. The first is the Canadian Charter of Rights and Freedoms, which, by offering legal guarantees, has cooled the homophobic ardour of some police officers. The other is the dialogue that has been established over time between queer communities and the police, which has been extensive enough that today policing of LGBTQ communities is much too subtle to involve the use of billy clubs, fists, and pepper spray; instead, it takes the form of dialogue and cooperation between police departments and LGBTQ communities in order to define the line between licit and illicit. Examples are committees for liaison between the police and LGBTQ communities (such as the Ottawa Police Liaison Committee), training sessions on LGBTQ issues prepared and led by LGBTQ people for police officers, proactive recruitment of LGBTQ people into police forces, the presence of LGBTQ patrol officers in the queer neighbourhoods of Canadian cities, and participation by a contingent of LGBTQ police officers in many queer pride parades across the country (see Warner 2002, 289–301).

In any event, the history of queer activism in Canada reveals that policing has far from broken the back of the movement. LGBTQ people have responded by deploying a wide variety of resistance strategies to secure equality rights and protection against discrimination; to compensate for government indifference and shortfalls, even hostility, in the struggle against HIV/AIDS; to counter governments' colonizing intentions regarding Aboriginal people; to destabilize heteronormative hegemony regarding intimate unions and extending parental and family rights to LGBTQ relationships; to react to homophobic and transphobic violence in schools and elsewhere; to combat state censorship on gender diversity, trans identities, and non-heteronormative sexualities; and more. It is these bilateral power relations between queer activism and public policy in Canada that *Queer Mobilizations* examines.

A few words should be said about the other basic theme underlying the issues discussed in this book: social movement theories. Basically, analyses of social movements are guided by four principal theoretical approaches. The first is collective behaviour theory, which suggests that collective protests outside of political institutions or within civil society result from the anger and grievances of people who feel deprived and discriminated against (see, for example, Blumer 1951; Gurney and Tierney 1982). The second is resource mobilization theory, which puts the emphasis on resources, organization, and opportunities to mobilize a social movement and to deploy collective action (see, among others, Gamson 1990; McCarthy and Zald 1973, 1977, 2002). The third is political process theory, which focuses both on the relationships between social movement actors and states and governments and on the role of opportunities (political, social, cultural, economic, discursive, or other) in collective actions and outcomes achieved by social movements (see, for instance, Meyer 2004; Tarrow 1994). The fourth is new social movement theory, so called because it pays particular attention to movements that flourished from the 1960s on and that are based on identity politics (see, among others, Habermas 1981; Melucci 1980, 1996). The authors in this book borrow less from collective behaviour theory and more from the last three approaches. That said, as Armstrong and Bernstein (2008) show, social movements are extremely complex entities, and understanding them requires a multifaceted approach based on several theoretical perspectives.

A Brief Look at Queer Activism in Canada

Kees Waaldijk (2000) suggests an interpretive framework for understanding the evolution of the rights of LGBTQ people in the West organized around three occurrences that were oriented towards seeking equality: first, homosexual acts were decriminalized; then, laws forbidding discrimination on the basis of sexual orientation were adopted; finally, lesbians and gays obtained various rights (e.g., with regard to employment, health care, civil union and marriage, and reproduction and parenting). I use this framework to orient my look at queer activism in Canada, notably because it is consistent with the liberal pluralist approach favoured in this book. Of course, the LGBTQ movement in Canada cannot be reduced to such a rights-seeking and human rights frameworks model, notably because it disappears lesbian and gay liberation narratives. Yet, as Warner (2002) demonstrates, since as far back as the 1960s queer activism in Canada has been torn between two orientations: (1) equality-seeking assimilationism and (2) liberationism. Warner's analysis suggests that followers of these two trends, although opposed, have occasionally collaborated; for instance, the Coalition for Lesbian and Gay Rights in Ontario (CLGRO), a liberationist group, was involved in struggles to secure legal recognition of same-sex relationships in Ontario – an obviously equality-seeking assimilationist issue (Warner 2002, 219–34).

In Canada, homosexuality came out of the closet in 1969, when Pierre Elliott Trudeau's Liberal government decriminalized buggery and gross indecency when engaged in by two consenting adults (twenty-one years of age and over) in private (Kinsman 2013), although other provisions in the Criminal Code related to policing gay sexuality (including sections dealing with bawdy houses and obscene material sent through the mail) were maintained.[5] The federal government took its lead from Britain's Wolfenden Report, which, in 1957, recommended that sex between men be partially decriminalized based on the principle that what people do in the privacy of their homes is not the state's business (Chambers 2010; Kollman and Waites 2011).

This is not to say that homosexuality was non-existent in Canada before 1969. In fact, the lesbian and gay activism that emerged in Canada following the 1969 reform of the Criminal Code had its roots in the development of gay cultures and communities in the 1950s and 1960s, which, in turn, made possible limited but important homophile activities and organizing in the second half of the 1960s (see Kinsman 1996, 161–69, 224–57; Kinsman 2013; Warner 2002, 42–60). Although the historical span of *Queer Mobilizations* focuses on the 1970s and beyond, it is worthwhile to write a few words on the decades before the 1969 reform of the Criminal Code because this is the period that set the stage for the emergence of queer activism in the 1970s.

The Second World War had a significant impact on the regime of heterosexual hegemony: by encouraging migration of people from rural to urban settings in order to work in war production it loosened the traditional heterosexual family ties, and by separating women and men it made possible same-sex relationships in both the army and in industry (Bérubé 1990; D'Emilio [1983] 1998). In the 1950s, several events took place that favoured public visibility of same-sex sex and raised questions about its nature: Was it a moral sin, a criminal offence, a mental and sexual disease, or something else? Which institution – the church, the social services and health care system, or the police – was best suited to handle these sexual deviants? In the United States, Alfred Kinsey published his studies on female and male sexual behaviour, showing that same-sex sex was much more prevalent than had been thought in 1948 and 1953. Kinsey's studies were important because they provided a scientific rationale for homophile groups arguing for the legitimization of their existence. In Great Britain, the Montagu-Wildeblood trial (a case involving several men accused of homosexual "offences") in 1954 received huge media coverage, and three years later the Wolfenden Report recommended a private/public regime of same-sex sex regulation under which homosexual acts would not lead to criminal prosecution unless committed in public or involving young people.

The period following the end of the Second World War also saw the creation of networks within which gay men (and, to a lesser extent, lesbians) appropriated spaces (basically bars and baths) where they could meet in Canada's larger cities. Although some women chose to live as lesbians in secret (Duder 2010), as early as the 1950s there was a vibrant working-class lesbian bar culture in some Canadian cities (Chamberland 1996a, 1996b; Chenier 2004), and lesbian and gay physique magazines, homoerotic novels, and "yellow press" newspapers were circulated (Fortier 1998; Waugh 1998). These materials were key to germinating a sense of belonging – of not being the only one of their kind – among lesbians and gays. In the 1950s, gay activist James Egan was writing columns in high-circulation newspapers denouncing what today is called heterosexism and pleading for recognition of the humanity of homosexual people (see Egan 1998; Kinsman 1996, 167–69). In 1954, Maurice Leznoff defended his doctoral dissertation, "The Homosexual in Urban Society." His research – now considered the first sociological survey of gay men in Canada – revealed the existence of a homosexual culture and gay networks in Montreal in the years following the end of the Second World War. Some gay men, whom Leznoff (1954) calls "overts" because they lived almost exclusively in gay networks, were in a way precursors of queer activism. Just as they "struggled for social space in the 1950s, so did working-class lesbian butch/femme cultures struggle for lesbian space and to affirm dyke identities" (Kinsman 1996, 165).

As the list of events compiled by Donald W. McLeod (1996, 1–39) shows, in the 1960s what was to become the gay liberation movement was well along in the gestational process: lesbian and gay themes appeared in literature, theatre, and film, and the number of bars and other gay meeting spaces, such as saunas, grew. The Association for Social Knowledge (ASK) was the most significant homophile activist group in the 1960s (on ASK, see Kinsman 1996, 230–48; Warner 2002, 59). Created in Vancouver in April 1964 and inspired by the Mattachine Society in the United States, ASK was the first and most enduring Canadian homophile group in Canada. It was established "to help society to understand and accept variations from the sexual norm" (quoted in McLeod 1996, 7). More specifically, ASK's purposes were to inform and educate about homosexuality (which was depicted as sharing several similarities with heterosexuality), to build and maintain a community centre, to encourage studies on homosexuality, to advocate and lobby for reforming criminal laws related to homosexuality, and to collaborate with similar homophile groups inside and outside of Canada (Kinsman 1996, 230–35). ASK was a mixed organization with a balanced number of lesbians and gay men not only as members but also in positions of leadership: for instance, Jaye Haris was the first executive advisor (McLeod 1996, 10) and Norma K. Mitchell was the president when ASK terminated its activities (Kinsman 1996, 235). The organization published *ASK Newsletter* from April 1964 to April 1965, and from December 1966 to May 1968; among other things, the newsletter informed members about events and issues relevant to homosexuality (Kinsman 1996, 233). It also sponsored public discussions on topics that were quite progressive – if not provocative – such as "Homosexual Marriages," "Drag and Transvestism," and "Sadism, Masochism, and Fetishism" during the summer of 1964 (McLeod 1996, 10).

ASK (or ASK members) also engaged in political and legal lobbying, such as submitting a brief to the Royal Commission on Security (McLeod 1996, 36, 37). Apparently, the organization disbanded in 1968.

Although it was the most significant and enduring group, ASK was not the only homophile group organizing in Canada in the 1960s. For instance, in 1963, the Committee on Social Hygiene was formed "to investigate the extent of homosexuality in eastern Canada and to quietly lobby for reforms to the Canadian Criminal Code" (McLeod 1996, 5). In May 1965, the committee was disbanded and the Canadian Council on Religion and the Homosexual was founded; it "urged Wolfenden-type reforms in Canada" (Warner 2002, 45). The short-lived Homophile Reform Society (HRS) was set up in August 1964 (Kinsman 2013). International Sex Equality Anonymous (ISEA), a homophile organization focusing on information and education, was formed in Montreal in August 1967 (Kimmel and Robinson 2001; Kinsman 1996, 250; McLeod 1996, 31). Two homophile magazines, *Gay* and *Two*, began to publish in Toronto in 1964.

Finally, it should be mentioned that the 1960s saw significant enough changes in social attitudes regarding homosexuality that the Liberal government could count on a good deal of public support when it announced its intention to decriminalize certain homosexual acts in private between consenting adults. This liberalization of attitudes towards same-sex sex had something to do with the fact that homosexuality had become a public issue increasingly (and positively) covered by the mass media, debated by different religious faiths and churches, and commented on by professionals such as lawyers, physicians, psychologists, and psychiatrists. In addition, the *Klippert* case spurred the impetus (already well under way) towards reforming the Criminal Code in the mid-1960s.[6] This public support, it should be noted, had been preceded by sweeping national security campaigns against queers that had been initiated in the late 1950s and early 1960s and that were epitomized by attempts to develop the famous "fruit machine" (Kinsman 1995; 1996, 177–81; Kinsman and Gentile 2010, 168–90).

Bill C-150, which decriminalized certain sexual acts ("gross indecency" and "buggery") committed in private between two consenting adults twenty-one years of age or older, was a liberal approach to sexual regulation, although it was oppressive in that it used the "sickness model" to regulate same-sex sex: in the spirit of the private/public regime of sex regulation advocated by the Wolfenden Report, there was the implication that, whereas what two adults did behind locked bedroom doors (thus defining "private" in very narrow terms) was not a crime, it could still be a sickness needing to be addressed by counsellors, doctors, psychiatrists, and psychologists. Quite paradoxically, although the 1969 reform was an attempt to confine queer sexualities to the private realm, people used it to become more public and visible (which led to police clampdowns due to the vagueness of the law with regard to the definition of "the public") (see Kinsman 2013). In fact, the adoption of Bill C-150 contributed to the emergence of LGBTQ activism, consciousness, and community building – that is, to the advent of the gay liberation movement. In ensuing years, LGBTQ people became political actors who took to the street to demand their rights; such demands were often rejected, of course, but the actors did sometimes make gains.

The 1970s were marked by a dynamic that swung between repression of homosexuality and construction of queer identities and communities. As mentioned above, Bill C-150 only partially decriminalized homosexual acts in Canada, and the Criminal Code still contained provisions allowing police forces and courts to repress homosexuality (Kinsman and Gentile 2010, 221–335; MacDougall 2000; Warner 2002, 99–118), as evidenced by the many police raids that took place in spaces of gay sociability (bars and saunas) and the existence of section 159 of the Criminal Code – which is still in effect (Knegt 2011, 52). It is in this spirit that, in August 1971, a brief was addressed to the federal government (see below) demanding, among other things, that the notions "gross indecency" and "indecent act" be removed from the Criminal Code. That said, in the 1970s LGBTQ people tackled the construction of a politicized sexual identity, defined as an essential precondition for the emergence and constitution of a "gay" community and of equality-seeking and rights-claiming political strategies (Smith 1999, 8–9). The first gay liberation groups started up in Canadian cities very soon after homosexuality was partially decriminalized. Without a doubt, they were influenced by the Stonewall Riots in New York City in June 1969 (Warner 2002, 62–95), even though "modern gay liberation was not born alone at the Stonewall Inn," as Altman (2013, 53) notes. These groups, with a wide array of missions, included the University of Toronto Homophile Association (October 1969); the Vancouver Gay Liberation Front (November 1970, the first gay liberation – non-homophile – group in Canada [Kinsman and Gentile 2010, 249]); the Front de libération homosexuel (Montreal, March 1971); the Gay Alliance towards Equality Saskatoon (April 1971); Toronto Gay Action and Gay Alliance towards Equality-Vancouver (June 1971); the Gay Alliance towards Equality (Edmonton, summer 1971); Gays of Ottawa/Gays d'Ottawa (September 1971); the Gay Alliance for Equality (Halifax, June 1972); Gays for Equality (Winnipeg, 1973; formerly the Campus Gay Club, University of Manitoba); Montreal Gay Women (March 1973); the Centre humanitaire d'aide et de libération (Quebec City, May 1973), which held the first pan-Canadian queer conference several months after it was founded; Lesbian Feminists (Saskatoon, autumn 1973); the Rights of Lesbians Subcommittee of the British Columbia Federation of Women (October 1974); the Coalition for Gay Rights in Ontario (January 1975); the Lesbian Organization of Ottawa Now (1976); the Association des gai(e)s du Québec (autumn 1976); and the Lesbian Organization of Toronto (late 1976; disbanded spring 1980) (McLeod 1996, 46–100, 138, 186, 225–27). Vancouver's first gay pride rally was organized in June 1972, and Toronto's first Gay Pride Week was held in August 1972. Regional gay newspapers (such as *Gaezette* in Halifax and *Gay Tide* in Vancouver) were started, and *Body Politic*, a Toronto-based magazine that was to play a leadership role in queer activism in Canada, was founded in late 1971 and published until 1987. As evidenced by the formation in 1975 of the first pan-Canadian queer rights group, the National Gay Rights Coalition/Coalition nationale pour les droits des homosexuels (in 1978 renamed the Canadian Lesbian and Gay Rights Coalition/Coalition canadienne pour les droits des lesbiennes et gais), the gay liberation groups that sprang up in the 1970s were not limited to local organizations.

The 1970s also saw the first attempts by LGBTQ people to gain equal rights. On 28 August 1971, the first queer demonstration in Canada took place: the August 28th Gay Day Committee, a coalition of twelve groups from Vancouver, Waterloo, Toronto, Ottawa, and Montreal, presented the federal government with a brief (entitled "We Demand") containing ten demands – a brief that was to frame the LGBTQ movement advocacy agenda for several years. The committee demanded equality for Canadian queer people in matters of criminal justice, immigration, divorce, employment, and promotion in the federal civil service (including in the Canadian Armed Forces and the Royal Canadian Mounted Police) as well as "all legal rights for homosexuals which currently exist for heterosexuals" (Jackson and Persky 1982, 219), and it denounced certain inequities that existed because lesbians and gays could not marry. Although it was certainly not a central concern, this last claim reflects the fact that, at the time, "gay marriage" may have been framed according to the canons of gay liberationism (see Chenier 2013). Although, in 1977, the Parti québécois government was the first in Canada to include sexual orientation among illegal grounds for discrimination (for an analysis of this decision, see Tremblay 2013), in 1971 GATE (Edmonton) lobbied the Alberta government on this issue and members of the University of Toronto Homophile Association demanded similar protection from the attorney general of Ontario (McLeod

1996, 72, 79; see also Jackson and Persky 1982, 221–23). In August 1973, the Saskatchewan Human Rights Commission recommended, albeit unsuccessfully, that the government provide such protection (McLeod 1996, 134). In October 1973, Toronto City Council became Canada's first legislative body to forbid discrimination due to sexual orientation (Rayside 2008, 93). The need to have discussions with the state to obtain rights may have convinced LGBTQ people to make their initial incursions into national electoral politics: in 1972, the National Gay Election Coalition (NGEC) was instituted for the federal elections of 1972 and 1974 (Kinsman and Gentile 2010, 317; Warner 2002, 76).

The 1980s offered a paradoxical juncture: on the one hand, the HIV/AIDS pandemic was ravaging the queer community; on the other hand, Canada voted in the Charter of Rights and Freedoms, section 15 of which, devoted to equality, left out discrimination on the basis of sexual orientation – discrimination that was hitting people with HIV/AIDS extremely hard, as evidenced by their difficulty gaining access to health care (Rayside and Lindquist 1992) and (shameful) proposals made in British Columbia and Nova Scotia to quarantine people suspected of carrying the virus (Knegt 2011, 93–94). The absence of the mention of sexual orientation in the Charter was even more disturbing because representations had been made to the federal government to have sexual orientation included among the proscribed grounds for discrimination (notably by Svend Robinson, an openly gay MP, and the Canadian Association of Lesbians and Gay Men, which, in December 1980, pleaded before a parliamentary committee for the inclusion of sexual orientation in the evolving Charter; see Rayside 1998, 193; Warner 2002, 158; 2010, 111) and Quebec had, several years earlier, added this criterion to its provincial charter of human rights and freedoms (Tremblay 2013). This lack of protection, fully endorsed by the state and as a consequence of its homophobia and heterosexism, combined with the many kinds of discrimination experienced by gays (and perpetrated by federal, provincial, and even municipal governments, which were slow to react to the pandemic, and by families, who sometimes purely and simply refused to allow a surviving spouse to inherit an estate accumulated over the course of a relationship with a deceased spouse) and lesbians (who, ignorantly, were also seen as carriers of the plague) led the movement to demand that the state focus on the area of rights, notably with regard to recognition of same-sex relationships. This was a strategy for securing both economic redistribution and social justice (Onishenko and Caragata 2010). In fact, as illustrated by the case studies presented in this collection, the HIV/AIDS crisis and the Charter were to dictate the agenda of Canadian LGBTQ activists for decades to come, whether the aim was to attain protection against discrimination, to gain recognition for same-sex unions and their families, to obtain health care services adapted to the needs of LGBTQ people, or to provide information to young people about sexuality. Put another way, the HIV/AIDS crisis boosted LGBTQ organizing around access to treatments, support for people living with HIV/AIDS, and information and education regarding safer sex. It also led to the formation of a plethora of groups embracing a wide array of ideological stances, from assimilationism to a more militant style (such as ACT UP and AIDS Action Now!). That said, although the HIV/AIDS crisis galvanized grassroots LGBTQ activism, it also led to a certain mainstreaming of HIV/AIDS issues through their appropriation by medical professionals and (partial and insufficient) financing by federal, municipal, and provincial governments.

From the second half of the 1980s to the late 1990s, LGBTQ people mobilized to amend provincial human rights laws (except in Quebec, where the criterion of sexual orientation was added to the Charter of Human Rights and Freedoms in 1977; on LGBTQ activism to amend provincial human rights laws, see Warner 2002, 197–211; more specifically, on Quebec, see Tremblay 2013). As a result of years of organizing to achieve protection against discrimination based on sexual orientation, Ontario (in 1986) and the Yukon and Manitoba (in 1987) followed Quebec by amending their human rights legislation to include sexual orientation as a prohibited ground for discrimination (Knegt 2011, 40). In 1986, Hamilton became the first large Canadian city to extend workplace benefits for its employees to same-sex partners. As a baby boom took place among lesbian women, the 1980s saw the first decisions favourable to LGBTQ people for both relationship and parental rights (Rayside 2008, 168–73). In June 1989, the Fifth International Conference on AIDS was held in Montreal, and queer activists took this opportunity to criticize how the federal government was managing the pandemic. The first steps towards activism also took place in the education sector, including regarding sex education, information on HIV/AIDS, and the fight against homophobia and heterosexism (Rayside 2008, 222–23).

On the organizational level, the Canadian queer movement was extremely active, and a plethora of groups was founded in the 1980s, including Calgary's Lesbian Mothers Defence Fund in the early 1980s and Gay Asians of Toronto in 1980; Zami, the first group in Canada for black and West Indian lesbians and gays, and Lesbians of Colour in 1984 (Warner 2002, 181, 185–86); the Nichiwakan Native Gay and Lesbian Society in Winnipeg in 1986; AIDS Action Now! in Toronto in 1988; the Gay and Lesbian Association of Nova Scotia and the Nova Scotia Coalition of People with AIDS, also in 1988; and the 2-Spirited People of the First Nations in Toronto in 1989. As well, in 1981 the first National Lesbian Conference was held in Vancouver. The sustained activism and organizational vitality of LGBTQ people in the heart of the HIV/ AIDS crisis was paralleled by growing activism in the social and religious conservative movement (Farney 2012, 106–12; Herman 1994a).

The 1990s saw a reformist and even, in the view of some, conservative and assimilationist activism (Knegt 2011, 7; Warner 2002, 218–46) oriented towards the state, its goal being to attain both negative rights (i.e., protection against discrimination) and positive rights for LGBTQ people. Equality for Gays and Lesbians Everywhere (EGALE) – the country's only national queer lobby group – embodied the reformist, legalistic orientation adopted by queer activists to promote rights claims. Nevertheless, the very conditions under which EGALE was formed indicated a position that favoured the search for equality for LGBTQ people as the group had deep roots in the 1985 parliamentary hearings on section 15 of the Canadian Charter. In addition to lobbying MPs and governments, one of EGALE's main goals was to take a role in Charter cases and litigation involving sexual orientation (Smith 1999, 77–101) – a role that it played effectively in trials such as *Mossop* (1993) and *Egan* (1995). Although it was important, EGALE was not alone as other groups also negotiated with the government to obtain queer rights. For example, in the early 1990s CLGRO mobilized in relation to Bill 167, the objective of which was to amend notions of "spouse" and "marital status" in some fifty Ontario laws to include LGBTQ people.

Although it was not completely successful, the reformist activism of the 1990s resulted in a number of rights gains. For instance, in 1992 the ban on queers serving in the Canadian Armed Forces was lifted. Following the *Haig and Birch v. Canada* ruling (1992), in 1996 the federal government amended the Canadian Human Rights Act to add sexual orientation to the list of prohibited grounds for discrimination. Six provinces and Nunavut did the same thing between 1991 and 1999. In addition, the courts made a series of rulings, many of which supported queers' equality-seeking rights claims (Smith 2005a). For example, in *Egan and Nesbitt v. Canada* (1995), the Supreme Court ruled that sexual orientation is analogous to other grounds for discrimination listed in the Canadian Charter section on equality. The ruling in *Vriend v. Alberta* (1998) resulted in sexual orientation being read into Alberta's human rights law. In *Rosenberg v. Canada* (1998) and *M v. H* (1999), the Supreme Court of Canada recognized same-sex relationships by attributing certain rights and obligations to them, notably regarding tax benefits for company pension plans and spousal support. In 1995, the government of British Columbia adopted Bill 51, which legalized the adoption of children by "two adults jointly" (Rayside

Manon Tremblay

2008, 174). During the second half of the 1990s, Ontario, Saskatchewan, and Alberta recognized same-sex couples' right to adoption (179). Also in the 1990s, benefits were extended to same-sex partners of employees of the federal government, nine provinces, and two territories (98) – gains that benefited from union support of queer demands.

Beyond rights claims lobbying by large organizations such as EGALE, LGBTQ activism in the 1990s was propelled by a wide range of groups involved in a multitude of regional and local projects. For example, in the 1990s the Foundation for the Advancement of Trans-Gender Equality was created and protests for transgendered human rights protections were organized, notably in Vancouver in 1998. In the same decade, LGBTQ-focused health organizations sprang up across Canada to compensate for the inadequate services available to queer people. In 1990–91, Toronto and Vancouver were the scenes of Queer Nation Acts Up activism. The Lesbian and Gay Immigration Task Force was founded in Vancouver in 1991. Also that year, the Nova Scotia Men's Project, dedicated to rural communities and marginalized groups such as male prostitutes, was launched; two years later, the Lesbian, Gay and Bisexual Youth Project was founded in Halifax. In 1995, the Triangle Program, a schooling initiative focusing on the needs of LGBTQ people, their identities, and their cultures, was set up in Toronto. Newfoundland Gays and Lesbians for Equality was created in 1995. The Lotus Root Conference for gay, lesbian, and bisexual East Asians was held in 1996. In the late 1990s and early 2000s, gay-straight alliances began to emerge, raising resistance on the part of some parents as well as Roman Catholic and Protestant schools. However, from the 1990s onward queer activism could count on the support of unions, as illustrated by the Marc Hall high school prom case (see Hunt and Eaton 2007).

The turn of the twenty-first century did not interrupt the queer movement's quest for rights. Although, earlier in the 1990s, some lesbians and gays had attempted to have their union recognized or to marry (Larocque 2006, 15–18), it was not until the late 1990s and early 2000s that this battle monopolized the lesbian and gay agenda. Over the course of this period, many resources were devoted to the fight for the recognition of unions between two women or two men and for the opening of civil marriage to same-sex couples. These battles, fought in the courts and the political arena, notably by EGALE and its offshoot, Canadians for Equal Marriage, clearly illustrate how the Charter served the equality rights of LGBTQ people. For instance, in its M $v.$ H decision (1999), the Supreme Court ruled that the definition of spouses as a "man and woman" in Ontario's Family Law Act was unconstitutional under the Charter. In response, in 2000 the federal government adopted the Modernization of

Benefits and Obligations Act, extending to same-sex couples a series of rights and social benefits. Between 2001 and 2005, eleven of the twelve provincial and territorial courts called upon to give rulings on cases brought by same-sex couples invalidated the traditional common-law definition of marriage and substituted a definition based on the right to equality provided in section 15 of the Charter (Hurley 2005, 6).

The opening of civil marriage to same-sex couples constituted an incontestable victory for the equality of lesbians and gays in Canada. However, this claim was not unanimously accepted within the movement as many (including numerous lesbian feminists) rejected marriage not only because of its non-egalitarian nature and its role in the oppression of women but also because making it accessible to lesbians and gays was a way of "heteronormalizing" them and marginalizing those who refused to marry (Cossman and Ryder 2001; Mulé 2010; Young and Boyd 2006). Peter Knegt (2011, 47) gives a succinct description of the reasons for this resistance: "Essentially, same-sex marriage only serves people who are in a position to take advantage of such expanded recognition. It also maintains the idea of heterosexual marriage as a 'norm' to which queer people should aspire. And ... it leaves many other important issues out in the cold." What is more, access to civil marriage for same-sex couples in no way meant that equality had been achieved for LGBTQ people in Canada, as evidenced by the police raids on men's bathhouses in Calgary and Hamilton as recently as 2004 (57) and the increase in the age of consent decreed by Stephen Harper's Conservative government in 2006 (Warner 2010, 85–93; see also Dauda 2010; Wong 2006). Despite its apparent normalization, "homosexuality remains contentious" (Altman 2013, 164).

Although the opening of civil marriage to same-sex couples monopolized the queer activist agenda at the turn of the twenty-first century, LGBTQ people had a number of other reasons to mobilize. The fight against discrimination, in the field of human rights, remained central to queer activism. For example, the Canadian Rainbow Health Coalition was formed in 2002 to educate about and advocate for LGBTQ health concerns. The International Conference on LGBT Community Human Rights was held in Montreal in 2006, leading to the creation of the International Day against Homophobia. A major source of homophobia is HIV/AIDS, which explains ongoing queer struggles on this terrain. This activism is worthwhile, as suggested by the adoption in Nova Scotia of the first provincial strategy on HIV/AIDS. In August 2011, a conference was held in Vancouver entitled "'We Demand': History/Sex/Activism in Canada/Nous demandons: Histoire/Sexe/Activisme au Canada."[7] The conference marked the fortieth anniversary of the demonstration held on 28 August 1971, when, for

Manon Tremblay

the first time, LGBTQ people – some two hundred of them – and their allies gathered on Parliament Hill in Ottawa to denounce discrimination against them and to demand their right to equality (see above for more details). This fight against discrimination went hand in hand with the question of human rights for transgender and transsexual people. Several provinces, including Manitoba and Ontario (since the summer of 2012) and the Northwest Territories, now offer these people protection against discrimination. However, homophobia and transphobia remain a particular concern in Canada. Governments are now becoming more aware of the issue, as evidenced by Nova Scotia's 2012 adoption of a policy mandating that no school can prohibit gay-straight alliances, by Ontario's 2012 adoption of the Accepting Schools Act, and by Quebec's 2009 adoption of the Policy against Homophobia and its 2011 adoption of the Government Action Plan against Homophobia, 2011–2016.

I cannot claim that this brief look at the Canadian queer movement is fully representative of LGBTQ activism in Canada. In fact, it positions at the forefront a privileged category of queer people – male, white, middle-class, living in urban areas, English-speakers, well-educated, able-bodied, and so on. Unfortunately, this kind of emphasis is a well-known phenomenon in history and in social sciences more generally – that is, the dominant group has the power to assimilate its own specific stories with history and to claim that its history is universal (i.e., neutral, non-gendered, non-coloured, non-classed, and so on) when in fact it is its own stories that are told. I do not claim that *Queer Mobilizations* escapes this hegemonic and assimilationist process; it is even possible that it exemplifies it. However, I dare to hope that several of the chapters in this collection allow this gap to be partially addressed by examining some specific queer groups (notably Aboriginals, Quebec francophones, and trans activists). Words have the power to cause a hermeneutic and ontological shift through the writing and publishing of different histories. More important, below I conduct a brief review of existing literature on the LGBTQ movement in Canada. My purpose is twofold: (1) to map research on queer activism in Canada – that is, to provide a reading of the current state of knowledge on the subject; and (2) to situate this collection in relation to works published up to now and (secondarily) to shed light on its contribution and originality.

The State of Knowledge about Queer Activism in Canada

What is most notable when examining works published on queer activism in Canada since the 1970s is their sheer number: it is impossible to claim that this field of research is underdeveloped. Of course, this does not mean that all topics have been covered and that there is no more research to be done. However, it does mean that this review cannot mention all the works published in the last fifty years. Moreover, my intention here is not to compile an exhaustive bibliography of all publications on LGBTQ activism in Canada since the 1970s (excellent databases on the subject exist) but, rather, to reveal major research niches. Consequently, as a general rule, I mention the best-known and most accessible titles for each niche, with an emphasis on books (although I also cite journal articles). Also notable is the diversity of themes that has inspired research on queer activism in Canada: from the homophile groups of the 1950s and 1960s to the social conservatism of the 1990s and 2000s via the HIV/AIDS pandemic, lesbian invisibility, homophobia and transphobia in schools and in the media, same-sex union recognition and resistance to this form of heteronormalization, transgender identities, and the clash between the right to equality and freedom of religion. Yet such diversity is hardly surprising since – as mentioned above – it can be interpreted as simply reflecting the diversity of LGBTQ activism in Canada. Below, I suggest a reading (without a doubt both subjective and selective) of the current state of research on queer activism in Canada.

This review is based on a cleavage that certainly is not beyond criticism: that between general works and particular, or thematic, works. The former provide a broad – one might say horizontal – look at LGBTQ activism, using a historical, theoretical, and/or comparative approach, while the latter provide a more focused – one might say vertical – look, concentrating on specific themes. By recounting the history, and offering an interpretation, of queer activism in Canada, historical works provide vital aspects of queer memories, identities, and communities. Published in 1972, *A Not So Gay World: Homosexuality in Canada*, by Marion Foster and Kent Murray (both pseudonyms), was the first book to use a sociological approach to look at the nascent lesbian and gay communities in Canada in the late 1960s and early 1970s (Foster and Murray 1972). That said, the most comprehensive books ever published on the history of queer activism in Canada – and written from a liberationist viewpoint – are Tom Warner's (2010) *Never Going Back: A History of Queer Activism in Canada* and Gary Kinsman's (1996) *The Regulation of Desire: Homo and Hetero Sexualities*. For those who do not have the time to read these two thick books, Peter Knegt's (2011) *About Canada: Queer Rights* is a highly recommended shortcut. People looking for dates and events may consult Donald W. McLeod's (1996) *Lesbian and Gay Liberation in Canada: A Selected Annotated Chronology, 1964–1975*, and those who want to revisit the times or read interpretations of the gay liberation movement from the mid-1970s to the early 1980s may read

Flaunting It! A Decade of Gay Journalism from The Body Politic, an anthology edited by Ed Jackson and Stan Persky (1982). Although they do not deal specifically with Canada, two books – *The Rise of a Gay and Lesbian Movement* by Barry D. Adam (1995) and *The Global Emergence of Gay and Lesbian Politics* edited by Barry D. Adam, Jan Willem Duyvendak, and André Krouwel (1999) – help to situate the emergence and early years of queer activism in Canada within the broader context of several Western countries. Biographies also give insight into the history of queer activism in Canada, such as Jim Egan's (1998) *Challenging the Conspiracy of Silence: My Life as a Canadian Gay Activist* and Ann Silversides's (2003) *AIDS Activist: Michael Lynch and the Politics of Community.*

The history of LGBTQ activism in Canada has also been addressed through the perspective of groups with more targeted identities within the queer movement. Lesbians have been the subject of several books, including *Lesbians in Canada,* edited by Sharon Dale Stone (1990), a very avant-garde anthology published in 1990 that deals with various aspects of living as a lesbian in Canada, including the invisibility of Afro-Caribbean lesbians, the life of lesbians living outside of major cities, and aging lesbians. *The House That Jill Built: A Lesbian Nation in Formation,* by Becki L. Ross (1995), offers a rare in-depth case study of a lesbian feminist group in the second half of the 1970s – the Lesbian Organization of Toronto (LOOT); in *Mémoires lesbiennes,* Line Chamberland (1996a) retraces the life of lesbians in Montreal during the 1950s and 1960s; and in *Awfully Devoted Women,* Cameron Duder (2010) examines sexuality, relationships, and community life of Canadian middle-class lesbians from the early twentieth century to 1965.

Some historical writings look at populations that have been widely ostracized within Canadian society, including First Nations people and trans people, and this marginalization unfortunately continues within an LGBTQ movement still dominated by white and cissexual people.[8] In "The Regulation of First Nations Sexuality," Martin Cannon (1998) shows in what ways the colonization of First Nations people led to the erasure of their traditional multiple genders and sexuality systems (see also the fascinating piece by Hérault 2010). Transsexual and transgender people have been the subject of much research in recent years. In *C'était du spectacle!,* Viviane Namaste (2005) recounts and analyzes the history of transsexual and transvestite artists in Montreal from 1955 to 1985, while bringing to light their strategies of resistance to the cisnormative and cissexist order.

Because Canada is a country of regions, more localized histories of LGBTQ activism have also been written. *Les homosexuels s'organisent au Québec et ailleurs,* by Paul-François Sylvestre (1979), was one of the first books to give a historical overview of queer activism in Quebec, although its narration ends in the 1970s. While its objective was not to give a history of LGBTQ activism in Quebec, Patrice Corriveau's (2011) *Judging Homosexuals: A History of Gay Persecution in Quebec and France* adopts a largely historical approach and covers a vast period of time from the New France era to the middle of the first decade of the twenty-first century. LGBTQ activism in Alberta between 1968 and 1998, and notably its progressive struggles to have the state respond to queer citizenship claims, is the subject of reflections by Laura L. Bonnett (2006; for a historical account since 1990, see Lloyd and Bonnett 2005). Applying a method akin to ethnology to innovative and original sources – trial dossiers on consensual sex between men – Gordon Brent Ingram (2003) suggests a reading of the history of male homosexuality in twentieth-century British Columbia (see also Ingram 2000 on the history in British Columbia). As queer activism was deployed mainly in cities, a number of authors limit their investigations to urban centres, including Irène Demczuk and Frank W. Remiggi (1998), Ross Higgins (1999), Fiona Meyer-Cook and Diane Labelle (2003), and Julie Podmore (2006) on Montreal; Catherine Jean Nash (2005, 2006, 2011) on Toronto; Anne-Marie Bouthillette (1997), Gordon Brent Ingram (2010), Jenny Lo and Theresa Healy (2000), Vincent Miller (2005), and Becki Ross and Rachael Sullivan (2012) on Vancouver. In comparison to this profusion of writings on queer activism in urban spaces, Michael Riordon's (1996) *Out Our Way: Gay and Lesbian Life in the Country* stands out for its view of LGBTQ life outside of the city.

Some general works on queer activism in Canada adopt a scholarly tone, with a thesis to verify, a theoretical framework to follow, and empirical results to present. One example is *Lesbian and Gay Rights in Canada: Social Movements and Equality-Seeking, 1971–1995,* in which Miriam Smith (1999) uses social movement theory to orient her historical reading of lesbian and gay activism in Canada. She demonstrates that rights claims and equality-seeking constituted both ideologies and strategies for lesbian and gay activism in Canada: before the Canadian Charter was adopted, claiming rights and seeking equality were used to build a lesbian and gay political identity and community; after the Charter was adopted, they were used to gain rights and to achieve political victories (more recently see Snow 2014). Other examples of books that link historical and theoretical perspectives are Patrice Corriveau's (2011) *Judging Homosexuals;* Pamela Dickey Young's (2012) *Religion, Sex and Politics: Christian Churches and Same-Sex Marriage in Canada;* Didi Herman's (1994b) *Rights of Passage: Struggles for Lesbian and Gay Legal Equality;* Gary Kinsman's

(1996) *The Regulation of Desire: Homo and Hetero Sexualities;* David Rayside's (2008) *Queer Inclusions, Continental Divisions;* Carolle Roy's (1985) *Les lesbiennes et le féminisme;* and Miriam Smith's (2008) *Political Institutions and Lesbian and Gay Rights in the United States and Canada.*

Rayside's and Smith's works exemplify another approach found in general works on queer activism in Canada: the comparative approach. Both compare Canada and the United States, as does *Faith, Politics, and Sexual Diversity in Canada and the United States,* edited by David Rayside and Clyde Wilcox (2011), although this book covers a very specific issue. LGBTQ activism in Canada and in the United States share several traits, which is not surprising given the two countries' geographic proximity, their similar philosophical and socio-cultural traditions, and their close economic ties. Yet their political institutions are profoundly different, and this difference has an effect on capacities for mobilization, resources, and the successes and failures of the Canadian and American queer movements.

As mentioned above, this literature review is articulated around a distinction between general works, which take a horizontal look at LGBTQ activism, and particular works, which take a vertical look, focusing on specific issues. The latter, in fact, comprises the lion's share of research on the subject. In the historical overview provided in the second section of this introduction, I describe some of the events that have marked queer activism in Canada – events that become meaningful in the light of an interpretive model suggested by Waaldijk (2000): (1) decriminalization of homosexual acts, (2) adoption of protection against discrimination, and (3) recognition of rights. Works that look at specific issues reflect this tripartite division. These important works not only testify to the diversity and richness of queer activism in Canada but also help to trace the boundary between the licit and the illicit, defining themes upon which it is legitimate to reflect, research that is "worthy" of funding, and works whose results meet the lofty standards of the scholarly press. For lack of space, only some of these themes are addressed here, all of which manifest themselves in a clear dialogue between queer activism and governments in Canada.

One extremely rich research issue concerns fights against discrimination and for acquisition of equality rights – gains that could be extracted only from the state. A book edited by Irène Demczuk (1998), *Des droits à reconnaître: Les lesbiennes face à la discrimination,* is devoted to describing and analyzing the manifest and latent discrimination experienced by lesbians in Quebec. In *The Canadian War on Queers: National Security as Sexual Regulation,* Gary Kinsman and Patrizia Gentile (2010) expose the witch hunt orchestrated by the federal government against queer civil servants and high-ranking officials in the late 1950s and early 1960s in the name of national security. Other works about changes in law and to statutes regarding queer people in Canada include Kathleen A. Lahey's (1999) *Are We 'Persons' Yet? Law and Sexuality in Canada* and Bruce MacDougall's (2000) *Queer Judgments: Homosexuality, Expression, and the Courts in Canada*.

Another theme to which much ink has been devoted is the HIV/AIDS crisis, especially in a country in which health care is essentially provided by the public sector. As mentioned above, the HIV/AIDS pandemic has had significant – and often unexpected – effects on LGBTQ activism in Canada. In *AIDS Activist: Michael Lynch and the Politics of Community,* Ann Silversides (2003) examines HIV/AIDS activism from within the LGBTQ movement – that is, through the eyes of an activist. Michael P. Brown's (1997) study of AIDS organizing and activism in Vancouver, *RePlacing Citizenship: AIDS Activism and Radical Democracy,* is an invitation to broaden understandings of democracy and citizenship as conceived of in the Western world (for a quick overview on HIV/AIDS activism in Canada, see Fung and McCaskell [2007] 2012). Rayside and Lindquist (1992) argue that the HIV/AIDS pandemic spurred queer activism partly because of the willingness of governments at all levels to provide funds to LGBTQ community groups. Yet these interactions with the state were not without deleterious effects on queer activism. For instance, it is possible that state funding helped to split the queer movement into institutionalized and professionalized "AIDS organizations," on the one side, and the LGBTQ community, on the other (Lavoie 1998). It is certainly possible that the mechanisms used by governments to manage the pandemic also formed an effective strategy for regulating queer activism (Kinsman 1997). It is also possible that the pandemic served as a pretext for governments to pursue their colonization of Aboriginal people, who responded with resistance strategies (see, for example, Morgensen 2008). Today, increased awareness of the complexity of queer identities and life experiences has resulted in highly sophisticated views of HIV/AIDS (see, for example, Adam, Betancourt, and Serrano-Sánchez 2011; Poon et al. 2005).

As mentioned above, same-sex union recognition and civil marriage monopolized lesbian and gay activism in the late 1990s and early 2000s, forcing a dialogue with the state. The many works published on the subject not only situate the debate but also bring to light the stakes for LGBTQ citizenship (see, among others, Dickey Young 2006, 2011, 2012; Larocque 2006; Matthews 2005; Nicol and Smith 2008; Pettinicchio 2010; Smith 2005b). Works looking more specifically at lesbian and gay marriage also reveal the many tensions generated by this issue, both inside and outside the LGBTQ movement. The view that civil marriage should be opened to same-sex couples was far from unanimously held among queer activists (Mulé 2010; Onishenko and Caragata 2010; Smith 2007; Young and Boyd 2006). What is more, this demand unleashed the most obvious adversary (or counter-movement) to queer activism: the social conservatism movement (Haskell 2011; Herman 1994a, 1994b, 1997; Rayside and Wilcox 2011; Warner 2010).

Although the problem of discrimination of all sorts against sexual minorities has preoccupied LGBTQ people for several decades, struggles over homophobia and transphobia have increasingly mobilized governments in recent years; in several provinces, policies have been adopted to combat these scourges. Some authors expose the sometimes extreme violence to which LGBTQ people may be subjected (see, for example, Field 2007; Janoff 2005). However, they also reveal that not only did homophobia and transphobia manifest as physical violence and even murder but they also took much more subtle forms that could lead to death. Research shows that queer people and those self-identified as heterosexual had very different relations with the health care system in Canada (see, among others, Mulé and Smith 2014; Tjepkema 2008). Starting from the principle that LGBTQ people do not form a homogeneous group, other authors emphasize that queer people who live on the edge of the edge – that is, those who display other traits lending themselves to discrimination, such as being a self-identified Two-Spirited person, an aging lesbian, or a trans person – might have even more problematic relations with the health care system than do "mainstream" LGBTQ people (see, for example, Brotman et al. 2002; Brotman, Ryan, and Cormier 2003; Mandlis 2011; Taylor 2009). Michel Foucault ([1976] 1978) shows that the health sciences, broadly defined (e.g., medicine, psychiatry, and psychology, among others), have constituted very powerful mechanisms for imposing heterosexuality on subjects defined as "deviating" from "normal" sexual behaviours, a theoretical approach that has inspired several Canadian researchers (Chenier 2008; Perreault 2011; see also Adams 1997; Filax 2006). That "reparative therapies" are gaining some popularity today shows that, in Canada, these heteronormalization mechanisms are not a thing of the past.

In addition to the health care system, homophobia and transphobia in the education sector have drawn more and more attention in the last few years, to the point at which EGALE has recently begun to campaign on the issue (see Taylor et al. 2011). A number of aspects of this issue have been explored, including bullying and harassment of LGBTQ youths in high schools (see, for example, Haskell and Burtch 2010; McCaskell 2005), fierce resistance from conservative and religious groups to sexual and gender diversity in schools (see, among others, Grace and Wells 2005; see also Rayside 2014; Wintemute 2002), and strategies deployed to resist homophobia and transphobia (such as gay-straight alliances; see, for example, Fetner et al. 2012; Smith 2004; see also Dorais and Verdier 2005). Homophobia and transphobia also affect teachers and school administrators, who either are subjected to a code of silence with regard to sexual diversity (forbidden to be "out" at work or forced to adopt a heteronormative framework for their syllabuses; see, for example, MacDougall 2002; Moon 2011) or are the object of manifest discrimination. What also emerges from these works is the fact that, in recent years, much effort has been expended to question the heteronormative parameters that frame the teaching profession (see, for example, McNinch and Cronin 2004).

One component of LGBTQ activism that, until now, has remained somewhat in the shadows but that has been gaining importance in recent years concerns transsexual/transgender people. The writings of Namaste (2000, 2005, 2011) are essential reading in this regard. Aside from transphobic violence, a number of challenges face trans activism, including trans human rights protection, trans identity recognition on legal documents such as passports, and public funding of sexual reassignment surgeries. Trans Lobby Group (2013) was set up in 2001 with two goals: to educate the public on trans issues and to pressure the political decision-making process on needs of trans people, notably regarding health care and human rights. The Association des transsexuels et transsexuelles du Québec (2013) and the Trans Equality Society of Alberta (2013) pursue similar objectives on the provincial level.

Although incomplete, this brief survey of works (to which should be added archival collections, such as the British Columbia Gay and Lesbian Archives located in Vancouver's West End, the Canadian Lesbian and Gay Archives in Toronto, and Les archives gaies du Québec in Montreal, and numerous websites on the subject, including www.fugues.com and www.dailyxtra.com) is nevertheless sufficient to reveal the wealth of knowledge accumulated to date – a wealth of knowledge that the case studies presented in the chapters below further flesh out. But if so much research exists on LGBTQ activism in Canada, why is this book necessary?

Outlining *Queer Mobilizations*

As mentioned above, the authors in *Queer Mobilizations: Social Movement Activism and Canadian Public Policy* explore the relations between LGBTQ activism and the federal, local, and provincial governments in Canada. More

Manon Tremblay

specifically, the analyses adopt two perspectives: one privileging the institutional aspect by looking at mechanisms deployed by governments in Canada to regulate (or repress) LGBTQ movements, the other focusing on the queer movement by examining how its activists attempt to influence the public decision-making process in Canada.

In order to look at the complexities that characterize relations between LGBTQ activism and governments in Canada, *Queer Mobilizations* takes a pluralistic approach that deploys a number of layers. First, by considering how public policy has or has not included queer dimensions, the contributors examine a broad array of policy areas. Second, they adopt and combine horizontal and vertical perspectives – the former consisting of a historical look at a given political jurisdiction (the federal government, a region, or a city), the latter consisting of thematic analyses (case studies). This mix of perspectives provides an original framework for investigating queer activism and public policy in Canada. Third, the contributors are leading researchers in a wide range of fields – criminology; gender, sexuality, and women's studies; geography; history; law; political science; and sociology. Fourth, they use diverse theoretical and methodological approaches. In fact, while they were constrained to follow a specific format for each chapter (see below), the contributors enjoyed full freedom to choose their theories, methods, and case studies. As a consequence, the chapters exhibit a broad range of theories (e.g., resource mobilization, political process theory, social constructivism and new social movements theories, liberal pluralism, institutionalism, and critical legal theory) and methodologies (e.g., case studies, interviews with activists, and content analysis [of newspapers, archival materials, and court decisions]), all of which are explored with rigour, openness, flexibility, and creativity.

The book contains thirteen chapters (including the Introduction and the Conclusion) and is divided into three parts in order to reflect not only the fact that Canadian governments are multi-layered but also to determine how local, federal, and provincial governments interact with queer activism. Part 1 consists of two chapters on the federal government and Aboriginal peoples. This grouping reflects the fact that the federal government and Aboriginal peoples are inescapable interlocutors since they are trapped in a colonial relationship in which the latter are dependent on and subjugated to the former. Part 2 consists of five chapters, each of which is devoted to a particular region of Canada: Atlantic Canada, Quebec, Ontario, Alberta, and British Columbia. The last two provinces are singled out because of their apparent contrast: while the latter is seen as an avant-gardist paradise for LGBTQ people, the former is often depicted as a bastion of backwardness. Part 2 is based on the rationale that region is a familiar tool for analyzing Canadian politics. However, it must be remembered that each region is heterogeneous as each encompasses a wide range of diversities and specificities. As becomes evident in this part, queer activism is also heterogeneous. Part 3 consists of four chapters, one of which deals with Vancouver, one with Toronto, one with Montreal, and one with Halifax. This section highlights the fact that queer activism was first deployed in urban spaces.

All chapters adopt a common format. Following a brief introduction, the first section, entitled "Historical Background," identifies the main aspects of LGBTQ activism to be discussed. The second section, entitled "Queer Activism Today," paints a portrait of present LGBTQ activism in the area to be discussed: its agenda, actors, and resources (the main groups, their membership, and other aspects), strategies (such as using the courts, pressuring governments, having allies within the political class and being active in political parties, electing lesbians and gays to the provincial legislative assembly or municipal council), and so on. The heart of each chapter is the third section, entitled "Queer Activism and Public Policy Changes: Case Studies," in which a relationship is established between the two analytic axes of this book – (1) how the government of a given political entity (e.g., the Alberta government or the Toronto city council) regulates (or represses) queer activism and (2) how LGBTQ activism has mobilized to shape public decisions and policies in this political space (e.g., the opening of civil marriage to same-sex couples at the federal level, the closer and better collaboration between the City of Montreal Police Service and the queer community). In each chapter three or four case studies are analyzed. Authors selected their own case studies to illustrate relationships between queer activism and public policy.

The result is that *Queer Mobilizations* offers a richly diverse palette of public policy topics: criminal law (age of consent; the *Bad Attitude, Little Sister's Art Emporium,* and *Vriend* cases); policing (in Montreal and Toronto); human rights (for lesbian and gays as well as for trans people; the case of Queers against Israeli Apartheid in the Toronto Pride Parade in 2010 and 2011; the adoption of Bill 44 in Alberta); health and social services (HIV/AIDS activism, education and prevention efforts); relationship recognition and parental and family rights (the *James Egan* case); education (anti-homophobic and transphobic initiatives in schools; residential schools for Aboriginal youth; Bill 44 in Alberta); queer space and infrastructure (in Montreal and Vancouver); Aboriginal issues (the Indian Act and residential schools); electoral politics (the "gay vote" in Montreal and Toronto and in the 2012 Alberta election). Each chapter concludes with a summary of its main observations and a glimpse of future challenges regarding queer activism and public policy in Canada.

Notes

1 Lesbian, gay, bisexual, transsexual, transgender, and queer.
2 The terms "LGBTQ" and "queer" are used synonymously to designate all non-heterosexual people. I employ particular terms (such as "lesbians and gays" and "trans people") when referring specifically to these groups.
3 This is much less true of bisexuals, transsexuals, transgenders, and queer people.
4 It is of interest to note that, in everyday language, the notions "heterosexism" and "homophobia" are used interchangeably, as if they were synonymous. However, they are not: "homophobia" borrows from the psychiatric and psychological discourses and tends to see the sources of discrimination against LGBTQ people in "phobic individuals," whereas "heterosexism" focuses on society – its values and norms, its organizing and functioning – and argues that heterosexuality imbues all social relations (see Bryant and Vidal-Ortiz 2008; Herek 2004).
5 The Criminal Code has played a more peripheral role in controlling lesbians, whose sexuality and morality have been managed through other laws, such as those governing family (e.g., parental rights and child custody) and medicine (e.g., regarding mental health and access to new technologies of reproduction).
6 In August 1965, after stating that he had engaged in sexual acts with consenting adult males on four occasions, Everett George Klippert was charged with four counts of gross indecency. In March 1966, he was declared a "dangerous sexual offender," which entailed a sentence of indefinite detention. In November 1967, the Supreme Court of Canada dismissed his appeal. This decision was very controversial and influenced Pierre Elliott Trudeau, then the justice minister, to expedite the reform of the Criminal Code that took place in 1969 (Kinsman 1996, 163; Kinsman and Gentile 2010, 215; McLeod 1996, 32).
7 The winter 2014 issue of the *Journal of Canadian Studies/Revue d'études canadiennes* was published in commemoration of the We Demand demonstration.
8 Julia Serano (2007, 12) uses the term "cissexual" to describe "people who are not transsexual and who have only ever experienced their mental and physical sexes as being aligned."

References

Adam, Barry D. 1995. *The Rise of a Gay and Lesbian Movement*. New York: Twayne.
Adam, Barry D., Gerardo Betancourt, and Angel Serrano-Sánchez. 2011. "Development of an HIV Prevention and Life Skills Program for Spanish-Speaking Gay and Bisexual Newcomers to Canada." *Canadian Journal of Human Sexuality* 20 (1–2): 11–7.
Adam, Barry D., Jan Willem Duyvendak, and André Krouwel, eds. 1999. *The Global Emergence of Gay and Lesbian Politics: National Imprints of a Worldwide Movement*. Philadelphia: Temple University Press.
Adams, Marie Louise. 1997. *The Trouble with Normal: Postwar Youth and the Making of Heterosexuality*. Toronto: University of Toronto Press.
Altman, Dennis. 2013. *The End of the Homosexual*. St. Luca: University of Queensland Press.
Armstrong, Elizabeth A., and Mary Bernstein. 2008. "Culture, Power, and Institutions: A Multi-Institutional Politics Approach to Social Movements." *Sociological Theory* 26 (1): 74–99. http://dx.doi.org/10.1111/j.1467-9558.2008.00319.x.
Association des transsexuels et transsexuelles du Québec. 2013. *À propos de nous*. http://www.atq1980.org/.

Bérubé, Allan. 1990. *Coming Out under Fire: The History of Gay Men and Women in World War Two*. New York: Free Press.

Blumer, Herbert. 1951. "Collective Behavior." In Alfred McClung Lee, ed., *Principles of Sociology*, 166–222. New York: Barnes and Noble.

Bonnett, Laura L. 2006. "Transgressing the Public/Private Divide: Gay, Lesbian, Bisexual and Transgender Citizenship Claims in Alberta, 1968–1998." PhD diss., University of Alberta.

Bouthillette, Anne-Marie. 1997. "Queer and Gendered Housing: A Tale of Two Neighbourhoods in Vancouver." In Gordon Brent Ingram, Anne-Marie Bouthillette, and Yolanda Retter, eds., *Queers in Space: Communities/Public Places/Sites of Resistance*, 213–32. Seattle: Bay Press.

Brotman, Shari, Bill Ryan, Yves Jalbert, and Bill Rowe. 2002. "Reclaiming Space-Regaining Health: The Health Care Experiences of Two-Spirit People in Canada." *Journal of Gay and Lesbian Social Services* 14 (1): 67–87. http://dx.doi.org/10.1300/J041v14n01_04.

Brotman, Shari, Bill Ryan, and Robert Cormier. 2003. "The Health and Social Service Needs of Gay and Lesbian Elders and Their Families in Canada." *Gerontologist* 43 (2): 192–202. http://dx.doi.org/10.1093/geront/43.2.192.

Brown, Michael P. 1997. *RePlacing Citizenship: AIDS Activism and Radical Democracy*. New York: Guilford Press.

Bryant, Karl, and Salvador Vidal-Ortiz. 2008. "Introduction to Retheorizing Homophobias." *Sexualities* 11 (4): 387–96. http://dx.doi.org/10.1177/1363460708091740.

Bunch, Charlotte. (1976) 2010. "Not for Lesbians Only." In Wendy K. Kolmar and Frances Burtkowski, eds., *Feminist Theory: A Reader*, 3rd ed., 211–14. Boston: McGraw Hill.

Cannon, Martin. 1998. "The Regulation of First Nations Sexuality." *Canadian Journal of Native Studies* 18 (1): 1–18.

Chamberland, Line. 1996a. *Mémoires lesbiennes, 1950–1972*. Montréal: Remue-ménage.

–. 1996b. "Remembering Lesbian Bars: Montreal, 1955–1975." In Wendy Mitchinson, Paula Bourne, Alison Prentice, Gail Cuthbert Brundt, Beth Light, and Naomi Black, eds., *Canadian Women: A Reader*, 352–79. Toronto: Harcourt Brace.

Chambers, Stuart. 2010. "Pierre Elliott Trudeau and Bill C-150: A Rational Approach to Homosexual Acts, 1968–69." *Journal of Homosexuality* 57 (2): 249–66. http://dx.doi.org/10.1080/00918360903489085.

Chenier, Elise. 2004. "Rethinking Class in Lesbian Bar Culture: Living 'the Gay Life' in Toronto, 1955–1965." *Left History* 9 (2): 85–118. Reprinted in Adele Perry and Mona Gleason, eds., *Rethinking Canada: The Promise of Women's History*, 5th ed., 301–22. Toronto: Oxford University Press, 2006.

–. 2008. *Strangers in Our Midst: Sexual Deviancy in Postwar Ontario*. Toronto: University of Toronto Press.

–. 2013. "Gay Marriage, 1970s Style." *Gay and Lesbian Review Worldwide* 20 (2): 19–21.

Corriveau, Patrice. 2011. *Judging Homosexuals: A History of Gay Persecution in Quebec and France*. Trans. Käthe Roth. Vancouver: UBC Press. Originally published as *La répression des homosexuels au Québec et en France: Du bûcher à la mairie* (Quebec City: Septentrion, 2006).

Cossman, Brenda, and Bruce Ryder. 2001. "What Is Marriage-Like Like? The Irrelevancy of Conjugality." *Canadian Journal of Family Law* 18 (2): 269–326.

Dauda, Carol L. 2010. "Childhood, Age of Consent and Moral Regulation in Canada and the UK." *Contemporary Politics* 16 (3): 227–47. http://dx.doi.org/10.1080/13569775.2010.501634.

Demczuk, Irène, ed. 1998. *Des droits à reconnaître: Les lesbiennes face à la discrimination.* Montréal: Remue-ménage.

Demczuk, Irène, and Frank W. Remiggi, eds. 1998. *Sortir de l'ombre: Histoires des communautés lesbienne et gaie de Montréal.* Montréal: VLB éditeur.

D'Emilio, John. (1983) 1998. *Sexual Politics, Sexual Communities: The Making of a Homosexual Minority in the United States, 1940–1970.* Chicago: University of Chicago Press. http://dx.doi.org/10.7208/chicago/9780226922454.001.0001.

Dickey Young, Pamela. 2006. "Same-Sex Marriage and the Christian Churches in Canada." *Studies in Religion/Sciences religieuses* 35 (1): 3–23.

–. 2011. "It's All about Sex: The Roots of Opposition to Gay and Lesbian Marriages in Some Christian Churches." In David Rayside and Clyde Wilcox, eds., *Faith Politics and Sexual Diversity*, 165–76. Vancouver: UBC Press.

–. 2012. *Religion, Sex and Politics: Christian Churches and Same-Sex Marriage in Canada.* Halifax: Fernwood.

Dorais, Michel, and Éric Verdier. 2005. *Sains et saufs: Petit manuel de lutte contre l'homophobie à l'usage des jeunes.* Montréal: VLB éditeur.

Duder, Cameron. 2010. *Awfully Devoted Women: Lesbian Lives in Canada, 1900–65.* Vancouver: UBC Press.

Egan, Jim. 1998. *Challenging the Conspiracy of Silence: My Life as a Canadian Gay Activist.* Comp. and ed. Donald W. McLeod. Toronto: Canadian Lesbian and Gay Archives and Homewood Books.

Everitt, Joanna, and Michael Camp. 2014. "In versus Out: LGBT Politicians in Canada." *Journal of Canadian Studies/Revue d'études canadiennes* 48 (1): 226–51.

Farney, James. 2012. *Social Conservatives and Party Politics in Canada and the United States.* Toronto: University of Toronto Press.

Fetner, Tina, Athena Elafros, Sandra Bortolin, and Coralee Drechsler. 2012. "Safe Spaces: Gay-Straight Alliances in High Schools." *Canadian Review of Sociology* 49 (2): 188–207.

Field, Anne-Marie. 2007. "Counter-Hegemonic Citizenship: LGBT Communities and the Politics of Hate Crimes in Canada." *Citizenship Studies* 11 (3): 247–62. http://dx.doi.org/10.1080/17450100701381813.

Filax, Gloria. 2006. *Queer Youth in the Province of the "Severely Normal."* Vancouver: UBC Press.

Fortier, Muriel. 1998. "Les *lesbian pulps*: un instrument de conscientisation." In Irène Demczuk and Frank W. Remiggi, eds., *Sortir de l'ombre: Histoires des communautés lesbienne et gaie de Montréal*, 27–52. Montréal: VLB éditeur.

Foster, Marion, and Kent Murray. 1972. *A Not So Gay World: Homosexuality in Canada.* Toronto: McClelland and Stewart.

Foucault, Michel. (1976) 1978. *La volonté de savoir.* Vol. 1, *Histoire de la sexualité.* Paris: Gallimard.

Fung, Richard, and Tim McCaskell. (2007) 2012. "Continental Drift: The Imaging of AIDS." In Maureen Fitzgerald and Scott Rayter, eds., *Queerly Canadian: An Introductory Reader in Sexuality Studies*, 191–96. Toronto: Canadian Scholars Press Inc.

Gamson, William A. 1990. *The Strategy of Social Protest.* 2nd ed. Belmont: Wadsworth.

Grace, André P., and Kristopher Wells. 2005. "The Marc Hall Prom Predicament: Queer Individual Rights v. Institutional Church Rights in Canadian Public Education." *Canadian Journal of Education* 28 (3): 237–70. http://dx.doi.org/10.2307/4126470.

Gurney, Joan Neff, and Kathleen J. Tierney. 1982. "Relative Deprivation and Social Movements: A Critical Look at Twenty Years of Theory and Research." *Sociological Quarterly* 23 (1): 33–47. http://dx.doi.org/10.1111/j.1533-8525.1982.tb02218.x.

Habermas, Jürgen. 1981. "New Social Movements." *Telos* 49 (1): 33–7. http://dx.doi.org/10.3817/0981049033.

Haskell, David M. 2011. "'What We Have Here Is a Failure to Communicate': Same-Sex Marriage, Evangelicals, and the Canadian News Media." *Journal of Religion and Popular Culture* 23 (3): 311–29. http://dx.doi.org/10.3138/jrpc.23.3.311.

Haskell, Rebecca, and Brian Burtch. 2010. *Get That Freak: Homophobia and Transphobia in High Schools*. Halifax: Fernwood Publishing.

Hérault, Laurence. 2010. "Transgression et désordre dans le genre: Les explorateurs français aux prises avec les 'berdaches' amérindiens." *Etnográfica* 14 (2): 337–60. http://dx.doi.org/10.4000/etnografica.316.

Herek, Gregory M. 2004. "Beyond 'Homophobia': Thinking about Sexual Prejudice and Stigma in the Twenty-First Century." *Sexuality Research and Social Policy* 1 (2): 6–24. http://dx.doi.org/10.1525/srsp.2004.1.2.6.

Herman, Didi. 1994a. "The Christian Right and the Politics of Morality in Canada." *Parliamentary Affairs* 47 (2): 268–79.

–. 1994b. *Rights of Passage: Struggles for Lesbian and Gay Legal Equality*. Toronto: University of Toronto Press.

–. 1997. *The Antigay Agenda: Orthodox Vision and the Christian Right*. Chicago: University of Chicago Press. http://dx.doi.org/10.7208/chicago/9780226327693.001.0001.

Higgins, Ross. 1999. *De la clandestinité à l'affirmation: Pour une histoire de la communauté gaie montréalaise*. Montréal: Comeau et Nadeau.

–. 2011. "La régulation sociale de l'homosexualité: De la répression policière à la normalisation." In Patrice Corriveau and Valérie Daoust, eds., *La régulation sociale des minorités sexuelles: L'inquiétude de la différence*, 67–102. Québec: Presses de l'Université du Québec.

Hunt, Gerald, and Jonathan Eaton. 2007. "We Are Family: Labour Responds to Gay, Lesbian, Bisexual, and Transgender Workers." In Gerald Hunt and David Rayside, eds., *Equity, Diversity, and Canadian Labour*, 130–55. Toronto: University of Toronto Press.

Hurley, Mary C. 2005. *Bill C-38: The Civil Marriage Act*, Ottawa: Library of Parliament, Parliamentary Information and Research Service, Law and Government Division, Legislative Summary #LS-502E. http://www.parl.gc.ca/Content/LOP/LegislativeSummaries/38/1/c38-e.pdf (viewed 10 February 2013).

Ingram, Gordon Brent. 2000. "Mapping Decolonisation of Male Homoerotic Space in Pacific Canada." In Richard Phillips, Diane Watt, and David Shuttleton, eds., *De-Centring Sexualities: Politics and Representations beyond the Metropolis*, 213–34. London: Routledge.

–. 2003. "Returning to the Scene of the Crime: Uses of Trial Dossiers on Consensual Male Homosexuality for Urban Research, with Examples from Twentieth-Century British Columbia." *GLQ: A Journal of Lesbian and Gay Studies* 10 (1): 77–110. http://dx.doi.org/10.1215/10642684-10-1-77.

–. 2010. "Fragments, Edges, and Matrices: Retheorizing the Formation of a So-Called Gay Ghetto through Queering Landscape Ecology." In Cate Sandilands and Bruce Erickson, eds., *Queer Ecologies: Sex, Nature, Politics and Desire*, 254–82. Bloomington: Indiana University Press.

Jackson, Ed, and Stan Persky, eds. 1982. *Flaunting It! A Decade of Gay Journalism from The Body Politic*. Vancouver/Toronto: New Star Books/Pink Triangle Press.

Janoff, Douglas. 2005. *Pink Blood: Homophobic Violence in Canada*. Toronto: University of Toronto Press.

Katz, Jonathan Ned. 1995. *The Invention of Heterosexuality*. New York: Dutton.

Kimmel, David, and Daniel J. Robinson. 2001. "Sex, Crime, Pathology: Homosexuality and Criminal Code Reform in Canada, 1949–1969." *Canadian Journal of Law and Society* 16 (1): 147–65.

Kinsman, Gary. 1995. "'Character Weaknesses' and 'Fruit Machines': Towards an Analysis of the Anti-Homosexual Security Campaign in the Canadian Civil Service." *Labour/Le Travail* 35 (Spring): 133–61. http://dx.doi.org/10.2307/25143914.

–. 1996. *The Regulation of Desire: Homo and Hetero Sexualities*. 2nd ed. Montreal: Black Rose Books.

–. 1997. "Managing AIDS Organizing: 'Consultation,' 'Partnership,' and 'Responsibility' as Strategies of Regulation." In William Carroll, ed., *Organizing Dissent: Contemporary Social Movements in Theory and Practice – Studies in the Politics of Counter-Hegemony*, 2nd ed., 213–39. Toronto: Garamond.

–. 2013. "Wolfenden in Canada: Within and Beyond Official Discourse in Law Reform Struggles." In Corinne Lennox and Matthew Waites, eds., *Human Rights, Sexual Orientation and Gender Identity in the Commonwealth*, 183–205. London: University of London, School of Advanced Study, Institute of Commonwealth Studies.

Kinsman, Gary, and Patrizia Gentile. 2010. *The Canadian War on Queers: National Security as Sexual Regulation*. Vancouver: UBC Press.

Knegt, Peter. 2011. *About Canada: Queer Rights*. Halifax: Fernwood.

Kollman, Kelly, and Matthew Waites. 2011. "United Kingdom: Changing Political Opportunity Structures, Policy Success and Continuing Challenges for Lesbian, Gay and Bisexual Movements." In Manon Tremblay, David Paternotte, and Carol Johnson, eds., *The Lesbian and Gay Movement and the State: Comparative Insights into a Transformed Relationship*, 181–95. Farnham: Ashgate.

Lahey, Kathleen A. 1999. *Are We 'Persons' Yet? Law and Sexuality in Canada*. Toronto: University of Toronto Press.

Larocque, Sylvain. 2006. *Gay Marriage: The Story of a Canadian Social Revolution*. Trans. Robert Chodos, Louisa Blair, and Benjamin Waterhouse. Toronto: Lorimer. Originally published as *Mariage gai: Les coulisses d'une révolution sociale* (Montréal: Flammarion, 2005).

Lavoie, René. 1998. "Deux solitudes: Les organismes sida et la communauté gaie." In Irène Demczuk and Frank W. Remiggi, eds., *Sortir de l'ombre: Histoires des communautés lesbienne et gaie de Montréal*, 337–62. Montréal: VLB éditeur.

Leznoff, Maurice. 1954. "The Homosexual in Urban Society." PhD diss., McGill University.

Lloyd, Julie, and Laura Bonnett. 2005. "The Arrested Development of Queer Rights in Alberta, 1990–2004." In Trevor W. Harrison, ed., *The Return of the Trojan Horse: Alberta and the New World (Dis)Order*, 328–41. Montreal: Black Rose Books.

Lo, Jenny, and Theresa Healy. 2000. "Flagrantly Flaunting It?: Contesting Perceptions of Locational Identity among Urban Vancouver Lesbians." *Journal of Lesbian Studies* 4 (1): 29–44. http://dx.doi.org/10.1300/J155v04n01_03.

Ludwig, Gundula. 2011. "From the 'Heterosexual Matrix' to a 'Heteronormative Hegemony': Initiating a Dialogue between Judith Butler and Antonio Gramsci about Queer Theory and Politics." In María do Mar Castro Varela, Nikita Dhawan, and Antke Engel, eds., *Hegemony and Heteronormativity: Revisiting "The Political" in Queer Politics*, 43–61. Farnham: Ashgate.

MacDougall, Bruce. 2000. *Queer Judgments: Homosexuality, Expression, and the Courts in Canada*. Toronto: University of Toronto Press.

–. 2002. "A Respectful Distance: Appellate Courts Consider Religious Motivation of Public Figures in Homosexual Equality Discourse – The Cases of *Chamberlain* and *Trinity Western University*." *UBC Law Review* 35 (2): 511–38.

Mandlis, Lane R. 2011. "Human Rights, Transsexed Bodies, and Health Care in Canada: What Counts as Legal Protection?" *Canadian Journal of Law and Society* 26 (3): 509–29. http://dx.doi.org/10.3138/cjls.26.3.509.

March, James G., and Johan P. Olsen. 2006. "Elaborating the 'New Institutionalism.'" In R.A.W. Rhodes, Sarah A. Binder, and Bert A. Rockman, eds., *The Oxford Handbook of Political Institutions*, 3–20. Oxford: Oxford University Press.

Matthews, J. Scott. 2005. "The Political Foundations of Support for Same-Sex Marriage in Canada." *Canadian Journal of Political Science* 38 (4): 841–66. http://dx.doi.org/10.1017/S0008423905040485.

McCarthy, John D., and Mayer N. Zald. 1973. *The Trend of Social Movements in America: Professionalization and Resource Mobilization*. Morristown. General Learning Press.

–. 1977. "Resource Mobilization and Social Movements: A Partial Theory." *American Journal of Sociology* 82 (6): 1212–41. http://dx.doi.org/10.1086/226464.

–. 2002. "The Enduring Vitality of the Resource Mobilization Theory of Social Movements." In Jonathan H. Turner, ed., *Handbook of Sociological Theory*, 533–65. New York: Kluwer Academic/Plenum.

McCaskell, Tim. 2005. *Race to Equity: Disrupting Educational Inequality*. Toronto: Between the Lines.

McLeod, Donald W. 1996. *Lesbian and Gay Liberation in Canada: A Selected Annotated Chronology, 1964–1975*. Toronto: ECW Press/Homewood Books.

McNinch, James, and Mary Cronin, eds. 2004. *"I Could Not Speak My Heart": Education and Social Justice for Gay and Lesbian Youth*. Regina: University of Regina, Canadian Plains Research Centre.

Melucci, Alberto. 1980. "The New Social Movements: A Theoretical Approach." *Social Sciences Information/Information sur les Sciences Sociales* 19 (2): 199–226. http://dx.doi.org/10.1177/053901848001900201.

–. 1996. *Challenging Codes: Collective Action in the Information Age*. Cambridge: Cambridge University Press. http://dx.doi.org/10.1017/CBO9780511520891.

Meyer, David S. 2004. "Protest and Political Opportunities." *Annual Review of Sociology* 30 (1): 125–45. http://dx.doi.org/10.1146/annurev.soc.30.012703.110545.

Meyer-Cook, Fiona, and Diane Labelle. 2003. "Namaji: Two-Spirit Organizing in Montreal, Canada." *Journal of Gay and Lesbian Social Services* 16 (1): 29–51. http://dx.doi.org/10.1300/J041v16n01_02.

Miller, Vincent. 2005. "Intertextuality, the Referential Illusion and the Production of a Gay Ghetto." *Social and Cultural Geography* 6 (1): 61–79. http://dx.doi.org/10.1080/14649360052000335973.

Moon, Richard. 2011. "The Supreme Court of Canada's Attempt to Reconcile Freedom of Religion and Sexual Orientation Equality in the Public Schools." In David Rayside and Clyde Wilcox, eds., *Faith, Politics, and Sexual Diversity in Canada and the United States*, 321–38. Vancouver: UBC Press.

Morgensen, Scott L. 2008. "Activist Media in Native AIDS Organizing: Theorizing the Colonial Conditions of AIDS." *American Indian Culture and Research Journal* 32 (1): 35–56.

Mulé, Nick J. 2010. "Same-Sex Marriage and Canadian Relationship Recognition – One Step Forward, Two Steps Back: A Critical Liberationist Perspective." *Journal of Gay and Lesbian Social Services* 22 (1–2): 74–90. http://dx.doi.org/10.1080/10538720903332354.

Mulé, Nick J., and Miriam Smith. 2014. "Invisible Populations: LGBTQ People and Federal Health Policy in Canada." *Canadian Public Administration* 57 (2): 234–55. http://dx.doi.org/10.1111/capa.12066.

Namaste, Viviane. 2000. *Invisible Lives: The Erasure of Transsexual and Transgendered People*. Chicago: University of Chicago Press.

–. 2005. *C'était du spectacle! L'histoire des artistes transsexuelles à Montréal*. Montreal and Kingston: McGill-Queen's University Press.

–. 2011. *Sex Change, Social Change: Reflections on Identity, Institutions, and Imperialism*. 2nd ed. Toronto: Women's Press.

Nash, Catherine Jean. 2005. "Contesting Identity: Politics of Gays and Lesbians in Toronto in the 1970s." *Gender, Place and Culture* 12 (1): 113–35. http://dx.doi.org/10.1080/09663690500083115.

–. 2006. "Toronto's Gay Village (1969–1982): Plotting the Politics of Gay Identity." *Canadian Geographer/Géographe canadien* 50 (1): 1–16. http://dx.doi.org/10.1111/j.0008-3658.2006.00123.x.

–. 2011. "Trans Experiences in Lesbian and Queer Space." *Canadian Geographer/Géographe canadien* 55 (2): 192–207. http://dx.doi.org/10.1111/j.1541-0064.2010.00337.x.

Nicol, Nancy, and Miriam Smith. 2008. "Legal Struggles and Political Resistance: Same-Sex Marriage in Canada and the USA." *Sexualities* 11 (6): 667–87. http://dx.doi.org/10.1177/1363460708096912.

Onishenko, Dawn, and Lea Caragata. 2010. "A Theoretically Critical Gaze on the Canadian Equal Marriage Debate: Breaking the Binaries." *Journal of Gay and Lesbian Social Services* 22 (1–2): 91–111. http://dx.doi.org/10.1080/10538720903332404.

Perreault, Isabelle. 2011. "Psychochirurgie et homosexualité. Quelques cas à l'Hôpital Saint-Jean-de-Dieu à la mi-XXe siècle." In Patrice Corriveau and Valérie Daoust, eds., *La régulation sociale des minorités sexuelles: L'inquiétude de la différence*, 27–44. Quebec City: Presses de l'Université du Québec.

Pettinicchio, David. 2010. "Public and Elite Policy Preferences: Gay Marriage in Canada." *International Journal of Canadian Studies* 42 (42): 125–53. http://dx.doi.org/10.7202/1002175ar.

Podmore, Julie. 2006. "Gone 'Underground'? Lesbian Visibility and the Consolidation of Queer Space in Montréal." *Social and Cultural Geography* 7 (4): 595–625. http://dx.doi.org/10.1080/14649360600825737.

Poon, Maurice Kwong-Lai, Peter Trung-Thu Ho, Josephine Pui-Hing Wong, Gabriel Wong, and Ruthann Lee. 2005. "Psychosocial Experiences of East and Southeast Asian Men Who Use Gay Chatrooms in Toronto: An Implication for HIV/AIDS Prevention." *Ethnicity and Health* 10 (2): 145–67. http://dx.doi.org/10.1080/13557850500071202.

Rayside, David. 1998. *On the Fringe: Gays and Lesbians in Politics*. Ithaca: Cornell University Press.

–. 2008. *Queer Inclusions, Continental Divisions: Public Recognition of Sexual Diversity in Canada and the United States*. Toronto: University of Toronto Press.

–. 2014. "The Inadequate Recognition of Sexual Diversity by Canadian Schools: LGBT Advocacy and Its Impact." *Journal of Canadian Studies/Revue d'études canadiennes* 48 (1): 190–225.

Rayside, David, and Evert Lindquist. 1992. "AIDS Activism and the State in Canada." *Studies in Political Economy* 39 (Autumn): 37–76.

Rayside, David, and Clyde Wilcox, eds. 2011. *Faith Politics and Sexual Diversity in Canada and the United States*. Vancouver: UBC Press.

Rich, Adrienne. 1980. "Compulsory Heterosexuality and Lesbian Existence." *Signs (Chicago, Ill.)* 5 (4): 631–60. http://dx.doi.org/10.1086/493756.

Riordon, Michael. 1996. *Out Our Way: Gay and Lesbian Life in the Country*. Toronto: Between the Lines.

Ross, Becki L. 1995. *The House That Jill Built: A Lesbian Nation in Formation*. Toronto: University of Toronto Press.

Ross, Becki, and Rachael Sullivan. 2012. "Tracing Lines of Horizontal Hostility: How Sex Workers and Gay Activists Battled for Space, Voice, and Belonging in Vancouver, 1975–1985." *Sexualities* 15 (5–6): 604–21. http://dx.doi.org/10.1177/1363460712446121.

Roy, Carolle. 1985. *Les lesbiennes et le féminisme*. Montréal: Saint-Martin.

Serano, Julia. 2007. *Whipping Girl: A Transsexual Woman on Sexism and the Scapegoating of Femininity*. Berkeley: Seal Press.

Silversides, Ann. 2003. *AIDS Activist: Michael Lynch and the Politics of Community*. Toronto: Between the Lines.

Smith, Miriam. 1999. *Lesbian and Gay Rights in Canada: Social Movements and Equality-Seeking, 1971–1995*. Toronto: University of Toronto Press.

–. 2004. "Questioning Heteronormativity: Lesbian and Gay Challenges to Education Practice in British Columbia, Canada." *Social Movement Studies* 3 (2): 131–45. http://dx.doi.org/10.1080/1474283042000266092.

–. 2005a. "Social Movements and Judicial Empowerment: Courts, Public Policy, and Lesbian and Gay Organizing in Canada." *Politics and Society* 33 (2): 327–53. http://dx.doi.org/10.1177/0032329205275193.

–. 2005b. "The Politics of Same-Sex Marriage in Canada and the United States." *PS: Political Science and Politics* 38 (2): 225–28.

–. 2007. "Framing Same-Sex Marriage in Canada and the United States: *Goodridge, Halpern*, and the National Boundaries of Political Discourse." *Social and Legal Studies* 16 (1): 5–26. http://dx.doi.org/10.1177/0964663907073444.

–. 2008. *Political Institutions and Lesbian and Gay Rights in the United States and Canada*. New York: Routledge.

Snow, Dave. 2014. "Reproductive Autonomy and the Evolving Family in the Supreme Court of Canada: Implications for Assisted Reproductive Technologies." *Journal of Canadian Studies/Revue d'études canadiennes* 48 (1): 153–89.

Stein, Marc. 2012. *Rethinking the Gay and Lesbian Movement*. New York: Routledge.

Stone, Sharon Dale, ed. 1990. *Lesbians in Canada*. Toronto: Between the Lines.

Sylvestre, Paul-François. 1979. *Les homosexuels s'organisent au Québec et ailleurs*. Montréal: Éditions Homeureux.

Tarrow, Sidney. 1994. *Power in Movement: Social Movements, Collective Action and Politics*. 2nd ed. Cambridge: Cambridge University Press.

Taylor, Catherine. 2009. "Health and Safety Issues for Aboriginal Transgender/Two Spirit People in Manitoba." *Canadian Journal of Aboriginal Community-Based HIV/AIDS Research* 2 (5): 63–84.

Taylor, Catherine and Tracey Peter, with T.L. McMinn, Tara Elliott, Stacey Beldom, Allison Ferry, Zoe Gross, Sarah Paquin, and Kevin Schachter. 2011. *Every Class in Every School:*

The First National Climate Survey on Homophobia, Biphobia, and Transphobia in Canadian Schools. Final Report. Toronto: EGALE Canada Human Rights Trust.

Tjepkema, Michael. 2008. Health Care Use among Gay, Lesbian and Bisexual Canadians. *Health Reports* 19 (1): 55–64 (Statistics Canada, 82-003-XPE). http://www.statcan.gc.ca/pub/82-003-x/2008001/article/10532/5002598-eng.htm.

Trans Equality Society of Alberta. 2013. *About Us.* http://www.tesaonline.org/.

Trans Lobby Group. 2013. *About Us.* https://www.facebook.com/TransLobbyGroup.

Tremblay, Manon. 2013. "Mouvements sociaux et opportunités politiques: Les lesbiennes et les gais et l'ajout de l'orientation sexuelle à la Charte québécoise des droits et liberté." *Revue canadienne de science politique* 46 (2): 295–322.

Vaid, Urvashi. 1995. *Virtual Equality: The Mainstreaming of Gay and Lesbian Liberation.* New York: Anchor Books.

Waaldijk, Kees. 2000. "Civil Developments: Patterns of Reform in the Legal Position of Same-Sex Partners in Europe." *Canadian Journal of Family Law* 17 (1): 62–88.

Warner, Tom. 2002. *Never Going Back: A History of Queer Activism in Canada.* Toronto: University of Toronto Press.

–. 2010. *Losing Control: Canada's Social Conservatives in the Age of Rights.* Toronto: Between the Lines.

Waugh, Thomas. 1998. "Des Adonis en quête d'immortalité: la photographie homoérotique." In Irène Demczuk and Frank W. Remiggi, eds., *Sortir de l'ombre: Histoires des communautés lesbienne et gaie de Montréal,* 53–79. Montréal: VLB éditeur.

Wintemute, Robert. 2002. "Religion vs. Sexual Orientation. A Clash of Human Rights?" *Journal of Law and Equality* 1 (2): 125–54.

Wittig, Monique. 1989. "On the Social Contract." *Feminist Issues* 9 (1): 3–12. http://dx.doi.org/10.1007/BF02685600.

Wong, Josephine P. 2006. "Age of Consent to Sexual Activity in Canada: Background to Proposed New Legislation on 'Age of Protection.'" *Canadian Journal of Human Sexuality* 15 (3/4): 163–69.

Young, Clare, and Susan Boyd. 2006. "Losing the Feminist Voice? Debates on the Legal Recognition of Same Sex Partnerships in Canada." *Feminist Legal Studies* 14 (2): 213–40. http://dx.doi.org/10.1007/s10691-006-9028-8.

The National Level

1

LGBTQ Activism: The Pan-Canadian Political Space

MIRIAM SMITH

Canada is often considered to be in the forefront of global LGBTQ rights. Beginning in 1969 with the partial decriminalization of homosexuality, the federal government has incrementally recognized LGBTQ rights in areas such as same-sex relationship recognition, federal human rights legislation, criminal law, and immigration and refugee policy. With the passage of the Civil Marriage Act in 2005, Canada became the fourth country in the world to legalize same-sex marriage. These policy successes resulted from long-standing political activism by the LGBTQ communities and, especially, from legal mobilization through the courts. LGBTQ people have benefited from the partisan and political institutional shifts of the Charter of Rights and Freedoms era, shifts that privileged legal mobilization, thus enhancing the political allure of constitutionally guaranteed human rights.

With the election of the Harper government in 2006, however, the political context for LGBTQ organizing at the Canadian level has shifted. The Conservative Party has deep roots in the social conservative and Christian evangelical movements (Farney 2012). While the government has not deliberately undertaken a rollback of existing LGBTQ rights, it has signalled an antipathy to the LGBTQ communities, symbolized by measures such as its refusal to equalize the age of consent, its failure to support trans rights, and its decision to remove LGBTQ rights from the Canadian citizenship guide. Has the election of successive Harper governments created new obstacles for political success for the LGBTQ movement?

In this chapter I explore LGBTQ political mobilization at the federal level in the post-same-sex marriage period in light of this partisan political shift. After a brief historical discussion of key turning points in LGBTQ policy and an overview of LGBTQ politics in the pan-Canadian political context, I consider three key issues that have been the subject of political and legal mobilization in the post-marriage period: (1) the debate over the age of consent and the way in which the federal state regulates queer sexuality through the criminal law; (2) the debate over homophobic bullying in schools, focusing on the role undertaken by the federal LGBTQ group Egale; and (3) attempts to pass amendments to the Canadian Human Rights Act to prohibit discrimination on the basis of gender expression and gender identity. These cases illustrate different types of political issues – criminal law, social policy, and human rights – as well as different policy dynamics. One of the issues – education – actually falls under provincial jurisdiction and yet has been taken up by Egale as a federal LGBTQ social movement organization. At the same time, the debates over the age of consent have mobilized urban and provincially based groups to target the federal state. Trans issues have moved forward in part because of support from opposition politicians and in part as a result of tribunal rulings in the provinces. I conclude by suggesting that the impact of political institutions and the impact of partisanship on policy development must be tempered with consideration of how political mobilization plays out over the multiple scales of Canadian politics.

Historical Background

The impact of political institutional factors and the challenges for LGBTQ organizing at the federal level are evident when one surveys historical developments from the late 1960s onward. In 1969, the Trudeau government amended the Criminal Code to partially decriminalize homosexuality. This action was facilitated by the federal government's legal jurisdiction over criminal law and by the Trudeau government's modernization of criminal and family law in a broad range of matters, including divorce, abortion, and homosexuality. Under the new law, sodomy was permitted between consenting adults, twenty-one years of age or over. As scholars such as Kinsman (1996, 210–17) and Corriveau (2011, 120–32) point out, this form of decriminalization restricted queer sexuality to the private realm. While the federal government had jurisdiction over the formal law of the Criminal Code, the administration of justice was in the hands of provincial governments and local authorities. Despite the Criminal Code change, the policing of gay sex in bathhouses, as well as other forms of

Miriam Smith

sexual regulation, continued unabated, although, over the course of the 1970s and 1980s, this was increasingly contested in urban areas by gay liberation groups, which were founded in all of Canada's urban centres. Policing practices at the local level were often important forms of sexual regulation. During the 1970s and 1980s, using other levers in the federal Criminal Code (including Victorian-era provisions such as being a "found-in" in a "bawdy house"), police in places such as Montreal, Vancouver, and Toronto sought to "clean up" their cities by arresting queers and by turning a blind eye to homophobic and transphobic violence in urban areas. Well-known clashes between police and the gay movement occurred in Montreal around the Olympic "clean up" of the city in 1976, the Toronto bath raids in 1981, and so on (Warner 2002, 99–118; see Chapter 8, this volume, for more details).

Gay liberation groups were established in all of Canada's major cities in the early 1970s. Gay liberation emphasized the importance of coming out, building community institutions, upending traditional sex and gender roles, and advocating sexual liberation. In August 1971, the first gay liberation demonstration was held on Parliament Hill, organized by homophile and gay liberation groups (see Kinsman and Gentile 2010, 255–65). Toronto Gay Action wrote and delivered a brief to the federal government outlining the demands of the gay movement, which was reprinted in full in the Toronto gay liberation newspaper, the *Body Politic*. Entitled "We Demand," it listed ten demands, including an end to discrimination against gay and lesbian applicants for immigration to Canada; the removal of crimes of "gross indecency," "buggery," and others from the Criminal Code; the right of gays and lesbians to serve in the armed forces; a uniform age of consent for sexual activity; an end to discrimination against lesbians and gays in federal employment; the removal of sodomy and homosexual acts as grounds for divorce under the federal Divorce Act and the right of homosexual parents to equal access in child custody; an end to harassment of lesbian and gay government employees by the RCMP; and the provision of "all legal rights for homosexuals which currently exist for heterosexuals" (Waite and DeNovo 1971, 4).

The 1971 demonstration typified an important dimension of LGBTQ organization in the federal space: local gay liberation groups were the driving force in political action. Youth-driven gay liberation organizations demanded human rights at the urban, provincial, and federal levels and, by 1974, had come together in the first pan-Canadian LGBTQ rights group, called the Canadian National Gay Election Coalition (NGEC) (later, the National Gay Rights Coalition and subsequently the Canadian Lesbian and Gay Rights Coalition [CLGRC]) (Smith 1999, 57–61, 63–66). The CLGRC was a coalition of gay liberation groups from across Canada, based in Ottawa. The federal nature of the organization meant that groups retained their autonomy while participating in the CLGRC. At the same time, given the CLGRC's lack of political and financial resources, its organization rested on the Ottawa-based gay liberation organization, Gays of Ottawa (GO). The 1970s marked the only period in which a Quebec-based queer political organization directly participated in a pan-Canadian organization. The *Association des gai(e)s du Québec* (ADGQ) was a major force in the CLGRC (Smith 1999, 54–57).

In 1980, the CLGRC was disbanded and, over the course of the early 1980s, two key developments shaped queer organizing in the federal space: (1) the advent of HIV/AIDS and the impact of the constitutional entrenchment of the Charter of Rights and Freedoms in 1982 and (2) the coming into effect of the equality rights section (section 15) in 1985. The HIV/AIDS crisis had a devastating effect on the gay liberation organizations of the 1970s as many key leaders were lost to the disease. In addition, new organizations were created to mobilize for health services and to advocate for people with AIDS. Many activists from the lesbian feminist, gay liberation, and women's movements of the 1970s turned to AIDS organizing in the 1980s. The advent of the Charter also shaped LGBTQ political mobilization by drawing queer activists into legal dialogue over the implementation of the Charter and the potential implications of litigation on equality rights. These factors led to a decline of gay liberation ideology in the movement.

A key catalyst for LGBTQ organizing in the 1980s at the federal level was the coming into force of section 15 of the Charter in 1985. Although the section did not include sexual orientation, in 1986 an informal network of lawyers and civil servants in Ottawa founded a new lesbian and gay rights group called Egale (Equality for Gays and Lesbians Everywhere), which aimed to secure the inclusion of sexual orientation in the Charter.[1] Egale was a very different organization than was its predecessor, the CLGRC. Based on individual membership, Egale did not advocate for gay liberation or sexual freedom but, rather, emphasized legally based rights protections. Led by the able and energetic lawyer John Fisher, its executive director from 1995 to 2003, Egale intervened in and helped to develop key lesbian and gay rights cases. Beginning with *Egan* in 1995 and continuing through the *Vriend* and *Rosenberg* cases in 1998, the *M v. H* case in 1999, and the *Halpern* case in 2003, Egale pushed for the recognition of same-sex couples in federal law and policy, the right of LGBTQ individuals to seek redress against discrimination in federal and provincial human rights legislation, and, following the establishment of full recognition for same-sex couples under "common law" (or *union de fait* in Quebec), for same-sex marriage. In 1999, in *M v. H*, the Supreme Court ruled that same-sex couples had the right to spousal support upon the breakdown of their relationships. This opened the door to litigation on same-sex marriage, which was undertaken by plaintiff couples in Quebec, British Columbia, and Ontario. Egale was heavily involved in the pan-Canadian litigation strategy on same-sex marriage, beginning with *Halpern* and ending with the full legalization of same-sex marriage by the Liberal government in 2005 (for details, see Hurley 2005; Rayside 2008, 92–125; Smith 1999, 111–40; 2008, 134–67).

The achievement of same-sex marriage in 2005 marked a turning point in LGBTQ politics in Canada. This policy outcome would have been unthinkable only a few years earlier. In 1996, the Liberal government only very reluctantly amended the Canadian Human Rights Act to include sexual orientation as a prohibited ground of discrimination. Yet, only nine years later, a Liberal government passed the Civil Marriage Act. Forced by the courts to act on LGBTQ rights, the Liberals made the best of it by integrating queer rights into their human rights and Charter-based vision of Canadian nationalism. While the courts pushed the government to act, disciplined political parties and the centralized parliamentary political system also facilitated policy change.

Queer Activism Today

In comparing the Canadian political system to similar systems, there are several important features of the pan-Canadian political space that stand out. First, Canada is a multinational state in which Aboriginal, Quebec, and English-speaking Canadian discourses on nationalism have often influenced LGBTQ organizing (Stychin 1998, 89–114). Both Quebec and Canadian nationalism have been deployed in favour of LGBTQ rights and used as symbols of progressive and modern politics. LGBTQ rights have been racialized in ways that have marginalized Aboriginal and non-Western perspectives (as applied to the United States, see Morgensen 2010; and Chapter 2, this volume). Second, Canada is a federal system that, although it is generally decentralized, is relatively centralized in terms of the legal framework that governs important areas of LGBTQ rights policy such as criminal law, marriage, and constitutional human rights. In contrast, other countries, such as the United States, allocate key areas of LGBTQ rights policy (e.g., criminal law and marriage) to the subnational level. Third, centralized parliamentary political institutions and disciplined political parties empower the government of the day to make decisions unchecked by legislative or caucus opposition. Governments are free to set the policy agenda and to respond to electoral calculations (Smith 2008,

1–30). Although, in the Charter era, the courts have provided a powerful check on government decisions and set constitutional requirements in the area of LGBTQ rights, the federal power of judicial appointment means that the courts' views on LGBTQ rights, as on other constitutional matters, could potentially shift over time in response to the government's policy agenda.

These structural-institutional features of the political environment in federal politics play out against the multiple internal diversities of the LGBTQ communities. Like other social movements that represent traditionally disadvantaged groups in Canada, it is very difficult for the LGBTQ communities to provide the political, organizational, and economic resources for successful and sustained mobilization in federal politics. The federal tax system does not provide generous tax incentives for the establishment of the non-profits, think tanks, and philanthropic endeavours that have proven to be so important to the success of large-scale fundraising for American LGBTQ organizations. The barriers of language, culture, and multinationalism have impeded partnerships between Quebec LGBTQ organizations and those in the rest of Canada. The multiracial and multicultural diversity of Canada has not been fully reflected in pan-Canadian organizing, which tends to have been dominated by white Canadians and to have provided a white "face" to LGBTQ perspectives (Lenon 2005). LGBTQ organizing at the pan-Canadian level also reflects the legacy of settler colonialism. Aboriginal people have been largely absent from the process of pan-Canadian LGBTQ rights claiming, and new scholarship calls attention to the implications of this exclusion for LGBT policy and politics (see Chapter 2, this volume). In addition, Canada's vaunted tolerance for LGBTQ rights claims may be used to pinkwash Canada's ongoing colonial relationship with First Nations and the violation of Aboriginal human rights (Center for Lesbian and Gay Studies 2013). The urban roots of LGBTQ communities and organizations have meant that political mobilization has often been strongest at the urban level. While governments seek unified and coherent organizations that can act as spokesgroups for particular communities, LGBTQ communities present an array of organizations in different fields, from the urban to the pan-Canadian level.

This picture has been further complicated by the impact of legal mobilization on LGBTQ communities. Legal mobilization through the Charter has privileged individual plaintiffs through networks of legal professionals and organizations such as Egale, which was founded in Ottawa in 1986 as an organization devoted to Charter litigation. Litigation played a key role in pushing forward policy issues in federal jurisdictions, and there were a number of struggles for legal and political control among plaintiffs, legal teams, and organizations in Ontario, Quebec, and British Columbia during the multi-year litigation over same-sex marriage. Litigation is not something that can be eas-ily directed from above or coordinated by a social movement organization. Individuals file cases and may do so regardless of the views of social movement elites. In the case of same-sex marriage in Canada, some cases were filed by claimants with their own distinctive histories of activism in LGBTQ commun-ities and with no real experience or interest in federal-level LGBTQ politics (Smith 2008, 134–60). These dynamics reinforced the fracturing effects experi-enced by LGBTQ organizing in the pan-Canadian political space.

Queer Activism and Public Policy Changes: Case Studies

Despite this rapid progress in the recognition of LGBTQ rights, there were a number of other LGBTQ political issues that came to the fore in the post-marriage period. This section examines three of the most important issues: (1) the age of consent for sexual activity, (2) the prevention of bullying and homophobia in schools, and (3) the prohibition of discrimination on the basis of gender expression and gender identity. The development of LGBTQ policies in these areas demonstrates that the political institutions that facilitated the recognition of LGBTQ rights (e.g., centralized parliamentary institutions) can also block further policy development (e.g., in the case of trans human rights recognition) as well as facilitate anti-LGBTQ policies (e.g., changes in the age of consent). The three cases also demonstrate the ways in which political mobilization crosses the jurisdictional boundaries of federalism, with urban LGBTQ groups intervening in federal policy issues and federally organized groups intervening in provincial matters. Moreover, the case of anti-bullying in education shows how the fluidity of political mobilization through social media can subvert the influence of political institutions on policy development.

Age of Consent

The age of consent issue illustrates the ways in which a determined government in the Canadian parliamentary system can undermine LGBTQ rights. Following the revision of the Criminal Code in 1969, the age of consent for sexual activity was eventually set at eighteen for anal sex (except for married couples) and fourteen for other sexual activity. In 2006, the Harper government proposed to increase the age of consent for sexual activity to sixteen, while retaining the dif-ferential age of consent for anal sex. The stated purpose was to protect children; however, LGBTQ groups interpreted the move as strengthening state regulation of sexuality, which had often been used against LGBTQ people.

During the late 1980s and throughout the 1990s, Egale had studiously avoided the issue and, when it did surface, it was evident that there were divisions in the queer community and within Egale over the position that should be taken on the age of consent (Kirkby 2005; McCann 2008). In the wake of the Supreme Court's *Butler* decision in 1992, there had been a struggle over the regulation of pornography, which had divided feminists and the queer community. Some pro-pornography feminists and LGBTQ people argued that the criminal regulation of pornography would inevitably marginalize the expression of queer sexualities, while other feminists, including some lesbian feminists, argued that pornography constituted harm to women and should be regulated (Bell, Cossman, and Gotell 1997, 3–47). The age of consent issue was also taken up in a series of cases in the 1980s and 1990s, in which plaintiffs challenged the criminalization of anal sex for those under the age of eighteen, and the differential age of consent was found to be unconstitutional in challenges before courts in Ontario and Quebec. By 2000, Egale had taken a clear position in favour of a uniform age of consent (Egale 2000).

While the Harper government repeatedly stated that it was not interested in opening up discussion of issues such as same-sex marriage or abortion, the "law-and-order" approach was widely seen as a measure intended to appeal to the base of the Conservative Party by promoting traditional values and social order (Dauda 2010). The name of the proposed legislation – the Tackling Violent Crime Act – seemed to further reinforce this impression as the change to the age of consent was packaged with other criminal law reforms such as increasing the sentencing for those convicted of gun crime (CBC 2008).

Over the period from 2006 to 2008, a number of groups mobilized around the proposed legislative changes. Two main types of groups were involved in opposing the age of consent legislation: (1) LGBTQ groups such as the Coalition for Lesbian and Gay Rights in Ontario (CLGRO, later Queer Ontario) and Egale, and (2) groups involved in sexual health policy such as the Canadian AIDS Society, Planned Parenthood, and the Canadian Federation for Sexual Health (Wong 2006, 164). CLGRO, for example, argued that the legislation did not address the exploitation of children but, rather, that it would discourage young people from seeking information for fear of criminalization. Moreover, CLGRO argued that the failure to equalize the age of consent for anal sex "sen[t] a strong message to the gay community that hostility toward same-sex relationships [was] a motivating factor behind this legislation" (cited in Hudler 2008). These views were strongly backed by Egale (Kirkby 2006). Groups involved in the promotion of sexual health

Miriam Smith

emphasized that the fear of criminalization would discourage youth from seeking information about sexual health or HIV testing. These groups also argued for a uniform age of consent for all types of sexual activity (Canadian AIDS Society 2006). In addition, several newer groups were also involved in opposing the increase in the age of consent. Toronto's Sex Laws Committee, a group of legal academics and others who oppose restrictive laws such as bawdy house laws and other provisions in the Criminal Code, campaigned against the Harper government proposals. Queer youth formed a new group – the Age of Consent Committee – to mobilize against the proposed policy changes. Along with other groups representing queer youth, they testified at the Senate Legal and Constitutional Affairs Committee in early 2008 when it considered the Harper government bill (Creelman 2008).

On the other side of the debate were a number of groups that supported the government and favoured the increase in the age of consent, including Christian groups and other religious groups as well as police representatives. The Canadian Association of Chiefs of Police, the Toronto Police Service, and the RCMP testified at the Senate Legal and Constitutional Affairs Committee in favour of the bill (Canada 2008). They claimed that Canada was becoming a haven for sex tourism because of the relatively low age of consent and that the existing law made it difficult for the police to prosecute sexual predators and for parents to protect children from sexual exploitation or recruitment into the sex trade (see also Hutchinson 2008, 2–3; Wong 2006, 163–64). The Christian Right associated the increased age of consent with protection of children and youth and with upholding the norm that people should not enter into sexual relationships before marriage. They also equated pedophilia with gay men and "stranger danger" and explained the Liberal Party's opposition to the legisla-tion as resulting from "political pressure from homosexuals" (cited in White 2006; see also Quist 2007).

In the end, the government was able to use its strong minority government position to pass the legislation unopposed as neither the Liberals nor the NDP were willing to bring down the government over the issue. This example dem-onstrates that the centralized parliamentary institutions that had served as a key lever for the advancement of LGBTQ rights so often in the past could also be used to stop or reverse the expansion of LGBTQ rights should a govern-ment in power favour such a course. The failure to stop the increase in the age of consent and the failure to equalize the age of consent for anal sex with other sexual activity were important defeats for the LGBTQ movement and strength-ened the ability of the state to regulate queer and youth sexuality through the deployment of criminal law.

Homophobia in Education

Education is a provincial responsibility and queer activism on the issue is focused mainly at the local and provincial levels. However, litigation on queer education issues brought it to country-wide attention. In the 1990s and early 2000s, the Surrey book banning grew out of teacher activism in the BC public school system, where teachers' attempts to use gay- and lesbian-positive reading materials led to a ban by the local school board (see Chapter 6, this volume). The book banning led to a divisive community debate over the stigma faced by queer teachers and students as well as over the challenges faced by children with same-sex parents. The queer teachers won their case in the Supreme Court in 2002 as the ban was struck down *(Chamberlain v. Surrey School Board)*.

Legal mobilization over queer education issues has also been taken up in other cases that have gained media attention across Canada, especially those focusing on conflicts between religious rights and education, including teacher training in British Columbia and the inclusion of same-sex couples at Roman Catholic school proms in Ontario (for more details, see Chapter 3 and Chapter 6, this volume). Bullying is another major issue that emerged in education: a number of teacher and parent activists have used provincial human rights codes to push school boards to enforce policies to stop the bullying of queer youth. In British Columbia, Glen Hansman, an LGBTQ education activist, has pressured the government to implement its own order to school boards to adopt codes of conduct that are compatible with the BC Human Rights Code. In Ontario, Ellen Chambers Picard filed two human rights complaints on behalf of her gay son under the Ontario Human Rights Code after his high school refused to act to stop homophobic bullying (Barsotti 2010; Smith 2004). Catholic schools in Ontario have been reluctant to permit gay-straight alliances (GSAs), which have been expanding in Canadian schools. And the anti-bullying It Gets Better (IGB) media campaign, which started in the United States, has spread through Canadian and global social media (see Chapter 5 and Chapter 11, this volume, for examples). At the same time, the IGB campaign has also been critiqued as presenting an assimilated, white, and affluent version of gay identity (although, to date, such critiques have not been heard directly in Canadian debates) (Puar 2010).

Moreover, a number of provincially or locally focused grassroots groups have worked on queer education issues, some very successfully. In Quebec, a new policy against homophobia in schools was developed in consultation with queer and queer-parent groups such as Coalition des familles homoparentales and Groupe de recherche et d'intervention sociale (GRIS). The policy, *La politique québécoise de lutte contre l'homophobie,* was developed in 2010 (see Chapter 4, this volume). In Ontario, TEACH is a local community group that has long made presentations on homophobia in the schools, and, in British Columbia, Out in Schools brings queer films to high schools in order to facilitate discussion about sexuality. Some of these initiatives entailed grassroots urban groups, operating through schools and school boards, while, in the case of Quebec, queer and queer-parent groups were able to successfully mobilize to push for policy change through the Quebec government. Ontario efforts resulted in the passage of an anti-bullying bill by the Liberal minority government of Dalton McGuinty in 2012, a bill that guarantees that all students in public schools in Ontario (including Catholic schools) have access to GSAs and that establishes anti-bullying programs to ensure a welcoming environment for LGBTQ youth. At the same time, however, Ontario was also the site of an earlier defeat for the revamping of sex education in schools, an initiative favoured by Queer Ontario and by Egale, which worked together on the issue (McCann 2010).

Despite provincial jurisdiction over education, Egale was pressured by activists from across Canada to develop a strong pan-Canadian network that could build on local and provincial efforts. In 2006, Egale commissioned a study on the climate for LGBTQ students in Canadian schools that was intended to provide an evidence base for LGBTQ claims about the need for queer-friendly education policies. The study, which was funded by Egale and its Human Rights Trust and was carried out by researchers from the University of Winnipeg, surveyed seventeen hundred high school students online and through in-school focus groups. Based on the online survey, the researchers reached the conclusions that: "despite Canada's leadership on human rights for LGBTQ people, a great deal of verbal and physical homophobic and transphobic harassment goes on in Canadian schools, that LGBTQ students are more likely to be aware of it than are other students who are not its main targets, and that the institutional response to harassment has more often than not been inadequate" (Taylor et al. 2009, 7). Consistent with the problems in establishing GSAs in Catholic schools in Ontario, most Catholic school boards did not agree to implement the in-school focus groups (ibid.).

Following the report, Egale established a website to bring together information for grassroots and local groups on how to establish GSAs. Similar to the school benchmarking tools developed by GLSEN in the United States (see Grundy and Smith 2007), Egale's website provided information that could be used by students and parents to assess the school environment as well as to establish and manage GSAs. In the case of Newfoundland and Labrador, Egale was invited to partner with the provincial ministry of education to deliver anti-bullying and LGBTQ training in the province's schools (Egale 2012).

Therefore, while education policy remains a local matter and the object of political mobilization by queer and queer-friendly groups at the level of school boards and provincial governments, Egale has played a role in facilitating policy change at the pan-Canadian level by bringing together resources, information, and communication through the internet. Rather than directly orchestrating legal challenges or political mobilization to influence the federal government, as was the case in the same-sex marriage debate or in debates over obtaining anti-discrimination protection, Egale has created networks and resources that can be used by groups at the local and provincial levels; joined coalitions such as Ontario GSA in support of the proposed Ontario anti-bullying legislation; built partnerships with provincial governments when invited, as in the case of Newfoundland and Labrador; and built policy resources and policy capacity that can be used by other groups. Still, Egale at times has been criticized for not reacting quickly and forcefully to anti-gay sallies perpetrated by the Harper government, such as the exclusion of LGBTQ people and issues from the new Canadian citizenship guide (Creelman 2010). In addition, Egale has sometimes been criticized for intervening in provincial issues (Rau 2008). The rise of social media means that advocacy groups such as Egale must react more quickly to unfolding events and must take public positions, even in cases such as education, in which the provinces play the key role.

Trans Human Rights Protection

Trans human rights is another important issue in the pan-Canadian queer political space. While the early gay liberation movement emphasized gender and sexual fluidity, the categories of gender and sexual orientation were gradually hardened in the movement's encounters with governments and courts. Litigation and constitutional reform encouraged a simplified view of the politics of gender in which binary categories of sex and sexual orientation were accorded legal status. Trans identities fit uneasily into these legal categories as some trans people seek to negotiate from one side of the gender binary to the other while others seek to disrupt gender binaries entirely (see discussion in Roen 2001). In addition, trans people do not necessarily identify as gay, lesbian, bisexual, or queer. Trans people express their identities in their own

Miriam Smith

specific languages, such as "FtM" (female to male), "MtF" (male to female), "genderqueer," "intersexed," "Two-Spirited," "bi-gendered," "transsexual," "drag king," "drag queen," or "gender variant." Discrimination on the basis of gender, gender expression, or gender identity may affect people of any sexual orientation. Some trans people transition through changes in gender expression without surgery and hormones, while others seek sexual reassignment surgery (SRS). Therefore, it is important to protect against discrimination based on gender, gender identity, and gender expression in order to encompass the full rights of trans people.

Like other areas of LGBTQ politics, trans human rights spans the federal and provincial levels. Demands for SRS funding fall under provincial jurisdiction. Currently, British Columbia, Ontario, Quebec, and a few of the Prairie provinces pay for SRS surgeries to a varying extent; however, even where provincial Medicare covers the surgery and expenses, such services are available only in a few sites in Canada and are governed by stringent requirements (Fagan 2009). Similarly, the protection of trans people in social institutions such as schools, hospitals, prisons, and jails often entails provincial involvement. Given that discrimination based on sex and sexual orientation are both prohibited under the Charter as a result of court decisions, some have argued that gender, gender expression, and gender identity are implicitly included in the Charter and in provincial human rights protections (Ontario 2000). However, unlike sexual orientation, gender identity and gender expression have yet to receive clear and explicit constitutional protection from the Supreme Court of Canada.

Like lesbian, gay, and bisexual plaintiffs, many trans people have sought human rights protections in recent years through courts and tribunals. Trans litigation has not been strategically undertaken as the deliberate tactic of a social movement seeking rights recognition, as was the case with litigation by the gay liberation movement during the 1970s; rather, individual plaintiffs have been at the forefront, although sometimes assisted by Egale, other LGBTQ organizations, or by the network of lawyers that was involved in earlier same-sex litigation. In recent years, Egale has been involved in the political mobilization for federal protection of trans human rights in the Canadian Human Rights Act. However, as with other areas of its political mobilization, Egale has also been criticized for its lack of effective outreach to the trans communities and for its lack of action on the trans file. The trans communities do not have a single effective organization that advocates at the Canadian level for their human rights, although Ontario's Trans Lobby Group (2012) has pushed for federal human rights protection. Like other queer movements, trans organizing is also carried out through the communities at the urban level, through the internet, through umbrella LGBTQ organizations, and/or through political parties such as the NDP.

There have been a number of key court and tribunal decisions on trans rights at the provincial level, which demonstrates the need for recognition of trans human rights at the pan-Canadian level. In a 2005 decision in the case of *Hogan v. Ontario (Health and Long-Term Care),* four complainants alleged that the 1998 delisting of SRS from OHIP coverage constituted discrimination based on sex; however, the tribunal ruled in favour only of those plaintiffs who also claimed the ground of disability. Following the *Hogan* case in Ontario, SRS funding has been increasingly framed as a human rights issue. A recent example is Vanida Plamondon, who has filed a case in the Nunavut Human Rights Tribunal contesting the denial of funding by the government of Nunavut (Murphy 2012). In another Ontario decision, the grounds of sex in the Ontario Human Rights Code were deemed to include gender identity (*Forrester v. Peel* 2006), while, in 2012, an Ontario human rights tribunal ruled in *XY v. Ontario* that trans people do not have to surgically alter their gender in order to change their gender on their Ontario birth certificate. In *Vancouver Rape Relief v. Nixon* (2005), the BC Court of Appeal held that discrimination against a trans woman occurred but that the discrimination was permitted, given the feminist goals of Vancouver Rape Relief. The Supreme Court of Canada declined to hear the appeal in 2007. These cases demonstrate an incremental recognition of trans rights, similar to the pattern that unfolded with lesbian and gay rights in the 1980s and 1090s.

In 2010, NDP MP Bill Siksay proposed to amend the Canadian Human Rights Act to include gender identity and gender expression as well as to amend the Criminal Code to include trans people in hate crimes sentencing. The law passed but died in the Senate in 2011 when the federal election was called. The bill has been reintroduced by Liberal MPs and passed by the House of Commons; however, it had not yet been passed by the Senate when Parliament disbanded for its summer recess in 2013. It is possible that policy change will be obtained through the courts. As it stands, SRS surgery is difficult to obtain in many parts of Canada. Besides, trans people may wish to express a different gender identity without necessarily undergoing surgery. In this case, they will present a different gender at the border than the gender that is specified in their passport, opening the door to discrimination and harassment (Houston 2011; see also Egale 2011). As is the case for many involved in lesbian, gay, and bisexual rights, many in the trans movement are also critical of the legal approach to rights protection (on the United States, see Spade 2011).

Miriam Smith

It is likely that a trans rights case will eventually be heard in the Supreme Court. When and if this occurs, the Charter-empowered courts will play a key role in advancing human rights in the LGBTQ area. The Harper government's recent actions in appointing more politically conservative judges to the Supreme Court and to other judicial positions may mean that the courts play a very different role than they played in the Liberal era, during which they ruled in favour of same-sex rights in a number of cases and effectively forced both federal and provincial governments to recognize lesbian and gay rights and the rights of same-sex couples. If the federal government appoints more socially conservative judges at the federal level and in key provinces such as Quebec and Ontario, this could lead to a blockage for the recognition of trans rights in the pan-Canadian space.

Conclusion

The pan-Canadian political level is challenging terrain for LGBTQ social movements. As for other social movements, the multiple diversities of a multi-national and multi-ethnic state create structural obstacles to movement coherence. LGBTQ organizing has been strong and vital in urban communities, especially in Vancouver, Montreal, and Toronto, Canada's three largest cities. It has been more difficult for these communities to organize nationally, or on a country-wide basis. Even organizations such as Egale (which defines its focus in terms of federal politics) have found it challenging to bridge the multiple linguistic, national, and regional divides in addition to dealing with the internal diversities of the LGBTQ communities.

The three case studies discussed here demonstrate that LGBTQ political mobilization crosses the lines and categories of federal and provincial jurisdiction. With regard to the age of consent, local urban groups were involved in pressuring the federal government. With regard to education, Egale has been involved in alliances with local and provincial groups in local education matters. In the case of trans human rights protections, the Trans Lobby, based in Ontario, has played an important role in pushing for federal human rights protections. As a federal-level lobby group, Egale has no special status among LGBTQ organizations in Canada. Local and urban organizations often have stronger community roots, and, particularly in Quebec, multinationalism undercuts Egale's "federal," or Ottawa-based, role. In the period prior to the attainment of same-sex marriage in 2005, legal mobilization was by far the most successful political strategy for LGBTQ organizing at the federal level; however, even then, successful campaigns were built on the strength of local and provincial organizations. In the case of relationship recognition, discrimination, and same-sex marriage, legal networks in Canada's major cities played an important role in creating a pan-Canadian dimension for LGBTQ; and Egale was built, in part, by lawyers who sought Charter-based human rights protections that would have been unimaginable to 1970s gay liberation activists. However, with the attainment of full marriage equality and the consequent decline of legal mobilization as a political strategy, country-wide networks have shifted to social media, which now play an important role in Canadian queer debates.

Just as political institutions and, in particular, the role of constitutionally empowered courts played a key role in facilitating rapid policy change for the LGBTQ movement in Canada from the 1980s to the 2000s, so, too, courts may prove to be an important ongoing venue for LGBTQ rights claims. The more that queer rights (including trans rights) have been pushed into courts and tribunals, the more successful they have been. Although the Harper government is seeking to shift judicial attitudes through conservative judicial appointments, this is a long-term strategy that may not succeed, given the jurisprudence that has already developed in the area. In addition, centralized parliamentary political institutions continue to facilitate policy change at the federal level. As in the case of the age of consent, if the federal government decides to limit or undermine LGBTQ rights, there is little that the movement can do to stop the change, barring court action. Similarly, during the period of LGBTQ rights expansion, LGBTQ rights opponents were similarly stymied by executive-dominated parliamentary institutions that were able to use parliamentary majorities to make decisions unchecked by legislative opposition. These realities mean that, for issues that fall clearly under federal jurisdiction, federalism will continue to play an important role in shaping the terrain of political battle. However, the urban-based strength of LGBTQ community organizations and Canada's multi-diversity mean that federal-level political organizations will never be the main source of the political strength of the communities; rather, urban-based and/or issue-based groups will continue to play a central role in LGBTQ organizing at the pan-Canadian level.

Note

1 Egale was originally named Equality for Gays and Lesbians Everywhere (EGALE). However, in 1995, it was renamed Egale Canada (Egale, for short) and incorporated as a non-profit. At the same time, Egale Human Rights Trust was founded as a charitable organization to undertake research and education. Throughout this article, I use the term Egale to reference the original EGALE and Egale Canada as advocacy organizations.

Miriam Smith

References

Barsotti, Natasha. 2010. "How the Canadian Education System Is Failing Queer Youth." *Xtra! Canada's Gay and Lesbian News*, 28 January. http://www.xtra.ca/public/National/ How_the_Canadian_education_system_is_failing_queer_youth-8159.aspx.

Bell, Shannon, Brenda Cossman, and Lise Gotell, eds. 1997. *Bad Attitude/s on Trial: Pornography, Feminism, and the* Butler *Decision.* Toronto: University of Toronto Press.

Canada. Senate of Canada. 2008. *Proceedings of the Standing Senate Committee on Legal and Constitutional Affairs, Issue 11 (February 25).* Ottawa: Library of Parliament. http:// www.parl.gc.ca/Content/SEN/Committee/392/lega/11evb-e.htm?Language=E&Parl=3 9&Ses=2&comm_id=11.

Canadian AIDS Society. 2006. *Position Statement: Age of Consent.* Ottawa: Canadian AIDS Society. http://www.cdnaids.ca/files.nsf/pages/age_of_consent_en_red/$file/Age_ of_Consent_En_Red.pdf.

CBC. 2008. "Canada's Age of Consent Raised by 2 Years." 1 May. Toronto: Canadian Broadcasting Corporation. http://www.cbc.ca/news/canada/story/2008/05/01/crime -bill.html.

Center for Lesbian and Gay Studies (New York City). 2013. *Queer Discourse of the Canadian Colonial Settler State* (July 6). Video. http://www.youtube.com/watch?v=3XK ZsgDYQlw&feature=youtube_gdata_player.

Corriveau, Patrice. 2011. *Judging Homosexuals: A History of Gay Persecution in Quebec and France.* Trans. Käthe Roth. Vancouver: UBC Press.

Creelman, Brent. 2008. "Youth Groups Tell Senate to Keep Consent Age at 14." *Xtra! Canada's Gay and Lesbian News*, 22 February. http://www.xtra.ca/public/viewstory. aspx?AFF_TYPE=1&STORY_ID=4379&PUB_TEMPLATE_ID=9.

–. 2010. "Twittersphere Slams EGALE's Response on Citizenship Guide Issue." *Xtra! Canada's Gay and Lesbian News*, 4 March. http://www.xtra.ca/public/National/Twittersphere_ slams_Egales_response_on_citizenship_guide_issue-8321.aspx.

Dauda, Carol L. 2010. "Childhood, Age of Consent and Moral Regulation in Canada and the UK." *Contemporary Politics* 16 (3): 227–47. http://dx.doi.org/10.1080/13569775.2010. 501634.

Egale. 2000. *EGALE's Submission on Age of Consent to the Department of Justice Canada.* Ottawa: Egale. 30 March. Document in possession of the author.

–. 2011. *Policy Paper: "Sex" Inscriptions on the Canadian Passport.* Egale: Toronto.

–. 2012. *EGALE Canada and Government of Newfoundland and Labrador Working Together to Promote Gay-Straight Alliances.* Press Release. Ottawa: Egale. http://egale. ca/wp-content/uploads/2012/09/Press-Egale-and-NL-promote-GSAs.pdf.

Fagan, Noreen. 2009. "Sex Reassignment Surgery in Canada: What's Covered and Where." *Xtra! Canada's Gay and Lesbian News*, 26 October. http://www.xtra.ca/public/National/ Sex_reassignment_surgery_in_Canada_whats_covered_and_where-7706.aspx .

Farney, James. 2012. *Social Conservatives and Party Politics in Canada and the United States.* Toronto: University of Toronto Press.

Grundy, John, and Miriam Smith. 2007. "Activist Knowledges in Queer Politics." *Economy and Society* 36 (2): 294–317. http://dx.doi.org/10.1080/03085140701254324.

Houston, Andrea. 2011. "Trans Canadians Fight for Recognition on Legal Documents." *Xtra! Canada's Gay and Lesbian News*, 16 April. http://www.xtra.ca/public/National/ Trans_Canadians_fight_for_recognition_on_legal_documents-11256.aspx.

Hudler, Richard. 2008. "Age of Consent." *Outwords*, April. http://queerontario.org/ archives/clgro-archives/clgro-newsletter/. Accessed 23 December 2011.

Hurley, Mary C. 2005. *Sexual Orientation and Legal Rights: A Chronological Overview*. Ottawa: Parliamentary Information and Research Service, Library of Parliament.

Hutchinson, Don. 2008. *Child Protection: Appearing as a Witness to the Standing Committee on Legal and Constitutional Affairs of the Senate of Canada on Bill C-2*. Ottawa: Evangelical Fellowship of Canada, 22 February. http://www.parl.gc.ca/Content/SEN/Committee/392/lega/pdf/10issue.pdf (viewed 18 February 2013).

Kinsman, Gary. 1996. *The Regulation of Desire: Homo and Hetero Sexualities*. 2nd ed. Montreal: Black Rose Rooks.

Kinsman, Gary, and Patrizia Gentile. 2010. *The Canadian War on Queers: National Security as Sexual Regulation*. Vancouver: UBC Press.

Kirkby, Gareth. 2005. "Age of Consent Changes Defeated." *Xtra! Canada's Gay and Lesbian News* (Ottawa). 6 October. http://dailyxtra.com/ottawa/news/age-consent-changes-defeated.

–. 2006. "EGALE Opposes Change in Age of Consent." *Xtra! Canada's Gay and Lesbian News* (Toronto), 26 May. http://www.xtra.ca/public/Toronto/Egale_opposes_change_in_age_of_consent-1693.aspx.

Lenon, Suzanne J. 2005. "Marrying Citizens! Raced Subjects? Re-Thinking the Terrain of Equal Marriage Discourse." *Canadian Journal of Women and the Law* 17 (2): 405–21.

McCann, Marcus. 2008. "Lessons Learned While Wrestling Age of Consent." *Xtra! Canada's Gay and Lesbian News*, 5 March. http://www.xtra.ca/public/viewstory.aspx?AFF_TYPE=1&STORY_ID=4443&PUB_TEMPLATE_ID=2.

–. 2010. "More Groups Endorse Ontario's 2010 Sex Ed Plan." *Xtra! Canada's Gay and Lesbian News*, 23 April. http://dailyxtra.com/ideas/blogs/latest-news-roundup/groups-endorse-ontarios-2010-sex-ed-plan.

Morgensen, Scott Lauria. 2010. "Settler Homonationalism: Theorizing Settler Colonialism Within Queer Modernities." *GLQ: A Journal of Lesbian and Gay Studies* 16 (1): 105–31. http://dx.doi.org/10.1215/10642684-2009-015.

Murphy, David. 2012. "Nunavut Won't Budge on Sex Reassignment Surgery Funding: Ma." *Nunatsiaq Online*, 17 May. http://www.nunatsiaqonline.ca/stories/article/65674nunavut_wont_on_sexual_reassignment_surgery_funding/.

Ontario. 2000. *Policy on Discrimination and Harrassment Because of Gender Identity*. Toronto: Ontario Human Rights Commission. http://www.ohrc.on.ca/en/policy-discrimination-and-harassment-because-gender-identity.

Puar, Jasbir. 2010. "In the Wake of *It Gets Better*." *Guardian*, 16 November. http://www.guardian.co.uk/commentisfree/cifamerica/2010/nov/16/wake-it-gets-better-campaign.

Quist, Dave. 2007. "Presentation before Justice Committee – Bill C22 Age of Sexual Consent." In *Report (2) 29 March*. Ottawa: Institute of Marriage and Family; http://www.imfcanada.org/article_files/Bill_C-22_Presentation.pdf. Accessed 20 December 2011. Summary document available at http://www.imfcanada.org/issues/presentation-justice-committee-house-commons.

Rau, Krishna. 2008. "EGALE Comes Under Fire." *Xtra! Canada's Gay and Lesbian News*, 8 May. http://www.xtra.ca/public/National/Egale_comes_under_fire-4740.aspx.

Rayside, David. 2008. *Queer Inclusions, Continental Divisions: Public Recognition of Sexual Diversity in Canada and the United States*. Toronto: University of Toronto Press.

Roen, Katrina. 2001. "'Either/Or' and 'Both/Neither': Discursive Tensions in Transgender Politics." *Signs* 27 (2): 501–22. http://dx.doi.org/10.1086/495695.

Smith, Miriam. 1999. *Lesbian and Gay Rights in Canada: Social Movements and Equality-Seeking, 1971–1995*. Toronto: University of Toronto Press.

–. 2004. "Questioning Heteronormativity: Lesbian and Gay Challenges to Educational Practice in British Columbia, Canada." *Social Movement Studies* 3 (2): 131–45. http://dx.doi.org/10.1080/1474283042000266092.

–. 2008. *Political Institutions and Lesbian and Gay Rights in the United States and Canada*. New York: Routledge.

Spade, Dean. 2011. *Normal Life: Administrative Violence, Critical Trans Politics, and the Limits of Law*. Brooklyn, NY: South End Press.

Stychin, Carl. 1998. *A Nation by Rights: National Cultures, Sexual Identity Politics and the Discourse of Rights*. Philadelphia: Temple University Press.

Taylor, Catherine, Tracey Peter, Kevin Schachter, Sarah Paquin, Stacey Beldom, Zoe Gross, and T.L. McMinn. 2009. *Youth Speak Up about Homophobia and Transphobia: The First National Climate Survey on Homophobia in Canadian Schools. Phase One Report*. Toronto: EGALE Canada Human Rights Trust. http://egale.ca/all/phase1/.

Trans Lobby Group. 2012. *About Us*. https://www.facebook.com/TransLobbyGroup/info.

Waite, Brian, and Cheri DeNovo. 1971. "We Demand." *Body Politic* 1 (November-December): 6–7.

Warner, Tom. 2002. *Never Going Back: A History of Queer Activism in Canada*. Toronto: University of Toronto Press.

White, Hillary. 2006. "Age of Consent at 14 Makes Canada Favoured Sex Tourism Destination." *LifeSiteNews.com*, 19 December. http://www.lifesitenews.com/news/archive/ldn/1961/21/6121905.

Wong, Josephine P. 2006. "Age of Consent to Sexual Activity in Canada: Background to Proposed New Legislation on 'Age of Protection.'" *Canadian Journal of Human Sexuality* 15 (3/4): 163–69.

Legal Cases

Chamberlain v. Surrey District School Board No. 36 [2002] 4 S.C.R. 710, 2002 SCC 86

Forrester v. Regional Municipality of Peel, Police Services Board (No. 2) [2006] HRTO 13

Halpern v. Canada (Attorney General) [2003] 65 O.R. (3d) 161 (C.A)

Hogan v. Ontario (Minister of Health and Long-Term Care) [2006] 58 C.H.R.R. D/317 (HRTO)

M v. H [1999] S.C.J. No. 23

R. v. Butler [1992] 1 S.C.R. 452

Rosenberg v. Canada (Attorney General) [1998] 38 O.R. (3d) 577

Vancouver Rape Relief Society v. Nixon [2005] BCCA 601 (CanLII)

Vriend v. Alberta [1998] 1 S.C.R. 493

XY v. Ontario (Government and Consumer Services) [2012] HRTO 726 (CanLII)

2

LGBTQ Issues as Indigenous Politics: Two-Spirit Mobilization in Canada

JULIE DEPELTEAU AND DALIE GIROUX

> As Native people, our erotic lives and identities have been colonized along
> with our homelands.
>
> – Qwo-Li Driskill, "Stolen from Our Bodies," 2004

This work examines the Two-Spirit movement and its relationship with regional and urban LGBTQ movements. Two-Spirit groups are more often than not located in cities, operate at a grassroots level, and position themselves at a distance from other LGBTQ groups. In the past twenty-five years, Two-Spirit mobilization in Canada has developed as a decentralized and open web of people and social organizations loosely linked to organizations created earlier in the United States. As a social and political movement, it presents a unique territoriality because it reflects, through its diverse practices, demands, and orientations, the multiple and complex identities at play in Indigenous LGBTQ issues. Reserve life, racism, homophobia, exile, HIV/AIDS, and urbanization are some of the themes through which LGBTQ and Indigenous issues intersect in the Two-Spirit movement.

In the first part of this chapter, we deal with the history of the Two-Spirit movement. In the second part, we illustrate its basic and enduring relationship to state power through three case studies: (1) the Indian Act, 1876, and its subsequent versions; (2) the regime of the residential schools; and (3) HIV/AIDS Two-Spirit activism. In both parts, we address the role of colonialism in the development of the Two-Spirit movement, with an emphasis on how colonial policy has potentially erased multiple-gender systems in Canada.

Next, we assess the contemporary Two-Spirit movement's political demands and how federal and provincial agencies meet those demands. Last, we show that the mobilization of Two-Spirited peoples in Canada has led to increased social activism and social and health programming – mostly related to the epidemic of HIV/AIDS in Indigenous communities and urban settings.

Historical Background

There is a rich history of multiple-gender traditions in the Indigenous Americas,[1] and, in the past few decades, these have been recorded orally by knowledge holders from different nations throughout the continent (Deschamps and 2-Spirited People of the 1st Nations 1998; Lang 2003, 203; Williams 1986, 18) and documented by historians and anthropologists (Roscoe 1998; Williams 1986). In the 1970s, urban LGBT Aboriginals began to reclaim those traditions (Lang 2003, 212).[2]

From Berdache to Two-Spirit

Since the seventeenth century, colonial states in North America have tried to erase those multiple-gender systems by imposing European and Christian moral codes on Indigenous peoples. The Canadian state, like others, directly and indirectly targeted those systems through a series of public policies.

The early voyageur and missionary accounts of alternative gender expression are often marked, if not by outrage, at least by a sense of dismissive astonishment that associates alternative genders with barbarism (see, for instance, renderings by Roscoe 1998 and Williams 1986). What was even more offensive to European eyes was that, among some nations, people identifying with an alternative gender were highly esteemed and sometimes held prestigious social or spiritual offices.[3]

During the land-grab known in the Euro-American imagination as the "Discovery of the New World," the church and the colonial state laid the cultural, social, moral, legal, and disciplinary groundwork for territorial despoliation. As Kinsman (1996, 95) suggests, the "civilization" of Indigenous bodies and ways of life appears as a founding element of the Canadian nation and state. Thus, when approaching multiple-gender traditions, we have to assess the multifarious and enduring social, economic, and political interventions into Indigenous societies within this historical-institutional context. The colonial church and state constructed a Euro-Christian gender system by regulating marriage and the sexual division of labour, by converting the Indigenous self-supporting and often nomadic economies into a cash economy, and by policing the Indigenous body – from clothing to shelter to eating to sex. The Indian Act facilitated these practices in Canada and led to the loss of traditional multiple-gender systems.[4]

We have to situate the Two-Spirit movement within this historical and political context. Having its roots in, and developing parallel to, the gay and lesbian movement of the 1970s (see the "Historical Background" sections of the various chapters of this book), the Two-Spirit movement forms its distinct identity by joining contemporary lives and practices in colonial societies with the pre-Columbian modes of thinking gender that were besieged during the "Discovery of the New World."

Two-Spirit Movement

"Two-Spirit" is a neologism that was coined in 1988 (Deschamps and 2-Spirited People of the 1st Nations 1998, 21; Meyer-Cook and Labelle 2004). It is used to describe a pan-Aboriginal set of traditional and contemporary multiple-gender identities. As an umbrella designation,[5] "Two-Spirit" does not replace the specific terms that appear in over 168 Native languages (still used mostly on reserves) and that refer to gender variant people (Tafoya 1997, 4; Thomas and Jacobs 1999, 92). The term was formalized in 1990 at the third Annual Native American Gay and Lesbian Gathering in Winnipeg, at which attendees changed the name of the gathering to the International Two-Spirit Gathering (Thomas and Jacobs 1999, 91; Walters et al. 2006, 127).[6]

"Two-Spirit" was meant to replace the derogatory term "berdache," which was still being used at that time, as well as to insist on the differences between the Indigenous movement and the dominant LGBTQ culture: "Two-Spirit identity articulates with and manipulates ideologies of gay and Indian despite the failure of gay and lesbian culture to recognize Native Americans as an important aspect of their society, as well as other Indians' denial of Two-Spirit existence" (Gilley 2006, 7).[7] It places the emphasis on gender diversity – rather than on sexual orientation – and its inclusion in a cultural and spiritual system.[8] Hence, scholars and activists insist on not reducing "Two-Spirit" to a sexual orientation or equating it with "gay," "homosexual," or even "berdache." (Gilley 2006, 54; Tafoya 1997, 5; Williams 1986, 223) From their perspective, sexual behaviour cannot be separated from the social roles occupied by Two-Spirited people and the world of relationships to which the term "Two-Spirit" refers.

Nonetheless, not all "LGBTQ Aboriginals" embrace the term: some identify with the LGBTQ movement, some with categories specific to their own

Julie Depelteau and Dalie Giroux

language, and some adopt different labels depending on the context (Driskill 2010, 72). There is tension regarding how to define Two-Spirit identity. This tension exists between those who see Two-Spirit as a suitable category for all LGBTQ Aboriginals and those who, in their critique of colonialism, see the importance of retaining certain traditional views. For the latter, the concept of "Two-Spirit," as an uncovered and reworked traditional identity, offers a way to reconcile marginalized people with their communities and to re-include them as mentors who can address social problems and take a stand against the homophobia and secrecy prompted by colonization (Alaers 2010, 77; Driskill 2010, 85–86; Gilley 2006, 135, 167–68; Williams 1986, 228). In this sense, "Two-Spirit" revisits cultural and spiritual traditions, and it articulates the connection between gender diversity, sexual behaviour, land, and sovereignty in a decolonizing discourse.[9]

Two-Spirit Activism Today

The urbanization of gay and lesbian Aboriginals started in the 1950s, at the same time as Canada's Department of Indian Affairs modified restrictions regarding Aboriginal people's ability to move off of reserves (Thoms and 2-Spirited People of the 1st Nations 2007, 21). In the context of the European binary gender system and corresponding heteronormativity,[10] many people left for urban centres in order to escape the homophobia and the alienation they would endure if their gender identity or sexual orientation were disclosed in small towns or rural areas (Monette et al. 2001, 26; Thoms and 2-Spirited People of the 1st Nations 2007, 22; Walters et al. 2006, 141). Susan Beaver recounts: "As a two-spirited man, you know there is no room for your life on the reserve. Your sexuality is not tolerated and many men leave to find urban centres where they can express themselves" (Deschamps and 2-Spirited People of the 1st Nations 1998, 14). As it was important to the repression of multiple-gender systems, land legislation, especially the gradual confinement of Aboriginal people to reserves (where Euro-American views about gender and sexuality were preached and implemented), became a turning point for the formation of an urban LGBTQ Aboriginal movement. That Two-Spirited people could leave reserves – with little chance of return – was also instrumental in the urbanization of two-spiritedness.

Notwithstanding, Lang (2003, 209) notes that some Aboriginal LGBTQ people stay on reserves and keep their gender identity/sexual orientation low profile, preferring not to "come out," as is sometimes encouraged in urban LGBTQ culture. According to Wilson (2007, 85), this might provide a way for

Two-Spirited individuals to "come in" to their community, to integrate themselves as LGBTQ, while also holding on to their Aboriginal culture and identity. This indicates that the reason for the separation between the Two-Spirit movement and the LGBTQ movement has to do with the importance of taking into account experiences of racism and colonialism, and of retaining the notions of gender variance and sexual orientation that existed in traditional Aboriginal cultures. In other words, at the heart of the effort to distinguish the Two-Spirit movement from the LGBTQ movement is the desire to escape a homophobic milieu while, at the same time, not being whitewashed and isolated from one's own culture. Hence the development of a social and political Two-Spirit identity distinct from that of the LGBTQ movement, which can be seen as a colonial institution that contributes to the continued erasure of Indigenous Two-Spirited persons. This distinction compelled people to form separate Aboriginal LGBTQ groups in the 1980s and a Two-Spirit movement in the 1990s.

Accordingly, Two-Spirit groups of various sizes emerged in several Canadian cities in the 1990s, as they did in the United States in the previous decade. Gays and Lesbians of the First Nations (in Toronto), which, in 1991, switched its name to 2-Spirited People of the 1st Nations; the Nichiwakan Native Gay and Lesbian Society, later to become the Two-Spirited People of Manitoba (in Winnipeg); and Vancouver Two-Spirit have, or had, important connections with their American counterparts. The Annual International Two-Spirit Gathering offers opportunities for networking as it is held on both sides of the border, alternating year to year. Other groups not especially dedicated to Two-Spirited people but active in advocating for them in their fight against HIV/AIDS are: Healing Our Spirit, and the Canadian Aboriginal AIDS Network (CAAN), both based in Vancouver; and the Ontario Aboriginal HIV/AIDS Strategy (OAHAS). These groups, especially 2-Spirited People of the 1st Nations, were formed in response to the HIV/AIDS epidemic (Morgensen 2008, 46).

The Two-Spirit movement came into sight in the late 1980s and the early 1990s in North American cities in which LGBTQ groups were already mobilizing and in which there were large populations of First Nations people. The movement was also contemporary with other critiques of the mainstream LGBTQ movement's cultural homogeneity, which led to the formation of distinct associations to deal with racism and colonialism (Walters et al. 2006, 133).

Queer Activism and Public Policy Changes: Case Studies

Because it sheds new light on the Two-Spirited experience and uncovers the stories obscured in colonial history, the formation of the Two-Spirit movement can be understood as a way to redress the devalorization of alternative identity

Julie Depelteau and Dalie Giroux

perpetrated by colonial eyes and policies. We demonstrate this through three cases: (1) the role of the Indian Act in establishing a binary gender system, particularly regarding the people colonial authorities called "berdache"; (2) the inculcation of the heteronormative productive family unit and further repression through the residential school system; and (3) how the HIV/AIDS epidemic affected Two-Spirit groups and Two-Spirited persons, and how it led to a critique of health care.

Gender Politics and the Indian Act

On the one hand, the imposition and consolidation of colonial law in "Canadian territory" is an ongoing and contested process as land, legal, and other disputes are still being negotiated between First Nations and the Crown; on the other hand, the Canadian private law regime, which applies to relations between persons and excludes those between state and administration, had been gradually enforced throughout the second half of the nineteenth century. This process may have directly and indirectly affected existing and potential multiple-gender systems in Indigenous societies, as Cannon (1998) convincingly demonstrates in his study of Two-Spirit and Canadian colonial policies.

Indigenous marriage laws are some of the most likely to affect traditional multiple-gender systems. Indigenous marriage has long been regulated in Canada, first through a series of legal disputes regarding the recognition of Aboriginal forms of marriage (the first case is *Connolly v. Woolrich* [1867]; see Carter 2008, 134–38) and then through the Indian Act, 1876. This last piece of legislation may be considered to be the cornerstone of Canadian colonial policy, erasing, to this day, the multiple-gender traditions, and newer expressions, of gender in this part of the Americas.

Under the Indian Act, during the nineteenth century to the late twentieth century, Indian status applied only to "male persons of Indian blood reputed to belong to a particular band" and, by extension, to their children and wives.[11] In this legal context, marriage became the key to the transmission of status, and First Nations conceptions of marriage and gender were disrupted: "In Western Canada," writes Sarah Carter (2008, 5) in her study of nineteenth-century marriage politics, "there existed diverse forms of marriage among Aboriginal people, including monogamy, polygamy, and same-sex marriage, and no marriage needed to be for life as divorce was easily obtained and remarriage was accepted and expected." This whole set of Indigenous American marital practices was thus nullified or extirpated by the Indian Act, which legally bound Indian status with Christian patriarchal marriage.

To obtain Aboriginal citizenship in colonial Canada meant, de facto, to adhere to Christian marriage and its binary and hierarchical conception of gender.

The purpose of controlling Indigenous marriage was not only to preclude divorce by defining it in Christian terms but also to control and reduce Indian identification by discriminating against women who engaged in interracial marriages. Monture-Angus (1995, 178) writes:

> The State constructed the Indian Act and saw to its implementation, which has continuously stripped Indian women and our children of basic rights such as citizenship. In the 1876 Indian Act, women were entitled to be registered based either on their marriage to an Indian man or because of their birth to an Indian man. Women were men's property. This was not an Aboriginal tradition.

As Cannon (1998, 10) shows, the Indian policy on Indigenous marriage was written in a language that has no category for same-sex marriage, let alone multiple-gender systems. The imposition of a European and Christian definition of marriage through early colonial legislation made any legal or social continuity of these alternative systems impossible.

Furthermore, relocation policies, reserve creation, and the economic reconfiguration of Aboriginal economies worked in conjunction with the Indian Act's heteronormativity to destroy the social and material basis for multiple-gender systems in Indigenous societies. "Indian husbands and wives," especially in the Prairies, were prepared and trained for agrarian life, in which a strict sexual division of labour prevailed, making no room for alternative gender roles or cross-gendered practices (Cannon 1998, 9). In this way, Two-Spirited persons (then still called "berdache") who did not comply with heterosexuality were refused citizenship status and became economically dependent on others, whereas, previously, they had been able to sustain themselves and their families, for instance by taking on some women's occupational activities.

Through land confiscation, the Indian Act destroyed the economic basis of multiple-gender systems and forced Indigenous peoples into a new, two-gender, patriarchal economy. With these actions, combined with a long-term politics of abjection directed at third-gender people, the colonial state declared Two-Spirited individuals, along with women, unfit to claim citizenship.

Julie Depelteau and Dalie Giroux

Residential Schools and the Production of Heterosexual Bodies

As heterosexual marriage became compulsory and the legal system criminalized alternative gender practices and homosexuality (Meyer-Cook and Labelle 2004, 34), those called "berdache" had to hide their genders. That being said, ideological forces were at work even before the legal elaboration of binary gender in the Indian Act. The churches and their personnel, all of whom were involved in the social colonization of Indigenous America, were instrumental in this process.

Indeed, the perceived obscenity of alternative genders was clearly an affront to the missionaries, who saw the feminine and spiritual roles associated with berdache as threats to social order and to the dominance of Christianity as a model of domestic and collective organization in the New World. From the early days, colonial authorities in Canada (i.e., the church and the state) forbade and severely punished cross-dressing on reserves. Later, they also forbade integrated education classes, making it impossible for youth to adopt cross-gender practices (Williams 1986, 178) and easy for missionaries to label them with one of the two genders admissible to Euro-Christian marriage (Roscoe 1998, 101).[12]

In this regard, the residential schools policy in Canada proved to be central to the implementation of the Indian Act and its heteronormativity. It was essential with regard to disciplining Aboriginal bodies to accept binary gender practices as well as a patriarchal, Christian conception of marriage, family, and the economy. The Canadian state and churches, operating together, designed the residential school system in order to assimilate Aboriginal children through education. As several chapters in *Queer Mobilizations* reveal, if today's schools fight against homophobia, residential schools functioned as homophobic machines to grind down Aboriginal identities. In her study of the disciplining of the Aboriginal body in colonial Canada, Mary-Ellen Kelm (1998, 59) reports on the Canadian government's explicit intent in creating and consolidating this system:

> After the passage of the Indian Act in 1876, the federal government commissioned Nicholas F. Davin to report on American industrial schools for Native people. Davin strongly recommended residential schooling, for in such institutions, Aboriginal children could be best educated while physically separated from their parents. Like Bagot [the Bagot Commission recommended residential schooling for Aboriginal children in its 1842 report to the Canadian

government], his recommendation was to seize the minds and bodies of Aboriginal youth by forcing them into residential schools where the values, language, and culture of Euro-Canadians would predominate.

Although residential schools had existed for Aboriginal children since the beginning of the eighteenth century and French settlement in the St. Lawrence Valley, they became fully operational only after 1920, when an Indian Act amendment made it compulsory for every "Indian" child to attend day school. This lasted well into the end of the twentieth century, the last boarding school for Aboriginal children being closed down in the 1990s.[13]

Residential schools was designed to strip Aboriginal children of their identity: they were separated from their parents and community for months every year; siblings were separated; children were physically punished for using Aboriginal languages; boys had their hair cut; children had to dress according to gender; and they were trained according to the economic needs of nascent Canadian capitalism (mainly in the farming and industrial domains). Children were also imbued with a sense of shame and scorn towards the ways of their parents and ancestors, especially with regard to hygiene, domestic life, motherhood, and health (Kelm 1998, 61).[14]

Most relevant to our issue, the residential schools policy effectively created spaces for the clergy to, with state authority, permanently settle Aboriginal bodies in two genitally based categories. Two body types were established within this non-mixed normative and disciplinary set-up, with two sexes corresponding to two genders – boy/girl, man/woman. Youth were accordingly separated and subjected to surveillance and were punished for gender variance: sex and gender, which, within multiple-gender traditions do not necessarily correspond, were, in the Euro-Canadian system, presented and enforced as overlapping.

In this structure, girls learned housekeeping, while boys learned the rudiments of farming or factory work; these two complementary activities were meant to form a sedentary, and low-class, productive unit. This set-up excluded other possible forms of economic and social organization, and made it possible for colonial powers to inculcate bourgeois norms of hygiene and sanitation. Through this disciplinary endeavour, younger generations of Aboriginal people learned to accept a strict sexual division of labour that reproduced notions of bourgeois cleanliness and morality and rejected traditional ways and habits, particularly the authority of female elders (Kelm 1998, 61). Alternative gender systems, those in which femininity and masculinity differed from the Euro-Canadian version, and whose notion of body types was not as clear-cut, were associated with dirt, disease, and death (57). Clearly, the

Julie Depelteau and Dalie Giroux

Euro-Canadian land grab relied on the disciplining of bodies and genders. This was undertaken through the Indian Act, in which the residential school, an institution regarded as genocidal according to the 1948 UN Geneva Convention on Genocide, played a central and decisive role.

Before closing this section, a few words must be said about the Truth and Reconciliation Commission of Canada, which was set up in 2009 to shed light on the various forms of abuse Aboriginal children and their families suffered in residential schools. The commission does not single out issues regarding the inculcation of a binary gender system and the treatment of students who did not fit its categories. However, that being said, the commission could be seen as receptive to this issue as it focuses on the effects of the residential schools on parenting skills, Aboriginal traditions and cultures in general, and spiritual traditions. In its interim report (Truth and Reconciliation Commission of Canada 2012, 25–26), the commission summarizes the students' experiences and refers to the replacement of clothes; the renaming of students; forced haircutting; and the forbidding of mother tongues, spiritual beliefs, and ways of life as assaults on Aboriginal people, cultures, and nations. The recognition of these experiences could provoke a discussion of gender and spiritual issues – a discussion that could be meaningful for former students or members of their families who identify as Two-Spirited or as traditional alternative gender figures. There seems to be an opportunity here for people to testify about how Aboriginal bodies were moulded in residential schools. However, whether or not the commission takes this road remains to be seen.

Two-Spirited People in Community: HIV/AIDS Social Mobilization

As a general rule, the HIV/AIDS epidemic played an important role in queer activism (see, for example, Chapter 11, this volume), as it did with regard to Aboriginal and Two-Spirit organization and mobilization. Just as anti-racist and anti-colonial critiques resulted in the emergence of groups distinct from the LGBTQ movement of the 1980s and 1990s, so the epidemic resulted in these urban groups devoting part of their activity towards providing information about HIV/AIDS (as it came available) and creating structures for supporting affected people. Because these urban groups were already reflecting on First Nations identities and traditions, they modelled their action on traditional conceptions of health and the traditional healing roles played by alternative gendered people in pre-Columbian societies. But these initiatives were not limited to urban settings: they also occurred in rural communities and remote reserves.

For Gilley (2006, 30), the epidemic created a space in which to talk about sexuality and Two-Spirited identity, Two-Spirited spirituality, and the discrimination faced by Two-Spirited people. A landmark in the battle against discrimination undertaken by Two-Spirited people in Canada is Susan Beaver's 1992 intervention in the Royal Commission on Aboriginal Peoples (available in Deschamps and 2-Spirited People of the 1st Nations 1998, 12–16), in which she introduced the Two-Spirited tradition to Canadian rulers. She demanded that this tradition be re-evaluated and that Two-Spirited people be reincluded in the communities from which they were excluded and that the discrimination they face be addressed.

Two-Spirited people face discrimination on many fronts, from racism to homophobia, from to classism to sexism, and from AIDSphobia to transphobia. Homophobia pushed many Two-Spirited persons out of their communities and into urban centres where they could live openly with their sexual orientation and gender identity. Unfortunately, Indigenous people still face discrimination in cities, where they experience racism and isolation (Brotman et al. 2002, 78). Should they return to their communities, whether in other cities, rural areas, or on reserves, they are quite likely to once again face homophobia or AIDSphobia (Alaers 2010, 76) and suffer the alienation and lack of services they experienced elsewhere (Brotman et al. 2002, 77). With this discrimination comes a greater risk of violence (including assault) against Two-Spirited people (appearing as men, women, trans, or queers) than against non-Aboriginal LGBTQ people. Accordingly, Two-Spirited people are subject to an array of health issues related to this violence, including low self-esteem and a sense of powerlessness (First Nations Centre 2012, 7). This makes counter-discrimination and the valorization of First Nations traditional multiple-gender systems a priority for the Two-Spirit movement.

This re-evaluation is important because the pervasive discrimination in health services limits health care access for Two-Spirited people: "Two-Spirited People's access to health care is uniquely problematized by the combination of homophobia, heterosexism, racism, cultural insensitivity, and a legacy of distrust towards health care professionals. One result is the diminished health status of our membership" (2-Spirited People of the 1st Nations 2004). These individuals cannot find safe spaces and barrier-free health services (Brotman et al. 2002, 79–80) in a context within which discrimination creates ever-more need for such things (a multi-layered stigma also experienced by trans people; see Chapter 1, this volume). The lack of awareness and respect for Two-Spirited people in the health care system – in First Nations communities and elsewhere –

Julie Depelteau and Dalie Giroux

leaves them vulnerable and without vital resources (Brotman et al. 2002, 75; Monette et al. 2001, 59–60).

In response to this problem, Two-Spirited people are demanding a form of health care attuned to their various realities and health needs, including the need to be heard (2-Spirited People of the 1st Nations 2004; Taylor 2009, 74–75). The listening is most important as one size does not fit all when it comes to health and well-being: not all First Nations LGBTQ are Two-Spirited, and not all First Nations LGBTQ identifying as Two-Spirited are traditionalists (Alaers 2010, 77). Nevertheless, some – even some non-traditionalists – seem to agree that spirituality and traditional culture, as sources of self-esteem and strength, might have a role to play in health care (Monette et al. 2001, 41). Culturally oriented support groups are one example of how this could work in practice, but Two-Spirited caregivers and their families often find, at least in the United States, that those groups are irrelevant, having been designed without any consideration of Two-Spiritedness and its realities (Evans-Campbell et al. 2007, 90).

For some Two-Spirit groups and academics, the solution is a health care system organized by First Nations, one that offers culturally appropriate services, in Native languages, to people in remote locations. Many health care propositions articulate this idea of First Nations health sovereignty. Even if not all of them are demands for absolute health care independence, in light of the link between colonization and health in Aboriginal communities most call for a reintegration of traditional knowledge, values, methods, and Aboriginal identity into health care (Morgensen 2011, 196). For example, the Canadian Aboriginal AIDS Network (CAAN) asserts the need for holistic healing approaches in the provision of care for HIV/AIDS patients and their families (Laforge and Canadian Aboriginal AIDS Network 2007, 19–21). These propositions make clear how Two-Spirited people can be actively involved in providing appropriate care to themselves and their communities. As people who traditionally occupy caring roles, they could share important health and healing knowledge with those around them (Morgensen 2011, 199). In this way, Two-Spirited people could play a fulfilling role in health and healing practices and, in so doing, move from a marginal position to one at the centre of their communities.

Correspondingly, the demands of the Two-Spirit movement are concerned with HIV/AIDS and its spread into rural and urban First Nations communities. The epidemic was also an occasion for Two-Spirited people living on reserves to assert themselves as the bearers of multiple-gender traditions and to take on public and political roles in their communities as caretakers, healers, teachers, and activists educating people about HIV/AIDS (Gilley 2006,

178; Walters et al. 2006, 146). These activities are in line with the traditional roles of third-gender people in Aboriginal communities and are of even greater importance today, especially as a bulwark against the HIV/AIDS, homophobia, and other forms of discrimination: "Two-Spirit men would conceptualize this subtle assertion of their presence in communities as a form of resistance having the potential to alter attitudes toward their differences" (Gilley 2006, 170–71). Furthermore, the Two-Spirit movement also publishes literature for both Two-Spirited people and health staff,[15] and it addresses advocacy documents to governments. Both forms of literature are often referenced in policy documents.[16] Through these de facto initiatives and declarations of self-government, we can see the movement taking a stand as a decolonizing force and occupying a space vacated by the Canadian state. Non-traditional Two-Spirited activists feel that it is important to participate in the decolonizing struggle in whatever way they can (Walters et al. 2006, 130).

This presence could also challenge the health care system's representation of Two-Spirited people as simply a population "at risk" of contracting HIV/AIDS and other diseases. When they raise awareness of health issues in their communities, groups and individuals who view health as a multifaceted (physical, spiritual, and emotional) state of well-being defy the vulnerable and passive characterization of Aboriginal peoples found in state policies and documents. Moreover, by asserting a holistic view of health, these same activists, teachers, and mentors resist the state's portrayal of Aboriginal concepts of health and gender as cultural particularisms in need of add-on services offered by the Canadian health care system. Therefore, along with a positive concept of their identity, Two-Spirited people bring new and decolonizing concepts of health and healing.

Conclusion

Government responses to the Two-Spirit movement's demands for recognition are scarce, informal, and widely disparate. The terms "Two-Spirit" and/or "Two-Spirited" do get included in some federal, provincial, and territorial government documents, mostly in research and reports on death and disease. As part of an obituary discourse on First Nations, "Two-Spirit" appears when HIV/AIDS, sexual health, substance abuse, suicide, and mental health are targeted as problems in specific populations, either LGBTQ or Aboriginal.

These rare occurrences can be seen as part of a larger history of colonial interference in multiple-gender traditions. As we show earlier, the Indian Act, 1876, has played a decisive role in the erasure of Aboriginal gender traditions

Julie Depelteau and Dalie Giroux

as well as in the suppression of non-conventional and innovative gender identities. In the same vein, residential schools functioned as disciplinary spaces for Aboriginal bodies and genders, where the clergy, sanctioned by the colonial state, enforced the Christian and Euro-Canadian gender system. State power continues to interfere with gender systems through policies that discredit, devalue, and ignore the alternative gender systems the Two-Spirit movement tries to establish. To date, Canadian governments have made no substantive efforts to recognize the unique situations and demands of Two-Spirited people, especially Two-Spirited people categorized as women and youth. Nor have those governments made any effort to recognize the value of Indigenous healing approaches and Two-Spirited people's participation in health care.

Of course, this recognition of Two-Spirited people could lead to their once again being labelled as a "risky" or "vulnerable" population in need of surveillance. This could be a future challenge for a movement that has thus far successfully formed and valued Two-Spirit identity as part of an Indigenous tradition that lets people find a place in their communities. Nevertheless, recognition is essential not only with regard to providing health services to and with Two-Spirited people but also with regard to facing the continuous colonial erasures of multiple-gender traditions and resulting discrimination.

Despite the Canadian government's ambivalence, the Two-Spirit movement has undertaken this decolonial work at both national and international levels. By revaluing alternative gender traditions, they counter the colonial imagery of the berdache and the subsequent erasure of the traditions it overlaid and the repressive practices it enabled. These acts involve confrontations between colonial and Aboriginal conceptions of bodies, gender, and normativity as they highlight the impact of state policies on all Aboriginal peoples (Morgensen 2011, 221) and create space for other views and practices. While this work is crucial, it is not a substitute for the Canadian government's participation in decolonization.

Notes

1 These traditions take and took various forms from nation to nation, going from what European observers described as "cross-dressing" (which we might as well see as "specific dressing" proper to specific gender roles) to "sodomy" (describing as much "improper" gender roles undertaken by "men" as sexual acts between them) and sexual activities understood by colonists as "homosexuality" (Kinsman 1996, 92–94).
2 It is noteworthy that those identified as women were generally neglected under European phallocentrism; hence a lack of information about third genders among "them" (Alaers 2010, 70). Smith (2008, xi) also notes that, if the presence of "women" (or, rather, those identified as women) in traditionalist movements in general is rather small, their visibility is even fainter.

3 For a convincing case in favour of reading the sixteenth- and early seventeenth-century European aversion to multiple-gender systems in the Americas in terms of the threat they posed to gender hierarchy (challenging the patriarchal and masculine value system) rather than a condemnation of multiple-gender systems as such, see Hérault (2010, 351), who writes: "Autrement dit, ce que les voyageurs voient c'est une version 'renversante' de la hiérarchie des genres et non pas une forme 'alternative' du système des genres."

4 Where Europeans condemn sodomy and "transvestism," we can interpret these occurrences as actual indications of gender-crossing practices and identities in Indigenous Americas, practices that did not find a place in the worldviews and laws of the colonizers' culture (hence their reduction to what was known to them: sodomy and transvestism). Pressures coming both from ecclesiastical authorities and state administrators pushed the tradition to engage in clandestine behaviour: individuals made themselves less visible by conforming to colonial gender practices (acting as men or women with the complicity of the community), by not occupying roles in religious ceremonies or by performing these ceremonies in secret, by avoiding talking about multiple-gender practices with white people (including anthropologists), or by asserting their disappearance (Williams 1986, 172, 187, 194). The absence or invisibility of legitimate persons to whom to transmit knowledge was detrimental to the existence of these practices as well as to the actual knowledge of multiple-gender traditions in Indigenous communities.

5 In the 1990s, like "queer" and "trans," "two-spirit" also came to be widely used for gender variance activism (Valentine 2008, 35).

6 Some authors also point to its academic formalization in 1993 (Alaers 2010, 69; Wilson 2007, 13) or 1994 (Gilley 2006, 25).

7 As summarized by Roscoe (1998, 110-11): "Given the way American social movements often turn upon strategic claims and redefinitions of words, symbols, and histories, it is not surprising that lesbian and gay native people would propose a label of their own to express and consolidate their self-awareness. Insisting that anthropologists and other representatives of elite discourse use this term is a symbolic gesture but one that alters the dynamics of an historical relationship that has all too often involved one-way transfers of knowledge. The creation of self-chosen terminology has been part of the history of African American, Latino/Chicano, lesbian/gay, and other movements. Indeed, native pantribalism in the twentieth century provides many examples of newly forged symbols of Indian identity. What is distinctive about the use of 'two-spirit' is that it has been deployed as a panhistorical as well as a pantribal term."

8 As Anguksuar ([Richard LaFortune] 1997, 221) explains in a source often referred to when defining Two-Spirits: "More essentially, it may refer to the fact that each human is born because a man and a woman have joined in creating each new life; all humans bear imprints of both, although some individuals may manifest both qualities more completely than others. In no way does the term define a person's social role and spiritual gifts. Some traditional teachers have expressed pointed concern that the term is being grossly equated with the concept of 'homosexual.' These teachers rigorously remind us that there is no resemblance between the two concepts."

9 As with those other traditions, it is at times misappropriated and romanticized (Walters et al. 2006, 133).

10 It is often pointed out that gendered violence and homophobia were introduced into Indigenous communities by residential schools (Smith 2005, 51).

Julie Depelteau and Dalie Giroux

11 See An Act to Amend and Consolidate the Laws Respecting Indians, S.C. 1880, c. 28, art. 3.
12 Morgensen (2010, 115–16) notes that members of the clergy went so far as to forbid ber-daches access to cemeteries, to blame them for any bad events in the community, to ignore and insult them, and to push them to exile or suicide.
13 See J.R. Miller (1996) for a history of residential schooling for Aboriginal people in Canada.
14 Smith (2005, 10–12) makes a compelling argument that the assertion of the dirtiness of Indigenous bodies served to enable violence against them (particularly sexual violence), as it implied that they were undeserving of bodily integrity. This sexual violence was part of the imposition of a patriarchal hierarchy upon Aboriginal peoples.
15 The 2-Spirited People of the 1st Nations website is particularly resourceful: http://www.2spirits.com.
16 Although they do not originate directly from Two-Spirited groups, two initiatives are of particular importance in the examination of the Two-Spirit movement's decolonizing stance as they share similar perspectives on HIV/AIDS and health: first, the Canadian Aboriginal AIDS Network's Aboriginal Strategy on HIV/AIDS in Canada (ASHAC) I and II, the implementation of which rests on the efforts of mostly non-governmental organizations; second, the Toronto Charter: Indigenous Peoples' Action Plan on HIV/AIDS 2006, an initiative of the International Indigenous Peoples Satellite, which comprises members of 2-Spirited People of the 1st Nations, CAAN, and OAHAS. See Canadian Aboriginal AIDS Network 2009; International Indigenous Peoples Satellite 2006. For an analysis of these documents, see Morgensen 2008, 2011). The International Strategic Plan on HIV and AIDS for Indigenous Peoples and Communities from 2011 to 2017 (ISPHA) is based on both strategies and also appears to integrate elements from the Toronto Charter.

References

2-Spirited People of the 1st Nations. 2004. What Health Providers Can Learn: There Are Two-Education Steps to a Healthy Patient Relationship with 2-Spirit People. http://www.2spirits.com/Healthcare.html.
Alaers, Jill. 2010. "Two-Spirited People and Social Work Practice: Exploring the History of Aboriginal Gender and Sexual Diversity." *Critical Social Work* 11 (1): 63–79.
Anguksuar, Richard LaFortune. 1997. "A Postcolonial Perspective on Western [Mis] Conceptions of the Cosmos and the Restoration of Indigenous Taxonomies." In Sue-Ellen Jacobs, Wesley Thomas, and Sabine Lang, eds., *Two-Spirit People: Native American Gender Identity, Sexuality, and Spirituality*, 217–22. Urbana: University of Illinois Press.
Brotman, Shari, Bill Ryan, Yves Jalbert, and Bill Rowe. 2002. "Reclaiming Space-Regaining Health: The Health Care Experiences of Two-Spirit People in Canada." *Journal of Gay and Lesbian Social Services* 14 (1): 67–87. http://dx.doi.org/10.1300/J041v14n01_04.
Canadian Aboriginal AIDS Network. 2009. *Aboriginal Strategy on HIV/AIDS in Canada II: For First Nations, Inuit and Métis Peoples from 2009 to 2014*. Ottawa: Canadian Aboriginal AIDS Network. http://www.caan.ca/national-aboriginal-strategies/strategies/.
Cannon, Martin. 1998. "The Regulation of First Nations Sexuality." *Canadian Journal of Native Studies* 18 (1): 1–18.

Carter, Sarah. 2008. *The Importance of Being Monogamous: Marriage and Nation Building in Western Canada to 1915*. Edmonton: University of Alberta Press.

Deschamps, Gilbert, and 2-Spirited People of the 1st Nations. 1998. *We Are Part of a Tradition: A Guide on Two-Spirited People for First Nations Communities*. http://www.2spirits.com/.

Driskill, Qwo-Li. 2004. "Stolen from Our Bodies: First Nations Two-Spirits/Queers and the Journey to a Sovereign Erotic." *Studies in American Indian Literatures* 16 (2): 50–64. http://dx.doi.org/10.1353/ail.2004.0020.

–. 2010. "Doubleweaving Two-Spirit Critiques: Building Alliances between Native and Queer Studies." *GLQ: A Journal of Lesbian and Gay Studies* 16 (1–2): 69–92. http://dx.doi.org/10.1215/10642684-2009-013.

Evans-Campbell, Teresa, Karen Fredriksen-Goldsen, Karina Walters, and Antony Stately. 2007. "Caregiving Experiences among American Indian Two-Spirit Men and Women." *Journal of Gay and Lesbian Social Services* 18 (3–4): 75–92. http://dx.doi.org/10.1300/J041v18n03_05.

First Nations Centre. 2012. *Suicide Prevention and Two-Spirited People*. Ottawa: National Aboriginal Health Organization. http://www.naho.ca/documents/fnc/english/2012_04_%20Guidebook_Suicide_Prevention.pdf.

Gilley, Brian Joseph. 2006. *Becoming Two-Spirit: Gay Identity and Social Acceptance in Indian Country*. Lincoln: University of Nebraska Press.

Hérault, Laurence. 2010. "Transgression et désordre dans le genre: Les explorateurs français aux prises avec les 'berdaches' amérindiens." *Etnografica Journal on Culture and Disability* 14 (2): 337–60. http://dx.doi.org/10.4000/etnografica.316.

International Indigenous Peoples Satellite. 2006. *The Toronto Charter: Indigenous Peoples' Action Plan on HIV/AIDS 2006*. See http://www.2spirits.com/.

Kelm, Mary-Ellen. 1998. *Colonizing Bodies: Aboriginal Health and Healing in British Columbia, 1900–1950*. Vancouver: UBC Press.

Kinsman, Gary William. 1996. "Sexual Colonization of the Indigenous Peoples." In *The Regulation of Desire: Homo and Hetero Sexualities*, 92–97. Montreal: Black Rose Books.

Laforge, Vicky, and the Canadian Aboriginal AIDS Network. 2007. *Walk With Me Pathways to Health: Harm Reduction Service Delivery Model for Aboriginal Women, Aboriginal Youth, Aboriginal People Who Are or Have Been in Prison and Aboriginal Two-Spirit Men*. http://caan.ca/wp-content/uploads/2012/05/WalkWithMe_en2.pdf.

Lang, Sabine. 2003. "Lesbians, Men-Women and Two-Spirits: Homosexuality and Gender in Native American Cultures." In Suzanne LaFont, ed., *Constructing Sexualities: Readings in Sexuality, Gender, and Culture*, 202–18. Upper Saddle River: Prentice Hall.

Meyer-Cook, Fiona, and Diane Labelle. 2004. "Namaji: Two-Spirit Organizing in Montreal, Canada." *Journal of Gay and Lesbian Social Services* 16 (1): 29–51. http://dx.doi.org/10.1300/J041v16n01_02.

Miller, James R. 1996. *Shingwauk's Vision: A History of Native Residential Schools*. Toronto: Toronto University Press.

Monette, LaVerne, Judith Kelly Waalen, Darcy Albert, 2-Spirited People of the 1st Nations, and Centre for Quality Service Research. 2001. *Voices of Two-Spirited Men*. Toronto: Centre for Quality Service Research.http://www.2spirits.com/.

Monture-Angus, Patricia. 1995. *Thunder in My Soul: A Mohawk Woman Speaks*. Halifax: Fernwood Publishing.

Morgensen, Scott Lauria. 2008. "Activist Media in Native AIDS Organizing: Theorizing the Colonial Conditions of AIDS." *American Indian Culture and Research Journal* 32 (1): 35–56.

–. 2010. "Settler Homonationalism: Theorizing Settler Colonialism within Queer Modernities." *GLQ: A Journal of Lesbian and Gay Studies* 16 (1–2): 105–31.

–. 2011. *Spaces Between Us: Queer Settler Colonialism and Indigenous Decolonization.* Minneapolis: University of Minnesota Press.

Roscoe, Will. 1998. *Changing Ones: Third and Fourth Genders in Native North America.* New York: St. Martin's Press.

Smith, Andrea. 2005. *Conquest: Sexual Violence and American Indian Genocide.* Cambridge, MA: South End Press.

–. 2008. *Native Americans and the Christian Right: The Gendered Politics of Unlikely Alliances.* Durham: Duke University Press. http://dx.doi.org/10.1215/9780822388876.

Tafoya, Terry. 1997. "Native Gay and Lesbian Issues." In Beverly Greene, ed., *Ethnic and Cultural Diversity among Lesbians and Gay Men*, 1–10. Thousand Oaks: Sage Publications.

Taylor, Catherine. 2009. "Health and Safety Issues for Aboriginal Transgender/Two-Spirit People in Manitoba." *Canadian Journal of Aboriginal Community-Based HIV-AIDS Research* 2 (5): 63–84.

Thomas, Wesley, and Sue-Ellen Jacobs. 1999. "'… And We Are Still Here': From Berdache to Two-Spirit People." *American Indian Culture and Research Journal* 23 (2): 91–107.

Thoms, J. Michael, and 2-Spirited People of the 1st Nations. 2007. *Leading an Extraordinary Life: Wise Practices for an HIV Prevention Campaign with Two-Spirit Men.* Toronto: 2-Spirited People of the 1st Nations. http://2spirits.com/PDFolder/Extraodinarylives.pdf.

Truth and Reconciliation Commission of Canada. 2012. *Truth and Reconciliation Commission of Canada Interim Report.* Winnipeg: Truth and Reconciliation Commission of Canada. http://www.myrobust.com/websites/trcinstitution/File/Interim%20report%20English%20electronic.pdf.

Valentine, David. 2008. *Imagining Transgender: An Ethnography of a Category.* Durham, NC: Duke University Press.

Walters, Karina L., Teresa Evans-Campbell, Jane M. Simoni, Theresa Ronquillo, and Rupaleem Bhuyan. 2006. "My Spirit in My Heart." *Journal of Lesbian Studies* 10 (1–2): 125–49. http://dx.doi.org/10.1300/J155v10n01_07.

Williams, Walter L. 1986. *The Spirit and the Flesh: Sexual Diversity in American Indian Culture.* Boston: Beacon Press.

Wilson, Alexandria M. 2007. *N'tacimowin inna nah': Coming in to Two-Spirit Identities.* Cambridge: Harvard University, Graduate School of Education.

Legal Case

Connolly v. Woolrich [1867] 17 R.J.R.Q. 75 (Que. S.C.)

PART 2

The Regional Level

3

Queer Advocacy in Ontario

DAVID RAYSIDE

For over forty years, and across a wide range of issues, Ontario has been the setting for remarkably sustained advocacy on the part of sexual minorities and their allies. That activist work, at both local and provincial levels, has produced pioneering court victories and policy changes in some issue areas, often in the face of political caution, concerted opposition from religious conservatives, and public anxiety.

The waves of advocacy in this province, as well as their successes and limitations, display a central contradiction in the story of Canadian LGBT politics. On the one hand, this is a profoundly local and regional story, amply illustrated by other chapters in *Queer Mobilizations*. The modern movement began with local groups, and today the majority of work that is done to address inequity and marginalization is effected at the local level. Canada is also a highly "regionalized" country, with significant jurisdictional decentralization in areas of most concern to equity advocates, and a strong sense of regional distinctiveness in places like British Columbia, Alberta, parts of Atlantic Canada, and, of course, Quebec. On the other hand, there are strong similarities in the LGBT political narrative across the country, more so, certainly, than in the United States, and in some ways more so than in countries like Brazil, Spain, and Australia.

Analyzing the strengths and weakness of LGBT activism in Ontario is challenging because of the province's large population and the number of distinct urban centres with their own activist histories. As everywhere else, too, there is a huge range of issue areas that affect the public recognition of sexual diversity. The present analysis draws heavily on the Greater Toronto Area (see also Chapter 9, this volume), but it tries to balance this by recognizing major developments in other cities and province-wide campaigns. It also limits itself to four policy areas, each of which can plausibly be claimed as crucial for advocates of change everywhere in Canada. The first of these is policing, particularly the prejudicial and oppressive policing practices that have been so common across Canada; the second is the establishment of basic legal and policy protections against discrimination based on sexual orientation and gender identity; the third is the public recognition of LGBT family rights, including both relational and parenting issues; and the fourth is schooling – the extent to which sexual diversity is recognized by state-regulated schools. What we see is great variation in success across these fields – an analysis much in line with what we would find across the country.

Historical Background

After the Second World War, Toronto, and to some extent Ottawa, saw the expansion of bars and public spaces where gay men, and to a more limited extent lesbians and trans people, could gather.[1] Rights advocacy developed more slowly in Ontario than in major American cities, Britain, and the Netherlands. In fact, there was no equivalent to the early formation of branches of the Mattachine Society and Daughters of Bilitis in US cities or the Centre for Culture and Leisure (*Cultuur-en Ontspanningscentrum,* known as the COC) in Amsterdam. Cautious restiveness was evident, however, in the 1964 appearance in Toronto of the magazine *Gay,* which was soon distributing thirty thousand copies across North America (see McLeod 2003). In that same year, a group of ministers in Ottawa formed the Council on Religion and the Homosexual, replaced within a year by the more broadly based (and multidenominational) Canadian Council on Religion and the Homosexual.

Early Political Organizing

In late 1969, the University of Toronto Homophile Association (UTHA) was established, representing (despite its name) the first Canadian manifestation of the radical liberationism that was surfacing in the United States and elsewhere. This was in the same year that homosexual activity was partially decriminalized through federal government amendments to the Criminal Code, a change made possible in part by the slow emergence of calls for reform in the 1960s. Soon after the birth of UTHA, in 1970, the Community

Homophile Association of Toronto (CHAT) was established, and Glad Day Bookshop (the first in Canada specializing in gay and/or lesbian material) was opened – also in Toronto. A "gay picnic" was held on the Toronto islands one year later, eventually growing into Toronto's massive pride celebration. In late 1971, the *Body Politic* was created – a gay magazine that would help define liberationist politics across North America for more than a decade. In 1972, the Gay Alliance Towards Equality (GATE) was constituted by those firmly committed to liberationist politics, though focused on gay rights and a human rights strategy. By the end of 1973, political groups had appeared in London, Waterloo, Guelph, Windsor, Hamilton, Kingston, and Sudbury – most based on university campuses. Gays of Ottawa, formed in 1971, was as large and long-lasting as any of these groups.

In this period, feminist groups such as Toronto Women's Liberation Movement were creating space for and recognition of lesbian issues at a time when gay activism was overwhelmingly male. Stand-alone lesbian groups were more challenging to organize, though a few emerged in the years to follow, including the Lesbian Organization of Toronto (LOOT), established in 1976 (Nash 2005; Ross 1995). Also at this time, advocacy groups were being created among people of faith, with Toronto Unitarian Universalist Gays formed in 1971, the Metropolitan Community Church (MCC) established in both Toronto and Ottawa two years after that, and other groups forming within the United Church, Anglican, and Catholic communities.

Based in part on this foundation, the Coalition for Gay Rights in Ontario (later the Coalition for Lesbian and Gay Rights in Ontario – CLGRO) was established in 1975 (Warner 2002, 2010). It was very much shaped by liberationist ideas, though its focus on provincial politics inevitably meant that it was directing most of its energies towards legislative outcomes – most notably the inclusion of sexual orientation in provincial human rights statutes. It regularly suffered the fate of many coalitional groups in that it brought together volunteer activists whose primary obligations were to other (in this case local) groups, so at times it had only a low profile. But it gave significant visibility to provincial-level policy demands, and it maintained a continuous provincial presence until its end in 2009.

Expansion of Mobilization in the 1980s

Police raids on institutions with significant gay and lesbian clientele continued throughout the 1970s, provoking activist surges from the late 1970s on. The largest and most provocative of these raids were those conducted in February

1981 on several Toronto bathhouses (Hannon 1982; McCaskell 1988). The arrest of three hundred men resulted in large-scale mobilization, led by the Right to Privacy Committee, which combined the confrontational demonstrations characteristic of liberationist politics with the skilful coordination of lawyers and the management of a legal defence fund more readily associated with mainstream politics. Also in this period, the *Body Politic* and Glad Day Bookshop were facing repeated charges of obscenity, and both mobilized a community response. The scale of opposition to police attacks, and the anger marshalled in the process, represented a turning point in the visibility and impact of Toronto-area activism, and it produced the largest and most sustained gay mobilization to that point in Canada.

As in other parts of Canada and the Western world, the onset of AIDS in the early 1980s introduced dramatic new challenges. The second half of that decade saw the LGBT movement as a whole focus much of its energy on defending its communities against discrimination and stigma, creating educational campaigns to stop the spread of HIV, providing services for those who were infected or ill, and pressing for change in government policy and health care institutions. AIDS community groups such as the AIDS Committee of Toronto (ACT) drew key leaders from the ranks of activist groups like the *Body Politic* and attracted women with experience in health care advocacy, partially bridging the activist gender divide. Within a few years, there were also AIDS groups in ethno-racial minority communities in which sexual diversity activism had been difficult to mobilize or to connect to "mainstream" LGBT advocacy. Activist mobilization was aided in part by access to state funding. Groups like Gay Asians Toronto, Zami, and Lesbians of Colour had already been formed, but the urgencies of AIDS created new initiatives, such as the Black Coalition for AIDS Prevention (in 1989) and various Toronto groups addressing AIDS in gay Asian communities.

The AIDS epidemic also led to more visible organizing by Two-Spirited Aboriginals. Across North America, lesbian and gay networks had begun forming, though with difficulty. They faced antagonism within their own societies, along with extraordinary social and cultural dislocation in the urban centres to which they migrated (see Chapter 2, this volume). In Ontario, the largest concentration of Two-Spirited Aboriginals was in Toronto, but social, economic, and cultural chasms separated them from the rest of the LGBT movement. 2-Spirited People of the 1st Nations was formed in Toronto in 1991, two years after the first Toronto gathering, to a large extent responding to the alarming spread of AIDS in Aboriginal communities (Warner 2002, 330).

David Rayside

Political openings were also widened by shifts in popular beliefs and the 1982 entrenchment of the Charter of Rights and Freedoms.[2] These changes, combined with the recognition by some state officials that they needed community expertise to slow the spread of HIV, created opportunities for equity advocates to develop connections with local governments, provincial ministries, professional associations in the legal and health care sectors, legal networks, and progressive politicians. Anger at the insufficiencies in state response to AIDS continued into the early 1990s, reviving activist radicalism – most notably in the Toronto-based AIDS Action Now. The ephemeral but important Toronto group Queer Nation also emerged in this period, directing activist anger at police inattention to anti-LGBT violence and re-energizing demands that there be more recognition of diversity within the sexual minority communities.

Mainstreaming in the 1990s

Despite this radical surge early in the decade, the 1990s were characterized more by reformist activism, or by activist tactics oriented towards the political opportunities for change created within left and centre-left political parties, government bureaucracies, unions, and courts. At the same time, this was a period, particularly in Toronto, marked by the proliferation of advocacy and support groups across ethno-racial, religious, and occupational lines.

Same-sex relationship recognition and parenting acquired a growing political profile from the late 1980s on. As Gerald Hunt and I argue, labour activists and other workplace groups saw the extension of workplace benefit programs to include same-sex partners as an obvious campaigning focus (Hunt 1999; Hunt and Rayside 2007). Several union organizations, including those with huge Ontario membership (e.g., the Canadian Auto Workers and the Canadian Union of Public Employees), were also supporting LGBT activist demands for political recognition. They had been allies in the mid-1980s struggles over basic rights protections and in the 1990s were more active than ever.

In Ontario, the recognition of same-sex relationships became the focus of large-scale community mobilization in 1994, aimed at the NDP provincial government's attempt to pass sweeping legislation on the rights of lesbian and gay couples. The defeat of Bill 167 represented only a temporary setback as activists (including union members) took constitutional challenges to the courts.

The early and mid-1990s also saw major activist work on schooling, particularly in Toronto (McCaskell 2005; Rayside 2008). Trans activism in Toronto was intensifying during this time, as it was in Vancouver and Montreal. The extreme marginalization of the various constituencies under the trans umbrella made the sustenance of advocacy very challenging, so no single group emerged with a lasting or substantial foundation, but enhanced political visibility had gained a foothold.

Important victories over rights sought by lesbian and gay couples in the 1990s ended up preparing the way for advocacy on marriage, led primarily by the national group EGALE. It is not clear that this struggle caught fire among Ontario activists, but major courtroom challenges were launched in Toronto going into the new millenium, at about the same time as legal actions were undertaken in other parts of the country.

Queer Activism Today

The strength of contemporary LGBT advocacy in Ontario lies in the proliferation of its forms and locations, and the range of constituencies that it speaks to. It is found in labour unions, professional organizations, academic centres, lawyer networks, workplace committees, campus student groups, social service agencies, community centres, pride organizations, queer cultural institutions, LGBT media outlets, HIV/AIDS groups, immigrant advisory networks, faith communities, and government-focused policy communities. Less activist energy is now devoted to multi-purpose all-embracing groups such as CLGRO and Queer Ontario than in the past – however important their work has been and remains – but that does not suggest a weaker movement overall.

In a list of LGBT resources relevant for high schools in Ontario, EGALE (2011) listed 139 local and provincial groups, networks, and programs. This includes groups and institutions as diverse as the 519 Church Street Community Centre in Toronto; 2-Spirited People of the 1st Nations; the Lesbian, Gay, Bi, Trans Youth Line; the LGBTQ Parenting Network; the Metropolitan Community Church; the Black Coalition for AIDS Prevention; Pride Toronto; Capital Pride; Rainbow Health Ontario; Salaam (Queer Muslim Community); Supporting Our Youth; the Canadian Lesbian and Gay Archives; Glad Day Bookshop; a large number of university student groups; and several local chapters of Parents and Friends of Lesbians and Gays.

There are weaknesses here. The most politically active provincial and local groups have usually had to do their work with only small numbers of volunteers, and, apart from groups focused on social service delivery (including AIDS-related services), with few paid staff – usually none. For most of its life, this was the case for CLGRO, the only multi-issue group operating at the provincial level, and it is even more the case for Queer Ontario, the group that took over CLGRO's mandate after 2009. As well, the important gains in law and policy secured during the 1990s and 2000s produced a degree of complacency, reducing the capacity of political groups to mobilize. There are also persistent inequalities and contrasts in public visibility along lines of gender, race, social class, and gender identity in the movement as a whole, and sometimes there is a degree of isolation (perhaps inevitable) between groups representing distinct constituencies or population sectors.

All this makes it harder than ever to characterize LGBT advocacy in the province as a whole. What can be said is that transformational radicalism and confrontational tactics have receded from their prominence in the movement during the 1970s, the early 1980s, and again during the very early 1990s. It is too easy and oversimplifying to characterize this as assimilationism (and, by implication, to imagine an earlier movement as being more inclusive than it was), but these shifts do reflect a mainstreaming of political advocacy across a wide range of groups.

Queer Activism and Public Policy Changes: Case Studies

Four policy areas have had particular relevance for advocates of change in Ontario and other jurisdictions across and beyond Canada: (1) policing, (2) human rights provisions with regard to discrimination, (3) family rights, and (4) schooling. These are areas that vary significantly in the jurisdictional role of various levels of government, in the timing of their prioritization by the LGBT movement, and in the impact that movement has had on them. In fact, any attempt to generalize about the immovability or deep embeddedness of state regulatory regimes is limited by the wide variation in impact and outcome evident across these issues.

Policing

Sexuality has been regulated or policed in many different ways – through the courts, schools, censorship practices, and community norms. Here, though, we focus specifically on the activity of police forces and the history of activist response to attacks on community institutions and particular sexual practices. This has been an important focus of community activism in several of Ontario's major urban centres.

Up to the 1980s, police raids against institutions frequented by gay men, lesbians, and trans people were commonplace in major Ontario cities, as they were in several other Canadian cities (see, for example, Chapter 8, this volume). Between 1975 and 1984, several large-scale and high-profile raids were undertaken against such institutions in Toronto and Ottawa, and, until the early 1980s, police attackers could rely on public support, media acquiescence, and guilty pleas from the majority of those arrested (see Hannon 1982; Warner 2002, 99–118).

The massive Toronto raids of February 1981 broke all records in the size of the operation and the number arrested (three hundred men). In a community in which activist networks had been slowly building, large numbers rallied to the Right to Privacy Committee (RTPC). With the support of other community groups, and the intense coverage of the raids and their aftermath by *The Body Politic,* the RTPC spearheaded a very public campaign targeting police practices and the criminal statutes facilitating that work.[3] It also mounted a systematic legal strategy and raised a defence fund to back up those who were willing to fight the charges. The vast majority did so and won in court. At the same time, blunt criticism of the police action was coming from a majority of Toronto's city council, civil libertarians, a wide range of other social movement allies, and much of the mass media – all provoked by the scale and ferocity of the police action targeting an increasingly visible and well organized gay and lesbian community.

This constituted a major setback for traditional policing responses to lesbian and gay visibility. There had been shifts towards more reformist approaches to policing in a number of American cities, but in the early 1980s this was barely evident in Canada. Among large Ontario cities, Ottawa, with the choice of Brian Ford as police chief in 1993, was the first to see moves (however uneven) in the direction of respect for sexual minorities. In Toronto, the 1995 selection of David Boothby as chief signalled a degree of movement towards reformism, though that was largely undone while Julian Fantino was chief from 2000 to 2005. Since then, Toronto's police leadership has, at the very least, embraced a rhetorical commitment to LGBT inclusivity, even in the face of persistent masculinist traditionalism in the force's organizational culture. In Toronto, as in other cities, there are still important irritants in the relationship between sexual minorities and police, though the large-scale concerted attacks on LGBT institutions that were once so commonplace are now much less likely.

Activists have sought more than just an end to police harassment: they have also wanted violence directed at sexual minorities taken more seriously. Police forces across Ontario, like their counterparts elsewhere, had a long record of almost entirely ignoring homophobic and transphobic violence, and

David Rayside

LGBT calls for change intensified in the early 1990s. Doug Janoff (2005, 158–98) reports that, since then, much has changed in responsiveness to such demands in major police forces across the country, with Toronto and Ottawa each taking creditable steps. However, he is quick to point out inadequacies or unevenness in police response – a point reinforced by the readiness of police officers in downtown Toronto to harass lesbian and gay institutions in the early 2000s.

It is still true that, among the majority of Ontario (and Canadian) police forces, only a tiny minority of officers are willing to be fully out as gay or lesbian. Within major segments of Ontario's police organizations, there remains a willingness to target those activities or groups considered not to be part of the "respectable" lesbian and gay community – sex workers or trans people, for example – or to underplay threats to their safety. There is still a tendency for erotic material that pushes the boundaries of queer sexuality to be more heavily policed, for example by customs officers, than other material (see the *Bad Attitude* case study and the Little Sister's challenge against Canada Customs in Chapter 9 and Chapter 6, respectively, this volume). There can be no serious doubt that the decades of work on policing issues have had a significant impact, but perhaps not yet transformative.

Human Rights

Even at the height of liberationist condemnation of existing social and political institutions, lesbian and gay activists were pressing human rights claims. In 1973, after sustained campaigning led by the Gay Alliance Towards Equality, Toronto became the first municipality in Canada, and one of the first in North America, to prohibit discrimination based on sexual orientation. In 1976, Ottawa became the second Canadian city to do so, and one year after that Windsor became the third (Rayside 2008, 96). As we have already seen, such change in formal policy did not stop police raids directed at institutions with gay and lesbian clientele, though it did provide a legal platform from which to press for further change, and it gave gays and lesbians a foothold in local mainstream politics.

At the provincial level, the 1975 establishment of the Coalition for Gay Rights in Ontario focused attention on the inclusion of sexual orientation in Ontario's Human Rights Code. Every time that changes to the code on other fronts were open for debate in the provincial legislature, CGRO and then CLGRO presented the case for including sexual orientation, first in its 1976 brief *The Homosexual Minority in Ontario*. The first serious opportunity for change, however, occurred only in the mid-1980s, with the electoral defeat of the Ontario Conservatives and the coming into force of section 15 of the Canadian Charter of Rights and Freedoms.

In 1985, a minority Liberal government took office, dependent on NDP support, at a time when lesbian and gay activism had expanded and deepened its foundations. A government bill to bring various provincial statutes into line with section 15 of the Charter, introduced by the provincial government in late 1985, then provided a potential vehicle for an amendment to the Human Rights Code on sexual orientation. Already, many judicial experts were arguing that courts would soon come to recognize sexual orientation as an equity ground analogous to those that were explicitly named in section 15, thereby prohibiting discrimination constitutionally.

This time, the Right to Privacy Committee, which had led the response to bathhouse raids in Toronto, joined CLGRO, adding its considerable experience in grassroots mobilization and the use of mainstream media (see Herman 1994; Rayside 1988; Warner 2002, 99–118). The previous work of both groups helped secure the support of labour unions, women's movement groups, progressive religious leaders (Christian and Jewish), and many politicians. The fact that the very high-profile Ian Scott, then justice minister, was eventually convinced of the worthiness of such an amendment added significantly to the leverage available for change. Bill 7, containing the provision adding sexual orientation to the OHRC, was passed at the end of 1986, making Ontario the second province (after Quebec) to acknowledge equal rights for lesbians and gays.

Transgender rights had been barely mentioned by activists or legislative reformers up to and including this time. The heightened visibility and activist mobilization around trans issues in the mid-1990s increased pressure for change. So did growing evidence of the prejudice and hardship facing trans people, born of persistent and profound unease with the kind of gender ambiguity or gender crossing that trans people are seen to embody. In 2000, the Ontario Human Rights Commission approved a policy prohibiting discrimination and harassment based on gender identity, interpreting this as covered under the category of "sex" (OHRC 2000). Trans advocates have long argued for explicit reference to gender identity, rather than coverage under other terms, and in this they were joined by other LGBT advocacy groups, several important labour unions, politicians from all parties in the provincial legislature, and Barbara Hall, chief commissioner of the Ontario Human Rights Commission.[4] In 2012, a private member's bill presented by NDP MLA Cheri DiNovo was passed adding gender identity and gender expression to the Ontario Human Rights Code.

David Rayside

Family Rights

The intensification of activist pressure to publicly recognize same-sex couples in the late 1980s and early 1990s soon had an impact on law, public policy, and the institutional practice of employers. What was at stake were hundreds of provincial statutes covering family law, medical decision making, inheritance, taxation, and access to social supports. There were also workplace benefits being sought for employee partners in both the public and private sectors, and access to religious blessings or full marriage within faith communities.

Demands for parenting rights were becoming more prominent at this time (Epstein 2009; Rayside 2008). These were not new issues, since lesbian mothers and gay fathers had long been threatened with loss of custody of children born of earlier heterosexual relationships. From the mid-1980s on, however, there were opportunities for lesbian couples in particular to gain access to anonymously donated sperm, often through American providers, widening the population of same-sex couples having children. This baby boom led to more couples going to court to secure adoption rights for the non-biological parent, thereby confronting judges with de facto functioning families.

In 1986, Hamilton became the first big city in Canada to extend workplace benefits to same-sex partners for its employees. Two years later, an Ontario court ruling denied a provincial health insurance benefit claim by Karen Andrews *(Andrews v. Ontario)*. However, within a very short time, the momentum behind the campaign for workplace recognition picked up speed. By decade's end, Toronto Public Libraries and Ryerson University extended their own benefit programs to cover same-sex couples. In 1990, Toronto became the second big city in the country to change its employee benefits, followed very quickly by Vancouver and Montreal. Within three years, Windsor, Ottawa, and Kitchener followed suit (see Rayside 2008, 167–91).

In 1991, Ontario and Manitoba became the second and third senior government jurisdictions in Canada (after the Yukon Territory, in 1988) to extend their employees' benefit plans, something that public-sector unions had been pressing for. In 1992, an Ontario appeal court ruled in a relationship case *(Haig and Birch v. Canada)* that the Canadian Human Rights Act ought to be read as though it included sexual orientation. One year later, the Supreme Court of Canada turned down Brian Mossop's claim for a partner benefit, but the ruling implied that an argument based on sexual orientation (as distinct from marital status) might have won the day. This sent a strong signal to courts and tribunals across the country, and the success rate of workplace grievances claiming benefits for same-sex partners suddenly increased (see Petersen 1999).

What seemed to be a period of "take-off" in wins for lesbian and gay couples was set back in 1994, with the defeat of legislation recognizing same-sex relationships introduced by the provincial NDP government (Rayside 1998, 141–78). Impressive LGBT activist mobilization in support of the measure was outgunned by the religious right and undermined by divisions inside the NDP. The opposition Liberal Party ended up almost entirely opposed to the bill, and the Conservatives condemned it from start to finish. The defeat of the legislation seemed likely to push family claims to the margins for some years.

That is not what happened. Relationship and parenting advocates escalated their court challenges as the number of same-sex couples with children grew, and they won with greater and greater frequency. In 1995, the Supreme Court of Canada ruled against a same-sex benefit claim in the *Egan* case but, in so doing, made it clear that sexual orientation discrimination was covered by section 15 of the Charter. In that same year, an Ontario court recognized the rights and obligations of non-biological parents in a case brought by four lesbian couples *(re K. and B.)* – a ruling that was soon interpreted as allowing simultaneous or joint parental adoption by same-sex couples. Taken together with legislative developments occurring at the same time in British Columbia, these were among the most significant early steps towards the official recognition of lesbian and gay parenting rights in the world.

In 1999, the Supreme Court of Canada delivered a monumentally important ruling in *M. v. H.*, striking down the exclusion of lesbian and gay couples from Ontario family law. This removed any doubts that de facto same-sex couples would be given the same treatment as heterosexual common law couples – this in a province (like most others) in which straight couples had acquired much of the legal recognition accorded to married couples.[5] Within a short time of that decision, Ontario's Conservative government introduced, grudgingly, a bill comprehensively recognizing same-sex relationships, securing agreement with other parties in the legislature to ensure rapid passage. There were still family issues to resolve, including the right to register two parents of the same sex on a child's birth certificate, a right established through a 2006 court ruling *(M.D.R. v. Ontario)*.

When marriage became a priority for at least some parts of the LGBT movement, after so many gains secured through claiming equivalence with heterosexual common law relationships, victory came quickly. Two of the carefully prepared constitutional challenges on marriage emerged in Ontario, one of them (begun in 2000) launched in Toronto on behalf of eight same-sex couples *(Halpern et al.)*. It was this case that resulted in a 2003 victory in the

Ontario Court of Appeal, which, unlike courts making similar judgments in other provinces, gave immediate effect to its ruling.[6] The decision by the federal government to not appeal that ruling made it clear that there was widespread judicial consensus on the constitutional impossibility of excluding lesbian and gay couples from marriage. In 2005, following the federal Parliament's approval of a formally inclusive definition of marriage, the Ontario legislature passed a bill altering 170 provincial statutes to bring them into line with the changed definition of marriage.

Schooling

There may well be no policy area in which significant change has been harder to effect than in schooling.[7] Activist groups at the school board and provincial levels in Ontario have been pressing for greater LGBT inclusiveness for as long as any similar groups in Canada, and they have made significant policy gains in several of the province's largest school boards. But indications at the level of individual schools and classrooms are that inclusive policies have had only an uneven effect even in Toronto, whose public school board has for so long taken the lead. At the provincial level, Ontario's education ministry has taken important steps, but only in recent years and in the face of considerable resistance. On this front no province or territory can claim to have leapt ahead of others in developing effective policies for challenging heterosexist school climates, and none has even come close to creating comprehensive policies for equitable school practices. To a disturbing extent, schools in Ontario, and across Canada, remain sites where traditional gender norms are reproduced, directly or indirectly, marginalizing deviation from those norms (Short 2013; Walton 2004).

In the 1970s, early activist attacks on discrimination against teachers produced no discernable change. The mid-1980s, though, saw increased and sustained activist attention to schools, especially in Toronto. The urgent need for public education in the early years of the AIDS epidemic provided some leverage for calls to enhance sex education in schools and to recognize sexual diversity. This led to the provincial government's requiring AIDS education in schools, though in retrospect it did not lead to the widespread change in approach to sex education for which advocates had hoped (see McCaskell 2005, chap. 9; Rayside 2008, 222–23; Rayside and Lindquist 1992).

From the mid-1980s on, there was increased advocacy and public policy interest in harassment and violence in schools. This led to provincial policies on bullying and discrimination (the 1994 "violence-free" schools policy and the 2001 Safe Schools Act) that formally included sexual orientation, but no attention was paid to the specificity of sexual diversity issues, and there were no significant resources allocated to combating the broader range of exclusionary practices.

The first indication of serious provincial attention came in the late 2000s. In 2008, Ontario's education minister, Kathleen Wynne, asked a school safety task force to follow up its earlier work by looking specifically at harassment and violence based on sexuality and gender. What came of that was *Shaping a Culture of Respect*, a report recommending a comprehensive strategy that included curricular change as well as other measures explicitly addressing the prevention of bullying based on sex and gender. In 2009, the provincial legislature approved the Keep Our Kids Safe at School Act, which increased the obligation for school staff to report harassment. In that year, the education ministry issued two policy memoranda requiring boards to develop equity and harassment policies and to ensure that those policies addressed sexual orientation (Ontario Ministry of Education 2009a, 2009b, 2009c).[8] In all these developments, in contrast to early legislative and administrative moves that referenced sexual diversity, these issues were now front and centre in policy discussions.

In late 2011, the provincial government introduced the Accepting Schools Act, which not only included sexual orientation and gender identity in strengthened policies addressing prejudice, but also required that boards support student groups intent upon countering it – including gay-straight alliances (GSAs). The bill encountered stiff opposition from the Conservative Party and from Catholic school trustees (and some school administrators) who objected to their schools being obliged to recognize LGBT-related student groups (Dabu Nonato 2012). The GSA name itself became a symbolic focal point, with many Catholic trustees seeing it as legitimizing homosexual activity. The Liberal government eventually pressed ahead and secured passage of its bill in 2012, including in it a requirement that all boards (including Catholic boards) had to recognize the name "GSA" if that was what students wanted to use.

In the midst of this policy expansion, a major controversy emerged over sex education, reminding LGBT activists and policymakers that no sea change was yet in prospect.[9] In 2008 and 2009, a new elementary school curriculum on health and physical education was being prepared, one that included sex education (as it had before). Following sustained pressure from educational reformers over many years, the new curriculum aimed to increase classroom recognition of the sexual diversity of students, their parents, and the wider

David Rayside

population. It also sought to keep up with the kind of sexual knowledge that students were acquiring at ever-younger ages. The new curriculum was released in early 2010 but then became the focus of an attack by religious conservatives in April of that year. This was the first time that any of the education ministry's initiatives on sexuality had come under fire. The provincial Conservatives immediately adopted a posture of outrage with regard to the curricular changes, contributing to distortions promoted by the most extreme of evangelical protesters. This was enough to lead Premier Dalton McGuinty to withdraw the sex education components for further consultation.

It is true that a generally cautious Ontario Liberal government, among all Canadian provincial governments, had taken among the first significant steps in recognizing the particular dimensions of schooling issues related to sexual diversity. There was no assurance that implementation would be seriously monitored or that significant resources would be attached to board initiatives, but these legislative and regulatory steps did reflect the sustained pressure from LGBT advocates across the province. Increased public concern over harassment and violence in schooling had provided an opening to consider a wider set of contributors to exclusionary school climates. Even now, though, curricular change was a more difficult challenge, amply illustrated by the heavy seas encountered by the provincial government over sexual health education. The willingness of Conservatives to side with moral traditionalists on this issue was likely to reinforce the caution of provincial policymakers for some time to come.

What about school boards? Some years before a serious provincial policy response to LGBT advocacy, pressure at the school board level – in Toronto, especially – had produced significant policy shifts (McCaskell 2005). In fact, that city's public school board was the first in Canada to adopt policies specifically addressing sexual diversity, though it could hardly claim to have moved early or rapidly. Between 1990 and 1992, led by openly gay trustee John Campey, reformist advocates succeeded in getting board approval for an instructional unit on sexual diversity in health education for senior high school students, the inclusion of sexual orientation in harassment and anti-discrimination policies, and the expansion of a new equity office's mandate to include sexual orientation. In 1995, the board launched the Triangle Program – an LGBT-positive alternative school for students who were having difficulty with these issues in their regular schools.

In 1998, municipal amalgamation presented new challenges when the board expanded to include areas of Metropolitan Toronto that had barely addressed sexual diversity. After much struggle, an equity policy was approved that included provisions on LGBT inclusivity that were as assertive and wide-ranging as those found in any major school board in North America (the only rival being San Francisco). In its entirety, this policy covered the full range of inequities, including those on race, ethnic, and gender lines, and notably insisted on curricular change as well as change in other school practices.

Since then, other Ontario boards have adopted LGBT-positive policies. These include Thames Valley (centred in London), Ottawa-Carleton, and Peel (in Mississauga). In some cases, there is an excessively narrow focus on harassment and bullying, though the urgency associated with this issue has at times provided leverage for a broader agenda.

Implementation is another matter. The systematic application of any equity policy is difficult enough, but it is even more challenging if teachers and administrators fear that some topics are especially controversial. This remains the case for sexuality generally, and for sexual diversity particularly (see Schneider and Dimito 2008). The attitudes and behaviours of students, and the expectations of so many of their parents, lead to deeply embedded reinforcements of traditional gender roles and a form of policing at the boundaries of gender norms. This applies across the country as well as in other countries (see the *Chamberlain v. Surrey School District* case study in Chapter 6, this volume; and the Bill 44 case study in Chapter 7, this volume). This affects what is expected of all students, but it has a particularly harsh impact on young people who feel or behave at variance with such gender constructs or who have friends and family who do not conform. Advocacy for LGBT inclusivity directed to schools, school boards, and the provincial education ministry has borne fruit in the policies of several school boards, in the creation of many GSAs, and in the belated development of provincial equity and harassment policies. These are the first steps in a long and difficult process, one that has produced some schools that are immensely better equipped to deal with sexual diversity than they were a generation ago, but many others have barely opened the windows to reformist air.

Conclusion

In Ontario, as elsewhere in Canada, there remains a sizeable minority of the population that is profoundly uneasy about the public recognition of sexual diversity. There are also areas of state policy in which change has been slow and very unevenly applied. That said, the larger story remains one of significant accomplishment on the part of an array of Ontario's LGBT advocacy groups. Across the province, including Toronto, the expansion of a politicized movement during the 1960s and 1970s was slower than it was in large US cities.

But when activist networks expanded in the 1980s, they faced a smaller and less well organized religious right than did their American counterparts, and they benefited from a more favourable legal and constitutional context. With far fewer resources than US groups were able to muster, they accomplished much more with regard to changing state policy, particularly during the 1980s and 1990s. The most notable advances have been made in formal non-discrimination policies and in the official recognition of lesbian and gay family rights. This change has been easier during NDP and Liberal governments (1985 to 1995 and from 2003 on) than when Conservatives have been in power (up to 1985 and from 1995 to 2003), though pressure imposed by the Charter, and by the courts interpreting it, have led to some changes in official policy under governments entirely unfriendly to sexual minorities. At the local level, major changes have also been easier during times when city councils have had reformist majorities, though not impossible in other periods.

There is no doubt, however, that there are limits to this change. The barriers to real inclusivity are particularly striking in schooling but are also evident in the attitudes and behaviour of many police officers. The official recognition of family rights for same-sex couples has been translated into equitable practices in some social agencies providing relevant services (e.g., in adoption and fostering) but not all. Faith-based organizations are often, though not always, particularly reluctant to recognize the legitimacy of LGBT families. Across the issue spectrum, the willingness to fully accept transgenderism or bisexuality is significantly more limited than is the preparedness to respond favourably to "straight-forward" homosexuality. And across all issue areas, there is no question that invidious distinctions are created between those lesbians and gays who appear "respectable," or who have other middle-class credentials, and those whose demeanour or social background deviates more drastically from what is thought normal or safe.

We also know from the controversy over sex education that the caution of state officials and the general public is substantially heightened when LGBT advocacy affects young people. Sexual desire among children and adolescents is widely viewed as fraught with danger, and talk of sexual diversity in such populations all too easily provokes deep anxieties. People who are otherwise supportive of the equitable treatment of sexual minorities often hesitate over questions like adoption, and even more over what is taught in schools.

In all these respects – the dramatic victories, the long struggles, the strengths of the activist movement and its weaknesses, and the timing of change in state policy – Ontario's story is part of a cross-country narrative that has more striking commonalities than differences. The priorities of LGBT advocates have not differed markedly from one region to another, or at least not for long, and the areas in which they have made the most gains have strong elements of similarity, particularly in the country's largest provinces. There are, to be sure, regions in which activist visibility has been harder to establish or sustain, and in which the forces of resistance have been more daunting; but even here we find enormous changes in public attitudes and public policy. In Ontario's cities, as in urban areas across much of the country, the activists who launched the modern LGBT movement decades ago could scarcely have imagined what impact their work would have.

Notes

This chapter has benefited greatly from comments by Manon Tremblay (University of Ottawa) and Jerry Sabin (University of Toronto), to whom I am very grateful.

1 On this and other aspects of early LGBT Canadian history, see Jackson and Persky (1982); Kinsman (1996); Kinsman and Gentile (2010); Knegt (2011); McLeod (1996); Ross (1995); and Warner (2002). On Ottawa, see Gentile (2011).

2 On the importance of institutions generally, and the Charter in particular, see Smith (1999, 2008). The Charter's section 15 was particularly significant for lesbian and gay advocates, and it came into force in 1985.

3 At that time, I was an active member of the Right to Privacy Committee, as well as a volunteer for *The Body Politic* and the Citizens' Independent Review of Police Activities (CIRPA).

4 In 2008, the provincial government "re-listed" reassignment surgery, technically opening the door to the coverage of costs through Medicare. But those seeking gender reassignment face huge administrative and screening hurdles that make such coverage exceedingly difficult to obtain. See Stratigacos (2009).

5 Quebec is an important exception since that province's Civil Code provided significantly fewer such rights than were available in the "common-law" provinces.

6 Favourable court rulings on marriage had come from other jurisdictions shortly before, but with delayed application pending appeal. The Ontario Court of Appeal ruled that its favourable decision would take effect immediately.

7 On schooling in Canada, see McCaskell (2005); McNinch and Cronin (2004); Rayside (2008, 221–47); Short (2013), Taylor and Peter (2011), Walton (2004), and Warner (2002). For an important Ontario government report on school climate, see Ontario Ministry of Education (2008).

8 Memorandum No. 119, *Developing and Implementing Equity and Inclusive Education Policies in Ontario Schools* (June) did not include gender identity, but No. 144, *Bullying Prevention and Intervention* (October) did. In the same year, the Ontario Ministry of Education (2009c) issued a strategy document – *Realizing the Promise of Diversity: Ontario's Equity and Inclusive Education Strategy*. Gender identity is not explicitly included in this document or in the strategy released prior to the memorandum.

9 More detail about this controversy can be found in Rayside (2010).

References

Dabu Nonato, Sheila. 2012. "Ontario, Catholic Schools Face Off Over Gay-Straight Alliances." *National Post*, 2 February. http://news.nationalpost.com/2012/02/02/ontario-catholic-schools-face-off-over-gay-straight-alliances/.

EGALE. 2011. *My GSA: Equity and Inclusive Education Resource Kit for Ontario High Schools*. Toronto: EGALE Canada. http://mygsa.ca/educators/lesson-plans-resources/.

Epstein, Rachel, ed. 2009. *Who's Your Daddy? And Other Writings on Queer Parenting*. Toronto: Sumach Press.

Gentile, Patrizia. 2011. "Capital Queers: Social Memory and Queer Place(s) in Cold War Ottawa." In James Opp and John Walsh, eds., *Placing Memory and Remembering Place in Canada*, 187–214. Vancouver: UBC Press.

Hannon, Gerald. 1982. "Raids, Rage and Bawdyhouses." In Ed Jackson and Stan Persky, eds., *Flaunting It! A Decade of Gay Journalism from* The Body Politic, 273-94. Vancouver/Toronto: New Star Books/Pink Triangle Press.

Herman, Didi. 1994. *Rights of Passage: Struggles for Lesbian and Gay Legal Equality*. Toronto: University of Toronto Press.

Hunt, Gerald, ed. 1999. *Laboring for Rights: Unions and Sexual Diversity Across Nations*. Philadelphia: Temple University Press.

Hunt, Gerald, and David Rayside, eds. 2007. *Equity and Diversity in Canadian Labour*. Toronto: University of Toronto Press.

Jackson, Ed, and Stan Persky. 1982. *Flaunting It! A Decade of Gay Journalism from* The Body Politic. Vancouver/Toronto: New Star Books/Pink Triangle Press.

Janoff, Douglas. 2005. *Pink Blood: Homophobic Violence in Canada*. Toronto: University of Toronto Press.

Kinsman, Gary. 1996. *The Regulation of Desire: Homo and Hetero Sexualities*. 2nd ed. Toronto: Black Rose Books.

Kinsman, Gary, and Patrizia Gentile. 2010. *The Canadian War on Queers: National Security as Sexual Regulation*. Vancouver: UBC Press.

Knegt, Peter. 2011. *About Canada: Queer Rights*. Halifax: Fernwood.

McCaskell, Tim. 1988. "The Bath Raids and Gay Politics." In Frank Cunningham, Sue Findlay, Marlene Kadar, and Alan Lennon, eds., *Social Movements/Social Change: The Politics and Practice of Organizing*, 169-88. Toronto: Between the Lines.

–. 2005. *Race to Equity: Disrupting Educational Inequality*. Toronto: Between the Lines.

McLeod, Donald W. 1996. *Lesbian and Gay Liberation in Canada: A Selected Annotated Chronology, 1964–1975*. Toronto: ECW Press/Homewood Books.

–. 2003. *A Brief History of GAY: Canada's First Gay Tabloid, 1964–1966*. Toronto: Homewood Books.

McNinch, James, and Mary Cronin, eds. 2004. *"I Could Not Speak My Heart": Education and Social Justice for Gay and Lesbian Youth*. Regina: University of Regina, Canadian Plains Research Centre.

Nash, Catherine Jean. 2005. "Contesting Identity: Politics of Gays and Lesbians in Toronto in the 1970s." *Gender, Place and Culture* 12 (1): 113–35. http://dx.doi.org/10.1080/09663690500083115.

Ontario Human Rights Commission (OHRC). 2000. *Policy on Discrimination and Harrassment Because of Gender Identity*. Toronto: Ontario Human Rights Commission. http://www.ohrc.on.ca/en/policy-discrimination-and-harassment-because-gender-identity.

Ontario Ministry of Education. 2008. *Shaping a Culture of Respect in Our Schools: Promoting Safe and Healthy Relationships. Safe Schools Action Team Report on Gender-based Violence, Homophobia, Sexual Harassment, and Inappropriate Sexual Behaviour in Schools.* Toronto: Ministry of Education. http://www.edu.gov.on.ca/eng/teachers/RespectCulture.pdf.
–. 2009a. *Policy/Program Memorandum No. 119: Developing and Implementing Equity and Inclusive Education Policies in Ontario Schools.* Toronto: Ministry of Education. http://www.edu.gov.on.ca/extra/eng/ppm/119.pdf.
–. 2009b. *Policy/Program Memorandum No. 144: Bullying Prevention and Intervention.* Toronto: Ministry of Education. http://www.edu.gov.on.ca/extra/eng/ppm/144.pdf.
–. 2009c. *Realizing the Promise of Diversity: Ontario's Equity and Inclusive Education Strategy.* Toronto: Ministry of Education. http://www.anti-racism.ca/content/realizing-promise-diversity-ontario%E2%80%99s-equity-and-inclusive-education-strategy-2009.
Petersen, Cynthia. 1999. "Fighting it Out in Canadian Courts." In Gerald Hunt, ed., *Laboring for Rights: Unions and Sexual Diversity across Nations,* 37–57. Philadelphia: Temple University Press.
Rayside, David. 1988. "Gay Rights and Family Values: The Passage of Bill 7 in Ontario." *Studies in Political Economy* 26 (Summer): 109–47.
–. 1998. *On the Fringe: Gays and Lesbians in Politics.* Ithaca: Cornell University Press.
–. 2008. *Queer Inclusions, Continental Divisions: Public Recognition of Sexual Diversity in Canada and the United States.* Toronto: University of Toronto Press.
–. 2010. "Sex Ed in Ontario: Religious Mobilization and Socio-Cultural Anxiety." Paper presented at the Annual Meeting of the Canadian Political Science Association, Montreal, June.
Rayside, David, and Evert Lindquist. 1992. "AIDS Activism and the State in Canada." *Studies in Political Economy* 39 (Autumn): 37–76.
Ross, Becki. 1995. *The House That Jill Built: A Lesbian Nation in Formation.* Toronto: University of Toronto Press.
Schneider, Margaret, and Anne Dimito. 2008. "Educators' Beliefs about Raising Lesbian, Gay, Bisexual, and Transgender Issues in the Schools: The Experience in Ontario, Canada." *Journal of LGBT Youth* 5 (4): 49–71. http://dx.doi.org/10.1080/19361650802223003.
Short, Donn. 2013. *"Don't Be So Gay!" Queers, Bullying, and Making Schools Safe.* Vancouver: UBC Press.
Smith, Miriam. 1999. *Lesbian and Gay Rights in Canada: Social Movements and Equality Seeking, 1971–1995.* Toronto: University of Toronto Press.
–. 2008. *Political Institutions and Lesbian and Gay Rights in the United States and Canada.* New York: Routledge.
Stratigacos, Nikki. 2009. "Sex for Sale: Prostitution, Government, and Regulation." Paper presented to Sex for Sale, a conference organized by the Sexual Diversity Studies Student Union, University of Toronto, March.
Taylor, Catherine, and Tracey Peter. with T.L. McMinn, Tara Elliott, Stacey Beldom, Allison Ferry, Zoe Gross, Sarah Paquin, and Kevin Schachter. 2011. *Every Class in Every School: The First National Climate Survey on Homophobia, Biphobia, and Transphobia in Canadian Schools. Final Report.* Toronto: EGALE Canada Human Rights Trust.

Walton, Gerald. 2004. "Bullying and Homophobia in Canadian Schools: The Politics of Policies, Programs, and Educational Leadership." *Journal of Gay and Lesbian Issues in Education* 1 (4): 23–36. http://dx.doi.org/10.1300/J367v01n04_03.

Warner, Tom. 2002. *Never Going Back: A History of Queer Activism in Canada*. Toronto: University of Toronto Press.

–. 2010. *Losing Control: Canada's Social Conservatives in the Age of Rights*. Toronto: Between the Lines.

4

Quebec and Sexual Diversity: From Repression to Citizenship?

MANON TREMBLAY

Quebec underwent major upheavals during the twentieth century. This transformation has been manifest with regard to sexual minorities, notably lesbians and gays: once criminalized under the law, condemned by the church, and labelled deviant by psychiatry, lesbians and gays now seem to enjoy full citizenship – especially because they can legally get married. But is this really the case? As I show in this chapter, a view that is polarized between social marginalization and full social and cultural equality for lesbians and gays is too simplistic. Nevertheless, it offers a certain heuristic potential if it is redefined in terms of a continuum: although legal equality and the accompanying negative rights constitute a gain, full social and cultural equality and the positive rights that it entails remain to be achieved. This is even truer for minority groups within the Quebec LGBT movement, such as Indigenous and Two-Spirited people. The lesson from past struggles is that, in their quests for equality, lesbians and gays have had to rely on the support of allies.

My objective in this chapter is to reveal the relationships between the government of Quebec and the lesbian and gay movement starting in the 1970s. I base my analysis on works written on the movement in Quebec, of course, but also on five interviews that I conducted with lesbians and gays from the activist elite. But before I go further, two points must be made with regard to the difficulty of speaking of a homogeneous "lesbian and gay movement." The first is that this label is misleading because lesbians and gays cannot easily be lumped together. In fact, in Quebec there is an important lesbian feminist current that has been very critical of a "male-focused" gay liberation movement and its ambient sexism. Moreover, not only do many lesbians not feel at home within the women's movement but they also confront each other over ideological orientation – lesbian feminists versus radical feminists (Hildebran 1998; Lamoureux 1998; Podmore and Tremblay forthcoming; Turcotte 1998). The second point has to do with other cleavages within the lesbian and gay movement in Quebec, including the linguistic cleavage between anglophones and francophones, and the cleavage between Montreal and the rest of Quebec (Podmore 2006).

First, I briefly describe some highlights in the evolution of the lesbian and gay movement in Quebec (for a specific point of view on Montreal, see Chapter 8, this volume). Then I examine current forms of activism. Finally, I analyze three policies adopted by the government of Quebec that have had immediate impacts on lesbians and gays.

Historical Background

In Higgins's (1999, 83–112) view, it is illusory to speak of a lesbian and gay movement in Quebec before the 1970s. In fact, the criminalization of homosexuality until 1969 impeded even the instigation of such a movement. Moreover, during the 1960s, unlike in English Canada – notably Vancouver (see Kinsman 1996, 161–69, 224–57; Warner 2002, 42–60) – in Quebec there were few homophile activities and little sustained organizing that would have established fertile ground for lesbian and gay activism (Podmore and Tremblay forthcoming).[1] Yet the Quiet Revolution, a vast movement of social, cultural, and economic modernization and national affirmation (notably the promotion of Québécois nationalism based on highlighting the "French fact") that swept through Quebec during the 1960s, may have played an indirect role in the expression of lesbian and gay activism in the early 1970s by advancing a modernizing nationalism with which lesbian and gay groups could associate. For instance, on 1 July 1971 a large anti-Confederation demonstration was held in Montreal in which the Front de libération homosexuel (FLH) took part – the group's first public demonstration. According to Higgins (1999, 113–14), the name testifies to the desire of lesbian and gay activists of the time to identify with the Front de libération du Québec (FLQ). It seems, however, that lesbians and gays were more eager to associate with nationalism than nationalists were to welcome them. Indeed, according to McLeod (1996, 73), at the 1 July 1971 anti-Confederation demonstration, "gay marchers were subjected to open hostility from other groups, and were condemned by René Lévesque, leader of the Parti Québécois." Previously, in its 1964 summer issue, the nationalist journal *Parti pris* referred to "fédérastes" and "Confédérastie," conflating Canadian federalists and pederasty (Schwartzwald 1991). In short, the relations between Quebec nationalism and lesbians and gays remain unclear, and further research is called for.

That said, in the wake of adoption by the House of Commons of an omnibus bill (C-150) on 14 May 1969, just a few weeks before the Stonewall Riots of 27 and 28 June, the 1970s saw the first steps towards the creation of lesbian and gay community life in Quebec, especially in Montreal. However, the handful of disparate groups listed in the chronology did not reach the critical threshold of what could be called a historically instituted lesbian and gay movement with a broad membership and a networked structural organization that could quickly mobilize for collective action. Noël (1998, 187 [my translation]) posits that "the history of gay activism in Montreal, if not Quebec, formally began" in 1971, with the creation of the FLH, whereas Higgins (1999, 125–26 [my translation]) dates "the beginning of the modern period of gay liberation in Montreal" to the creation, in 1976, of the Comité homosexuel anti-répression (CHAR). This group was created in reaction to police violence against lesbians and gays that was part of a broader clean-up campaign in preparation for the Olympic Games (Kinsman and Gentile 2010, 310–19).

But whenever – in 1971 with the FLH or in 1976 with CHAR – lesbian and gay activism began in Quebec, the creation in the autumn of 1976 of the Association pour les droits des gai(e)s du Québec (ADGQ) definitively marking the advent of lesbian and gay activism espousing gay liberation ideology (Smith 1999, 55–57). Founded in the wake of CHAR, the ADGQ was one of the largest gay liberation groups in Canada. Among other things, it played a prominent role in having the Quebec Charter of Human Rights and Freedoms modified in 1977 to include sexual orientation as an illegal ground for discrimination (Ontario was the second province to do so, in 1986; see Chapter 3, this volume), testifying to its support not only for the consistent strategy of positioning the struggles of lesbians and gays as a core human right but also for promoting a certain degree of homonationalism (Tremblay 2013).[2] Yet, according to Smith (1999, 57), this victory may have had the perverse effect of sounding the death knell of gay liberation activism in Quebec. What is more, unlike what occurred in English Canada, the adoption of the Canadian Charter of Rights and Freedoms and the coming into effect of section 15 in 1985 did not whip up lesbian and gay activism in Quebec (Smith 1998).

In Quebec, as elsewhere in the West, the 1980s were marked by the HIV/AIDS crisis, which, overall, had contradictory effects on the lesbian and gay

Manon Tremblay

movements. On the one hand, the crisis helped to reinforce public disap-proval of homosexuality, although at the same time it promoted and strengthened the construction of a gay identity. On the other hand, it brought homosexuality out of the shadows by placing it on the public agenda: people, especially men, were dying, and action had to be taken. The crisis also brought to light the consequences, sometimes tragic, of the lack of recognition of same-sex unions, and, at the same time, it energized the struggles for recognition of these unions. Finally, the crisis helped to institu-tionalize the relationships between lesbian and gay communities and the government of Quebec as the former advocated for people with HIV/AIDS and the latter provided and funded (though not always adequately) interventions.

Whereas a clear liberationist, or "radical," current had inspired the move-ment since the 1970s, the mood began to change during the first half of the 1990s, when dialogue started to develop between the government of Quebec and the lesbian and gay communities. In the early 1990s, a series of homo-phobic murders, about which the police seemed to care little, mobilized these communities. Responding to pressure by the Table de concertation des lesbi-ennes et des gais du Québec, the Quebec Human Rights Commission (QHRC), the public agency responsible for ensuring compliance with the Quebec Charter of Human Rights and Freedoms, held public hearings on violence and discrimination against lesbians and gays in November 1993. The Quebec les-bian and gay communities were energized as briefs were submitted by thirty agencies devoted to the defence and promotion of their rights or to being pro-vided with services (including an Indigenous group, the Centre d'amitié autochtone de Montréal). The hearings resulted in the publication in 1994 of the report *De l'illégalité à l'égalité,* which served as an action plan for relations between the lesbian and gay community and the government of Quebec for years to come (Smith 1999, 126–32; one of the interviewees). By providing a sort of arena for discussion between the state and the lesbian and gay com-munities, the report helped to institutionalize the lesbian and gay movement by "deradicalizing" its demands and even by heteronormalizing lesbians and gays. The establishment of civil union in Quebec in 1999 and the opening of civil marriage to same-sex couples by the federal government in 2005 are no doubt the clearest manifestations of the process of normalization of lesbians and gays (Higgins 2011).[3]

In sum, over time, the lesbian and gay movement navigated through a sea of political opportunities, its members transitioning from the status of pariah to that of respectable citizen. Things have progressed to the point at which today the lesbian and gay movement maintains close ties with the government of Quebec – allowing for exchanges that fall within the broader project of achieving full social equality for lesbians and gays.

Queer Activism Today

Resource mobilization theory looks at resources available to a social move-ment to enable it to emerge and become involved in collective action (see, among others, Jenkins 1983; McCarthy and Zald 1977). These resources take various forms: cultural, moral, socio-organizational, human, and material (Edwards and McCarthy 2004, 125–28). By 2013, the lesbian and gay move-ment in Quebec encompassed a wide range of resources, as demonstrated by the panoply of groups and a wide variety of activities: huge tourism events with economic benefits (such as the gay pride parade and Divers/Cité in Montreal and, to a lesser extent, the Fête Arc-en-ciel in Quebec City); groups devoted to defending rights (including the Coalition gaie et lesbienne du Québec, the Conseil québécois des gais et lesbiennes, and the Réseau des les-biennes du Québec); help lines and assistance (including Gai Écoute); educa-tion and awareness raising (Fondation Émergence, Gris-Montréal, and Gris-Québec); and the fight against homophobia (such as GLBT Québec/Lutte à l'homophobie); professional groups (such as the Chambre de commerce gaie du Québec); and a plethora of ethno-cultural groups and groups focusing on recreation and sports, health, and other issues. However, the vast majority of these groups are concentrated in Montreal.

State repression is a well-documented factor in terms of exerting heavy influence on the activities of social movements (Earl 2003, 2011); however, good relations with the state form a resource that is too often minimized in – though very important to – the deployment of lesbian and gay activism. Today, in the mid-2010s, the government of Quebec and the lesbian and gay move-ment have a close connection. On the one hand, the state regulates the lesbian and gay movement through its departments (e.g., the Ministère de la Justice, de la Santé et des services sociaux, and the Ministère du Travail) and specific or inter-ministerial policies (as illustrated in the *Québec Policy against Homophobia* and the *Government Action Plan against Homophobia, 2011–2016*), through targeted financial support (for events such as the gay pride parade and services such as Gai Écoute), and in other ways. On the other hand, the movement is not clay that can be modelled by the state; rather, it influences the state, for example by advocating services (the Gris groups are one example of this) or by offering expertise with regard to sexual diversity (e.g., the research

Manon Tremblay

chair on homophobia at UQAM). Three case studies illustrate the influence that the lesbian and gay movement can have on the state.

Queer Activism and Public Policy Changes: Case Studies

The guiding idea of this chapter is that, although it is no longer possible to think of lesbians and gays as living on the margins of Quebec society, it is also not possible to believe that they have full social and cultural citizenship. Since the late 1990s, lesbians and gays have gained rights and acquired recognition that, without a shadow of a doubt, have contributed to their equality. These advances are the result of demands and struggles by lesbians and gays, with the support of allied institutions and individuals. In using the notion of "alliance," I am referring to actors outside the lesbian and gay communities that share these communities' values, objectives, strategies, and struggles: these include interest groups, political parties, media outlets, and political and intellectual elites (Rucht 2004). Below, I examine three public policies: (1) the recognition of same-sex common-law unions, (2) the establishment of new filiation rules open to same-sex parenting, and (3) the struggle against homophobia.

Recognition of Same-Sex Unions and Same-Sex Parenting

In 1999, the National Assembly of Quebec unanimously adopted the Act to Amend Various Legislative Provisions Concerning de Facto Spouses. This statute conferred the same rights and privileges on all common-law spouses, both same-sex and opposite-sex. Three years later, in 2002, the National Assembly adopted, again unanimously, the Act Instituting Civil Unions and Establishing New Rules of Filiation. Aside from creating a new conjugal institution (civil union), this statute made it possible to record the names of two mothers or two fathers on a child's birth certificate. Both statutes posed a serious challenge to what Lahey (1999, 52) calls "the presumption of heterosexuality," the postulate that every individual is heterosexual and that the state must protect, promote, and favour heterosexual relations through a series of rights and privileges, notably because they constitute the fertile soil for the future of society. Why did the Quebec government, with the Parti québécois (PQ) then in power, turn its back on the presumption of heterosexuality by adopting these statutes? Essentially, it was a positive effect of the pressure asserted by the lesbian and gay movement, which was able to count among its resources, aside from positive court rulings, the support of allies within the state apparatus.

An Act to Amend Various Legislative Provisions Concerning de Facto Spouses
Recognition of same-sex unions was a long-standing demand by the lesbian and gay movement and its allies. As far back as January 1975, during their testimony before the Standing Committee on Justice, which was responsible for holding public hearings in preparation for the formulation of the Quebec Charter, representatives of lesbian and gay associations demanded better protection for couples formed of two individuals of the same sex (Quebec 1975, B-447). Whereas the Civil Code of Lower Canada did not specify that marriage consisted exclusively of the union of a woman and a man, the Civil Code of Quebec, which came into effect in 1994, added this detail (sec. 365) – a worrisome development in the view of some lesbians and gays (according to an interview with an activist in the Quebec LGBT movement). During public hearings on violence and discrimination against lesbians and gays in November 1993, all of the briefs received (except for one) dealing with same-sex spouses advocated recognition of these unions on the same terms as opposite-sex unions. In its report *De l'illégalité à l'égalité,* the QHRC recommended, for the first time in Quebec, that same-sex couples benefit from the same recognition and social benefits as couples formed of a woman and a man. More specifically, the QHRC recommended (rec. 33) that section 137 of the Quebec Charter, which allowed for different treatment on the basis of sexual orientation in pension and retirement plans, personal insurance, and all other social benefits plans, be abrogated. As it was, because same-sex unions were not recognized, lesbians and gays living in a common-law union were refused benefits from such plans. Section 137 was abrogated in 1996. The QHRC also asked the Quebec government to review all laws and regulations to bring them into compliance with the Quebec Charter so that people in homosexual and heterosexual common-law marriages would benefit from the same rights (rec. 34). This began the battle for recognition of same-sex spouses.

In 1998, the Table de concertation des lesbiennes et des gais du Grand Montréal initiated the creation of the Coalition québécoise pour la reconnaissance des conjoints et conjointes de même sexe. The coalition's objectives were to promote social and legal recognition of same-sex couples and their families and to ensure their equality through the elimination of discrimination against them in society in general – and especially in the statutes. The coalition included some twenty associations from the lesbian and gay community, of course, but also allied groups from outside that community, including the three labour confederations, women's groups (such as the Fédération des femmes du Québec), and the Ligue des droits et libertés. The coalition favoured a lobbying strategy, based on dialogue rather than confrontation, with politicians of all

Manon Tremblay

parties so that, when the bill was presented to the National Assembly, all parties would support it (according to one of the interviewees). In fact, not only had the question of recognition of common-law spouses spurred activism within the PQ for a number of years, but it also had the support of solid allies within the party, including MNAs Louise Harel and Pauline Marois, the ministers of justice from 1994 to 1999 (Paul Bégin, Serge Ménard, and Linda Goupil), and Premier Lucien Bouchard himself (Bureau and Papy 2006; one of the interviewees). In any case, as if to underline the importance that his government accorded to this question and to follow up on the PQ's commitment made during its 1996 national congress to "standardize in the laws the criteria defining common-law spouses, including same-sex common-law spouses" (Parti québécois 1997, 16; my translation), in June 1998 Premier Bouchard tabled a bill providing for recognition of common-law spouses. In the end, by creating an alliance among the lesbian and gay movement, major civil society organizations, and Quebec political parties, the coalition was able to generate consensus with regard to recognition of common-law unions between two lesbians and between two gay men.

An Act Instituting Civil Unions and Establishing New Rules of Filiation
As its title indicates, Act 84, An Act Instituting Civil Unions and Establishing New Rules of Filiation, created a new institution (civil union) open to both same-sex and opposite-sex couples and involving essentially the same rights and obligations as marriage.[4] Above all, Act 84 spelled out the right of couples in a civil union to filiation. It explicitly recognized the right of a spouse to adopt her or his spouse's child and created a presumption of parenthood for both same-sex and opposite-sex spouses. Act 84 thus amended section 115 of the Civil Code of Quebec such that when two women or two men are the parents of a child they are designated as the mothers or fathers on the declaration of birth, thus eliminating the step of adoption by the co-parent. This was a first in Canada (according to an interview with an activist in the Quebec LGBT movement). What made it possible?

In 1994, the QHRC advised the Quebec government, in its report *De l'illégalité à l'égalité*, to take into account the recommendation made by the Royal Commission on New Reproductive Technologies that access to insemination services should not be subject to any type of discrimination, including by sexual orientation (rec. 41). In the QHRC's view, this went hand in hand with the recognition of women's equality rights (CDPQ 1994, 122). At the time, insemination clinics were refusing services to lesbians, and that may be why they were very present, "often in the majority[,] around the [coalition's] table" (Demczuk quoted in Dupuis 2012, 14; my translation). As a sign of the high priority of parenthood rights on the lesbian and gay community's agenda, in

1998 the Coalition québécoise pour la reconnaissance des conjoints et conjointes de même sexe and the Association des mères lesbiennes du Québec were founded; one of the goals of the latter was to gain rights for lesbian mothers and lesbians who wanted to become mothers. Indeed, there were same-sex-parent families in Quebec with no legal recognition in that the spouse of the legal parent had no legal status or rights with regard to that parent's children, even if she or he participated actively in their education. It also had to be established that children of same-sex parents would not suffer prejudice and would have the same rights as did children whose parents were opposite-sex. The late 1990s were also marked by a growing number of court decisions ruling that same-sex conjugal relationships should have the same constitutional recognition as do heterosexual conjugal relationships (e.g., the *M. v. H.* ruling in 1999).

It was in this context that, in December 2001, Minister of Justice Paul Bégin tabled a bill on same-sex civil union in the National Assembly. The bill both created a conjugal status reserved exclusively for same-sex couples and excluded the recognition of parental rights for lesbian and gay families, basically because there was no consensus on the subject in the PQ caucus (Nicol 2005). This omission caused grumbling among certain groups, including the Coalition québécoise pour la reconnaissance des conjoints et conjointes de même sexe and the Table de concertation des lesbiennes et des gais du Québec, which felt that it was in the interest of children living in same-sex families to have parental rights for same-sex couples recognized (Lafontaine 2001; see also Bureau and Papy 2006). Following a meeting with representatives of the lesbian and gay communities, the minister agreed to submit the bill to a parliamentary committee for examination. Lesbians and gays then relied on a visibility and information strategy aimed at bringing the existence of same-sex families into the public eye and winning over public opinion, notably through media appearances. Situations had to be exposed and demystified, and prejudices fought, by associating faces with "lived realities." In this perspective, three young adults who had grown up in same-sex families testified at the Committee on Institutions in February 2002, describing episodes of discrimination that had marked their childhood and adolescence due to their parents' sexual orientation (see Nicol 2005). This strategy seems to have been connected to the government's decision to amend the bill to include recognition of the parental rights of lesbian and gay families. The decision is also explained by intense lobbying by certain actors in the lesbian and gay communities with Minister Bégin (according to an interview with an activist in the Quebec LGBT movement), an ally without whom the rules of filiation would never have been redefined to include same-sex parenting.[5]

Manon Tremblay

Now that legal equality has been acquired, social and cultural equality remains to be addressed.[6] In other words, even though equality before the law is crucial, for lesbians and gay men equality in everyday life would mean that they could live free of the invisible and visible regulations and strictures that heteronormative hegemony imposes in order to marginalize, denigrate, and oppress queer sexualities. With social and cultural equality, the heterosexual lifestyle would no longer hold a monopoly on legitimacy regarding sexualities by embodying the model that must be mimicked in order to be respectable and to have access to a broad range of advantages; it would mean that several sexualities are possible, publicly coexist, and benefit from the same respectability and opportunities. Put simply, social and cultural equality implies that the choice people make regarding how to organize their daily lives would in no way be related to the entitlements of full citizenship.

Struggles against Homophobia

As elsewhere in Canada, lesbians and gays in Quebec are not spared from homophobia – a scourge whose devastating effects multiply when combined with other minority social characteristics, such as being non-white, underschooled, and poor; living in a rural area or small town; and having a physical or mental handicap. Thus, in December 2009, the Quebec government adopted the *Québec Policy against Homophobia* – the outcome of a number of years of activism by the lesbian and gay movement and dialogue with the Quebec government with the goal of instituting measures to counter homophobia.[7] The *Policy* also benefited from the support of allies both inside the state apparatus, notably the Quebec Commission of Human Rights and Youth Rights, and outside of it (e.g., the feminist and labour movements).[8] Finally, the *Policy* drew on a number of recommendations made in two reports delivered by the commission and designed to fight homophobia.

In the first report, *De l'illégalité à l'égalité*, the commission made forty-one recommendations for fighting homophobia in the areas of health and social services, relations with the police, and compliance of laws with the Quebec Charter. Taken together, these recommendations proposed to combat homophobia through raising awareness of homosexuality, education and training, adaptation of existing services or creation of specific structures, research and funding of programs for lesbians and gays, review of federal and provincial laws, and other measures. In other words, the recommendations aimed to adapt lesbians and gays to Quebec society without challenging that society's heteronormative foundations or the privileges that it conferred on heterosexuals –

privileges that poorly concealed a degree of heterosexism. The second report, from which the *Policy* was generated, was *De l'égalité juridique à l'égalité sociale*, published in March 2007. Its tone was clearly different from that in *De l'illégalité à l'égalité*: the commission adopted an approach used by LGBT groups, as revealed by the use of terms such as "heterosexism."[9] Resulting from the demands and struggles of Quebec LGBT communities, *De l'égalité juridique à l'égalité sociale* was the fruit of close collaboration between these communities and the Quebec government in the battle against homophobia; it no doubt would not have been published without the cooperation of institutional and individual allies.

De l'égalité juridique à l'égalité sociale was the result of the LGBT communities' initiative and leadership. Following the Liberal victory in the provincial election of 2003, representatives from the LGBT communities undertook to canvass the minister of citizens' relations and immigration, Michelle Courchesne, who then positioned herself as an ally for lesbians and gays by agreeing to set up a working group called the Groupe de travail mixte contre l'homophobie (CDPDJ 2007, 8). It must be said that the "gay lobby" successfully used a powerful method of pressuring the minister by arriving at her office with members of the media (according to an interview with an activist in the Quebec LGBT movement). The important influence exerted by the LGBT communities on the working group was also evident in the areas of reflection initially chosen – those designated as a high priority at the États généraux des communautés LGBT du Québec, held on 2–3 September 2004: health and social services, education, and support for LGBT community groups (ibid.). Following a cabinet shuffle in February 2005, the working group came under the aegis of the minister of justice, Yvon Marcoux, who passed responsibility for it on to the commission. The working group's mandate included painting a portrait of homophobia and heterosexism in Quebec, identifying the institutional mechanisms already in place for government services to meet the needs of sexual minorities, inventorying the problems resulting from homophobia, and making recommendations for the highest-priority measures to fight it (CDPDJ 2007, 9). To carry out this mandate, the working group created seven ad hoc sector-based committees composed of representatives from government departments, unions, academe, and LGBT communities. The last category consisted of a wide range of groups – testifying to the diversity of realities experienced by sexual minorities in Quebec and the complexity of the issues engendered by homophobia – including Action Séro Zéro, the Association des mères lesbiennes, the Coalition des transsexuel(le)s et transsexué(e)s du Québec, the Conseil québécois des gais et lesbiennes, the

Fondation Émergence and Gai Écoute, the Organisation des êtres bispirituels du Québec, the Regroupement d'entraide pour la jeunesse allosexuelle du Québec, and the Réseau des lesbiennes du Québec. In a word, the advisory report of the Groupe de travail mixte contre l'homophobie was the result of efforts made by the LGBT communities and expressed their concerns. Of course, the recommendations "fell under the complete responsibility of the Commission of Human Rights and Youth Rights" (11; my translation). However, the commission was positioned as an ally of the LGBT communities because, due to its power to make recommendations, it acted as a liaison between the communities and the Quebec government. The fact remains that the commission formulated a galaxy of recommendations, one of which consisted of adoption of a national policy of eradication of homophobia.

The *Québec Policy against Homophobia* was the government's response to this recommendation. Why did the government act in this way? According to one of the LGBT activists interviewed, there are at least three reasons. First, the minister responsible for this portfolio, Kathleen Weil, was an ally of the LGBT communities. Second, these communities had a demographic weight that a government would find hard to ignore. Finally, it is possible that the Liberal government wanted to broaden its electoral base to the LGBT communities, historically more favourable to the PQ, which had amended the Quebec Charter to include sexual orientation under illegal reasons for discrimination in 1977 (Tremblay 2013).

The overall objective of the *Policy* is to "[improve] the situation of the sexual minorities in Québec in order to achieve social equality" (Quebec 2009, 16). The premises upon which the *Policy* is based are those of human rights: respecting the dignity, rights, and freedoms of LGBT people, eliminating discrimination against them in compliance with the right to equality, recognizing their legitimate aspirations to well-being, and eradicating homophobia – an issue that should concern everyone, not just the government. The *Policy* was followed by the adoption, in May 2011, of the *Government Action Plan against Homophobia, 2011–2016*. Written by a working group that included eleven government departments, the *Plan* listed sixty practical measures "in all spheres of activity to combat homophobic behaviour" (Quebec 2011, iii). That such a wide array of departments was involved indicates that there was cooperation by a number of allies within the Quebec government. Moreover, the measures proposed were the fruit of consultations conducted with several groups in the LGBT communities. The range of organizations consulted proved to be much more modest than those that had participated in the deliberations of the Groupe de travail mixte contre l'homophobie. Nevertheless, the

Plan adopted two notions that testified to a desire to cover a broad array of manifestations of homophobia. The first notion is that of transphobia, defined to encompass not only transsexuals, transgenders, and transvestites, but also "persons who cross the lines of gender and sex or of gender and sex representations" (Quebec 2011, ix). Thus conceptualized, transphobia includes, for instance, tomboys and heterosexual men whose appearance is perceived as effeminate. The second notion is gender-differentiated analysis. This analytic tool is based on the postulate that women and men have different realities and divergent needs and that they differently experience the consequences of public policies. Its use thus kept the realities and needs of lesbians from being assimilated with those of gays (and heterosexual women) and even made it possible to work on traditionally neglected issues that specifically affect lesbians (e.g., taking lesbians into shelters in the context of conjugal violence). Although it is too early to assess the effectiveness of the *Policy* and the *Plan*, it is to be hoped that these governmental strategies, based on communication with civil society and a socially integrated approach, will not instrumentalize lesbians, gays, bisexuals, transsexuals, and transgenders as simply beneficiaries of state services, condemned to become good citizens normalized to the heterosexual lifestyle. Indeed, the *Policy* and the *Plan* may be criticized because they do not question and challenge the heterosexist foundations of Quebec society but, rather, are mechanisms of regulation in the form of long shopping lists of apparently LGBT-friendly measures designed to ensure that sanitized and respectable lesbians and gays will fit within Quebec's inherently heteronormative society.

Conclusion

In Quebec, as in the other regions of Canada covered in this book, lesbians and gays have evolved from the status of pariah to that of respectable citizen: from the starting point, in 1969, of partial decriminalization of buggery and gross indecency when engaged in by two adults (twenty-one years of age and over) in private, lesbians and gays have, over subsequent decades, attained equality before the law. In this regard, the Act to Amend Various Legislative Provisions Concerning de Facto Spouses and the Act Instituting Civil Unions and Establishing New Rules of Filiation constitute important victories for Quebec lesbians and gays – victories resulting from battles that they have led, with the support of allies. More than a negative rights measure (such as banning discrimination on the basis of sexual orientation following amendment of the Quebec Charter in 1977), these statutes confer rights (and obligations) on lesbians and gays, contributing to the project of their full social and cultural equality. Yet social and cultural equality remains a mirage as long as prejudices against lesbians and gays endure – especially for lesbians and gays who are not part of the mainstream due to the colour of their skin and their ethno-cultural background, their lower social class, if they reside outside of large urban areas, and so on. In this perspective, the LGBT communities and the Quebec government have been engaging in dialogue for a long time, often via the intermediary of allies such as the Commission of Human Rights and Youth Rights, and have resolved to fight together against homophobia.

Much work remains to be done to attain full social and cultural equality for LGBT people in Quebec – and this is even more the case for LGBT people who are labelled "different," such as Aboriginal people. The fight against homophobia (including transphobia and biphobia) constitutes an important challenge for the coming years – a challenge that will have to be addressed in the light of transformations in Quebec's socio-demographic fabric as the population ages and diversifies. It will also be important for government services offered to respond to the needs of LGBT clienteles, which, like the heterosexual population, are getting older – but, contrary to the latter, having frequently been rejected by their families, will need state assistance even more. Ethno-cultural groups offer unequal receptiveness to LGBT people, with resistance sometimes stronger towards lesbians than gays, a fact that will have to be taken into account in the fight against homophobia. It is encouraging to observe that the *Government Action Plan against Homophobia, 2011–2016* suggests a number of practical measures for fighting homophobia that are sensitive to age and ethno-cultural diversity.

Despite this, it may be that the coming years will not bring as much success to lesbians and gays as has the recent past. One reason is the socially conservative climate that has prevailed in Canada over the past few years (Farney 2012; McDonald 2010; Nadeau 2011; Warner 2010). Social conservatism seeks to protect and promote traditional (heterosexual) sexual and family morals. An example of this is the Harper government's announcement in 2014 regarding the family income splitting opportunity, a measure which will first and foremost benefit rich heterofamilies with a stay-at-home mom and a highly paid breadwinner dad. Miriam Smith provides another example in her chapter in this book, where she shows that one of the arguments advanced in 2006 for the amendment of the Criminal Code (which covers Quebec) to increase the age of consent was protection of youth – an age group that is idealized as pure and innocent because it is not "sullied" by sexual activity. Paradoxically, it is possible that social conservatism is helping to normalize certain homoerotic customs (Johnson 2013). Recognition of unions formed of two women or two men and parental rights for families composed of same-sex parents clearly illustrate this normalization. Or, more precisely, heteronormalization: equality has served as the pretext for normalization of lesbians and gays who agree to mimic the heterosexual, middle-class way of life – that of a monogamous, faithful couple who may be parents and joint property owners and have a joint bank account and Registered Retirement Savings Plans (RRSPs). What becomes of lesbians and gays who refuse to conform with this heterosexual lifestyle? Could it be that their resistance to being "heteronormalized" keeps them on the fringes of society as unacceptable and unrespectable? It is such subtle manifestations of heterosexism – that is, invisible and unconscious, yet performatively engraved on citizens and citizenship through repetitive *habituses* and discourses – to which attention will have to be paid in coming years.

Chronology

1969   Adoption of the omnibus bill (federal), which partially decriminalizes buggery and gross indecency when committed in private between two consenting adults aged twenty-one and over (August).

1970   Publication of the first issue of the magazine *Le tiers* (September).
        Publication of the first issue of the magazine *Mainmise* (October).

1971   Founding of the Front de libération homosexuel (FLH) (March; dissolved in August 1972).

1972   Founding of the Association homophile de Québec (June).
        Founding of Gay McGill (September).

1973   Founding of Montreal Gay Women (March).
        In Quebec City, founding of the Centre humanitaire d'aide et de libération (CHAL) (May).
        Publication of the lesbian magazine *Long Time Coming* (July).
        Opening of the bookstore Androgyny (later renamed L'Androgyne) (October).
        Founding of the Association homophile de Montréal/Gay Montreal Association, officially incorporated in early 1974 (December).

1974   Founding of the Centre homophile urbain de Montréal (CHUM) (January).
        Founding of Service d'entraide homophile de Québec (January).
        Founding of the Front homosexuel québécois de libération (FHQL) (spring).
        Founding of Labyris Montreal (December).

1975–77 A wave of police repression descends on gay bars in Montreal.
        Founding of Groupe homosexuel d'action politique (GHAP) (March 1975; dissolved in May 1976).

1976   Publication of the newspaper *Gay Montreal*.
        Creation of the Comité homosexuel anti-répression (CHAR), from which the Association pour les droits des gai(e)s du Québec emerges (May).

First large-scale lesbian and gay demonstration in Quebec: almost three hundred lesbians and gays march in downtown Montreal to denounce police repression (19 June).

Founding of Gay Women of Montreal and the Montreal Lesbian Organization (June) and Montreal Lesbian Women (November).

Founding of the Association pour les droits des gai(e)s du Québec (ADGQ), which became the Association pour les droits des gais et des lesbiennes du Québec (ADGLQ) (October; dissolved in 1988).

1977   Founding of Coop-Femmes (February).

Holding of the first Congrès national des gai(e)s du Québec (15–16 October).

On 21 October, the Montreal Urban Community police force conducts a major raid on the gay bar Truxx, arresting 146 men. The next day, the Association pour les droits des gai(e)s et des lesbiennes organizes a demonstration in Montreal to denounce the raid; 2,000 people participate.

Bill 88 is passed, which incorporates sexual orientation into the Quebec Charter of Human Rights and Freedoms as a prohibited reason for discrimination (15 December).

1978   Creation of the Regroupement national des lesbiennes et gais du Québec (RNLGQ) (dissolved in 1980).

1979   First gay pride parade held in Montreal (June).

Publication of the first issue of the newspaper *Le Berdache* (June).

Sources: Higgins (1999, 2011); McLeod (1996).

Notes

I would like to thank Julie Podmore and Miriam Smith for reading and commenting on this chapter. I alone am responsible for any errors.

1 Kimmel and Robinson (2001), Kinsman (1996, 250), and McLeod (1996, 31) mention the existence of International Sex Equality Anonymous (ISEA), a homophile group created in Montreal in August 1967, whose mandate dealt mainly with information and education. That said, ISEA was quite marginal and certainly did not exhibit a sustained level of homophile activities and organizing. In addition, before the 1969 reform of the Criminal Code homosexual themes were explored in the arts, including theatre and literature (see Higgins 1999, 39-71; McLeod 1996, 1-44).

2 Other factors to explain the Quebec Charter amendment are the police harassment of lesbians and gay men, as sadly exemplified by the police raid on the gay bar Truxx in October 1977, and the need to protect certain closeted gay ministers within the first Parti québécois cabinet, who were in a position of extreme vulnerability (see Bureau and Papy 2006, 119).

3 Defined as "processes of social acceptance, so that LGBT people are not seen as different from anyone else" (Richardson and Monro 2012, 1).

4 Except with regard to age (one must be sixteen years old to marry but eighteen to enter a civil union) and dissolution (civil unions are dissolved by a notary; marriage, by court order).

5 On the idea that Bégin positioned himself as an ally of lesbians and gays, see Dupuis (2012) and Nicol (2005).

6 Pakulski (1997, 73) defines "cultural citizenship" as "cultural rights that involve the right to symbolic presence, dignifying representation, propagation of identity and maintenance of lifestyles." For lesbians and gays, cultural citizenship implies, at minimum, overcoming the marginalization, stigmatization, and assimilation intrinsic to heterosexist society.

7 It is interesting to note that the title of the *Policy* focuses on homophobia and not heterosexism (even though the *Policy* uses this notion within its pages). Such an approach implies that "phobic individuals," rather than "heterosexist society," are responsible for bullying, harassment, and other types of violence that are part of LGBT people's daily lives and that solutions are to be found in changing individuals and not in changing social processes and discourses.

8 The Commission of Human Rights and Youth Rights resulted from the merger, in 1995, of the Quebec Commission of Human Rights and the Commission of Protection of Youth Rights. In this section, the term "commission" refers to all of these entities without distinction.

9 In this section, I use the abbreviation LGBT (for lesbians, gays, bisexuals, transsexuals, and transgenders), as this is the language used in the report *De l'égalité juridique à l'égalité sociale*.

References

Bureau, Marie-France, and Jacques Papy. 2006. "L'orientation sexuelle et la Charte des droits et libertés de la personne: récit d'une trajectoire." *Revue du Barreau du Québec.* "La Charte québécoise: origines, enjeux et perspectives." Numéro thématique hors série de la Revue du Barreau en marge du trentième anniversaire de l'entrée en vigueur de la Charte des droits et libertés de la personne, 109–41.

Commission des droits de la personne (CDPQ). 1994. *De l'illégalité à l'égalité: Rapport de la consultation publique sur la violence et la discrimination envers les gais et lesbiennes.* Montréal: La Commission, May.

Commission des droits de la personne et des droits de la jeunesse (CDPDJ). 2007. *De l'égalité juridique à l'égalité sociale: Vers une stratégie nationale de lutte contre l'homophobie.* Ville de Québec and Montréal: CDPDJ.

Dupuis, Jacinthe. 2012. "L'union civile: Jamais deux sans droits." *Entre Elles* 120–21: 14, 16.

Earl, Jennifer. 2003. "Tanks, Tear Gas, and Taxes: Toward a Theory of Movement Repression." *Sociological Theory* 21 (1): 44–68. http://dx.doi.org/10.1111/1467-9558.00175.

–. 2011. "Political Repression: Iron Fists, Velvet Gloves, and Diffuse Control." *Annual Review of Sociology* 37 (1): 261–84. http://dx.doi.org/10.1146/annurev.soc.012809. 102609.

Edwards, Bob, and John D. McCarthy. 2004. "Resources and Social Movement Mobilization." In David A. Snow, Sarah Anne Soule, and Hanspeter Kriesi, eds., *The Blackwell Companion to Social Movements*, 116–52. Oxford: Blackwell.

Farney, James. 2012. *Social Conservatives and Party Politics in Canada and the United States.* Toronto: University of Toronto Press.

Higgins, Ross. 1999. *De la clandestinité à l'affirmation: Pour une histoire de la communauté gaie montréalaise.* Montréal: Comeau and Nadeau.

–. 2011. "La régulation sociale de l'homosexualité: De la répression policière à la normalisation." In Patrice Corriveau and Valérie Daoust, eds., *La régulation sociale des minorités sexuelles: L'inquiétude de la différence*, 67–102. Quebec City: Presses de l'Université du Québec.

Manon Tremblay

Hildebran, Andrea. 1998. "Genèse d'une communauté lesbienne: Un récit des années 1970." In Irène Demczuk and Frank W. Remiggi, eds., *Sortir de l'ombre: Histoires des communautés lesbienne et gaie de Montréal*, 207–33. Montréal: VLB éditeur.

Jenkins, J. Craig. 1983. "Resource Mobilization Theory and the Study of Social Movements." *Annual Review of Sociology* 9 (1): 527–53. http://dx.doi.org/10.1146/annurev.so.09.080183.002523.

Johnson, Carol. 2013. "Fixing the Meaning of Marriage: Political Symbolism and Citizen Identity in the Same-Sex Marriage Debate." *Continuum* (Perth) 27 (2): 242–53. http://dx.doi.org/10.1080/10304312.2013.766308.

Kimmel, David, and Daniel J. Robinson. 2001. "Sex, Crime, Pathology: Homosexuality and Criminal Code Reform in Canada, 1949–1969." *Canadian Journal of Law and Society* 16 (1): 147–65.

Kinsman, Gary. 1996. *The Regulation of Desire: Homo and Hetero Sexualities*. 2nd ed. Montreal: Black Rose Books.

Kinsman, Gary, and Patrizia Gentile. 2010. *The Canadian War on Queers: National Security as Sexual Regulation*. Vancouver: UBC Press.

Lafontaine, Yves. 2001. "L'union civile pour les couples homosexuels: L'union civile, un pas dans la bonne direction." *Fugues*, 20 December. http://www.fugues.com/main.cfm?l=fr&p=100_Article&article_id=742&rubrique_ID=40.

Lahey, Kathleen A. 1999. *Are We 'Persons' Yet? Law and Sexuality in Canada*. Toronto: University of Toronto Press.

Lamoureux, Diane. 1998. "La question lesbienne dans le féminisme montréalais: Un chassé-croisé." In Irène Demczuk and Frank W. Remiggi, eds., *Sortir de l'ombre: Histoires des communautés lesbienne et gaie de Montréal*, 167–85. Montréal: VLB éditeur.

McCarthy, John D., and Mayer N. Zald. 1977. "Resource Mobilization and Social Movements: A Partial Theory." *American Journal of Sociology* 82 (6): 1212–41. http://dx.doi.org/10.1086/226464.

McDonald, Marci. 2010. *The Armageddon Factor: The Rise of Christian Nationalism in Canada*. Toronto: Random House Canada.

McLeod, Donald W. 1996. *Lesbian and Gay Liberation in Canada: A Selected Annotated Chronology, 1964–1975*. Toronto: ECW Press/Homewood Books.

Nadeau, Christian. 2011. *Rogue in Power: Why Stephen Harper Is Remaking Canada by Stealth*. Toronto: James Lorimer.

Nicol, Nancy. 2005. *Politics of the Heart*. Toronto: V Tape.

Noël, Roger. 1998. "Libération homosexuelle ou révolution socialiste? L'expérience du GHAP." In Irène Demczuk and Frank W. Remiggi, eds., *Sortir de l'ombre: Histoires des communautés lesbienne et gaie de Montréal*, 187–206. Montréal: VLB éditeur.

Pakulski, Jan. 1997. "Cultural Citizenship." *Citizenship Studies* 1 (1): 73–86. http://dx.doi.org/10.1080/13621029708420648.

Parti québécois. 1997. La volonté de réussir. Programme et statuts du Parti québécois. Adoptés lors du XIII congrès national, novembre 1996. Montréal: Parti québécois. http://pq.org/sites/default/files/Programme1996.pdf (accessed 25 October 2012).

Podmore, Julie. 2006. "Gone 'Underground'? Lesbian Visibility and the Consolidation of Queer Space in Montréal." *Social and Cultural Geography* 7 (4): 595–625. http://dx.doi.org/10.1080/14649360600825737.

Podmore, Julie, and Manon Tremblay. Forthcoming. "Lesbians, Second-Wave Feminism and Gay Liberation." In David Paternotte and Manon Tremblay, eds., *The Ashgate Research Companion to Lesbian and Gay Activism*. Farnham: Ashgate.

Quebec. 2009. *Québec Policy against Homophobia: Moving Together towards Social Equality*. Ville de Québec: Ministère de la Justice. http://www.justice.gouv.qc.ca/english/publications/rapports/pdf/homophobie-a.pdf.

–. 2011. *Government Action Plan against Homophobia, 2011–2016*. Ville de Québec: Ministère de la Justice. http://www.justice.gouv.qc.ca/english/ministere/dossiers/homophobie/plan_action_homo_AN.pdf.

Quebec (Assemblée nationale). 1975. Journal des débats. Commissions parlementaires. Commission permanente de la justice. Étude du projet de loi n° 50 – Loi concernant les droits et les libertés de la personne. Troisième session – 30ᵉ législature. No. 8, 23 January.

Richardson, Diane, and Surya Monro. 2012. *Sexuality, Equality and Diversity*. Basingstoke: Palgrave Macmillan.

Rucht, Dieter. 2004. "Movement Allies, Adversaries, and Third Parties." In David A. Snow, Sarah A. Soule, and Hanspeter Kriesi, eds., *The Blackwell Companion to Social Movements*, 197–216. Oxford: Blackwell.

Schwartzwald, Robert. 1991. "Fear of Federasty: Québec's Inverted Fictions." In Hortense J. Spillers, ed., *Comparative American Identities: Race, Sex, and Nationality in the Modern Text*, 175–95. New York: Routledge.

Smith, Miriam. 1998. "Nationalisme et politiques des mouvements sociaux: Les droits des gais et lesbiennes et l'incidence de la Charte canadienne au Québec." *Politique et Sociétés* 17 (3): 113–40. http://dx.doi.org/10.7202/040131ar.

–. 1999. *Lesbian and Gay Rights in Canada: Social Movements and Equality-Seeking, 1971–1995*. Toronto: University of Toronto Press.

Tremblay, Manon. 2013. "Mouvements sociaux et opportunités politiques: Les lesbiennes et les gais et l'ajout de l'orientation sexuelle à la Charte québécoise des droits et liberté." *Revue canadienne de science politique* 46 (2): 295–322.

Turcotte, Louise. 1998. "Itinéraire d'un courant politique: Le lesbianisme radical au Québec." In Irène Demczuk and Frank W. Remiggi, eds., *Sortir de l'ombre: Histoires des communautés lesbienne et gaie de Montréal*, 363–98. Montréal: VLB éditeur.

Warner, Tom. 2002. *Never Going Back: A History of Queer Activism in Canada*. Toronto: University of Toronto Press.

–. 2010. *Losing Control: Canada's Social Conservatives in the Age of Rights*. Toronto: Between the Lines.

Legal Case

M v. H [1999] S.C.J. No. 23.

5

Mobilization on the Periphery: LGBT Activism and Success in Atlantic Canada

JOANNA EVERITT

If little has been written about the policy impact of queer movement mobilization in Canada, even less is known about its impact in the smaller, less urban, and more traditional provinces of Atlantic Canada. Indeed, Atlantic Canada's reputation for having a rural, homogeneous, strongly religious,[1] and conservative political culture might make it appear more unwelcoming to LGBT individuals than more populous and cosmopolitan areas of the country.[2] The fact that the Greater Halifax area is the largest urban centre, with just under 400,000 residents,[3] may lead many to expect that the first thing any LGBT youth would do is leave the region as small towns are known for being less supportive of LGBT rights (Langstaff 2011, 62). Certainly much of the literature on lesbians, gays, bisexual, and transgendered people assumes that cities, with greater anonymity and heterogeneity (and therefore presumably greater tolerance for difference), have acted as a beacon for LGBT migration out of rural areas (Kassler 1983). The national attention to homophobic statements by local politicians like Liberal Roseanne Skoke in 1994 and Progressive Conservative Elsie Wayne in 2003 have only strengthened this reputation.

Yet, despite their reputations, vibrant LGBT communities have developed over the past three decades in the four Atlantic Canadian provinces. While the range of organizations or activities are not as extensive as might be found in larger urban centres, there are a surprising variety of options that go beyond the yearly pride parades or Parents, Families and Friends of Lesbian and Gays (PFLAG) organizations. Although often social and non-political in nature, these organizations and activities have helped to establish networks within the community that have been used to advocate around key policy issues.

In this chapter I explore the occurrence of LGBT mobilization and advocacy in New Brunswick, Nova Scotia, Prince Edward Island, and Newfoundland and Labrador and the impact of this activity on provincial public policy surrounding key issues of interest to the LGBT movement. I begin by identifying the network of groups and actors that has been active in the region in recent decades and describe the resources that it has used to promote policy change. I conclude by focusing on three key policy issues (relationship recognition, family and adoption rights, and the fight against homophobia) and assessing the factors that have (or have not) contributed to the LGBT movement's success in promoting its agenda relating to them.

Historical Background

As elsewhere in the country, organizing within the Atlantic Canadian LGBT community has been social in nature, providing opportunities for LGBT individuals to come together to meet others and share experiences and fellowship. Early activities were often low key (e.g., a men's supper club in Saint John, Thanksgiving potluck suppers in PEI, or the lesbian brunch circuit in Halifax); however, increasingly, as public attitudes have changed, these activities have become more public, involving dances, soft ball leagues, theatre events, and gala dinners to fundraise for community needs.

The movement also developed around the provision of information about issues central to the homosexual, bisexual, or transgendered population. AIDS organizations appeared across the region in the 1980s and 1990s and provided critical early support for those living with HIV/AIDS as well as supplying important resources and opportunities for LGBT individuals to connect with others in their communities (see also Chapter 11, this volume). AIDS organizations in the region were among the earliest to be established in the country, with AIDS NB, based in Fredericton, appearing in 1985, and other organizations appearing in Halifax (1986), St. John's (1986), Saint John (1988), Moncton (1989), and Charlottetown (1990) shortly thereafter.

Other organizations were also established to provide crisis counselling or support. Gayline was a volunteer-staffed support line established in 1972, and it provided a quarter-century of information, counselling, and referral service to the LGBT communities in Nova Scotia. In other areas, however, efforts to provide support have been more challenging due to lack of continued resources. For example, Newfoundland Gays and Lesbians for Equality's

Joanna Everitt

(NGALE) efforts in the mid-1990s to offer a support number that could be called once a week was terminated after a few years and was only recently re-established.

Other support was provided by the Friends of Lesbians and Gays (FLAG) and later Parents and Friends of Lesbians and Gays (PFLAG) organizations, which began to spring up in towns across the region between the mid-1990s and 2000s, developing into important focal points for support, education, and resources for LGBT individuals and their parents. Many key activists in the region (Eldon Hayes of Sackville, NB; Gemma Schlamp-Hickey of St. John's, NL; Wayne Harrison of Saint John, NB; Cherie MacLeod of Moncton, NB) have played an active role not only in their local organizations but also in PFLAG Canada. PFLAG's national headquarters has been located in New Brunswick since the organization was established.

Another key organization in the region with a focus on youth is the Lesbian, Gay and Bisexual Youth Project, a Halifax-based organization. It began in 1993 and was originally in partnership with Planned Parenthood of Nova Scotia. Over the last two decades it has provided homophobia/heterosexism work-shops and training across Nova Scotia, New Brunswick, and PEI and has estab-lished a toll-free hotline – OUTline – for queer youth calling from Nova Scotia (Droesbeck 1997). It also offers supportive counselling, a resource library, edu-cational workshops, social activities, a summer camp, and a food bank (www. youthproject.ns.ca). The Lesbian, Gay and Bisexual Youth Project is closely connected to the broader LGBT community in Halifax and throughout Nova Scotia, and it has worked to educate schools, community organizations, and professionals by providing them with an awareness of the needs and experien-ces of LGBT youth. Through its efforts the first Gay-Straight Alliance in Nova Scotia was established.

The increasingly broader range of support that these organizations are able to provide reflects an important change in public acceptance of the LGBT community in the region. LGBT organizations began to appear in the 1970s. These included the Gay Alliance for Equality (GAE) in 1973, and the Community Homophile Association of Newfoundland (CHAN) in St. John's and the Gay Friends of Fredericton in 1974. Public demands for rights and recognitions began in the 1970s with picnics (1973), protests against the CBC Radio's refusal to air gay public service announcements (1977), the organizing of an Atlantic Canada Gay Conference (1977), sit-ins in Halifax bars that had previously banned gay patrons (1978–79), and the first gay rights parade in the region (Halifax 1978), when GAE hosted the sixth national conference of the Canadian Lesbian and Gay Rights Coalition.

Regularized and organized pride parades and other pride events began in the late 1980s with the first Halifax Pride Parade occurring in 1988. This event involved about seventy-five men and women marching down Spring Garden Road, about ten to fifteen of whom concealed their faces with paper bags to protect their identities (Chapin 2008). Other pride parades appeared around the region over the next dozen years, and, by the summer of 2011, pride weeks were held in Fredericton, Saint John, Moncton, Charlottetown, Corner Brook, St. John's, Antigonish, Halifax, and Sydney. The Halifax Pride Parade, which currently draws almost seventy thousand spectators and sixteen hundred participants (although, at its peak in 2007, it claimed to have seven thousand participants) has become the fourth largest pride parade in the country. In addition to pride parade or Pride Week festivities, activists participate in other parades or marches, including Labour Day parades, Santa Claus parades, AIDS walks, and Rainbow Peace marches (the latter occurring on 17 May). There are also regional networks of organizations that have been established, such as Newfoundland Gays and Lesbians for Equality (NGALE), which formed in 1994; the Nova Scotia Rainbow Action Project (NSRAP), which formed in 1995; the Abegweit Rainbow Collective in PEI (ARCPEI), which formed in 1999; and the New Brunswick Rainbow Alliance, which formed in 2001.

Queer Activism Today

Although some of these organizations have developed strong institutional support structures that allow them to grow from one year to the next, most have few resources and are built around committed volunteers. When interest flags or conflicts arise between key members of an organization it becomes difficult to maintain continued activity, and this may lead to the cancellation of pride weeks or other events. Likewise, local or regional organizations also suffer from volunteer fatigue, as is the case for ARCPEI, which threatened to disband in the spring of 2012 due to the lack of volunteer interest (CBC 2012).

As social movement organizations they have sought both social and political change. Social change, including a general acceptance of lesbians and gays, has occurred at a noteworthy pace in the region. Figure 5.1 shows changes in the attitudes of Atlantic Canadians towards gays and lesbians based on the following question, which appeared in four Canadian Election Studies: "How do you feel about gays and lesbians?" The studies used a scale from zero to one hundred, with zero indicating respondents really disliked gays and lesbians and one hundred indicating that they really liked them. These data indicate

Figure 5.1 Change in Atlantic Canadian attitudes toward gays and lesbians (feeling thermometer)

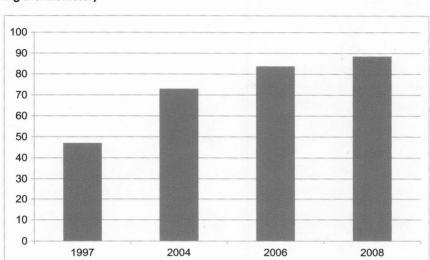

Sources: Blais et al. 1997; Gidengil et al. 2004–08.

that feelings measured using these feeling thermometers were almost twice as positive in 2008 as they were in 1997.

While the LGBT movement has made significant progress in the Atlantic region, there has been, and remains, some resistance, often tied to religious beliefs (which is also true elsewhere in Canada, as is shown in Chapters 3, 6, and 7 [on Ontario, British Columbia, and Alberta, respectively], this volume). For example, in 1998, LGBT activists had to file a complaint with the New Brunswick Human Rights Commission to force long-time Fredericton mayor Brad Woodside to read a proclamation pertaining to gay pride days. In protest, Woodside turned off his microphone and read the proclamation in such a low voice that it was impossible for any in the council chamber to hear him. Other examples of cities or towns refusing to recognize pride days or to fly the pride flag abound. In Nova Scotia, the mayor and city council of the town of Truro refused to declare Pride Week in 2007, then banned all festival proclamations in 2008. Other towns, such as Pictou and Antigonish, have also refused to fly the pride flag due to town policies.

Such responses are clear evidence of the continued resistance to sexual diversity, yet they also serve as rallying points for support for the LGBT community. Woodside's resistance to making a Pride Day proclamation resulted in heightened awareness of, and debate around, human rights issues and led to a greater awareness of the LGBT community in Fredericton. Truro's pride flag stance resulted in a rally of more than a hundred people who protested the council's lack of support for the LGBT community. According to Charles Thompson (2007, 3): "In a way [Truro] Mayor Bill Mills did the gay community a great service by refusing our request to fly the pride flag: if Council agreed we would have been lucky to get a write up in the Truro Daily News, whereas we continue to receive requests from media outlets."

Other rallying points for LGBT activism have occurred around key policy issues, in particular human rights issues. Nova Scotia amended its human rights legislation to prohibit sexual orientation discrimination in 1991, followed by New Brunswick in 1992. A Newfoundland court ruled in 1995 that sexual orientation must be read into the Newfoundland Human Rights Act, and this was later affirmed in legislation in 1997. Prince Edward Island followed in 1998.

These changes were not made without significant efforts on the part of the LGBT community. The first demonstration for the inclusion of lesbian and gay rights in the Nova Scotia Human Rights Act was held on 12 April 1989, years before the change was enacted. It took hundreds of letters to Newfoundland members of the House of Assembly after the court ruling to ensure that action was actually taken on this issue. Brian Tobin had promised to make changes to the act when he was elected in 1996, but the introduction of the amendments was put off three times before it finally passed.

However, despite these protections, there are still egregious examples of homophobic behaviour. For instance, in the spring of 2012 Crandall University (formerly the Atlantic Baptist University), a private university in Moncton that has received some public funding from all levels of government, had its anti-gay policies regarding students and faculty members brought to public attention. Students and faculty are required by the university's statement of moral standards "to be sexually pure, reserving sexual intimacy for within a traditional marriage between one man and one woman, and refraining from the use of pornographic materials" (http://www.crandallu.ca/cu/mission-statement/statement-of-moral-standards).[4] A previous version of the code, which actually banned staff from participating in homosexual activity, was only eliminated in 2010. The university defends its position, arguing that the legislative act that created the university in 1983 gave it the right to grant degrees and to educate based on its Christian beliefs (Rankin 2012). In drawing attention to this issue the LGBT community in Moncton pressured governments to reduce funding to the university.

Joanna Everitt

Queer Activism and Public Policy Changes: Case Studies

In Atlantic Canada, three issues highlight the impact of the LGBT movement on expanding human rights and associated public policy: (1) relationship recognition, (2) family and adoption rights, and (3) the fight against homophobia.

Relationship Recognition

Relationship recognition is a policy area that extends beyond just the legalization of same-sex marriage. In fact, as Smith (2008, 5) argues, same-sex marriage is a "final and to some extent symbolic step in a long campaign for same sex relationship recognition in Canadian law and policy." Relationship recognition also involves government and public recognition of same-sex rights in the areas of employee benefits to same-sex partners, pension benefits, and spousal support in the event of a termination of a relationship.

Among the first rights extended to same-sex couples were employee benefits (see also the "From Pensions to Partners" section in Chapter 11, this volume). Much of the extension of government employee health-related benefits to same-sex partners occurred in the 1990s, even before governments found themselves pushed to extend benefits as a result of court challenges. The province of New Brunswick was the first in the region to extend these benefits (1993), followed by Nova Scotia (1995), Newfoundland (1998), and Prince Edward Island (1999) (Rayside 2008, 98).

There is little question, however, that Supreme Court rulings in the 1990s paved the way for an expansion of the rights of same-sex couples across the country, and provinces in Atlantic Canada responded accordingly. In the late 1990s and early 2000s, the provinces began to reform their family law legislation to include provisions for same-sex couples in the event either of the death of one of the partners or a breakup. In 1998, Nova Scotia extended survivor benefits to same-sex partners, and, two years later, in late 2000, it passed the Law Reform Act, which added the gender-neutral term "common-law partner" to much of its legislation. This effectively restricted the term "spouse" to married individuals but allowed same-sex couples to register as domestic partners and to assume all the rights and obligations of married spouses (Hurley 2005, 12).

New Brunswick extended survivor benefits to individuals who had been in same-sex relationships shortly after Nova Scotia (Hurley 2005, 9) changed its Family Services Act in 2000 to provide spousal benefits to separating couples

(Rayside 2008, 106). That same year Newfoundland amended its Family Law Act, changing some aspects of family law to recognize same-sex partners. In 2001, it introduced the Same-Sex Amendment Act, which further amended several statutes, extending rights to same-sex partners in relation to pension benefits, workplace compensation, survivor benefits, along with other matters. PEI was the last to move on issues of relationship recognition, waiting until 2002 to amend its Family Law Act to extended provisions pertaining to spousal support upon separation to same-sex couples (Rayside 2008, 106).

In some cases the extension of these rights was the result of human rights challenges to current legislation by same-sex couples who were prepared to publicly demand their rights. In other instances their extension resulted from challenges by heterosexual couples, as in the case of *Attorney General of Nova Scotia v. Walsh* (2002), which led to the creation of a domestic partnership registry that gave unmarried couples many rights that married couples have (including property rights) (Bailey 2004, 155). While this decision was not directly concerned with LGBT rights, the fact that "domestic partners" were defined as individuals cohabitating in a conjugal relationship (with no mention of sex) in effect gave same-sex couples domestic property rights that they had not previously had. Finally, court challenges elsewhere were also instrumental in pushing governments to take proactive action in reforming their statutes to afford same-sex couples the same rights as heterosexual couples.

This was the case with respect to same-sex marriage. Just as elsewhere across the country, courts in Nova Scotia (September 2004) and Newfoundland and Labrador (December 2004) allowed Charter challenges to provincial laws defining marriage, effectively legalizing same-sex marriage.[5] PEI and New Brunswick both insisted they would recognize marriage only as an arrangement between a man and a woman until the federal government dictated otherwise. As it turned out, however, in the spring of 2005 four same-sex couples in New Brunswick challenged the province's policy of issuing marriage licences only to heterosexual couples, and in June 2005 New Brunswick's Court of Queen's Bench issued a ruling that redefined civil marriage in the province in gender-neutral terms.[6] This made New Brunswick the eighth province to have legalized same-sex marriage before the federal legislation to codify a gender-neutral definition of marriage was enacted and took effect across the country. PEI began the process of updating its laws to recognize same-sex marriage only after the federal legislation had been passed. Initially, licences were not going to be issued until the fall of 2005, when the legislation would have been updated; however, public outcry and complaints that such delays

Joanna Everitt

were illegal and violated same-sex couples' rights led the province to reverse its position.

The federal nature of Canada, according to which the federal government has control over the definition of marriage (thereby requiring provinces to adapt their provincial policies), and the Charter of Rights of Freedoms (which includes an equality clause that has been successfully used to secure LGBT rights) are both critical to the success of LGBT movements with regard to achieving relationship recognition and same-sex marriage. There have, however, been efforts to minimize this success, such as the attempt of the New Brunswick and PEI governments to introduce legislation that allows a person who solemnizes weddings to refuse to do so for same-sex couples if it is against his or her religious beliefs. The Newfoundland and Labrador government took a completely opposite approach by warning its civil marriage commissioners that, as these marriages are now legal, all mayors or justices of the peace must either perform them or resign. Another way that provinces attempted to retain control over the definition of marriage was through gender-specific wording in their legislation. For example, PEI took until 2008 to remove terms like "bride" and "groom" from more than forty provincial statutes and replace them with more gender-neutral terms. These changes were important as they dealt with issues such as adoption or the right of spouses to speak for each other should there be a medical emergency.

Family and Adoption Rights

With relationship recognition came attention to family and adoption rights. Whereas in the past lesbians and gays had to fight for custody of their children upon the termination of relationships, such discrimination is no longer the case. LGBT parents have the same full parenting rights and obligations as do all Canadian citizens. Where recent change has occurred it has been in respect to the rights of non-biological parents, or step-parents.

For the most part, family law legislation that changed to acknowledge same-sex couples and to provide spousal benefits was written in gender neutral language, making it possible for same-sex couples to adopt. Such rights, however, were not straightforward, and, like the extension of other rights, frequently required court challenges to produce legislative change. For example, when Nova Scotia reformed many of its laws in 2000, it specifically excluded adoption from its legislation. In a subsequent court hearing in 2001, the courts ruled that such an exclusion was unconstitutional, and changes were made to recognize step-parent and joint custody (Rayside 2008, 178–79). Newfoundland

and Labrador followed suit in changing its legislation in 2002. New Brunswick required a challenge through a human rights tribunal before recognizing step-parent rights in 2004 (179).

An area of continuing contestation, however, is that of parental recognition on birth certificates – a battle that has been won elsewhere (see Chapter 4, this volume, with regard to Quebec). New Brunswick birth certificate applications continue to ask for both a mother's and a father's information, and the NB Vital Statistics Act often uses gendered language such as "mother," "father," "married woman," and "husband" when discussing birth registration procedures and parental rights. Similarly, the PEI Vital Statistics Act usually refers to a "mother" and a "father" in reference to birth registrations and the name of the child; however, the actual birth certificate asks only for the mother's and second parent's information.

A wider degree of acceptance appears to have developed in Nova Scotia and Newfoundland and Labrador. Nova Scotia birth registrations ask for a mother's and father's or "other parent's" information, and its Vital Statistics Act generally uses gender-neutral wording. This was the result of a court challenge in 2006, when Nova Scotian lesbian couples won the right to put both mothers' names on a child's birth certificate.

Like Nova Scotia's policies, Newfoundland and Labrador's policies were changed in November 2007 to allow for an "other parent" option on birth certificates after an official complaint was submitted to the Human Rights Commission in the fall of that year. Its legislation governing the registration of births uses gender-neutral language and specifically states: "5(5) The birth registration of a child born as a result of artificial insemination shall be completed showing, with the written consent of the woman and her spouse or cohabiting partner, the particulars of the spouse or cohabiting partner as being the father or other parent of the child." This is the only Vital Statistics Act in Atlantic Canada to mention this specifically. The Newfoundland and Labrador act also covers surrogacy arrangements and the use of both partners' surnames for the child.

Due to earlier changes recognizing same-sex relationships, new rights involving adoption or parental recognition were easier to achieve. Yet, as with relationship recognition, it often required human rights challenges initiated by LGBT individuals before governments took the requisite steps to extend these rights.

Fight against Homophobia

A third policy area that has received significant LGBT attention in recent years concerns the fight against homophobia (see also Chapter 1, this volume).

Joanna Everitt

While not all queer oppression can be categorized as homophobia, over the years several events have highlighted the LGBT population's vulnerability to hate crimes.

It is thought that between 1990 and 2007, at least nine Maritimers were killed because they were homosexual (*Wayves* 2007). The fatal attack against Raymond Taavel in Halifax in the spring of 2012 is just the most recent of these events. Other events, such as the firebombing of the home of a gay couple in PEI in the fall of 2010 and the attack against two men outside of a Pride Cape Breton dance in 2010 are also evidence of the continued persistence of homophobia in the Atlantic region. What has changed over time, however, is the degree of public tolerance of such activity. When Taavel was killed outside of a Halifax bar, the public outpouring of grief and outrage was enormous, with politicians and community leaders expressing their concern. The Halifax police even added a rainbow flag to its Facebook webpage in honour of Taavel's contribution to the community over the years. The PEI and Cape Breton attacks were also greeted with public outrage and an indication from the police that there was no tolerance for such crimes.

Homophobia among youth is of particular concern, with a growing number of studies showing that LGBT youth are far more likely to suffer from depression or to commit suicide than are other youth. LGBT organizations have been giving increasing attention to combatting homophobia among youth. The Safe Spaces Project offered by CIDA/AIDS Moncton and the Lesbian, Gay and Bisexual Youth Project in Halifax (which was also piloted in Montreal and Kamloops) began in 1999 and was designed to help identify the challenges facing LGBT youth and to enable them to break their isolation and to accept their sexual orientation in a safe and healthy environment. In 2004, the Moncton organization eventually partnered with ANKORS (AIDS Network Outreach and Support Society) in the Kootenay and Boundary Region of British Columbia to produce the National Safe Spaces Project and to create a training manual for service providers and youth in rural communities regarding the development of gay, lesbian, bisexual, transgendered, two-spirited, and queer (GLBTTQ) youth support services. Over the last several years, these organizations have also worked in conjunction with school districts to provide materials for educators to assist schools in confronting homophobia and other forms of discrimination in high school environments. In Nova Scotia, the LGB Youth Project has also been actively involved in accrediting and recognizing allies of LGBT youth in schools – allies who can be approached by students without fear of rejection. As a result of all this, there are now gay-straight alliances (GSAs) in all regions of the province.

In addition, recent years have seen the establishment of the Wapanaki Two-Spirit Alliance, a support and social network of Two-Spirited people from the Mi'kma'kik, Wulustook, Passaquoddy, and Penobscot communities in the region. One of its primary goals has been to develop "a Two-Spirited suicide prevention and intervention module that other organizations, health centres or crisis counsellors can use when working with Two-Spirited people" (Wapanaki Two-Spirit Alliance 2011, 2). This organization has also produced an "It Gets Better!" YouTube video targeted at Two-Spirited Aboriginal youth.[7]

Governments have also stepped up to try to address homophobia among youth. In 1998, the Newfoundland and Labrador government established a homophobia poster project in which it asked students to create posters to be used to fight homophobia. In 2003, the PEI Teachers' Federation adopted a policy on homophobia that was committed to making schools a safe place for all LGBT students and staff. Since 2008, an organization named Pride in Education (PIE) New Brunswick has worked to advocate for teacher awareness and to provide education seminars around anti-homophobia and anti-heterosexism. In the spring of 2009, the government allowed a series of presentations on homophobia, entitled "Making Queerness Visible," to be held in schools across western New Brunswick (Werner 2009). In 2012, the province of Newfoundland and Labrador announced new teacher resources for administrators, teachers, and students who wish to establish GSAs in schools.

While the ministries are not mandating GSAs, they are indicating high levels of support for such organizations. The number of GSAs has grown throughout the region, so that now EGALE's website (mygsa.ca) lists fifteen GSAs in Nova Scotia, fifteen in New Brunswick, and seven in Newfoundland and Labrador. Only Prince Edward Island does not have a listed GSA in its schools. Along with introducing more resources for addressing issues of homophobia, all of the provinces are introducing stronger legislation surrounding bullying in their schools, which, along with bullying, covers gender-based violence and incidents based on homophobia.

There is some evidence that these efforts are having an effect and that attitudes among youth are changing. For example, in 2007, when a Grade 9 student at Central Kings Rural High School in Nova Scotia was bullied and called "gay" for wearing a pink shirt to school on the first day of classes, older students reacted. They distributed pink shirts to all of their friends and organized a pink shirt day to make a statement that such bullying would not be tolerated. This action caught the attention of others around the country and across the world, leading to an international movement against homophobic bullying.

Joanna Everitt

The Nova Scotia government has since officially designated 9 September as Anti-Bullying Day.

The experience of Woodstock High's Lady Thunder Hockey provides another example of how peers are stepping up to demonstrate that homophobia should not be tolerated. When team members faced homophobic slurs and unsportsmanlike behaviour from competing teams because they were lesbians, the rest of the team responded by wearing rainbow-striped pins, upon which the words "No Homophobia" were printed, to their games. Coaches and parents and even rival teams began to wear them as well, communicating the message that such behaviour was unacceptable. The team's fight against homophobia led it to be awarded the New Brunswick Human Rights Award in October 2009. As Gordon Porter, chair of the New Brunswick Human Rights Council, said when he presented the award, it was unsurprising that the girls stood up for gay rights, given that the school had had a GSA since 2003 and had a long history of promoting diversity. In fact, Richard Blaquiere, the founder of the school's GSA, won the same award in 1993 for his work in human rights education (Logan 2009).

Homophobia and intolerance remain issues in the Atlantic region, particularly among youth. However, attitudes are changing and efforts on the part of LGBT organizations, ministries of education, school officials, and individuals are contributing to those changes. Learning is shared from one community to another, and, as in the case of the Safe Spaces Project, knowledge that has been developed in the region is being shared with other parts of the country.

Conclusion

Policy change has occurred at a different pace around the Atlantic region. In most instances, Nova Scotia is a policy leader, which is not surprising given the fact that the largest and most active LGBT community is found in Halifax (see Chapter 11, this volume). It is also the Atlantic province in which the New Democratic Party, the party that has been most open to LGBT issues and concerns, has had the greatest success, serving as the official opposition since 1998 and eventually forming a one-term majority government in 2009. These two factors may have resulted in an environment that is more receptive to policy change. The opposite would be true of provinces such as PEI and New Brunswick, where the population is predominately rural or living in small towns, or is split between three small cities (Saint John, Moncton, and Fredericton), making LGBT activism less focused. Added to this are a large Catholic population (approximately 50 percent) and significant conservative Baptist and Pentacostal populations whose beliefs are critical of homosexuality and opposed to policies such as same-sex marriage (Statistics Canada 2001). Finally, these provinces possess weak provincial New Democratic parties that seldom hold seats. PEI has never received more than 8 percent of the vote and New Brunswick has never received more than 11 percent. Given these factors, it is no wonder that these provinces have lagged behind the others in terms of policy change.

Nonetheless, changes have occurred over the past few decades, and these changes have significantly improved the lives of LGBT individuals in the region. Along with providing social, educational, and counselling support, the wide range of organizations and activists involved in the community have helped to bring these changes about by challenging governments to address key policy demands and by expanding public recognition of their rights and concerns.

As some issues are addressed, new ones appear on the movement's agenda. For example, there has been growing concern among activists regarding issues of gender identity and gender expression. This concern can be seen by the appearance of transgendered support groups in Halifax and at the Université de Moncton; workshops hosted around the region, such as the Transgendered Health Workshop held in St John's in the fall of 2010; or the multi-part Main Street series that CBC Radio One produced about what it is like to be a trans-sexual teenager in Nova Scotia. In 2011, the Nova Scotia Rainbow Alliance Project (NSRAP) began to lobby for LGBT human rights legislation to include "gender identity" and "gender expression" as prohibited grounds of discrimination (things that have yet to be included in regional human rights legislation) and to request that gender transition surgery be covered in Nova Scotia as it is in other provinces in Canada.

Another area of growing concern is LGBT seniors. These individuals have often lived most of their lives keeping their sexual orientation and relationships private; however, as they age they are confronted with the challenges of finding appropriate health care or social support services. In the spring of 2010, the NDP government of Nova Scotia gave ten thousand dollars to NSRAP to study senior citizens and long-term care facilities that are safe and welcoming. To assist with this effort and to ensure that the broader needs of LGBT seniors are addressed, the organization held several meetings in Halifax to hear seniors' concerns. The result of these consultations were written up in a NSRAP document entitled "Towards a Home for the LGBT Community in Nova Scotia," which can be found on the organization's website and which includes a series of recommendations for ensuring that the needs of senior members of the LGBT community receive the appropriate attention and concern.

Joanna Everitt

Yet, despite the fact that areas in need of improvement remain, there can be little doubt that attitudes have changed. Public support and sympathy for LGBT individuals is much stronger now than it has been in the past, and examples of this, such as the growing number of GSAs in schools, the development of the Pink Shirt Anti-Bullying Campaign, and the continued expansion of LGBT rights, suggest a growing (albeit not full) acceptance of gays and lesbians in the region. As Barry Adam (1999, 15) argues: "This proliferation and decentralization of movement organizations has profoundly impacted the larger society as many non-gay Canadians, in various spheres of their lives, encounter openly lesbian and gay people who work with them, share their interests, and participate in their cultural activities." Religious intolerance, homophobia, and discomfort with diversity continue to be issues within the community; however, the growing number of organizations providing support to the LGBT community, a heightened public profile of LGBT interests and concerns, and the development of an organization that has taken on an active lobbying role have all had an important impact on changing overall public attitudes towards LGBT rights.

Notes

1 Some of the highest rates of church attendance and religious identification in the country are found in this region (Valpy and Friesen 2010). As well there is a significant presence of evangelical Protestants and conservative Catholics in the area, which has been put forth as a limiting factor with regard to support for LGBT rights (Adam 1999, 17; Herman 1994; Langstaff 2011, 61).
2 While there is some debate as to whether Atlantic Canadians hold more conservative views than do other regions of the country (see O'Neill and Erickson 2003), the dominant role of religion, the persistent two-party system in most of the provinces, and the weakness of the NDP make public policy more conservative in this region than elsewhere.
3 Halifax is roughly the same size as cities such as London or Kitchener, Ontario. St. John's has a population of roughly 165,000. The three New Brunswick cities (Moncton, Saint John, and Fredericton) have between sixty thousand and 110,000 residents, and Charlottetown, the capital of Prince Edward Island, has only forty-two thousand residents.
4 This statement has since been removed from the website. Now they have a line in their job advertisements indicating that "to be considered for appointment candidates must be committed to teaching and pursuing scholarship from a Christian perspective and to the mission and the statement of faith of the university."
5 In Nova Scotia, the partners were Brian Mombourquette and Ross Bouthilier, Kim Vance and Samantha Meehan, and Ron and Bryan Garnett-Doucette. In Newfoundland and Labrador, they were Jacqueline Pottle and Noelle French, and Lisa Zigler and Theresa Walsh.
6 The New Brunswick couples were Art Vautour-Toole and Wayne Toole, Catherine Sidney and Bridget McGale, Wayne Harrison and Ross Leavitt, and Jim Crooks and Carl Trickey.
7 http://www.youtube.com/watch?v=bgG1o-JcKdw.

References

Adam, Barry. 1999. "Moral Regulation and the Disintegrating Canadian State." In Barry Adam, Jan Willen Duyvendak, and Andre Krovwel, eds., *The Global Emergence of Gay and Lesbian Politics: National Imprints of a Worldwide Movement*, 12–29. Philadelphia: Temple University Press.

Bailey, Martha. 2004. "Regulation of Cohabitation and Marriage in Canada." *Law and Policy* 26 (1): 153–75. http://dx.doi.org/10.1111/j.0265-8240.2004.00166.x.

Blais, André, Elisabeth Gidengil, Richard Nadeau, and Neil Nevitte. 1997. *Canadian Election Study, 1997*. Dataset [computer file].

CBC. 2012. "Island LGBT Group in Danger of Disbanding." *CBC News*, 7 April. http://www.cbc.ca/news/canada/prince-edward-island/story/2012/04/07/pei-lgbt-group-needs-volunteers-584.html.

Chapin, Angelina. 2008. "Halifax Pride Grand Marshals Humbly Accept Their Honours." *Xtra! Canada's Gay and Lesbian News*, 28 July. http://www.xtra.ca/public/National/Halifax_Pride_grand_marshals_humbly_accept_their_honours-5178.aspx.

Droesbeck, Trevor S. 1997. "Not the Lady's Auxiliary: Exploring the Politics of Gender Relations in the Halifax Queer Youth Movement." MA thesis, Dalhousie University.

Gidengil, Elisabeth, Joanna Everitt, Patrick Fournier, and Neil Nevitte. 2004–08. *Canadian Election Study, 2004–2008*. Panel data set [computer file]. Toronto: York University/Institute for Social Research.

Herman, Didi. 1994. *Rights of Passage: Struggles for Lesbian and Gay Legal Equality*. Toronto: University of Toronto Press.

Hurley, Mary C. 2005. *Sexual Orientation and Legal Rights*. Ottawa: Parliamentary Information and Research Service. http://www.parl.gc.ca/content/LOP/ResearchPublications/921-e.htm.

Kassler, Jeanne. 1983. *Gay Men's Health: A Guide to the AID Syndrome and Other Sexually Transmitted Diseases*. New York: Harper and Row.

Langstaff, Amy. 2011. "A Twenty-Year Survey of Canadian Attitudes towards Homosexuality and Gay Rights." In David Rayside and Clyde Wilcox, eds., *Faith Politics and Sexual Diversity in Canada and the United States*, 49–66. Vancouver: UBC Press.

Logan, Nick. 2009. "NB Hockey Team Battles Homophobia on the Rink." *Xtra! Canada's Gay and Lesbian News*, 18 September. http://www.xtra.ca/public/National/NB_hockey_team_battles_homophobia_on_the_rink-7501.aspx.

O'Neill, Brenda, and Lynda Erickson. 2003. "Evaluating Traditionalism in the Atlantic Provinces: Voting, Public Opinion and the Electoral Project." *Atlantis* 27 (2): 113–22.

Rankin, Andrew. 2012. "New Brunswick University under Fire for Anti-Gay Hiring Policy." *Toronto Star*, 1 June. http://www.thestar.com/news/canada/article/1204607-new-brunswick-university-under-fire-for-anti-gay-hiring-policy.

Rayside, David. 2008. *Queer Inclusions, Continental Divisions: Public Recognition of Sexual Diversity in Canada and the United States*. Toronto: University of Toronto Press.

Smith, Miriam. 2008. *Political Institutions and Gay Rights in the United States and Canada*. New York: Routledge.

Statistics Canada. 2001. *Population by Religion, by Province and Territory: Summary Tables*. Ottawa: Statistics Canada. http://www.statcan.gc.ca/tables-tableaux/sum-som/l01/cst01/demo30a-eng.htm.

Thompson, Charles. 2007. "Truro Mayor: Passing the Flag to the County." *Wayves*, September, 1, 3.

Valpy, Michael, and Joe Friesen. 2010. "Canada Marching from Religion to Secularization." *Globe and Mail*, 10 December.

Wapanaki Two-Spirit Alliance. 2011. *Mawita' jij Puoinaq: A Gathering of 2-Spirited People! A Gathering of Gay/Lesbian/Bisexual and Transgendered L'nuk aq Wolastoqiyik! A Gathering of Spiritually Powerful People!* http://gay.hfxns.org/picsMawita'jikPuoinaq/2011_Mawita'jij_Puoinaq_Final_Report.pdf.

Wayves. 2007. "Hundreds Attend Halifax IDAH Rally." July, 1.

Werner, Sarah Rose. 2009. "We've Come a Long Way Baby ... or Have We?" *Wayves*, August, 8.

6

LGBTQ Movements in Western Canada: British Columbia

BRIAN BURTCH, AYNSLEY PESCITELLI, AND REBECCA HASKELL

British Columbia has a distinctive legacy of groundbreaking struggles relating to social policies, legal rights, and social acceptance of lesbian, gay, bisexual, Two-Spirited, and queer (LGBTQ) individuals and groups. This provincial legacy and ongoing initiatives involve the mobilization of resources on many fronts, including mass media, alternative media, social networking sites, LGBTQ-friendly bookstores, street rallies and demonstrations, legal cases, petitions to government, cases heard by human rights tribunals, and a general promotion of cultural expressions that question heteronormativity. This chapter presents some key developments in the history of the LGBTQ movement in BC. We recognize that there are various groups and activist outlooks and that not all are included (nor would they want to be included) as part of more LGBTQ mainstream movements.

Like other provinces and territories discussed elsewhere in *Queer Mobilizations,* BC has had many notable individuals who have broken new ground with regard to LGBTQ rights and recognition. Gay rights activist Jim Egan was elected as a regional director in Comox-Strathcona in 1981, making him the "first openly gay man living in an openly gay relationship to be elected to public office in Canada" (Egan 1998, 97; on other gays elected in politics in the 1980s, see Chapter 8 [Montreal] and Chapter 9 [Toronto], this volume). He served in this capacity until 1993, and was re-elected two times. In 1988, former MP Svend Robinson was the first federal politician to come out as openly gay (Carlson 2012; Matas 1999), and, in 1996, provincial MLA Tim Stevenson was the first provincial politician to come out as openly gay (Beatty and

McInnes 2000). Former liberal MLA Lorne Mayencourt and NDP MLA Nicholas Simons are both openly gay (Mason 2011), as is NDP MP Libby Davies. Of course, politicians in other provinces have also come out, including provincial cabinet ministers Jim Rondeau and Jennifer Howard in Manitoba, and Kathleen Wynne and George Smitherman in Ontario (Barber 2007).

The prominence of politicians is but one facet of a complex and ongoing social movement that has achieved a national impact with regard to challenging discrimination against LGBTQ people and setting important precedents in the acceptance of sexual orientation. These achievements include extending basic human rights and benefits in BC and fostering social acceptance of and personal safety for LGBTQ individuals. This social movement seeks to redress harassment and exclusion, and to celebrate the diversity that is part and parcel of sexual orientation. The work continues on several fronts, such as court challenges, actions under the BC Human Rights Code, use of mainstream media such as the *Vancouver Sun* and alternative media such as *Xtra!*, and establishing community-based organizations such as Qmunity, which offers a wide range of LGBTQ services to youth, adults, and seniors.

First, we outline some pivotal events in BC as they pertain to public policy, social change, and queer social movements. Second, we outline some of the early groups advocating for LGBTQ rights. Third, we discuss three case studies: (1) Little Sister's challenges to government officials seizing sexually explicit materials at the border, (2) anti-homophobic and anti-transphobic initiatives in BC schools, and (3) James Egan's battle to secure Old Age Security benefits for same-sex partners. We conclude with some thoughts on future areas for LGBTQ research and activism in BC and in society in general.

Historical Background

One of the first formal gay activist groups in Canada – the Association for Social Knowledge (ASK) – was formed in Vancouver in 1964. ASK was part of the ferment associated with grassroots associations linked with lesbian and gay liberation in the 1960s and early 1970s (e.g., Gay Sisters, Gay People of UBC [University of British Columbia], among others) (McLeod 1996, 253–54). According to the Canadian Lesbian and Gay Archives (2012), another organization, Gay Alliance Towards Equality (GATE), was founded in Vancouver in 1971. Its key focus was "education, along with research and law reform. Committees dealt with membership ($10), programming, library, research and education, and publications. The goal of ASK was 'to help society to understand and accept variations from the sexual norm.'" ASK published a newsletter until 1968 and opened Canada's first community centre to serve the needs of homosexuals. In November 1970, the Vancouver Gay Liberation Front was established (Canadian Lesbian and Gay Archives 1997). GATE became one of the most prominent organizations seeking equality for gays and lesbians in the 1970s. The GATE example is linked with the establishment of a provincial human rights code in 1973 through the New Democratic Party. The passage of the code was accompanied by the creation of a human rights branch, which received complaints about violations of human rights and a stronger mandate for the BC Human Rights Commission to foster public knowledge about human rights.

GATE took on causes linked with the national movement for gay rights, including discriminatory age of consent laws. In the 1970s, for example, people had to be at least twenty-one years old to legally consent to anal sex, compared with a threshold of at least fourteen years old to consent to other forms of sex. While some activists insisted on a uniform age of consent that would apply to homosexuals and heterosexuals alike, others took a more radical turn, questioning the repression of youth sexuality by the church and the state (see Warner 2002, 120–21). GATE Vancouver, along with other radical gay liberation groups, sought the abolition of discriminatory age of sexual consent laws. GATE's short-lived (1973–76) publication *Gay Tide* highlighted many forms of oppression and resistance for gay people. During the 1972 BC election campaign, the Vancouver branch of GATE issued questionnaires to every candidate, asking for their position on various forms of legislation. The NDP candidates were generally more favourable to reforming the BC Human Rights Act, while the right-wing Social Credit Party candidates were much less favourable, with some offering outright homophobic comments (Canada's Human Rights History n.d.).

The lack of progress in securing human rights status based on sexual orientation led GATE to lodge a complaint to the BC Human Rights Branch in 1974 following a refusal by the *Vancouver Sun* newspaper staff to publish a classified ad promoting *Gay Tide*. Ostensibly, the decision not to publish the advertisement was based on concerns that it might be offensive to some readers. The Human Rights Branch decided in favour of GATE as the *Vancouver Sun* was seen to have violated section 3(1) of the BC Human Rights Code, alleging denial of a service usually available to the public. The case was heard by the Supreme Court of Canada (SCC). By a six to three margin, the justices ruled in favour of the *Sun,* citing freedom of the press. The *Sun* continued to be pressured and eventually published the advertisement in 1980 (Canada's Human Rights History n.d.; Warner 2002, 146).

Brian Burtch, Aynsley Pescitelli, and Rebecca Haskell

Other events include the failure to include gender identity in the BC Human Rights Code and the abolition of the provincial Human Rights Commission in 2002 by then premier Gordon Campbell (Goldstein 2007). The BC Human Rights Code remains in place and outlines numerous grounds of discrimination: for example, race, religion, disability, sexual harassment, and sexual orientation (Ministry of Attorney General 2008). Even so, in 2011, John Cummins, leader of the BC Conservative Party, issued a call to remove sexual orientation as a ground of discrimination under the code. A spokesperson from the University of Victoria's Pride Collective countered that verbal and physical harassment is still evident in the province and that many LGBTQ advocates would challenge Cummins's simplistic stance that sexual orientation is a "choice"(CBC News 2011).

Queer Activism Today

Miriam Smith (2008, viii) observes that states foster systemic social power by either recognizing or not recognizing "specific gendered relationships and sexual preferences." This observation holds true for the BC context, from the early days of the gay liberation movement through to present-day struggles. Many BC residents have been at the forefront of political action, including attempts by BC MLAs and MPs to have gender identity protected under human rights bills in BC (Spencer Chandra Herbert) and under the Canadian Human Rights Act and Criminal Code (Bill Siksay). People who identify as transgender have also become more prominent in bringing their concerns to public attention through the courts and human rights tribunals. One example of this is the *Kimberly Nixon* case against Rape Relief.

This case arose when Vancouver Rape Relief and Women's Shelter refused to allow Kimberly Nixon, a post-operative male-to-female transsexual woman, to be included in its volunteer training program. Nixon, who had suffered sexual and relational violence following gender reassignment surgery, had received support from Battered Women's Support Services, another violence against women organization in Vancouver. Although, initially, Rape Relief had accepted Nixon for its training program following a screening, she was later rejected after a program facilitator identified her as being a transsexual. Rape Relief justified its response by positing that it ran a women-only program, providing services to physically and sexually abused women. In its determination, Nixon was not a "real" woman (findlay 2003; *Nixon v. Vancouver Rape Relief Society* 2002; *Vancouver Rape Relief Society v. British Columbia [Human Rights Commission]* 2000).

Nixon filed a complaint with the BC Human Rights Commission on the basis of sex-based discrimination. This case was heard under the British Columbia Human Rights Code, with respect to provisions against discrimination tied to publicly available services or facilities and sex-based refusal of employment. Rape Relief applied for judicial review, alleging that the human rights complaint should not be heard by the tribunal. Its argument was that transsexuals are not entitled to protection under existing grounds in the code and that sex-based discrimination claims cannot be advanced by transsexual individuals. Finally, it argued that the delay in proceedings actually served to remove this case from the tribunal's jurisdiction. The application was dismissed, and it was determined that the tribunal held appropriate jurisdiction over this matter (*Vancouver Rape Relief Society v. British Columbia [Human Rights Commission]* 2000; findlay 2003).

The tribunal heard Nixon's case against Rape Relief in 2002. It decided that this was a prima facie case of discrimination and that Rape Relief's actions could not be justified by section 41 of the code (common political belief exemption based on the nature of the organization). Rape Relief was ordered to cease this type of discrimination, in accordance with section 37(2) of the code (remedial powers of the tribunal). The tribunal also awarded Nixon $7,500 as compensation, based on injury to her feelings, dignity, and self-respect (*Nixon v. Vancouver Rape Relief Society* 2002). Rape Relief applied for judicial review for a second time, alleging that the tribunal's decision was flawed. Its argument surrounded its entitlement to decide volunteer qualifications and the non-objective finding of damage to Nixon's dignity. The court decided in favour of Rape Relief and set aside the tribunal's decision, agreeing with each of Rape Relief's assertions. The compensation order was also set aside (*Vancouver Rape Relief Society v. Nixon* 2003). Nixon appealed the court's decision, but the appeal was dismissed (*Vancouver Rape Relief Society v. Nixon* 2005).

Following the court's decision, Rape Relief still appears unwilling to accept trans women into their volunteer community (Perelle 2007). This has led to recent activism on the part of local groups, including an active presence at Rape Relief's Annual Walkathon in Stanley Park in May 2012. Individuals were on hand to provide alternative information, including material concerning Rape Relief's ongoing exclusion of trans individuals and sex workers. Pamphlets included information about harm reduction, trans women's and sex workers' rights, as well as support information for sexual violence survivors. Rape Relief took photographs of the activists and called the police, who informed the group that it could no longer distribute its pamphlets without a

Brian Burtch, Aynsley Pescitelli, and Rebecca Haskell

valid permit. After leaving the area, activists went to the location where the Walkathon would finish and, on the walkway, wrote several messages about equality. Rape Relief volunteers then poured buckets of water on these messages and attempted to confiscate the remaining pamphlets (Homomilitia 2012).

Struggles for gay and lesbian rights were undermined by lack of organizational support for specific cases: "In its 1989 annual report, the Court Challenges Program noted that sexual orientation applications were the single largest group of cases of discrimination not specifically enumerated in section 15 (equality rights) of the Canadian Charter of Rights and Freedoms and that 'the program feels that the fact that women and persons with disabilities have brought lots of cases is in part due to the fact that they have organizations in place to bring cases'" (Smith 1999, 88). Courts are clearly more apt "to recognize lesbian and gay rights than other political actors" (Smith 2008, 185).

Queer Activism and Public Policy Changes: Case Studies

Smith (2008, 19) maintains that court challenges and court decisions have played a vital part in establishing lesbian and gay rights policies in Canada and the United States. As we demonstrate, LGBTQ-related struggles in BC have had an impact nationwide, a point that is fleshed out in the three case studies set out below.

Little Sister's Book and Art Emporium versus Canada Customs

The Little Sister's challenge against Canada Customs (now, Canada Customs and Revenue Agency) is one of the most prominent cases of a struggle for queer expression (in the same vein, see the *Bad Attitude* case study in Chapter 9, this volume). Little Sister's, a small independent and queer bookstore, was established in 1983 in Vancouver's West End. Beginning in 1985, the owners and the BC Civil Liberties Association initiated a challenge to Canada Customs' practice of seizing gay-themed works, including books, at the border rather than permitting their delivery to Little Sister's (Busby 2006). This challenge was significant in its protest of the overreach of Canadian Criminal Code provisions against obscenity and of a homophobic undercurrent among Canada Customs officials.

Little Sister's alleged that, for over a period of approximately fifteen years, customs officials violated its equality rights through the confiscation, damage, and wrongful delay of store materials imported from the United States. Due to a lack of availability of erotica published in Canada, Little Sister's imports nearly all (80 to 90 percent) of its erotic books and magazines from the United States. This resulted in much of its imported erotica being detained and examined at Canada Customs for obscenity reasons under section 163(8) of the Criminal Code, despite the fact that the supposed erotica in question was not necessarily obscene in nature. Seizures included safe-sex education materials, award-winning novels, magazines, and videos. Interestingly, many of these same items were imported by conventional bookstores without difficulty. Further, other small-scale bookstores catering to specific clientele reported being subjected to similar searches. These customs activities had been occurring for fifteen years, causing considerable financial and supply-related issues for Little Sister's. An even bigger issue concerned the lack of availability of this gay-themed material for sexual and ethno-cultural minorities who had great difficulty gaining access to it (*Little Sister's Book and Art Emporium v. Canada* 2000).

The BC Supreme Court judge (Smith J.) found that the store's imports were "systematically targeted" by customs officials and that customs legislation infringed the bookstore's right to freedom of expression under section 2(b) of the Charter of Rights and Freedoms. However, he determined that this infringement could be saved as a reasonable limit under section 1 as the aim of the legislation (protection from harm produced by the distribution of such materials) was both pressing and substantial. He also stated that the customs legislation did not infringe upon section 15(1) and that there was no violation of the bookstore's equality rights. While he denied a section 52(1) remedy (declaration of invalidity), Smith proposed a section 24(1) declaration that was related to customs administration. He found that the legislation, while valid, had been applied in an unconstitutional manner. This was related to significant issues with customs administration applying the legislation in a homophobic and indefensible fashion (*Little Sister's Book and Art Emporium v. Canada* 2000; Cossman and Ryder 1996). This judgment has been subject to critique, with some arguing that it was crafted to appease both sides of the case, and others pointing out that there continues to be a shortfall between the promise of the Charter and its utility in understanding and extending issues of sexualities and sexual representation. Cossman and Ryder (1996, 103) argue that Justice Smith "managed to vindicate, and sought to preserve, both Little Sister's and Customs by affirming the importance to the life of the nation of both homosexual literature and the existing legislative regime of border censorship." In her incisive and future-oriented analysis, Cossman (2013) contends that censorship of lesbian and gay sexual expression – and non-normative sexual expression more generally – has a legacy of being used against stakeholders such as gay and lesbian bookstores and that there continue to be struggles with explicit expressions on online sites and digital technologies. She adds that, "unlike in the earlier days of gay and lesbian resistance to censorship, there is no longer a politicized grass roots movement mobilized to contest the censorship. Multiple shifts in gay and lesbian activism, as well as a degree of political complacency that accompanied the achievement of formal equality rights, leaves those concerned with the censorship of gay and lesbian fetish material rather more isolated" (27).

A majority judgment of the Court of Appeal dismissed the appeal by Little Sister's. The majority argued that the customs legislation was not overly vague and that the internal manual used by Canada Customs officers was merely a guideline. No section 15(1) violation was found, and the majority held that the legislation was not discriminatory. If applied as intended, non-obscene materials should not be targeted by this legislation. In a dissenting opinion, Finch J.A. stated that he would have allowed the appeal. He also would have declared the customs legislation of no force and effect (*Little Sister's Book and Art Emporium v. Canada* 2000).

The case was eventually heard by the Supreme Court of Canada, where the majority (six to three) allowed the appeal in part. This allowance related to the "reverse onus" provision related to section 152(3) of the Customs Act, which charges the importer with the task of proving that the items in question are not obscene. It was held that the importer cannot be expected to disprove obscenity and has the right under the Charter to receive material unless its detainment can be justified by the state. The majority agreed with the trial judge that there was a discrepancy in Canada Customs' treatment of homosexually and heterosexually explicit materials, with the former being much more likely to be deemed obscene. This treatment was even more glaring when compared to the treatment of general bookstores that were importing erotica. While the customs legislation was seen to infringe section 2(b) of the Charter, the majority argued that it could be justified under section 1. Furthermore, nothing was found to indicate that this legislation itself discriminates against those with a homosexual orientation (*Little Sister's Book and Art Emporium v. Canada* 2000).

Three justices (Iacobucci J., Arbour J., and LeBel J.) dissented in part to the majority judgment. The dissenting justices argued that, while the customs legislation itself does not violate section 15(1) of the Charter, the application of this legislation does. Not only had the legislation been applied in an unconstitutional fashion, but the legislation itself is responsible for many of these violations. This legislation violated Little Sister's section 2(b) rights. Further, the dissenting justices maintained that this violation could not be justified under section 1 because the legislation requires procedural protections to curtail abuses of power. The existing legislation has a high rate of error in intercepting obscene materials, affects importers financially, serves to stigmatize authors and artists, and denies access to consumers. Their recommendation involved striking down the offending section (Code 9956[a] of the Customs Tariff). They would have allowed the appeal and declared this section of the code to be of no force and effect, and would have suspended this order for eighteen months to allow time for corrective action (Cossman 2003).

Cossman (2003) gives several examples of dominant discourses about what constitutes "good sex" and "bad sex" and how this distinction plays out in repressing various kinds of sexual expression as well as designating people and organizations as "sexual outlaws." Little Sister's is cited as a prominent example of a bookseller whose staff and supporters have resisted such designations and have fought for freedom of sexual expression and against harassment of LGBTQ artists, patrons, and other stakeholders. While Little Sister's is best known for its long-standing conflict with Canada Customs, it is also active on many fronts, ranging from supplying pride parade items and free publications, having an in-store bulletin board, and social networking (including Facebook) (Babineau 2008). As one activist put it, "Little Sister's is like the general store ... it's where you go to find out what's going on and get the gossip. They know everything" (ibid.).

Following its long-standing court struggles, Little Sister's has inspired many local events for the queer community. Vancouver's annual queer art festival, Queerotica, was established in 1999 following the pitched battles with Canada Customs. The bookstore was approached by the event's artistic director, S.D. Holman, who volunteered to donate any proceeds from the event to the Little Sister's Defence Fund for the store's Supreme Court challenge. When the defence fund was no longer needed, proceeds were designated to contributing artists. Queerotica continues to run every year in Vancouver, celebrating artistic contributions from members of the queer community (Queer Arts Festival 2014). Since 2005, the bookstore has also been involved in obtaining out-of-print gay and lesbian literature and publishing it in volumes entitled "Little Sister's Classics" (Little Sister's Book and Art Emporium 2011). Notwithstanding these ongoing initiatives, concerns remain, again, about the limited use of Charter provisions and equality rights in challenging state censorship (e.g., Cossman 2013).

Anti-Homophobic Initiatives in Schools

Concerns over LGBTQ-themed books in schools and over bullying of LGBTQ students have also become especially newsworthy since 2009, when several students in Canada and the United States took their lives after being

Brian Burtch, Aynsley Pescitelli, and Rebecca Haskell

bullied. There have been several efforts to protect LGBTQ students – and those who are seen as gender variant, more generally – from such bullying. Specific examples include the It Gets Better campaign, Make It Better, and Out in Schools. A minority of BC school districts have adopted specific policies to expressly support queer students and staff, and there was a considerable struggle that ensued before the successful adoption of such a policy in the Burnaby School District. Key events, including the *Azmi Jubran* case, which has left school boards liable if they do not foster a safe environment for LGBTQ youth; the Surrey book banning, in which books depicting LGBTQ people were banned; and the "Corren agreement" are reviewed here.

North Vancouver School District v. Jubran

Azmi Jubran, a student at Handsworth Secondary School in North Vancouver, was harassed by classmates from 1993 to 1998. Although Jubran is not homosexual, the verbal harassment he experienced was homophobic in nature. This harassment was witnessed by teachers and administrators. While school administrators investigated and responded to these incidents, students continued to harass Jubran after others were punished.

Jubran lodged a complaint with the BC Human Rights Commission in 1996, when he was a Grade 10 student. In 2002, the commission found that Jubran was subject to sexual orientation-based discrimination. Due to this harassment, Jubran was unable to fully participate in and benefit from his high school experience. The commission also found the school district responsible for the discrimination as it did not adequately provide a discrimination-free environment. The commission recommended additional staff training in the area of sensitive topics, such as sexual orientation. Jubran was awarded $4,500 in damages. The commission's decision was subject to judicial review. The judge found that Jubran could not qualify under the category of discrimination based on sexual orientation because he did not identify as homosexual, and the students who engaged in the harassment claimed that they did not perceive him to be homosexual. His harassers claimed that they knew he was not homosexual and that the insults (e.g., "gay," "faggot") did not have a homophobic connotation.

On appeal, Levine J.A. allowed the appeal and restored the commission's original order. She argued that the effects of this harassment were still linked to sexual orientation. Such harassment essentially labelled Jubran as a homosexual and "attributed to him the negative perceptions, myths, and stereotypes attributed to homosexuals" (*North Vancouver School District No. 44 v. Jubran* 2005, 47). Now an anti-bullying activist, Jubran continues to speak out about his struggles with homophobic bullying in high school. He spoke about his court case and high school experiences in April 2012 at CUPE (Canadian Union of Public Employees) BC's Forty-Ninth Annual Convention. His talk was part of an equality forum, and Jubran discussed his transformation from victim into activist (CUPE 2012).

Chamberlain v. Surrey School District

The *Chamberlain* case concerns three books (*Asha's Mum; Belinda's Bouquet;* and *One Dad, Two Dads, Brown Dads, Blue Dads*) submitted to the Surrey School Board for use in kindergarten classrooms. These books, which feature same-sex parent families, were put forward by James Chamberlain, an elementary teacher in the Surrey School District. One learning objective in kindergarten involves comparing and contrasting different family models. The Surrey School Board did not approve the classroom use of these books, predominantly because it believed the controversial subject matter might upset parents with opposing viewpoints. There were also concerns regarding the age-appropriateness of such materials. This Charter challenge was brought by teachers, a parent, a student, and an author of one of the three books, and it was supported by the British Columbia Civil Liberties Association. Joseph Arvay, who previously served as counsel for both the *Egan* and the *Little Sister's* cases, was the lawyer in this case as well.

The majority judgment (six to two) of the Supreme Court of Canada was that the board acted outside of its mandate by improperly applying the criteria for approval of supplementary materials. The majority argued that the decision not to approve the books contradicted the principles of tolerance and secularism under section 76 of the School Act because the decision to refuse recommendation stemmed from religious considerations. The board's decision not to approve these books was deemed unreasonable. McLachlin C.J. referred the approval of the books back to the school board (*Chamberlain v. Surrey School District No. 36* 2002; MacDougall and Clarke 2004; Moon 2011; Smith 2004).

Dissenting justices – Gonthier J. and Bastarache J. – argued that the decision not to approve the use of the three books was within the mandate of the board and that the board's decision should be reinstated. They held that the board's decision was reasonable and that the decision not to approve the books did not offend the School Act, as the majority argued. It was thus important to weigh the rights of all individuals in terms of freedom from discrimination and parental rights regarding children's moral education (*Chamberlain v. Surrey School District No. 36* 2002; MacDougall and Clarke 2004). Following this decision, the Surrey School Board approved two books (*ABC: A Family Alphabet Book* and *Who's in a Family*) featuring same-sex parents for use in kindergarten and Grade 1 classrooms. This occurred only weeks after the Supreme Court judgment, and the recommendations were submitted by a committee consisting of teachers, administrators, trustees, and parents from the Surrey School District. This committee intends to continue submitting related resources for school board consideration (MacDougall and Clarke 2004).

Recently, the Surrey School Board unanimously supported the creation of a working group to review anti-discrimination policy, with a heavy focus on homophobia. Laurie Larsen, a school trustee in the Surrey district, was at the forefront of this proposal. She argued that homophobia is far too common in schools and that anti-homophobic initiatives and policies are needed. Recommendations include "leadership from school administrators, professional development for staff, curricular integration of queer issues, support for gay-straight alliances (GSAs), training for counsellors and education for parents" (Barsotti 2012). Although a decade has passed since the book-banning case, Larsen believes that community education is still necessary to get these recommendations passed.

The Corren Agreement

The Corren Agreement followed a 1999 human rights complaint lodged by Peter and Murray Corren (formerly Peter Cook and Murray Warren) against the BC Ministry of Education (Steffenhagen 2010). The complaint related to discrimination against non-heterosexual students and their parents through a lack of representation in the school curriculum (*Corren v. British Columbia [Ministry of Education]* 2005). Before going to trial, a settlement was reached with the provincial government in 2006. Terms included the development of a social justice elective course for Grade 12 students that addresses sexual orientation and gender identity, and the development of guidelines for curriculum delivery for kindergarten through Grade 12, with attention to diversity and equality. Finally, it was decided that the Correns would be ongoing consultants in terms of curriculum development (Settlement Agreement between Murray Corren and Peter Corren 2006; Steffenhagen 2010). In 2008, the Correns lodged a complaint under the Human Rights Code when the Social Justice 12 elective was withdrawn from Abbotsford's W.J. Mouat Secondary School's course offerings, despite the fact that more than ninety students had enrolled in the course. The complaint was backed by ten students initially enrolled in the class. The Abbotsford School Board justified their decision, claiming it had received several complaints from parents. The Correns' complaint was revised in 2009 to assert further discrimination, when the Abbotsford School Board established a policy requiring parental consent for student enrolment in Social Justice 12 (*Abbotsford School District No. 34 v. Corren* 2011). These decisions resulted in sizeable student and parent protests (Steffenhagen 2011). Peter Corren died in 2009, so Murray Corren has since taken full responsibility for the complaint.

In 2009, the Abbotsford School Board contended that the complaint should not be considered as the Correns were not students or parents in this district, and it argued that the Human Rights Tribunal should dismiss the complaint. The year after, in 2010, the tribunal ordered that, as long as the complaint was amended to indicate the group it represented, it could be filed at a later date. The school board then applied for judicial review of the tribunal's decision, asserting that the case should not go forward without a properly identified group. The application for review took place before Murray Corren was able to file his amended complaint and before the tribunal made a final decision. In 2011, Smith J. decided that this application for review was premature and did not fit within the proscribed guidelines (*Abbotsford School District No. 34 v. Corren* 2011). This case remains undecided.

Corren continues to speak out about these issues, both publicly and to students in Coquitlam-area Social Justice 12 classrooms. He shares his personal history with students, discussing his difficult youth, coming out, and his adult life as an educator and activist. He discusses his role in GALE BC (Gay and Lesbian Educators of British Columbia) as well as his role in the Surrey book-banning case (McDonald 2010a). Although the Social Justice 12 course has been reinstated and approved for use in the Abbotsford School District since 2009, it has not been without controversy. Shortly after the district agreed to offer the course, a parent, student, and teacher conference was held in Abbotsford to discuss the tensions in the educational curriculum between religion, sexuality, and parental involvement and consent. Yet much of the conference's discussions centred on the parental consent provision rather than on the broader themes sought by community activists. Conference participants acknowledged that awareness had been raised about sexuality and gender orientation through earlier protests, and they hoped that this conference would have a similar effect (Barsotti 2009).

Access to Old Age Security (OAS) Provisions for Same-Sex Couples (James Egan)

Social movements rely on a host of contributors, including high-profile, relentless activists such as James Egan. Egan, hailed as one of Canada's first gay activists, wrote a series of editorial commentaries in the 1950s and 1960s, using his initials – G.L.E. – at a time when gays and lesbians were subject to a matrix of denunciation: police raids, arrests and criminal prosecution,

Brian Burtch, Aynsley Pescitelli, and Rebecca Haskell

expulsion from churches, being treated as mentally ill, and dismissal from the military and civil service (see Kinsman and Gentile 2010, 70, 110, 211, 214). Taking on what he termed a "conspiracy of silence" (Egan 1998), Egan wrote more than eighty commentaries and articles in the 1950s to contest sensationalist, lurid stories about homosexuals and homosexuality (Churchill 2004) and to set the record straight (so to speak). Through his own writing and a documentary film, *Jim Loves Jack* (Adkin 2007), Egan is best known for a landmark case to end discrimination against same-sex partners, using section 15 of the Charter of Rights and Freedoms. Section 15 provides protection against discrimination, including specific grounds such as racial discrimination. Sexual orientation was not listed as an enumerated ground of discrimination. In the Supreme Court of Canada ruling, sexual orientation was recognized as an analogous ground, and this inclusion was seen as a victory for LGBTQ people.

The initial trial regarding whether sexual orientation could be interpreted as a prohibited ground for discrimination took place in 1991 in the Trial Division of the Federal Court. The action was funded by the Court Challenges Program, a federally sponsored program "to support the cost of litigation in selected text cases related to equality issues under the Charter" (Egan 1998, 100). This was an appeal of Health and Welfare Canada's 1987 refusal of a spousal benefit for Jim Egan's partner Jack Nesbitt. Justice Leonard Martin ruled that the OAS Act was not discriminatory in terms of sexual orientation or gender. The legislation was not intended to grant benefits to same-sex couples or to other types of non-spousal couples (e.g., siblings, parents, friends who are ineligible for spousal benefits). Essentially, Jim Egan and James Nesbitt's long-term relationship was deemed to be non-spousal (Egan 1998, 100–1; *Egan v. Canada* 1991).

The 1992 appeal to the BC Supreme Court was also initially funded by the Court Challenges Program, a program later abolished by the federal government.[1] Egan and Nesbitt's lawyer, Joseph Arvay, agreed to continue to represent them in a pro bono capacity (Egan 1998, 101). In 1993, the majority (two to one) supported the trial court, finding that there was no sexual orientation-based discrimination. Dissenting Justice Allen Linden argued that same-sex partnerships meet all other requirements of the legislation and that benefits should be extended. He added that homosexuals should be protected under section 15(1). He believed that the appropriate remedy would be to amend the definition of section 2 of the OAS to include analogous relationships, and he would have allowed the appeal (Egan 1998, 101; *Egan v. Canada (C.A.)* 1993).

By the time the case made its way to the Supreme Court of Canada in 1994, the Court Challenges Program had been restored and funding was provided for the trial (Egan 1998, 101). In their 1995 ruling, all nine Supreme Court justices held that sexual orientation was analogous to existing grounds for discrimination under section 15. While the majority (five to four) held that the definition of spouse in this act was discriminatory, they nevertheless held that such discrimination could be upheld under section 1 of the Charter. Their argument was that "the Government of Canada is entitled to take time to bring its laws into conformity with the Charter" (102), and the appeal was dismissed (*Egan v. Canada* 1995).

Dissenting justices L'Heureux-Dubé J., Cory J., McLachlin J., and Iacobucci J. would have allowed the appeal. Iacobucci recommended reading out the opposite-sex requirement of section 2 of the OAS as a remedy but allowing a one-year period for Parliament to ensure proper application and amendment. He would not grant individual remedy to the appellants (retroactive spousal allowance payment) as he felt the larger-scale remedy was a better fit.

In addition to retirement concerns, aging same-sex couples also have to consider altering their activities and living arrangements, particularly if they require additional care. Dalhousie master's student Alex Sangha, originally from Vancouver, is attempting to raise funds for a study that will address whether developing retirement homes for elderly LGBTQ individuals is feasible. Sangha points to the discrimination faced by elderly LGBTQ individuals in retirement and long-term care facilities, both on the part of other residents and staff. Allowing the elderly the opportunity to live in an LGBTQ-friendly environment has the potential to engender a sense of community and support, which could be particularly beneficial to individuals who do not have this support from family or friends. Vancouver is an ideal setting for such establishments because many of the local gay communities are located in areas that are cost-prohibitive to elderly citizens. This can lead to their seeking housing outside of these areas and losing their sense of community and acceptance. Several similar establishments exist in the United States, while Montreal hosts the only Canadian example (Canadian Press 2012).

Conclusion

Our focus reveals some of the richness of LGBTQ activism in BC at all levels of politics, from municipal to provincial and federal, from courts and tribunals to classrooms and streets. This includes court challenges, demonstrations, political resolutions, legislation, human rights tribunals, and advocacy for LGBTQ people outside of Canada. As noted earlier in this chapter, BC and other jurisdictions have had high-profile, often long-serving gay and lesbian politicians such as former

Brian Burtch, Aynsley Pescitelli, and Rebecca Haskell

MP Svend Robinson (BC MP 1979–2004), Nova Scotia MP Scott Brison (1997 to present), and MP Libby Davies (1997 to present) as well as younger politicians such as MLA Spencer Chandra Herbert (Vancouver-West End riding, 2008 to present) and MLA Nicholas Simons (Powell River-Sunshine Coast, 2005 to present). Despite such LGBTQ federal and provincial politicians in BC and elsewhere in Canada, doubts remain about their general acceptability to citizens. News columnist Gary Mason cited David Brindle, an open-line radio host, and Spencer Chandra Herbert, an NDP MLA, both of whom are out. Both men gave examples of homophobic – even hateful – messages they receive as well as examples of being shunned, for example, when holding hands with their partners in public (Mason 2011). There have also been concerns about supposedly elevated rates of homophobia in non-urban areas and among members of specific ethno-cultural groups – sometimes referred to as visible minorities (Mason 2011). Morrison (2008, 200) makes the general point that "ethnic or cultural group mores generally affect the development of identity for ethnic or cultural group minority persons ... there may be considerable emphasis placed on the family unit ... [along with bolstering] the normality of a heterosexual orientation, expectations surrounding entry into marriage, and eventual reproduction and continuation of one's familial line." In this vein, we see the importance of appreciating how one's culture, ethnicity, and geographic location influence one's experiences of being LGBTQ and experiences of homophobia in unique ways and that these need to be examined. This approach ties in with the concept of intersectionality as well as the importance of avoiding overgeneralizations. We are more comfortable with this more nuanced approach than we are with identifying – or oversimplifying – the complex dynamics of specific groups as more (or less) homophobic. These issues are just too complex to make such statements without taking more time and space to unpack them.

Clearly, political struggles over LGBTQ issues have been taken to the courts, where, for the most part, judges have affirmed the importance of diversity. In response to the Surrey School Board action, Chief Justice McLachlin of the Supreme Court of Canada stated: "Parental views, however important, cannot override the imperative placed upon the British Columbia public schools to mirror the diversity of the community, and teach tolerance and understanding of difference" (cited in McDonald 2010b, 213). We should appreciate that Canada has witnessed numerous progressive decisions in LGBTQ cases: "by 2004, all jurisdictions prohibited discrimination based on sexual orientation, several prohibited gender identity discrimination, and all provided clear procedures for bringing a claim of discrimination on these grounds against governments or in the private sector" (Smith 2008, 2). BC was one of the first provinces to enable same-sex parents to legally adopt children (see also the case study on family rights in Chapter 3, this volume). The gradual acceptance of LGBTQ rights in BC stands in marked contrast to the situation in approximately seventy countries where homosexuality is illegal and where LGBTQ people can face imprisonment, deportation, and even the death penalty (e.g., Iran, Sudan, Burundi, Qatar, Jamaica, and Russia, to name only a few) (Haskell and Burtch 2010, 321; Kordunsky 2013).

This chapter highlights parts of a complex, multi-layered legacy for LGBTQ individuals and groups. Future accounts of these struggles could include the intersection of LGBTQ with other identities – for example, ableism, ethnicity, age, gender – given that the queer community has been criticized for not always being very inclusive of queer people of colour (see also the analysis of the group Queers against Israeli Apartheid in Chapter 9, this volume). Accordingly, we are coming to a greater understanding of and focus on how experiences of being LGBTQ intersect with experiences of our proclaimed or perceived ethnicity, age, and gender. This has led to the creation of queer people of colour (QPOC) groups. In British Columbia, the Urban Youth Native Association (Lerat and Gray 2004) explored the needs of Two-Spirited people, documenting barriers to acceptance in some First Nations communities and in mainstream, urban settings: "Today, many Two-spirit youth leave their communities hoping to find, safety, acceptance, and fulfillment in the big city. Unfortunately when they arrive, they face harsh realities when being confronted with racism, a lack of skills and training to find employment, a lack of familial support, a lack of support within the larger GLBT community, and even homophobia. Hence, Two-spirit youth are finding themselves living on the streets of the big city, which puts them at great risk of sexual exploitation, chemical dependency, suicide, and contracting HIV" (5). In 2006, Embracing Our Spirits: A Gathering of Two Spirit, Family, and Friends, the first-ever event exploring Two-Spirit issues, was held in the Vancouver area (Christopher 2006). As Julie Depelteau and Dalie Giroux emphasize in Chapter 2 (this volume), and as others have underscored (Driskell et al. 2011), it is important to explore the legacy of colonialism for Two-Spirited people, and ongoing work is needed to reclaim Two-Spirit identities and to build communities in which social acceptance and progressive public policies are secured. This sensitivity to social harms (Yar 2011) is clearly applicable not only to Two-Spirited youth but also as part of a critical approach to social exclusion, especially as it affects Aboriginal people in Canada (Galabuzi 2012, 106).

Note

1 The Court Challenges Program was defunded by the Mulroney (Progressive Conservative) government in 1992, reinstated by the Chrétien (Liberal) government in 1994, and then defunded by the Harper (Conservative) government in 2006.

References

Adkin, David, producer/director. 2007. *Jim Loves Jack: The James Egan Story* (video recording). New York: Cinema Guild.

Babineau, Guy. 2008. "Little Sister's: 25 Years of Determination." *Xtra! Canada's Gay and Lesbian News*, 23 April. http://dailyxtra.com/canada/news/little-sisters-25-years -determination-53360.

Barber, J. 2007. "The New Face of Toronto Gets a Well-Deserved Wynne." *Globe and Mail*, 13 October.

Barsotti, Natasha. 2009. "Activists Hold Social Justice Conference in Abbotsford: Last Fall's Rally Galvanized People." *Xtra! Canada's Gay and Lesbian News*, 26 February. http://www.xtra.ca/public/Vancouver/Activists_hold_social_justice_conference_in_ Abbotsford-6372.aspx.

–. 2012. "Surrey Agrees to Consider Anti-Homophobia Policy: Superintendent Tasked with Creating Working Group." *Xtra! Canada's Gay and Lesbian News*, 22 June. http:// www.xtra.ca/public/Vancouver/Surrey_agrees_to_consider_antihomophobia_policy -12187.aspx.

Beatty, Jim, and Craig McInnes. 2000. "Meet the New Ministers: Appointments Include First Openly Gay Man to Serve in a BC Cabinet and the Man with the Record as the Longest-Serving MLA without a Cabinet Post." *Vancouver Sun*, 2 November.

Busby, Karen. 2006. "*Little Sister's v. Canada*: What Did the Queer-Sensitive Interveners Argue about Equality Rights and Free Expression?" In Brian Burtch and Nick Larsen, eds., *Law in Society: Canadian Readings*, 2nd ed., 4–17. Toronto: Nelson.

Canada's Human Rights History (CHRA)/Dominique Clément. n.d. *The GATE Case*. Edmonton: Canada's Human Rights History. http://www.historyofrights.com/events/ GATE.html.

Canadian Press. 2012. "LGBT Retirement Home Mooted for BC." 2 September. Toronto: Canadian Broadcasting Corporation. http://www.cbc.ca/news/canada/british-columbia/ story/2012/09/02/bc-lgbt-retirement-home.html.

Canadian Lesbian and Gay Archives. 2012. *Association for Social Knowledge (ASK)*. http:// www.clga.ca/association-social-knowledge-ask.

–. 1997. *Chronology from Flaunting It! 1964–1982*. http://www.clga.ca/Material/Records/ docs/flitchro/80.htm.

Carlson, Kathryn Blaze. 2012. "The True North LGBT: New Poll Reveals Landscape of Gay Canada." *National Post*, 6 July. http://news.nationalpost.com/2012/07/06/the-true -north-lgbt-new-poll-reveals-landscape-of-gay-canada/.

CBC News. 2011. "Sexual Orientation Rights Questioned by BC Tory." 12 May. Toronto: Canadian Broadcasting Corporation. http://www.cbc.ca/news/canada/british-columbia/ story/2011/05/12/bc-john-cummins-gay-rights.html.

Christopher, Nathaniel. 2006. "Building a Stronger Two-Spirited Community: Ground-breaking Event Aims to Bring Queer Aboriginals Together." *DailyXTRA*, 18 July. http:// dailyxtra.com/vancouver/news/building-stronger-two-spirited-community-10988.

Churchill, David S. 2004. "Mother Goose's Map: Tabloid Geographies and Gay Male Experience in 1950s Toronto." *Journal of Urban History* 30 (6): 826–52. http://dx.doi.org/10.1177/0096144204266743.

Cossman, Brenda. 2003. "Disciplining the Unruly: Sexual Outlaws, Little Sister's and the Legacy of Butler." *UBC Law Review* 36 (1): 77–99.

–. 2013. "Censor, Resist, Repeat: A History of Censorship of Gay and Lesbian Sexual Representation in Canada." http://works.bepress.com/cgi/viewcontent.cgi?article=1000&context=brenda_cossman.

Cossman, Brenda, and Bruce Ryder. 1996. "Customs Censorship and the Charter: The *Little Sister's* Case." *Constitutional Forum* 7 (4): 103–12.

CUPE. 2012. *Delegates Shaken and Stirred at Equality Forum.* 27 April. http://www.cupe.bc.ca/news/2563.

Driskell, Quo-Li, Chris Finley, Brian Joseph Gilley, and Scott Laurie Morgensen, eds. 2011. *Queer Indigenous Studies: Critical Interventions in Theory, Politics, and Literature.* Tucson: University of Arizona Press.

Egan, Jim. 1998. *Challenging the Conspiracy of Silence: My Life as a Canadian Gay Activist.* Comp. and ed. Donald W. McLeod. Toronto: Canadian Lesbian and Gay Archives.

findlay, barbara. 2003. "Real Women: *Kimberly Nixon v. Vancouver Rape Relief.*" *University of British Columbia Law Review* 36 (1): 57–76.

Galabuzi, Grace-Edward. 2012. "Social Exclusion as a Determinant of Health." In Elizabeth A. McGibbon, ed., *Oppression: A Social Determinant of Health*, 97–112. Black Point, NS: Fernwood Publishing.

Goldstein, Aaron. 2007. "Is Abolishing Canada's Human Rights Necessary?" *Madashell.com*, 22 December. http://madashell.com/more.php?id=1531_0_1_0_M.

Haskell, Rebecca, and Brian Burtch. 2010. "Teachers Don't Hear the Word 'Fag.'" In Nick Larsen and Brian Burtch, eds., in *Law in Society: Canadian Readings*, 3rd ed., 4–17. Toronto: Nelson Education.

Homomilitia. 2012. "All Survivors Deserve Support: Activists Intervene at Rape Relief Walkathon." *Vancouver Media Co-op*, 28 May. http://vancouver.mediacoop.ca/blog/flux/11077.

Kinsman, Gary, and Patrizia Gentile. 2010. *The Canadian War on Queers: National Security as Sexual Regulation.* Vancouver: UBC Press.

Kordunsky, Anna. 2013. "Russia Not Only Country with Anti-Gay Laws: Many Other Countries, from Iran to Cameroon, Have Harsh Anti-Gay Laws." *National Geographic Daily News*, 13 August. http://news.nationalgeographic.com/news/2013/08/130814-russia-anti-gay-propaganda-law-world-olympics-africa-gay-rights/.

Lerat, Gil, and Lynda Gray. 2004. *Two-Spirit Youth Speak Out: Analysis of the Needs Assessment Tool.* Vancouver: Urban Native Youth Association/Health Canada. http://www.unya.bc.ca/downloads/glbtq-twospirit-final-report.pdf.

Little Sister's Book and Art Emporium. 2011. *About Us.* Vancouver: Little Sister's Book and Art Emporium. http://littlesisters.ca/blog/?page_id=143.

MacDougall, Bruce, and Paul T. Clarke. 2004. "Teaching Tolerance, Mirroring Diversity, Understanding Difference: The Effect and Implications of the *Chamberlain* Case." In James McNinch and Mary Cronin, eds., *"I Could Not Speak My Heart": Education and Social Justice for Gay and Lesbian Youth*, 193–19. Regina: University of Regina, Canadian Plains Research Centre.

Mason, Gary. 2011. "Is BC Ready for an Openly Gay Party Leader?" *Globe and Mail*, 24 January. http://m.theglobeandmail.com/news/british-columbia/is-bc-ready-for-an -openly-gay-party-leader/article621859/ ?service=mobile.

Matas, Robert. 1999. "There's No Stopping Svend: Once Married, Now Openly Gay, the NDP Activist Is a Born Fighter." *Globe and Mail*, 19 June.

McDonald, Marci. 2010a. "British Columbia, Test Bed for Harper's Religious Base." *Tyee*, 19 July. http://thetyee.ca/News/2010/07/19/ReligiousBase/.

–. 2010b. *The Armageddon Factor: The Rise of Christian Nationalism in Canada*. Toronto: Random House.

McLeod, Donald W. 1996. *Lesbian and Gay Liberation in Canada: A Selected Annotated Chronology, 1964–1975*. Toronto: ECW Press/Homewood Books.

Ministry of Attorney General. 2008. *Human Rights in British Columbia*. January. Victoria: Ministry of Attorney General. http://www.ag.gov.bc.ca/human-rights-protection/pdfs/ ProtectDiscrimination.pdf.

Moon, Richard. 2011. "The Supreme Court of Canada's Attempt to Reconcile Freedom of Religion and Sexual Orientation Equality in the Public Schools." In David Rayside and Clyde Wilcox, eds., *Faith, Politics, and Sexual Diversity in Canada and the United States*, 321–38. Vancouver: UBC Press.

Morrison, Melanie A. 2008. "Navigating Sexual and Ethno-Cultural Identities in Canada: Perspectives from Aboriginal and Chinese Sexual Minority Men." In Shari Brotman and Joseph J. Levy, eds., *Intersections: Cultures, Sexualities, and Genders*, 193–218. Quebec: University of Quebec Press.

Perelle, Robin. 2007. "Rape Relief Wins: Supreme Court Refuses to Hear Trans Woman's Appeal." *Xtra! Canada's Gay and Lesbian News*, 14 February. http://dailyxtra.com/ vancouver/news/rape-relief-wins-10251.

Queer Arts Festival. 2014. *Queerotica*. Vancouver: Pride in Art Society. http://queerartsfestival. com/.

Settlement Agreement between Murry Corren and Peter Corren. 2006. *Settlement Agreement between Murray Corren and Peter Corren (Complainants) and the Ministry of Education*. 28 April. Surrey, BC: Parents and Teachers for Life. http://www.bcptl.org/Corren.pdf.

Smith, Miriam Catherine. 1999. *Lesbian and Gay Rights in Canada: Social Movements and Equality-Seeking, 1971–1995*. Toronto: University of Toronto Press.

Smith, Miriam Catherine. 2004. "Questioning Heteronormativity: Lesbian and Gay Challenges to Education Practice in British Columbia, Canada." *Social Movement Studies* 3 (2): 131–45. http://dx.doi.org/10.1080/1474283042000266092.

–. 2008. *Political Institutions and Lesbian and Gay Rights in the United States and Canada*. New York: Taylor and Francis.

Steffenhagen, Janet. 2010. "CLARIFICATION: The Corren Agreement." *Vancouver Sun*, 3 January. http://blogs.vancouversun.com/2010/01/03/clarification-the-corren -agreement-2006/.

–. 2011. "Court Won't Halt Human-Rights Case over Social Justice 12." *Vancouver Sun*, 4 May. http://blogs.vancouversun.com/2011/05/04/court-wont-halt-human-rights-case -over-social-justice-12/.

Warner, Tom. 2002. *Never Going Back: A History of Queer Activism in Canada*. Toronto: University of Toronto Press.

Yar, Majid. 2011. "Critical Criminology, Critical Theory, and Social Harm." In Steve Hall and Simon Winlow, eds., *New Directions in Criminological Theory*, 52–65. Abingdon, Oxon: Routledge.

Legal Cases

Abbotsford School District No. 34 v. Corren [2011] B.C.J. No. 788
Chamberlain v. Surrey School District No. 36 [2002] 4 S.C.R. 710
Corren v. British Columbia (Ministry of Education) [2005] B.C.H.R.T.D. No. 497
Egan v. Canada [1991] F.C.J. No. 1252
Egan v. Canada [1993] 3 F.C. 401
Egan v. Canada [1995] 2 S.C.R. 513
Little Sister's Book and Art Emporium v. Canada (Minister of Justice) [2000] 2 S.C.R. 1120
Nixon v. Vancouver Rape Relief Society (c.o.b. Rape Relief and Women's Shelter) [2002] B.C.R.T.D. No. 1
North Vancouver School District No. 44 v. Jubran [2005] B.C.J. No. 733
Vancouver Rape Relief Society v. British Columbia (Human Rights Commission) [2000] B.C.J. No. 1143
Vancouver Rape Relief Society v. Nixon [2003] B.C.J. No. 2899
Vancouver Rape Relief Society v. Nixon [2005] B.C.J. No. 2647.

Brian Burtch, Aynsley Pescitelli, and Rebecca Haskell

7

"Severely Queer" in Western Canada: LGBT2Q Activism in Alberta

ALEXA DEGAGNE

Over the past forty-one years, Alberta has gained a reputation as the most conservative and homophobic province in Canada. Since 1971, the Progressive Conservative (PC) government – which has governed the province with over-whelming legislative majorities – has maintained power, in part, by continu-ously appeasing their religious and socially conservative base. Alberta's one-party government has accordingly implemented laws and policies that have been punitive and regulatory with regard to Alberta's LGBT2Q citizens.[1]

In the 1970s and 1980s, the PC government was representing the will of the majority of Albertans as it created and upheld pro-family and homophobic legislation and governance practices. By the mid-1990s, however, Albertans' ideological and political beliefs began to shift as the secular urban population grew and started to become a formidable challenge to traditional rural social conservative politics (Bonnett 2006, 76–78). Sensing this shift among the elec-torate, PC premier Ralph Klein attempted to appease his religious and socially conservative base without losing the support of the ever-more moderate urban voters. To win favour from both camps, Klein practised a politics of inaction with regard to LGBT2Q rights and protections. Specifically, in reaction to the 1998 Supreme Court decision in the *Vriend* case, Klein simply refused to add sexual orientation as prohibited grounds of discrimination to the province's Individual Rights Protection Act (IRPA). In 2009, PC premier Ed Stelmach did add sexual orientation to the act, but he also introduced parental rights to the same act (through Bill 44) and defunded gender reassignment surgery (GRS), thus targeting and punishing LGBT2Q Albertans.

In the eleven years during which the PC government stalled on affording LGB Albertans provincial rights and protections, Albertans' ideological and political views shifted even further to the centre of the spectrum, and support for LGB rights grew. Still, Klein's and Stelmach's governments perpetuated the myth that the majority of Albertans – who are "severely normal" – will always be more socially conservative than the rest of Canadians (on this issue of conservatism, see also Chapter 5 and Chapter 11, this volume). In tandem with this worldview, PC governments have argued that LGBT2Q Albertans are a small special interest group and that LGBT2Q equality and rights are of little concern to the majority of "severely normal" Albertans (Filax 2006, xiii; Lloyd and Bonnett 2005, 329). Such arguments are made to minimize and to delegitimize the lived experiences and political demands of LGBT2Q citizens, activists, and organizations. These myths were challenged, however, when LGBT2Q activists and organizations were joined by dozens of human rights, civil liberties, and education-focused organizations to protest Bill 44. Moreover, these myths have been nearly shattered as the socially conservative and libertarian Wildrose Party was rejected in the 2012 provincial election by the majority of Albertans, who opposed its anti-human rights policies as well as its homophobic and racists candidates.

This chapter traces the evolving relationship between Alberta's PC governments and provincial political parties, its ever-more moderate electorate, and its LGBT2Q activists and organizations. I take the *Vriend* case (1998), Bill 44 (2009), and the 2012 provincial election as my case studies, and I trace two important and interrelated trends in Albertan LGBT2Q politics. First, I argue that, contrary to PC governments' propagation, the majority of Albertans do not support social conservative and anti-LGB politics. Second, I argue that Alberta's political climate has actually fostered diverse, and conflicting, LGB, transgender, and queer activisms in the province.

Historical Background

Alberta's political culture has been characterized by social and economic conservatism, and influenced by orthodox Protestant Christianity (Filax 2006, xiii). Historically, social conservatives have depended on churches, community organizations, families, and the government to teach and reinforce moral order and community loyalty (Lakoff 1996, 143). For social conservatives, the family, in particular, is foundational to the creation of a proper society because it instills tradition, religious devotion, morality, responsibility, and appropriate gender roles. The social conservative ideal family is heterosexual and

Alexa DeGagne

patriarchal. This model is based partially on tradition that has developed since the Industrial Revolution and partially on religious doctrine (Cossman 2005).

In Alberta, religious fundamentalism and social conservatism have been concentrated largely in rural communities. As such, religious and socially conservative groups lost influence briefly in the early 1970s as the industrial economy expanded and Alberta's cities attracted secular and well-educated citizens, and produced a growing middle class (Clement 2013). The PC party's base and leadership accordingly changed from "a party led by 'teachers, farmers and small businessmen from rural areas and small towns [with] a new, young, and largely urban middle class leadership'" (Palmer quoted in Clement 2013, 61–62). PC premier Peter Lougheed thus focused on resource and economic development, as well as human rights legislation, rather than on moral and religious issues (Bonnett 2006, 76–78). As Clement (2013, 66) argues: "The election of the Progressive Conservative Party in 1971 after decades of Social Credit government was a turning point in ushering the rights revolution to Alberta. The period following the election has been dubbed by one historian James Marsh as 'Alberta's Quiet Revolution.'" In 1972, the government passed the Alberta Bill of Rights, the Individual Rights Protection Act, and established the Human Rights Commission (Clement 2013).[2] While these initiatives did not address the specific needs and concerns of LGBT Albertans, they were seen as indicating a shift in Alberta's human rights history.

The 1960s and 1970s also saw the emergence of feminist and gay and lesbian liberation movements that challenged, among many other things, the patriarchal family and the primacy of heterosexuality in Canadian and Albertan society (Fetner 2001). In reaction to these social and political movements, and Alberta's "Quiet Revolution," a backlash developed in the 1970s among social conservatives who wanted to maintain the importance and prominence of the traditional family in society. A new wave of social conservatives started to pressure the Alberta government to create laws and policies that would reinforce the importance and strength of traditional families (Bonnett 2006, 70). Throughout the 1980s and 1990s, Alberta's PC premiers and MLAs folded to this pressure, largely out of fear of losing their legislative stronghold.

In this political climate, LGBT2Q Albertans have struggled to gain rights and protections, and they have in many ways lagged behind their counterparts in other provinces (Shogan and Filax 2003, 167; see also other chapters in this volume). In this section, I offer a brief history of LGBT2Q human rights struggles in the province between 1998 and 2012. I do this by discussing five major events that have affected the relationship between the provincial governments and LGBT2Q citizens and activism: (1) the *Vriend* case (1998), (2) the battle over same-sex marriage (2005), (3) the passage of Bill 44 (2009), (4) the delisting and relisting of gender reassignment surgery (2009 and 2012), and (5) the 2012 provincial election.

The PC government's tumultuous relationship with LGBT2Q citizens and organizations is well exemplified in its handling of the Supreme Court of Canada's decision in the 1998 *Vriend* case. In this case, the Supreme Court decided that Alberta's Individual Rights Protection Act violated section 15(1) of the Canadian Charter of Rights and Freedoms by failing to list sexual orientation as an illegal ground for discrimination (Lloyd and Bonnett 2005, 333). The *Vriend* decision produced progressive effects for Canadian LGB citizens: it reinforced the fact that section 15 of the Charter prohibits discrimination against the gay and lesbian individuals; and it "established that employer pronouncements of sin would not take precedence over fundamental human rights" (Shogan and Filax 2003, 167).

Despite these progressive advances outside of Alberta, the Klein government acted out of fear of alienating its base. Bucking pressure from his party, Klein did not implement the Notwithstanding Clause of the Charter. Instead, he and his party took the route of inaction and waited eleven years before amending the act to include the protection of sexual orientation (Hurley 2010). In the next section, I take the *Vriend* case as my point of departure and trace how the Alberta government's reaction to it has conditioned the focus and tactics of queer activism in the province in the 1990s and 2000s.

The Klein government handled same-sex marriage much the same way as it did the *Vriend* decision: by choosing not to make a decision. As Lloyd and Bonnett (2005, 339) recount: "Upon receiving the Supreme Court of Canada reference on same-sex marriage ... Premier Klein vowed to continue the fight on behalf of Albertans ... Many in the party and government secretly [appeared] to admit there is little the government [could] do beyond the use of rhetoric." Thus, while rhetorically placating their base, the PCs were able to avoid making any overt political moves that would dissuade Albertan voters, 40 percent of whom actually supported same-sex marriage in 2002 (EKOS Research Associates Inc. 2002). Still, the PC government claimed it was following the will of the people as it enacted an entrenched social conservative ideology until 2005, when Klein, "much to [his] chagrin," afforded same-sex couples marriage licences (CTV News Online 2005).

In what was supposed to be a "good news" bill the PCs, led by Ed Stelmach, finally agreed in May 2009 to abide by the Supreme Court's ruling in the *Vriend* case. As part of these amendments to the IRPA, the Stelmach government passed Bill 44. This bill established a new section of the IRPA that introduced parental rights provisions requiring school boards to notify parents or guardians "where courses of study, educational programs or instructional materials, or instruction or exercises, prescribed under that [School] Act include subject-matter that deals explicitly with religion, sexuality or sexual orientation" (section 11.1[1]). On the same basis, Bill 44 also allows a student's parent/guardian to exclude a student from the classroom or participation in related educational activities without academic penalty.

There was substantial public outcry against Bill 44, marking a moment in which opposition political parties and non-LGBT2Q-focused organizations (e.g., the Alberta Teachers' Association) acted in solidarity with Alberta's LGBT2Q citizens, activists, and organizations. LGBT2Q activists and groups, and their allied groups, argued that the bill stifled free speech, demonized homosexuality, and infringed on teachers' and students' educational rights and freedoms (Kerr 2009e). These LGBT2Q and allied groups represent the ever-more moderate political priorities of Alberta voters. In the face of this shift, Stelmach chose to cater to his social conservative base by actively silencing discussion of sexuality and sexual orientation.

In tandem with Bill 44, the Stelmach government removed gender reassignment surgery from the list of medical procedures covered by the Alberta Health Care Insurance Plan (on GRS and trans human rights protection, see also Chapter 1). Citing budgetary constraints, the government argued that it would save $700,000 annually by delisting the surgery, but critics held that this was another attempt to placate the base (Canadian Press 2012a). Members of Alberta's transgender, LGB, and queer communities and their allies responded by rallying outside the legislature and by filing complaints with the Alberta Human Rights and Citizenship Commission (Young 2009). The Trans Equality Society of Alberta (TESA) presented several MLAs with letters requesting that the Minister's Advisory Committee on Health review the GRS funding cuts because they had been made without consulting medical professionals or anyone directly affected by the decision (Padfield 2009). Months after winning the 2012 provincial election, Premier Redford relisted GRSs (Canadian Press 2012a). This surprising change in policy, however, appears to have been motivated by the government's desire to distance itself from the unpopular social policies of the Wildrose Party.

The mounting battle and tension between Alberta's old Protestant social conservative roots and the more moderate, or even progressive, beliefs of the majority of voters was manifest in the 2012 provincial election.[3] Leading up to the election the Wildrose Party's true colours began to bleed through as leader Danielle Smith supported the idea of establishing conscience rights that would enable public servants to opt out of performing services (i.e., abortions and same-sex marriages); threatened to dismantle the Human Rights Commission; promised referendums to vote on contentious moral issues and, ultimately, on the rights of minorities; and stood in solidarity with two candidates who had made racist and homophobic public statements (Climenhaga 2012; Craigie 2012; Howell 2011; Kaufmann 2012; Simons 2012a). Smith espoused right-wing libertarian solutions to social problems, pledging to remove government intervention and to allow the public to vote on moral issues and social policy. Panic spread among Alberta's centrist voters. The provincial Liberal, NDP, and PC parties; the mayors of Edmonton and Calgary; LGBT2Q citizens and organizations; and many political and community organizations condemned Smith and her party's policies and candidates (Wood 2012). Surprising many, the Wildrose Party did not stop the PC party from winning its twelfth con-secutive majority government (Henderson 2012). With the majority of Alberta's religious and socially conservative voters supporting the Wildrose Party, Alison Redford's PCs claimed that they were ready to divorce their social conservative partners of forty years. With social conservatism engrained in PC governance, however, this was only a trial separation.

Queer Activism Today

Since the 1960s, LGBT2Q activist organizations have formed and disbanded in Alberta's three main centres: Calgary, Red Deer, and Edmonton (Bonnett 2006, 116–17). These cities' LGBT2Q organizations have been quite autono-mous, and few province-wide organizations have emerged. In addition, while the same individual activists or politicians may have been involved in more than one of the cases studied here, few organizations have been involved in more than one of them.

The organizations studied here may be broadly categorized according to two criteria: (1) structure (grassroots/community-based versus non-grassroots/ institutionalized) and (2) ideology (mainstream/liberal LGB versus queer). Non-grassroots/institutionalized organizations have structured and hier-archal governance models, relatively stable membership and leaders, and dependable or semi-dependable sources of funding. Grassroots/community-based organizations tend to have less structured governance models (they may reject hierarchical models), fluctuating and ever-changing members, revolving leaders (if they have leaders at all), and few, if any, sources of fund-ing and/or resources (see Chapter 10, this volume, for another way of conceiv-ing of LGBT groups).

Alexa DeGagne

Mainstream/liberal LGB organizations tend to focus on attaining liberal rights and equality through formal political avenues, including working with political parties and politicians, lobbying provincial and federal governments, and initiating and supporting challenges to law through the courts (Bernstein 2003). Queer organizations, on the other hand, argue that while the liberal equal rights framework may afford people formal protections, it does little to challenge common assumptions of acceptable sexuality and the ways in which heteronormativity permeates society (DeGagne 2012). Accordingly, many queer organizations reject the liberal rights and equality project, seeking instead to challenge and dismantle racist, sexist, and heteronormal systems of oppression. The subcategories within each criterion are not mutually exclusive: grassroots/community organizations do adopt some elements of non-grassroots/institutionalized organizations, and mainstream/liberal LGB and queer ideologies can and do exist within the same organization. Moreover, it is predominantly, but not universally, the case that non-grassroots/ institutionalized organizations practise mainstream/liberal LGB politics and that grassroots/community-based organizations practise queer politics. In the next section, I outline and discuss the structure and ideology of the organizations involved in the *Vriend* case, Bill 44, and the 2012 election.

In all three cases, LGBT2Q organizations did not fight alone for their respective causes; rather, in each of these cases activist organizations that have not been traditionally affiliated with or focused on LGBT2Q issues fought in solidarity with LGBT2Q activist citizens and organizations. These alliances between LGBT2Q activists/organizations and allied organizations demonstrate two important realities pertaining to Albertan politics. First, these cases and issues are intersectional in nature: they concern not only sexuality but also race, gender, class/employment, and religion. As such, organizations that are focused solely or predominantly on sexuality could not and did not fully represent every facet of each issue. Thus, solidarity among many organizations was necessary. Second, the solidarity between groups demonstrates the changing nature of Albertans' political ideologies, affiliations, and priorities. The implicated groups represent predominantly moderate and/or progressive ideologies and perspectives. That said, the organizations involved in each case approached the issues from different perspectives and with different goals. Accordingly, the organizations (LGBT2Q and allied) that were involved in each case had divergent, and at times conflicting, principles, goals, and strategies. The nuanced differences between the organizations' principles, goals, and strategies is addressed throughout this chapter.

Queer Activism and Public Policy Changes: Case Studies

I now examine the *Vriend* case (1998), Bill 44 (2009), and the 2012 provincial election. My intention is to demonstrate that (1) a majority of Albertans do not agree with social conservative and anti-LGB politics and that (2) the current political climate encourages diversified, yet conflicting, queer activisms in Alberta.

The 1998 *Vriend* Decision

The *Vriend* case marked a flashpoint between the homophobia rooted in Protestant beliefs, LGBT2Q citizens and activists, and the emergence of a moderate electorate in the province. Lloyd and Bonnett (2005, 329) argue that, in the 1990s, the PC government used its powers to engrain and bolster the province's conservative culture, often at the expense of LGBT Albertans. The early 1990s saw the emergence of the national Reform Party and rumours of a provincial wing. To counter Reform momentum the PCs veered further right, embraced the anti-Charter politics of the Reform Party, and PC MLAs began to openly shun the inclusion of human rights for LGB people (Bonnett 2006, 96) – this despite the fact that public opinion was starting to support the establishment of LGB rights. After the *Vriend* case had surfaced, the Human Rights Commission started taking complaints on the basis of sexual orientation even though it was not included in the IRPA. Community Development Minister Dianne Mirosh stopped the Human Rights Commission from taking these complaints as she mistakenly thought sexual orientation was covered under the IRPA. Deploying "special rights" discourse, Mirosh argued: "Gays and lesbians are having more rights than anyone else" (Bonnett 2006, 95).

LGB activists had been trying to get sexual orientation into the IRPA during the 1980s and 1990s. Facing an antagonistic government, many of them stopped lobbying MLAs, the provincial political parties, and the Human Rights Commission, choosing instead to engage in activism through the courts. In 1994, Court of Queen's Bench Justice Anne Russell ruled in Delwin Vriend's favour. Vriend was fired from King's College because he was a homosexual. Justice Russell found that the IRPA contravened the Charter, and she gave the province thirty days before sexual orientation would be read into the act. The PC government appealed Justice Russell's decision, and the Alberta Court of Appeal overturned it in 1996 (Bonnett 2006, 102). By the time the case was headed to the Supreme Court of Canada, several Albertan LGB

Alexa DeGagne

groups (Gala-Gay and Lesbian Awareness Society of Edmonton, Gay and Lesbian Community Centre of Edmonton, Society and Dignity Canada, and Dignité for Gay Catholics and Supporters) were joined by diverse provincial and national interveners, including women's groups,[4] civil liberties groups, lawyers and human rights groups,[5] religious denominations,[6] labour organizations,[7] and national LGBTQ organizations (Equality for Gays and Lesbians Everywhere, Foundation for Equal Families and Canadian AIDS Society). In April 1998, the Supreme Court ruled that sexual orientation must be "read-in" to the IRPA as prohibited grounds of discrimination.

Klein reacted to the *Vriend* Supreme Court decision by demonizing the judiciary, saying that this was a case of the courts versus "ordinary people." The premier then threatened, but declined, to invoke the Notwithstanding Clause. Under pressure from his caucus, Klein did take action in establishing a committee to review the situation and in creating "legislative fences" to protect the province from any implications that may have arisen for the ruling: the Alberta government refused to include gays and lesbians in extant legislative structures and vocabulary previously applicable only to heterosexuals (Lloyd and Bonnett 2005, 333).

Across Canada, LGBTQ and human rights groups celebrated the *Vriend* ruling as a monumental victory. In Alberta, the decision was met with a homophobic backlash. The *Edmonton Journal* and the *Calgary Herald* were filled with letters to the editor accusing the Supreme Court of giving homosexuals special rights and of supporting everything from pedophilia to the destruction of the family (Shogan and Filax 2003, 167). Yet, according to Edmonton LGBTQ activist Kristy Harcourt, the backlash had some positive effects: moderate and centrist Albertans who were not completely supportive of LGBT rights came to stand in solidarity to oppose the discrimination against LGBT people (Harris 2008).

The *Vriend* victory marked the end of a particular era of LGBT activism in Alberta. LGBT2Q activists largely abandoned provincial lobbying efforts and engagement with provincial parties and politicians. Instead, LGBT2Q activism continued along two main tracks: (1) equality seekers depended on lawyers and the Charter to challenge discriminatory laws, and (2) queer activists formed grassroots responses to social and political heteronormativity through alternative systems of care and community building and organizing (see also Chapter 10, this volume). By 2009, Alberta's LGBT2Q communities and activist organizations had grown, diversified, and were ready to respond to Premier Stelmach's changes to the IRPA.

Bill 44: Human Rights, Citizenship and Multiculturalism Amendment Act, 2009

In 2009, breaking with eleven years of PC avoidance, Premier Ed Stelmach took action and initiated Bill 44, which would add sexual orientation to Alberta's IRPA as a prohibited ground of discrimination (Simons 2012b). Opposition MLAs had attempted to amend Bill 44 to include gender identity and Aboriginal heritage as prohibited grounds of discrimination, but both amendments were rejected (Kerr 2009b). Stelmach, however, did add parental rights to the IRPA under Bill 44.

While the PCs initially sold the bill as a leap forward for human rights, queer Albertans quickly became its strongest opponents (Kerr 2009a, 2009e). Mike Gary was the communications chair of the Alberta chapter of the Centre for Inquiry, a non-profit group committed to promoting sceptical, secular, rational, and humanistic enquiry. In response to the bill, Gary stated: "As a gay man, I am prepared to wait for my human rights to be enshrined by the Alberta government ... I am offended that the acknowledgement of homosexual rights in our province is only being used to make an otherwise intolerable bill sound more appealing. Mr. Premier, do not use the appearance of gay rights as a cover to advance a fundamentalist agenda" (Kerr 2009b).

The Alberta Teachers' Association clarified that the Alberta School Act already protects a parent's rights with regard to what her or his children are taught (ATA 2009). The parental rights section of Bill 44, therefore, is functionally redundant. With this revelation in mind, many opponents of the bill argued that the legislation seemed to "come out of nowhere." But this bill is actually a product of Alberta's Protestant and socially conservative roots.

In the early 2000s, Ted Morton, then University of Calgary professor and conservative activist, delivered a speech to the World Congress of Families in which he attacked what he called "gender feminists" and the gay rights movement, and argued that governments, when drafting all new legislation, must consider the impact on parental rights, especially the right to educate children in the moral and spiritual traditions of their choice (Simons 2009). Ted Morton became a prominent member of Stelmach's government, and, although he never spoke publicly about Bill 44, he was largely acknowledged to be its intellectual godfather (Simons 2012b). Liberal MLA Laurie Blakeman stated that the PC government's tabling of Bill 44 had "caused its own caucus to become divided between Red Tories, who tend to be fiscally conservative but socially progressive, and rural MLAs, who preach so-called family values" (Hasselriis 2009). MLA Morton belonged to the latter group, a minority of MLAs in the legislature, who represented the voice of deeply socially conservative and religious Albertans.

LGBT2Q activists and opposition MLAs were quick to argue that the majority of Albertans did not subscribe to the socially conservative values and ideology that were being espoused by the PC government. While debating Bill 44, then Alberta Liberal leader Dr. David Swann addressed Premier Stelmach:

> By placating certain interest groups at the expense of public education, this administration has made Albertans both angry and embarrassed. Ordinary citizens, parents, teachers, academics and religious groups have all joined together to support public education, and oppose enshrining parental rights in the human rights code. To the premier, why is the government unwilling to accept the voice of the majority and protect public education? (Alberta 2009, 1199)

Stelmach failed to answer Swann's question and simply reiterated his party's commitment to supporting the socially conservative notion that (particular kinds of) families are the foundation of society. Several of his ministers, however, were adamant that Bill 44 actually did represent the will of the majority of Albertans. Culture Minister Lindsay Blackett, who officially introduced Bill 44, insisted that the "silent majority" of Albertans wanted parental rights (Simons 2012b). PC MLA Rob Anderson also argued that the "silent majority," which was comprised of "severely normal" (a term borrowed from Klein) Albertans, wanted parental rights. He stated: "There are thousands and thousands of parents, the silent majority, severely normal Albertans that are extremely happy with this legislation, that believe it's right to affirm the right of parents as being the primary educators of their children on these subjects" (CBC News 2009).

Blackett's and Anderson's unfounded assertions that the "silent majority" of Albertans support socially conservative policies were challenged as politicians and organizations that have not historically focused on LGBT2Q issues joined provincial and national liberal rights organizations, along with Alberta's LGBT2Q activists and organizations, against Bill 44. Referring to the province's education-focused organizations, Liberal MLA Laurie Blakeman stated: "These are not usually groups who come together and support each other. It's quite remarkable" (Hasselriis 2009). The Alberta School Boards Association, the Alberta School Councils' Association, the College of Alberta School Superintendents, the Alberta Teachers' Association, the Alberta Civil Liberties Research Centre, the Canadian Civil Liberties Association, NDP and Liberal opposition MLAs, and mainstream/liberal LGB and queer activists and organizations pointed to Bill 44's several potentially dangerous implications. These opponents of Bill 44 warned that the legislation would stifle free speech and would punish teachers who could not or would not end discussions about religion, sexuality, and sexual orientation (ATA 2009; CCLA 2009; Hasselriis 2009).

Mainstream/liberal LGB and queer activism against Bill 44 took many forms: blog and internet campaigns, attempts to gain media attention for the issue, protests at the legislature, and a satirical video to raise awareness and spur debate and protest over the bill. For the purposes of this chapter, I address the latter two activist strategies because they highlight the difference between the mainstream/liberal LGB efforts and queer efforts.

Prominent Albertan LGB activists attended protests at the provincial legislature before and after Bill 44 was passed. The most publicized and attended protest occurred on 26 May 2009, the day before the vote on Bill 44. During this "Day of Protest against Bill 44," LGB and queer activists, predominantly from Edmonton, held a press conference on the steps of the legislature. The protest focused on the history and current state of LGB liberal rights and equality politics in Alberta. The group included lawyer Julie Lloyd, who was involved in the *Vriend* case; Michael Phair, who was one of the province's first openly gay politicians; and Lance Anderson, a gay father of two who, along with his husband, won a major adoption battle in Alberta (Kerr 2009c).

On 1 September 2009, one year before the legislation was to be implemented, the Queer Allied Network (QAN) organized another rally at the legislature. QAN seeks to mobilize Albertans on issues that affect the queer community and its allies and is committed to fighting for equal rights and to ending discrimination against LGBT people (QAN 2012). In November 2009, members of QAN actually gave the government a "work list" of liberal and equal rights demands: repeal Bill 44 and introduce a new bill to revise the Alberta Human Rights Code; reinstate GRS as a provincially funded medical procedure; and revise the Education Act in a fair and equitable way (Kerr 2009f). Justifying their continued action, Bethany Padfield, QAN media relations officer, stated:

> Ideally, we would love for the Alberta Legislature to seriously look at the work list and realize that it is their duty to represent and protect all citizens ... Being a bit more realistic, knowing that the Alberta government is much more likely to ignore anything coming from the queer community, we simply want them and the larger population to be aware that we haven't forgotten what the issues are. (Kerr 2009f)

One month after Bill 44 was passed, a group of queer artists and activists from Edmonton produced a satirical film entitled *Smaller Classes, Smaller Minds* to protest the new legislation. Daniel Peers, one of the film's creators, explained that *Smaller Classes, Smaller Minds* was a DIWYC (do it with your community) project created through grassroots collaboration with many members and organizations in Edmonton's queer communities (Kerr 2009d). The video, which has garnered more than three thousand views on YouTube, is a mock public service announcement from the Coalition for the Reduction of Alberta Class Sizes (CRACS). The video's announcer, Mrs. Trixie Cane, states: "Bill 44 encourages parents to remove their children from classes in which religion, sexuality or sexual orientation is discussed, allowing parents to keep their children's minds and lives as limited as possible" (Coalition for the Reduction of Alberta Class Sizes 2009). Cane then offers Albertan teachers tips on how they can use Bill 44 to reduce their class sizes by injecting queer material into every class. Cane's first example: "At an elementary level, simply create problems like the following: If in 2008 Suzanne had four polyamorous lovers but in December two of her lovers formed a monogamous couple, how many polyamorous lovers did Suzanne have at the beginning of 2009?" (ibid.). Here CRACS pushes the terms of the debate concerning Bill 44 beyond whether or not equal rights and homosexuality should be discussed in classrooms (both of these topics were the focus of the above-mentioned rallies). The video subtly and satirically argues that sexuality is always present in all areas of life and learning. Math, science, languages, and social studies courses are imbued with heteronormal assumptions, examples, and knowledges. Ultimately, CRACS's video offers a queer critique of public education as a heteronormative institution. CRACS presents the possibility of a public education system that goes beyond the heterosexual/homosexual binary and that actually embraces polyamorous, transgendered, and queer lived experiences and worldviews.

Despite public opposition – and the various protests from Albertan education associations, opposition MLAs, provincial and federal civil liberties organizations, mainstream/liberal LGB activists and organizations, and queer academics and activists – the Stelmach government passed Bill 44 on 26 May 2009 and implemented its legislative changes in September 2010. Red Tories in the caucus, including Dave Hancock, publicly opposed the bill but did not vote against it, choosing instead to miss the vote. Rob Anderson, who was the bill's most vocal public advocate, crossed the floor to the Wildrose Party in January 2010, eight months after the bill was passed. As *Edmonton Journal* columnist Simons (2012b) observed: "Stelmach missed out on the chance to be a true human rights champion, to appease the so-cons in his caucus, only to be betrayed by them in the end."

Alison Redford was justice minister when the bill was passed, and she did not publicly speak against the legislation or its possible legal repercussions (Simons 2012b). Yet, as I discuss in the next section, during the 2012 provincial election Premier Redford claimed that she, and her party, would uphold and defend gay rights in the legislature. And it seemed that some mainstream/liberal LGB activists were completely willing to forget the recent past and to believe that the PC party would no longer side with its socially conservative base.

The 2012 Provincial Election

At first approach, the emergence of the libertarian and socially conservative Wildrose Party was thought to signal Albertans' unwavering commitment to right-wing ideology and politics. Late polls indicated that Wildrose would topple the PCs and win a majority in the 2012 election (Craigie 2012; Larson 2012). Yet Wildrose did not come close to forming a majority government as it won only seventeen of eighty-seven possible seats. The perpetual tension between the province's Protestant and socially conservative roots, red Tories, the ever-more moderate majority, and mainstream/liberal LGB and queer activists was starkly played out in this election, ultimately showing that Albertan voters are moving to the centre and that the vast majority do not support social conservative and homophobic politics.

The Wildrose Party was born in 2008, largely as a backlash to the Stelmach government's oil and gas royalty program, a record deficit, and liberal spending (Kleiss 2012). According to its 2011 Constitution, the Wildrose Party believes that the provincial government exists to "reflect, strengthen and efficiently serve the common-sense values of Albertans." These values include: the lowest possible taxation, a strong and enterprising work ethic, self-directed communities, and stable families and a growing population (Wildrose 2012).

The party's unique combination of social conservatism and libertarianism was slowly revealed to the electorate. Imploring populist political strategy, Smith promised that the party's libertarianism would contain the social conservative leanings of its candidates: Albertan voters, not government, would have control over social and moral issues and policy. First, Smith stated that she would support the establishment of conscience rights to ensure that marriage commissioners and health professionals could opt out of performing services that run counter to their personal and/or religious beliefs (i.e., abortions and same-sex marriages) (Howell 2011). Second, Smith threatened to dismantle the Human Rights Commission in the name of free speech (Climenhaga 2012). Third, she promised that referendums would be used to vote on contentious moral issues and, ultimately, on the rights of minorities (Simons 2012a).

Finally, in the last weeks of the election, support for the Wildrose Party fell when Smith stood by two of its candidates who had made public comments that were both homophobic and racist (Kaufmann 2012). In June 2011, Wildrose candidate Allan Hunsperger, a leader in Alberta's Christian private school movement and a pastor at an evangelical church (Simons 2012c), published a pastoral letter on his church website that stated that homosexuals who do not change their orientation or lifestyles "will suffer the rest of eternity in the lake of fire, hell, a place of eternal suffering" (ibid.). Smith claimed that candidates' personal views would not affect their ability to represent the will of Albertans. According to her: "Mr. Hunsperger understands that the views he expressed were his personal views in the context of him being a pastor and I'm not going to discriminate against anyone" (CBC News 2012). In further defence of Hunsperger, Smith reiterated that her party would not legislate on "contentious social issues" (Simons 2012c). Here Smith and the Wildrose Party deployed the right-wing libertarian fallacy that social and moral issues – such as religious freedom and gender equality – do not infuse all areas of politics and governance. By claiming that these social and moral issues can and should be isolated from other areas of politics, such as the economy and education, parties and politicians negate complex systems of power relations and ultimately abdicate their responsibility to account for their effects.

Given the rapid pace of the election, there was little opportunity for coordinated and extensive protests from Alberta's LGBT2Q activists and organizations. In an article entitled "Gay Activists Demand Wildrose Remove Candidate," CBC News cited only Kris Wells, who works for the University of Alberta's Institute for Sexual Minority Studies and Services. Wells focused on equality, referred to two-tiered citizenship, and told CBC News: "Danielle Smith should immediately apologize. The candidate should be removed from this election and Danielle Smith should clarify that there isn't a two-tiered approach to equality in this province" (CBC News 2012).

Opposition parties were quick to criticize Smith. Redford vowed to uphold gay and lesbian rights, but her comments came only after Wildrose's homophobia began to surface. Centrist and moderate voters panicked, and some suggested that voters must strategically support the PCs in order to ensure that Wildrose did not form the next government.

Championing strategic voting, a group called Proud of Alberta published large advertisements in the *Calgary Herald* and the *Edmonton Journal* entitled "Read This and Pray for Alberta," three days before the election. The advertisement, printed in the shape of the province, quoted excerpts from Hunsperger's homophobic blog post. It then stated: "The Wildrose Party is committed to shut[ting] down the Human Rights Commission. Alison Redford is committed to protecting gay rights and human rights in Alberta. Which is your Alberta?" (Proud of Alberta 2012). Proud of Alberta, which has no connection with PCs (Climenhaga 2012), presented two different possibilities for Alberta: (1) that of the socially conservative and homophobic Wildrose Party and (2) that of the supposedly softening PCs. According to strategic voters, these two different visions of Alberta were the only realistic possibilities for the province. Voters could choose the "old Alberta" replete with racism and homophobia, or they could chose the newer Alberta of the reformed and progressive PCs. This division negates the possibility that Alberta (and Albertans) could become, or is actually in the midst of becoming, a moderate and/or progressive province. Proud of Alberta reinforced the myth of the either/or choice by calling on all LGBT2Q voters and their allies to vote for the PCs, ignoring that party's deplorable history and current practices of demonizing and punishing LGBT2Q Albertans.

Conclusion

Before the election, Redford apparently consulted with a select few LGBT Albertans (including prominent members of Edmonton's LGB community and media organizations active in Proud of Alberta), and together they determined the priorities for Alberta's LGBT2Q communities, one of which was the refunding of GRSs. Shortly after the election, the PC government decided to refund GRSs. As Health Minister Fred Horne explained: "Alberta is a very progressive province and policy needs to catch up to where Albertans are. I think this reflects a decision of a government that is very much in tune with Albertans and their views" (Canadian Press 2012a). While the PCs seem to be catching up to the ever-more progressive electorate, it must be remembered that Redford made the political decisions on her terms, always careful not to spook the social conservatives who still support her party.

Premier Redford spoke at the Edmonton Pride Festival's 2012 opening celebration, making her the first sitting premier to do so. Some in the crowd chanted "Redford, Redford, Redford," and others shouted that her government needed to retract the parental rights section in Bill 44 (Canadian Press 2012b). Redford did not utter the words "gay," "lesbian," "bisexual," "transgender," or "queer"; instead, she used neutral and safe words like "diversity," "equality," and "freedom." This subjectless language renders invisible the reality that Alberta's LGBT2Q communities have diverse lived experiences, needs, and political views.

If the PC government is going to actually hold true to its election promise to fight for LGBT Albertans, it needs to speak with Alberta's many LGBTQ individuals, activists, and organizations. Doing so would reveal that, in the eleven-year gap between the *Vriend* decision and Bill 44, Alberta's LGBT2Q activist communities have grown, diversified, and strengthened. Groups like TESA, CRACS, and QAN, as well as Queers against Israeli Apartheid (Edmonton and Calgary chapters; see also Chapter 9, this volume) and the Community Response Project (Edmonton), have been working on critical and radical queer projects birthed in grassroots community organizing. As well, the Two Spirit Circle of Edmonton Society has formed to support and advocate for Indigenous Two-Spirited individuals and communities in Alberta (see Chapter 2, this volume).

Speaking to these diverse LGBT2Q groups and communities would reveal that LGBT2Q Albertans have different lived experiences and needs based on their gender, gender expression, race, ability, class, and/or occupation: LGBT2Q Albertans' lives are differently affected by poverty; systemic and daily violence; and homophobic, transmisogynic, and racist policing, justice, and prison systems. Accordingly, alliances have been forged between many anti-oppression communities working on myriad issues affecting the province's marginalized communities.

Yet, to date, the PC government has interacted with and taken cues from a select few LGBT organizations in the province – organizations that largely represent the will of those who are privileged within Alberta's LGBT2Q communities, including middle- and upper-class white gay males. The PCs may be a desirable option for white, affluent gay Albertans whose gender, race, class, and ability needs are met by the current government. However, Albertans who have long suffered under PC rule because of their gender, race, class, ability, and sexuality will find neither support nor representation in a party that prioritizes individual freedom, corporate rights, and the deterioration of the social welfare system.

Notes

1 Throughout this chapter, I shift between using "LGB," "LGBT2Q," "LGBT," and "queer" to refer to different organizations and communities. I have respected the identification organizations and communities use to describe themselves. When organizations and communities have not described themselves, I choose a description that seems to best suit their politics, location, and time period.

2 "The Alberta Bill of Rights dealt with fundamental freedoms, whereas the Individual Rights Protection Act prohibited discrimination in accommodation, employment and services" (Clement 2013, 74).

3 While the PC party was re-elected in 2012, thus indicating that the province's voters are not yet moderate or progressive, it is argued that its victory is partially the result of factors that have engendered Alberta's party system for the past several decades. First, the PC party has ruled with strong majority governments for forty years, indicating that it is difficult for opposition and new parties to challenge its dominance, regardless of changing popular opinion (Craigie 2012). Second, as discussed, rural ridings are predominantly socially conservative. Moreover, rural ridings are overrepresented in the Alberta legislature due to improperly drawn constituency boundaries. As such, rural ridings have disproportionate power in influencing parties' platforms and governments' agendas (Johnscrude 2010). While the Wildrose Party secured many of these rural ridings, its failure to win either a minority or a majority indicates that courting rural social conservative ridings is no longer a guarantee for victory in the province. The "2012 Provincial Election" section of this chapter discusses how the PCs managed to maintain power in relation to the ever-more moderate Alberta electorate.

4 Alberta Federation of Women, and Women's Legal Education and Action Fund.

5 Alberta Civil Liberties Association, Canadian Bar Association Alberta Branch, Canadian Human Rights Commission, and Canadian Association of Statutory Human Rights Agencies.

6 Alberta and North West Conference of the United Church of Canada, and the Canadian Jewish Congress.

7 Canadian Labour Congress.

References

Alberta (Provincial Legislature). 2009. *Alberta Hansard, Question Period, Second Session, 27th Legislature, 25 May (Afternoon)*. Edmonton: Legislative Assembly of Alberta. http://www.assembly.ab.ca/ISYS/LADDAR_files/docs/hansards/han/legislature_27/session_2/20090525_1330_01_han.pdf.

Alberta Teachers' Association (ATA). 2009. *Media Release: Parents, Teachers, Superintendents and Elected School Boards Line up against Bill 44*. 6 May. Edmonton: Alberta Teachers' Association. http://www.asba.ab.ca/perspectives/media-releases/2009/may06_09.asp.

Bernstein, Mary. 2003. "Nothing Ventured, Nothing Gained? Conceptualizing Social Movement 'Success' in the Lesbian and Gay Movement." *Sociological Perspectives* 46 (3): 353–79. http://dx.doi.org/10.1525/sop.2003.46.3.353.

Bonnett, Laura L. 2006. "Transgressing the Public/Private Divide: Gay, Lesbian, Bisexual and Transgender Citizenship Claims in Alberta, 1968–1998." PhD. diss., University of Alberta.

Canadian Civil Liberties Association (CCLA). 2009. *CCLA Criticizes Alberta's Bill 44, Saying It Undermines the Critical Educational Goals of Fostering Democratic Debate, Diversity and Respect for Fundamental Freedoms*. 22 May. Toronto: Canadian Civil Liberties Association. http://ccla.org/2009/05/22/ccla-criticizes-alberta%E2%80%99s-bill-44/.

Canadian Press. 2012a. "Alberta Reinstates Funding for Gender Reassignment after Delisting Surgery in 2009." *National Post*, 7 June. http://news.nationalpost.com/2012/06/07/alberta-gender-reassignment-surgery/.

–. 2012b. "Alison Redford at Gay Pride: Cheers Greet First Alberta Premier to Speak at Gay Pride Event in Edmonton." *Huffington Post*, 9 June. http://www.huffingtonpost.ca/2012/06/09/alison-redford-gay-pride_n_1583769.html.

CBC News. 2009. "Alberta Passes Law Allowing Parents to Pull Kids Out of Class." 2 June. Toronto: Canadian Broadcasting Corporation http://www.cbc.ca/news/canada/story/2009/06/02/alberta-human-rights-school-gay-education-law.html.

–. 2012. "Gay Activists Demand Wildrose Remove Candidate." 16 April. http://www.cbc.ca/news/canada/albertavotes2012/story/2012/04/16/albertavotes2012-wildrose-hunsperger-gay.html.

Clement, Dominique. 2013. "Alberta's Rights Revolution." *British Journal of Canadian Studies* 26 (1): 59–77. http://dx.doi.org/10.3828/bjcs.2013.4.

Climenhaga, David J. 2012. "Are Candidates' 19th-Century Views Actually Helping the Wildrose Party?" *Rabble.ca*, 21 April. http://rabble.ca/blogs/bloggers/djclimenhaga/2012/04/are-candidates%E2%80%99-19th-century-views-actually-helping-wildrose-par.

Coalition for the Reduction of Alberta Class Sizes (CRACS). 2009. *Bill 44: Smaller Classes, Smaller Minds.* http://www.youtube.com/watch?v=DRAI2eTTzQ0.

Cossman, Brenda. 2005. "Contesting Conservatisms, Family Feuds and the Privatization of Dependency." *Journal of Gender, Social Policy and the Law* 13 (3): 415–510.

Craigie, Allan. 2012. "From the Jaws of Defeat: The Alberta General Election of 2012." *Regional and Federal Studies* 22 (5): 633–44. http://dx.doi.org/10.1080/13597566.2012.736384.

CTV News Online. 2005. "Alberta Backs Down on Same-Sex Marriage." *CTV News.* http://www.ctv.ca/CTVNews/Canada/20050713/klein_marriage_050712/.

DeGagne, Alexa. 2012. "Queering the Language of 'Sexual Minorities' in Canada." In Malinda Smith and Fatima Jaffer, eds., *Beyond the Queer Alphabet: Conversations on Gender, Sexuality and Intersectionality*, 24–27. Ottawa: Canadian Federation for the Humanities and Social Sciences.

EKOS Research Associates Inc. 2002. *CBC/EKOS Poll for the CBC Sunday News Public Attitudes Toward Same-Sex Marriage.* Ottawa: EKOS Research Associates Inc. http://www.ekos.com/admin/articles/CBCSundayNews6.pdf (accessed 3 April 2012).

Fetner, Tina. 2001. "Working Anita Bryant: The Impact of Christian Anti-Gay Activism on Lesbian and Gay Movement Claims." *Social Problems* 48 (3): 411–28. http://dx.doi.org/10.1525/sp.2001.48.3.411.

Filax, Gloria. 2006. *Queer Youth in the Province of the "Severely Normal."* Vancouver: UBC Press.

Harris, Scott. 2008. "Vriend at 10: Ten Years after the Watershed *Vriend v. Alberta* Decision." *Vue Weekly Magazine*, 2 April. http://www.vueweekly.com/vriend_at_10/.

Hasselriis, Kaj. 2009. "Alberta Bill Threatens Lessons on Gay Life." *Xtra! Canada's Gay and Lesbian News*, 21 May. http://www.xtra.ca/public/National/Alberta_bill_threatens_lessons_on_gay_life-6816.aspx.

Henderson, Peter. 2012. "Polls Missed Wildrose Fade in Closing Days of Alberta Election." *Montreal Gazette*, 24 April. http://www.canada.com/news/Polls+missed+Wildrose+fade+closing+days+Alberta+election/6511012/story.html#ixzz1x03J0p4C.

Howell, Trevor Scott. 2011. "'Conscience Rights Need Protection: Wildrose Leader." *Fast Forward Weekly Magazine*, 1 September. http://www.ffwdweekly.com/article/news-views/news/conscience-rights-need-protection-wildrose-leader-8013/.

Hurley, Mary C. 2010. *Sexual Orientation and Legal Rights.* Ottawa: Library of Parliament.

Johnscrude, Larry. 2010. "The Value of Your Vote: Rural Votes Are Worth Up to Three Times as Much as Urban Votes." Alberta Views Magazine, March. http://www.albertaviews.ab.ca/2012/04/04/the-value-of-your-vote-march-2010/.

Kaufmann, Bill. 2012. "Wildrose Support Slips: Poll." *Edmonton Sun Online*, 20 April. http://www.edmontonsun.com/2012/04/20/wildrose-support-slips-poll.

Kerr, Ted. 2009a. "Opponents of Alberta's Bill 44 Set to Rally." *Xtra! Canada's Gay and Lesbian News,* 25 May. http://dailyxtra.com/canada/news/opponents-albertas-bill-44-set-rally.
–. 2009b. "Alberta's Bill 44 Unchanged after Marathon Debate." *Xtra! Canada's Gay and Lesbian News,* 27 May. http://www.xtra.ca/public/National/Albertas_Bill_44_unchanged_after_marathon_debate-6841.aspx.
–. 2009c. "Gay Albertans Vow to Keep up the Fight against Bill 44." *Xtra! Canada's Gay and Lesbian News,* 2 June. http://www.xtra.ca/public/National/Gay_Albertans_vow_to_keep_up_the_fight_against_Bill_44-6871.aspx.
–. 2009d. "Satirical Short Film Pokes Fun at Alberta's Bill 44." *Xtra! Canada's Gay and Lesbian News,* 20 July. http://www.xtra.ca/public/National/Satirical_short_film_pokes_fun_at_Albertas_Bill_44-7161.aspx.
–. 2009e. "Yanking Kids from Sex Ed.: Implementation of Alberta's Bill 44 Delayed One Year." *Xtra! Canada's Gay and Lesbian News,* 31 August. http://www.xtra.ca/public/National/Yanking_kids_from_sex_ed-7395.aspx.
–. 2009f. "Alberta Activists Demand Action on Queer Issues." *Xtra! Canada's Gay and Lesbian News,* 9 November. http://www.xtra.ca/public/National/Alberta_activists_demand_action_on_queer_issues-7814.aspx.
Kleiss, Karen. 2012. "Alberta Election Pits PC's 'Red' versus Wildrose's 'Blue' Conservatives, Experts Say." *National Post,* 9 April. http://news.nationalpost.com/2012/04/09/alberta-election-pits-pcs-red-versus-wildroses-blue-conservatives-experts-say/.
Lakoff, George. 1996. *Moral Politics: What Conservatives Know That Liberals Don't.* Chicago: University of Chicago Press.
Larson, Jackie L. 2012. "Wildrose Party Would Form Majority Alberta Government: Poll." *Canoe.ca,* 28 March. http://cnews.canoe.ca/CNEWS/Politics/2012/03/28/19559491.html.
Lloyd, Julie, and Laura Bonnett. 2005. "The Arrested Development of Queer Rights in Alberta, 1990–2004." In Trevor W. Harrison, ed., *The Return of the Trojan Horse: Alberta and the New World (Dis)Order,* 328–41. Montreal: Black Rose Books.
Padfield, Bethany. 2009. "Alberta Trans Activists Call for Review of GRS Funding Cuts." *Xtra! Canada's Gay and Lesbian News,* 27 October. http://www.xtra.ca/public/National/Alberta_trans_activists_call_for_review_of_GRS_funding_cuts-7742.aspx.
Proud of Alberta. 2012. "Read This and Pray for Alberta." *Calgary Herald,* 20 April.
QAN (Queer Allied Network). 2012. Queer Allied Network website. http://www.mygsa.ca/node/2865.
Shogan, Debra, and Gloria Filax. 2003. "Sexual Minorities in Canada." In Janine Brodie and Linda Trimble, eds., *Re-inventing Canada: Politics of the 21st Century,* 164–74. Toronto: Prentice Hall.
Simons, Paula. 2009. *Speech: The Child's Right to an Education: Bill 44 Re-Visited from a Broader Perspective.* Calgary: Sheldon Chumir Foundation for Ethics in Leadership, November. http://www.chumirethicsfoundation.ca/main/page.php?page_id=263.
–. 2012a. "Wildrose Must Say How Citizen Referendums Would Work." *Edmonton Journal,* 7 April. http://www.edmontonjournal.com/life/Wildrose+must+citizen+referendums+would+work/6422388/story.html.
–. 2012b. "Alberta Election: Smith and Redford and Pots and Kettles." *Edmonton Journal,* 17 April. http://blogs.edmontonjournal.com/2012/04/17/alberta-election-smith-and-redford-and-pots-and-kettles/.
–. 2012c. "Smith Fails Leadership Test on Issue of Candidate's Anti-Gay Blog." *Edmonton Journal,* 17 April. http://www.edmontonjournal.com/opinion/venting/Simons+Smith+fails+leadership+test+issue+candidate+anti+blog/6468850/story.html.

Wildrose. 2012. Wildrose Party official website. http://www.wildrose.ca.

Wood, James. 2012. "Wildrose Candidate Tells Gays in Lady Gaga-Inspired Blog Post: 'You Will Suffer the Rest of Eternity in the Lake of Fire, Hell.'" *National Post*, 15 April. http://news.nationalpost.com/2012/04/15/allan-hunsperger-wildrose-blog/.

Young, Jim. 2009. *Human Rights in Question as Alberta Delists Gender Reassignment Surgery*. Edmonton: University of Alberta, Centre for Constitutional Studies.

Legal Case
Vriend v. Alberta [1998] 1 S.C.R. 493.

PART 3

The Municipal Level

8

From Contestation to Incorporation: LGBT Activism and Urban Politics in Montreal

JULIE PODMORE

Over the past forty years, LGBT identities and communities in Canadian cities have been increasingly visible and central to urban social movements, neighbourhood formation, and urban regeneration projects. This chapter examines LGBT activism in relation to city politics in Montreal from the early 1970s to the present. As in Toronto (see Chapter 9, this volume), Montreal LGBT activists have had diverse approaches to activism, ranging from the assimilationist current that began with the homophile movement to the more socially radical gay liberationist stance. By the 1980s, the formation of the city's Village gai (or, the Village) also led to a territorial politics and the framing of gays and lesbians as a minority group. However, there are a number of local factors that distinguish Montreal's history of LGBT activism within Canada, including the postcolonial nationalist movement, the constitutional status of Quebec, language politics, local history, and forms of municipal governance.

In this chapter, my objective is to examine the specific interplay between LGBT activism and urban politics in Montreal. I trace the complex shifts in the struggle for the "right to the city" (Harvey 2003) on the part of LGBT activists from the 1970s onwards. As Harvey (939) argues, the collective right to the city, "beyond the right to individual access to the resources that the city embodies," should be seen as a basic human right, a platform from which we can begin to rework our cities to reflect more socially just ideals. This argument provides a framework within which to ground LGBT rights struggles – more often analyzed for their impact on federal and provincial policy – in urban space. However, as Bell and Binnie (2000, 3) argue, the predominant choice of a politics of rights through which to express sexual citizenship in liberal democracies also creates a burden of compromise between gaining those rights and their implicit normative responsibilities. I argue, therefore, that the struggle to claim LGBT "rights to the city" in Montreal has been shaped by this tension, initially involving collective struggles for social justice but increasingly moving towards political incorporation into municipal governance as more rights are gained at other political scales. In order to trace these patterns, I begin by providing a chronology of LGBT activism in Montreal. Next, I use a set of case studies of events that, as they move forward in time, illustrate the tension between the fight against societal repression and the processes of municipal incorporation into LGBT struggles to claim the right to the city.

Historical Background

While there is no generally accepted chronology of LGBT activist events in Montreal that spans the past forty years, there are sources that chart this activism in Canada (Smith 1999; Warner 2002) and in Quebec (Higgins 1999, 2011; Smith 1998; Sylvestre 1979). In Warner's (2002) overview of the Canadian context, a sustained LGBT activist movement begins in 1975 and ends in the aftermath of the inclusion of sexual orientation in the Canadian Charter of Rights and Freedoms in 1982. Smith's (1998) analysis also views 1982 as a national turning point; however, she notes that, after 1977, activism in Quebec makes a significant departure from that of the rest of Canada due to inclusion in the provincial Charter and the nationalist social project. Differences in the legal system, local history, and ideology are also notable in projects that situate Quebec and Montreal within broader LGBT social movements (Corriveau 2011; Côté and Boucher 2008; Higgins 1999, 2011; Léobon 2006). The following chronology of Montreal accounts for these differences, dividing its LGBT activist history before 1993 into three time periods. A fourth section on contemporary political issues accounts for LGBT activist histories after 1993. This chronology's turning points are marked by a combination of locally specific events and local interpretations of broader social processes and movements.

Contesting Repression, Building Institutions, 1971 to 1977

The suspension of civil liberties that came with the 1970 October Crisis, news of the gay liberation movements in Paris and New York, and the partial decriminalization of homosexual acts in Canada's 1969 omnibus bill (Bill C-150) all contributed to the mobilization of LGBT activists in Montreal. Visible and organized activism begins with the Front de libération homosexuel (FLH), a neo-Marxist, anti-colonial, gay liberationist group that, reflecting the political climate of the time, made its first public appearance during an anti-Confederation demonstration on Canada Day in 1971. Inspired by New York's Gay Liberation Front and Paris's Front homosexuel d'action révolutionnaire, the FLH was equally short-lived: it was active until 1972, when, after repeated police raids of its premises, it disbanded (Higgins 1999, 115).

Except for this public appearance of the FLH, we can characterize the period between 1971 and 1976 as one that focused on the initial organization of the lesbian and gay populations rather than on demonstrations. After the disbanding of the FLH, the city's anglophone sector became more active and many new groups formed, most of which began with the university group Gay McGill, including the community-based, bilingual Gay Montreal Association and Montreal Gay Women (*Le Berdache* 1981). Throughout the 1970s, these groups concentrated on building services, creating meeting places, and hosting social events. They also produced some of the first gay and lesbian publications and created the collective that founded the city's gay, lesbian, and feminist bookstore Androgyny in 1973 (Higgins 1999, 119). The mobilization and interaction created by these activities also led to the proliferation of new groups, as ideological, gender, and linguistic differences were confronted. For example, in 1976, tired of straddling the gap between the anglophone lesbian movement and the francophone feminist movement, francophone lesbians launched their own lesbian-feminist group, Coop-Femmes (Lamoureux 1998).[1]

By the mid-1970s, a series of events mobilized Montreal gay and lesbian activists to fight police repression, leading to provincial protections for gay and lesbian rights. The first event was the exclusion of sexual orientation from the non-discrimination clause of the newly adopted Quebec Charter of Rights and Freedoms in 1975. This exclusion set the stage for the development of the rights movement in Quebec (Sylvestre 1979, 55; Warner 2002, 148). The second event was the summer Olympics in 1976 and the corresponding "cleanup" campaign adopted by Montreal's municipal government. Raids on gay and lesbian commercial spaces mobilized the various activist groups in the city to form the first coalition against police repression, the Comité homosexuelle anti-répression (CHAR), and mount some of the first major lesbian and gay demonstrations in 1976 (see Case Study 1). Once the Olympics and the arrests had ended, the formal rights movement was launched with the founding of the Association pour les droits des gai(e)s du Québec (ADGQ) (Sivry 1998). Now, activists were ready to confront a third event, the post-Olympic raid on the Truxx. On 22 October 1977, the Montreal police raided this downtown gay bar and arrested 146 men as found-ins in a bawdy house. This sparked the largest anti-repression demonstration of the period when, the following night, the ADGQ organized a demonstration of two thousand people to protest. Two months later, under pressure from the ADGQ, the Quebec Human Rights Commission, and a public that was alarmed by the level of police brutality in the Truxx raid (Higgins 1999, 131; Sylvestre 1979, 60), the newly elected Parti Québécois amended the Charter to include protections on the basis of sexual orientation. Law 88 was passed by Quebec's National Assembly on 15 December 1977, making Quebec the first of any Canadian jurisdiction to offer such protections, globally second to the Netherlands (Côté and Boucher 2008).

Claiming Lesbian and Gay Spaces, 1978 to 1990

By the early 1980s, there were new dynamics shaping lesbian and gay activism in Montreal. The ADGQ now focused on mounting campaigns against discrimination, contesting the legal status of arrests, and influencing municipal politics by working with opposition parties. Activists also focused on institution building and the claiming of space in the city – a process that followed distinctive gender and linguistic patterns (Léobon 2006). The slow emigration of the anglophone population after 1976, the expansion of the central business district, and the Olympic clean-up campaign all contributed to the eastward movement of lesbian and gay territories (Podmore 2006; Remiggi 2000). Now predominantly francophone, lesbian and gay activists and their spaces were also divided along gender lines. Lesbians had long been involved in the feminist networks developing in the Plateau Mont Royal District in the 1970s (Hildebran 1998), and, after 1982, their place-making practices would expand throughout this district, building community in feminist bookstores, creating community centres, and opening their own lesbian-operated bars and cafés (Podmore 2006). By this year, gay men were also establishing themselves in the Village located in the Centre-Sud district along Saint Catherine Street East (Remiggi 2000). This new location created an anchor for gay commerce and political mobilization.

Over the course of the 1980s, gay institutional and political development in the Village intensified, culminating, towards the end of the decade, in a common movement for building lesbian and gay institutions. Homophobic violence in the Village combined with the increased incidence of HIV/AIDS among gay men meant that institution building and political representation became a central aspect of gay activism in the 1980s: confronting HIV/AIDS required community-based care, support, and prevention programs (Lavoie 1998), and dealing with gay bashing in the public spaces in the Village required improved relations with the police force (Blain 1987a). Both issues pointed towards mobilizing gay political power from the growing constituency in the Village. In the early 1980s, the first community AIDS resource groups were formed, expanding and developing into Comité SIDA Aide Montréal (C-SAM) and AIDS Community Care Montreal (ACCM). In 1986, residents of the Village also elected Quebec's first openly gay political official, Raymond Blain, to the city's municipal council (see Case Study 2). By the end of the 1980s, the political gains of the growing gay constituency led to a movement to represent "gays and lesbians" at the metropolitan scale through the creation of common institutions, including the Centre communautaire des gais et lesbiennes de Montréal (CCGLM) and the Coalition des organismes des minorités sexuelles du Montréal métropolitain (COMSM).

"Queering" Community and Space, 1990 to 1993

Events and social movements in the early 1990s significantly reshaped LGBT activism in Montreal. During the 5th Annual International AIDS Conference in Montreal in 1989, queer activist groups such as the AIDS Coalition to Unleash the Power (ACT UP) and AIDS Action Now! came to the city to demonstrate with local groups.[2] By 1990, both ACT UP and Queer Nation had established Montreal chapters (Lavoie 1998). Continued police repression of gay spaces and the lack of government attention to the AIDS crisis radicalized a new generation of "queer-identified" activists. Inspired by the more public and transgressive politics of these groups, queer activists now adopted a more militant form of activism and took to the city's streets.

The catalyst for queer militancy in Montreal came in July 1990, when the Montreal Urban Community police force raided Sex Garage, a warehouse party of four hundred people, on the pretext that the operators did not have a liquor licence (Demczuk and Remiggi 1998; Higgins 2011). While only eight people were arrested, the brutality of the police force during the raid mobilized a new generation (Crawford and Herland 2014). In the two days following the raid, protestors used ACT UP and Queer Nation tactics to fight this repression, holding a sit-in of 150 people in the Village on 16 July and, the following day, a kiss-in of four hundred in front of a downtown police station (Burnett 2009). The arrest and beating of forty-eight of these participants mobilized an organized movement against police repression and violence.

While the 1990s began with a militant queer agenda, activism in this decade would quickly be redirected towards advancing gay and lesbian rights (Demczuk and Remiggi 1998, 403). The movement against police repression and brutality expanded with the formation of Lesbians and Gays against Violence (LGV). This group lobbied for greater attention to a series of unsolved murders of gay men, police brutality in the city, and homophobic violence in the Village. By 1993, a coalition of such lobby groups convinced the Quebec Human Rights Commission to conduct an inquiry into the conditions of gays and lesbians. The commission's final report, *De l'illégalité à l'égalité*, addressed three areas of concern: community-police relations, access to services and health, and the application of Law 88 banning discrimination based on sexual orientation (Commission des droits de la personne 1994). Recommendations in these areas provided the framework for a new rights movement centred on gaining legal recognition of same-sex relationships. The commission's recommendations also led to institutional outcomes such as the creation of the anti-violence agency Dire enfin la violence (DELV) in 1995.

LGBT Activism Today

Since the 1993 commission, LGBT activism in Montreal has become diverse and complex. As the mainstream movement mobilized around the commission, the differences between particular populations within the LGBT coalition became increasingly apparent.[3] In addition, the 1990s brought a wide range of activist stances – ranging from assimilationist to separatist to queer – that were compounded by the coexistence of at least three generations of activists (Côté and Boucher 2008). While there is a notable "radical queer" movement currently developing among younger activists, many of the projects of the first "queer" generation have developed as the primary commercial institutions of the current movement. For example, Divers/Cité, the city's long-standing gay pride organization, and Black and Blue, a large circuit party that raises funds for AIDS research, began as small queer activist projects in the early 1990s. Along the same lines, the Village has also evolved from a "safe haven" for gay bars and bathhouses into a landscape that is marketed by an expansive gay commercial press as a cosmopolitan consumer landscape that is both distinctively gay and open to all consumers (Hunt and Zacharias 2008; Ray 2004).

Over the last decade, there have also been important gains in the struggle for rights that have intensified the incorporation of LGBT citizens at all levels of government. Canada granted common-law status to same-sex couples in 1999 and full marriage rights in 2005, while Quebec granted civil union rights in 2002. In 2006, the provincial Human Rights Commission held its second inquiry, focusing on the transition from legal to social equality, resulting in an activist focus on eradicating social homophobia and advancing trans rights (see Chapter 4, this volume, for details). At the municipal level, the World Outgames in 2006 had a significant impact on the relationship between LGBT communities and City Hall. At the international human rights conference that launched this event, representatives from all over the world drafted the *Montreal Declaration on Lesbian, Gay, Bisexual, and Transgender Human Rights,* which was adopted by the local city council and submitted to the United Nations. As shown in the third case study, the city also accepted a proposal from the Village merchants association to form a public-private partnership by designating the Village as one of the city's fourteen business improvement areas (see also Chapter 9, this volume).

LGBT Activism and Public Policy Changes: Case Studies

This section presents three case studies that exemplify the ways in which LGBT activists in Montreal have sought to claim rights to the city in different time periods. I begin by describing how activists fought a police morality squad campaign to repress homosexuality during the Olympic clean-up campaign in 1976. I then look at the 1980s, analyzing how the Village was mobilized as a source of gay political power with the election of the city's first openly gay city councillor. I conclude by examining how the formation of a business improve-ment area in the Village has led to the incorporation of LGBT claims to urban space into neoliberal processes of municipal governance. Specifically, I discuss how business interests have used renovation, festivalization, and securitization to limit access to urban public space in the area.

Fighting the Olympic "Clean-up" Campaign, 1975–76

In June 1976, three hundred gays and lesbians took to the streets of Montreal to contest the local police morality squad's sustained attack on their spaces in preparation for the 1976 Summer Olympics. Because it sparked resistance among activists and led to the mobilization of a linguistically divided gay and lesbian community, this event is often described as Montreal's "Stonewall" (see Corriveau 2011, 141). However, as Armstrong and Crage (2006) argue, mobil-ization among American lesbian and gay communities in the 1960s and 1970s was highly dependent on local conditions, including local politics, forms of police repression, levels of organization, and community orientation towards public protest. With these arguments in mind, this section examines how a very large police repression campaign, supported by Canadian criminal law, was met with significant resistance by gay and lesbian activists, leading ultimately to the expansion of the gay liberation movement and the first claims to the right to the city in Montreal.

In terms of police repression in Canada, the period between the passing of Bill C-150 in 1969 and 1975, when the intensification of police raids led activists to believe that there was a campaign to recriminalize gays and lesbians (Warner 2002, 107), is considered to be one of relative calm (Corriveau 2011, 139; Higgins 1999, 122). In Montreal, the increase in police repression in 1975 was linked to the city's preparations to host the Summer Olympics in July 1976.[4] The Drapeau regime and the Montreal police force launched a new morality campaign in order to achieve their ultimate goal: to diminish the presence of "non-conforming populations" in the downtown core at a time when the eyes of the world would be on the city (*Body Politic* 1976; Kinsman and Gentile 2009, 310; Warner 2002, 107). Implemented in 1975, the strategy involved using a pre-existing law for a new purpose. The law regarding "bawdy houses" in the Canadian Criminal Code was originally created to enable the police to raid brothels following a period of surveillance in which they had established evidence of prostitution. An amendment in 1917, however, set the stage for the application of this law to gay establishments: in order to increase police access to massage parlours, "habitual acts of indecency" were added to the definition of a bawdy house (Kinsman and Gentile 2009, 311). Until this time, gay men were primarily policed under the section of the code related to "gross indecency," which, once private acts between consenting adults were decriminalized in 1969, could only be applied in public places such as toilets and parks (Corriveau 2011, 124; Higgins 2011).[5] However, gay sex could still be interpreted as "indecent" and "public" in private spaces where there was a third person present. Therefore, any establishment in which this took place could then be considered public and be treated as a bawdy house (Kinsman and Gentile 2009, 311). Therefore, in 1975, the Montreal police morality squad prepared for raids by surveying the premises for "habitual acts of indecency." They would then forcibly raid them and arrest the found-ins and the operators. By refusing passkeys and choosing forcible entry, they converted the private space of a bathhouse into a public space. As the *Body Politic* (1976, 1) described it: "By this means the police convert sexual activity in private – perfectly lawful – into sexual acts in the presence of a third party: gross indecency."

On 4 February 1975, after six hours of surveillance, the Montreal police broke down the door and raided Sauna Aquarius, a bathhouse in the down-

Julie Podmore

town core, arresting thirty-six men as found-ins in a bawdy house. This was the first time this law had been used for a gay establishment in Canada, and it would set an important precedent in Canadian criminal law (Corriveau 2011, 140; Higgins 1999, 122). After about six months of relative calm, the police suddenly raided five gay bars on the evening of 17 October, all of which were located in the downtown core in close proximity to one another. These raids were described by police as "routine checks" (*Body Politic* 1976). Two weeks later on Halloween, there were more "routine checks" in two downtown establishments, the Limelight and the lesbian bar Baby Face. By November of that year, there were also reports that more than eighty gay men had been arrested that fall for gross indecency in the public spaces of the downtown core (Higgins 2011).

In January and February 1976, the raids began to intensify and their geographical range was extended. In Montreal, the police began to raid gay bathhouses in other areas of the city: uptown, thirteen arrests were made in a raid on Sauna Club, and Sauna Cristal was raided; in the East End, thirty-five men were arrested at Club Baths. In March, Toronto activists also reported that the RCMP had begun to investigate their activities, looking for evidence of plans to demonstrate in Montreal during the Olympics. However, the most intense repression in Montreal was witnessed just before the Olympics when, on the weekend of 13 May, four downtown bars were raided, including the lesbian discotheque Chez Jilly's, and eighty-nine arrests were made at Sauna Neptune. Just to finalize this clampdown, a week later the police raided Club Baths in both Montreal and Ottawa. As the *Body Politic* (1976) summarized the situation, the fifteen months leading up to the Olympics had brought eighteen raids on gay and lesbian establishments, one visit from the RCMP, and had spanned the area from Montreal to Toronto, including Ottawa.

Montreal's gays and lesbians mounted the first communal response in May 1976, and it was organized, visible, and militant. As Sivry (1998, 240) points out, the magnitude of these raids had not been seen in Montreal since the October Crisis in 1970, and the raids in Toronto and Ottawa had made it clear that this police operation was large in scale. The demonstration was organized by CHAR, a broad coalition of gay groups, including gay socialists, university groups, and social services activists and many unaffiliated participants, including a large number of francophone gay men and some lesbians (*Le Berdache* 1981). Their collective demand was for "the immediate retreat of all accusations made against the people arrested during these recent police raids, and an immediate end to police repression against the homosexual community of Montréal, Ottawa and elsewhere" (Faubert 1976).

Representing "the gay community," three hundred people from the coalition took to Montreal's streets on 19 June 1976. This demonstration was notable because of the size and breadth of community representation. It was also notable for the way in which this coalition occupied the streets to claim the right to the city. The demonstrators moved through the central area carrying French and English placards that read "Down with police repression," "God loves us but not the police," and "We want to make love in peace." Some of their messages were also calls to solidarity, such as "Gay women in the streets" and "Lesbian sisters and gay brothers unite."

These claims to the right to the city were underscored by the route of the demonstration. It began at Dominion Square, a place that would become highly symbolic in the late 1970s and early 1980s due to its proximity to the gay bars of the downtown core (Guindon 2001, 7). As the demonstrators moved eastward along Dorchester Street (Boulevard René-Lévesque), they passed the offices of the provincial premier and the Olympic Organizing Committee (Kinsman and Gentile 2009, 313; Sylvestre 1979, 144). Turning south down Saint-Laurent Boulevard they headed towards the headquarters of their repression, and, on Notre-Dame Street, they turned east to march past the court houses, the police headquarters, and City Hall. They finally made their way north to Viger Square, where they held a rally that featured speakers from local groups as well as gay and lesbian activists from other cities (Sylvestre 1979, 144). For the first time, Montreal's "gay community," supported by an emerging pan-Canadian network of activists, claimed the right to the city by moving from the bars of the downtown core into the city's streets.

Mobilizing the Gay Village Vote, 1986

In 1986, Raymond Blain became the first openly gay politician to be elected to public office in Quebec when he was elected to represent the emerging gay village (the Saint-Jacques District) on the Montreal city council.[6] As in other North American cities, the spatial concentration of gay commerce and residence in Montreal's emerging gay village had created the possibility of political representation (Knopp 1997; Nash 2006). As Castells (1983, 163) argues in his famous study of San Francisco, a combination of the social, economic, and physical characteristics of the Castro District created the conditions for the appropriation of this neighbourhood by gay men, resulting in organization and, ultimately, political representation with the election of Harvey Milk to the Board of Supervisors in 1977. In this section, I examine the particular local conditions that led to the election of Blain in 1986. I argue that, in addition to the concentration of the gay population in the Village in the 1980s, other neighbourhood characteristics and municipal regime change were influential factors in his election.

The first expression of an attempt by lesbian and gay activists to influence municipal politics came just before the November 1978 election, when the ADGQ demonstrated in front of City Hall asking the public to vote the Drapeau regime out of office (MacKinnon 1978). However, gay activists would have to wait until the 1986 election to gain formal influence in the municipal arena. For gay activists and the emerging gay village constituency, this election was pivotal as it brought three significant changes to local politics. First, this election made Blain the first openly gay politician to be elected to a large Canadian metropolitan city council, which, in and of itself, was an important event. Second, Blain's party, the Montréal Citizens' Movement (MCM), was the party that finally ousted Drapeau and his Civic Party regime, which had controlled City Hall since 1960. Moreover, it did so by taking a significant portion of the vote: the MCM and its mayoralty candidate, Jean Doré, beat the Civic Party and Claude Dupras (Drapeau's chosen successor) by garnering 67 percent of the vote and winning fifty-five of the fifty-eight seats on the council (Léveillée and Léonard 1987). Finally, the election of Blain, as both a representative of the Saint-Jacques District and a councillor with the majority MCM party, meant that the issues facing the gay constituency could finally be brought into the municipal political arena.

While Blain's election was not necessarily predictable, it is possible to argue that the conditions were just right. Perhaps the most important factor in his success was that he was a candidate with the MCM. Like other progressive reform parties emerging in Canadian inner-city areas in the 1970s and 1980s, the MCM stood for the democratization and decentralization of municipal governance (Lustiger-Thaler and Shragge 1998; Whelan 1991). Backed by the unions and community groups, it stressed the improvement of the quality of life in the urban environment over the megaprojects preferred by the Civic Party. Promoting a new "openness" at City Hall, the integration of grassroots movements, and the local neighbourhood as the arena of engagement, the MCM formula provided excellent conditions for the election of an openly gay candidate in Saint-Jacques in 1986. Indeed, the MCM made a strategic decision before the election to be open about Blain's sexuality, viewing this openness as evidence of its transparent political platform (*Fugues* 1986; Pleau 1990a).

Blain could also rely on the fact that Drapeau's regime had been behind every raid on gay and lesbian bars and gay bathhouses that had taken place in the city since the early 1970s. With an estimated 30 percent of the electorate of the Saint-Jacques District being gay or lesbian (Leclerc 1986), Blain's candidacy created the opportunity to have community-based representation against the Civic Party. His 1986 campaign played to this electorate, encouraging it to be proud by supporting a candidate who had "declared his pride." However, with only 30 percent identifying with this form of solidarity, Blain had to have support from other components of the electorate. Again, the MCM's platform of working with community groups to improve the quality of life in neighbourhoods was crucial. Like many progressive reform parties at the municipal level in Canadian cities in the 1980s, the MCM was a party that brought together working-class community groups and the progressive ideals of the "new urban middle class" who were moving into inner-city neighbourhoods (Ley 1996, 272; Whelan 1991). The MCM had estimated that the remaining 70 percent of the Saint-Jacques electorate was composed of a small group of "yuppies" (20 percent) and a much larger group of "traditional" (50 percent), or working-class, residents (*Body Politic* 1987; Leclerc 1986). Blain was also conscious of the fact that, while the "traditional" residents felt invaded by "yuppies and gays" (Leclerc 1986, 28), an MCM poll showed that 87 percent had no objection to being represented by a gay councillor, as long as he or she represented their interests (*Body Politic* 1987). Therefore, Blain not only made clear that he wanted to be known as "the councillor who is gay rather than the gay councillor," he also sought out support from anti-poverty and tenants rights groups. Furthermore, he chose themes for his campaign that built on common interests: the decentralization of the municipal administration and public security were issues that resonated with both groups, while affordable housing and support for youth were of greater concern for the traditional population (Leclerc 1986, 28). Public security and affordable housing emerged as the predominant themes of his tenure, each, respectively, securing the gay and the working-class vote.

While Blain certainly represented the interests of all of his constituents, he did create a number of initiatives that specifically dealt with municipal issues facing the gay community and the complex politics of claiming gay rights to the city in the Village. While two of the primary concerns of his gay constituency (the AIDS crisis and the application of the rights guaranteed in the Charter) had to be addressed at the provincial and federal levels, he did find innovative ways to work on both of these issues at City Hall. He lobbied the municipal government to extend insurance benefits to employees in same-sex relationships. He also worked to develop a non-disclosure policy for city employees living with HIV, enabling workers to declare their status without fear of exposure and prejudice (Pleau 1988). He worked with AIDS Community

Julie Podmore

Care Montréal (C-SAM) to lobby the provincial government for funding and initiated a campaign that would see safe-sex information posted in all municipal buildings (Blain 1987b; Pleau 1988). In terms of claiming space in the Village, Blain focused on ensuring public security and building community infrastructure. Throughout his tenure, Blain fought for an increase in police foot patrols in order to decrease attacks on gay men leaving Village bars at night. He also formed community-police relations committees to improve the relationship between the gay community and the police (Blain 1987b; Pleau 1988). Finally, in terms of helping to build community infrastructure, Blain provided vacant municipal spaces for the incubation of new institutions. The main institutions he provided for were C-SAM, the new community centre (CCGLM), and the Association of Village Business Owners (ACV) (Pleau 1990b).

Private Claims on Public Gay Village Space

In 2006, the main streets of Montreal's gay village were incorporated and designated as a business improvement area (BIA). Like BIAs elsewhere, the Société de développement commercial du Village (SDC du Village) is a public-private partnership between local business owners and the city of Montreal. Because they galvanize the property and commercial interests of an area, BIAs give these interests the power to rework an area's physical infrastructure, raising important issues related to urban citizenship, political representation, and access to public space (Clough and Vanderbeck 2006; Lewis 2010). In this section, I examine the impact of the creation of the SDC du Village on the politics of public space of the Village since 2006. I argue that, by incorporating gay commercial and property interests in the Village into the process of neoliberal urban governance, the SDC has increased the power of these interests to shape public space, ultimately rendering the Village a politically contested space.

The lobby for the creation of the SDC du Village has its roots in a particular form of LGBT activism that began to develop in the late 1980s: gay business and property interests in the district identified an identity-based consumer market in the area and promoted it as gay commercial and political territory (Collins 2004; Knopp 1997). By the late 1990s, Village business interests were consolidated by founding gay-specific institutions, including the Chambre de commerce gaie du Québec (CCGQ) and the Association des commerçants et professionnels du Village (ACPV) (Passiour 2002). The CCGQ was central to the Rendez-vous Montréal movement, a long-term project to bid for the Gay Games. The push for an SDC in the Village developed alongside this movement as a group of merchants within the ACPV sought to increase its power to secure funding for renovations and influence municipal decision making through the formation of an SDC (Passiour 2002). The ACPV proposal for the SDC was finally accepted by the city in 2005, and the organization was launched in July 2006, just in time for the World Outgames.

Through the SDC du Village, business owners gained more power to shape gay Village space through three primary processes: renovation, festivalization, and securitization. Like SDCs throughout the province, the primary function of the SDC du Village is to bolster the business environment by improving the infrastructure in the area and assisting in its renovation (Québec 2009). This is done by securing and distributing funds for the renovation of local private property (such as the facades of businesses) and lobbying governments for the renovation of public spaces and infrastructure. Another primary task of an SDC is to ensure the maintenance of the environment. The SDC du Village offers a graffiti-removal service and has launched a volunteer cleanliness brigade. The festivalization of the public spaces of the Village is also an important component of its objectives, reflecting the city's plans to make Montreal a "city of culture" by promoting the revitalization of commercial areas through festivalization (Ville de Montréal 2005). Promotional materials celebrate the festival networks of the Village, including partnerships with LGBT festivals such as Gay Pride and the gay and lesbian film festival, and city-wide events such as the fireworks and winter festivals. Finally, a very important component of the SDC's objectives is the securitization of public spaces of the Village. After its founding, the SDC commissioned diagnostic planning studies of the area that highlight "problem" areas (Convercité 2007). Based on these studies, the SDC has pushed for increased lighting in parks, an increase in police patrols, and the displacement of street sex work and drug dealing from the public spaces of the district. Its annual reports also specifically celebrate increases in the number of hours of police patrols in the Village.

The formation of the SDC du Village, therefore, has increased the power of commercial and property interests to influence the physical and social aspects of public spaces in the Village. Exemplary of this aspect of the SDC's activities is the summer Aires Libres, or "Free Space," project. Aires Libres is a pedestrianization project in which the main commercial street of the Village is closed to automobiles for four months during the summer. Free of cars, the road is transformed into a space for pedestrians, and the sidewalks are appropriated by restaurant and bar owners for outdoor terraces. The SDC's production of "free space" distinctively festivalizes the public space of the area. During the summer, the street is transformed through the appropriation and decoration of the public spaces. It is also used to support a number of LGBT festivals, such as Divers/Cité and the pride parade known as Fierté Montréal Pride as well as a two-week open-air arts festival known as GaleRue d'Art. The public spaces are also decorated with art and installations that specifically reflect LGBT identities and the SDC's vision of the Village.

While the production of the Village as a free space has opened this LGBT commercial area to a larger consumer base, it has also raised issues regarding access to its public spaces. As Hanhardt's (2008) research on New York and San Francisco suggests, discourses of anti-gay violence in gentrifying LGBT districts are often mobilized to defend homonormative property interests against "undesirable" street life. In the case of Montreal, a chaotic discourse regarding public space, property, and security is being promoted by the SDC. On the one hand, this discourse highlights the victimizaton of LGBT populations, stressing a recent increase in gay bashing in the Village (see Lefebvre 2012); on the other hand, it also specifically identifies "undesirable" street life as the source of that vulnerability. The SDC has been lobbying the government to address what it argues is an increase in the presence of homeless people and drug dealing in the mini-parks and on the streets of the Village.

Two events in 2011 demonstrated the power of the SDC to shape social outcomes in the Village using this discourse. First, business owners successfully rallied together to contest a proposal for a safe-injection site in the area (Passiour 2011). Second, two thousand Village business owners and residents signed an SDC petition requesting significant improvements to public security in the area (Lafontaine 2011). The petition was launched by a local business owner following an incident with a group of homeless people in front of his business. Supporters of the petition argued that, by turning a blind eye to the increase in homelessness in the area, "the city and province expect an already vulnerable community – gays and lesbians – to take on the responsibility of integrating these people back into society" (de la Cuetra 2011).

Reactions to the petition highlight the specific ways in which, through the creation of the SDC, gay commercial interests have been empowered at the expense of other interests in the area. The SDC du Village argues that problems of security in the Village are due to the disproportionate concentration of social service agencies in the area. Groups representing homeless populations and drug users argue that the district has long been an important site of social service provision for these populations and that the location has been central to building outreach programs (*2B Magazine* 2011). The petition also caused controversy among queer activists who questioned the SDC's normative assumptions and its capacity to fully represent the city's LGBT populations. For example, Queer McGill's Political Action Working Group held a demonstration in the Village against the petition in October 2011. It denounced the petition for its claims to represent all people who use the Village, and it opposed increased police repression and the gentrification of the Village (Temmerman 2011). PolitiQ Queers, a radical queer community organization, argued that the petition to rid the Village of homelessness amounted to the criminalization of poverty (Pieuvre 2011).

Although the city's initial reaction to the petition was to cede to police observations that there had been no statistical increase in crimes committed in the Village in recent years, it eventually supported two of the SDC's proposed securitization projects. The "J'aime mon village" campaign was launched in March 2012 to combat crime and homophobic violence in the Village. The stated objective of this pilot project is to promote "pride" in the Village in order to encourage victims of violence to report crimes to police (Passiour 2012a, para. 3). Local Village celebrities, many of whom are business owners, are figured as "superheroes" defending queer populations from violence and cleaning up crime in the Village. A second city-funded pilot project, "Une cohabitation à maintenir," targets "vagrancy" in the public spaces of the Village (Passiour 2012b, 16). Two LGBT social workers have been hired to patrol the streets and to intervene when conflicts arise by connecting street-identified people with the appropriate social service agencies. The stated goals of this project are to reduce "undesirable behaviours" and "incivility" in the Village and to increase the overall sense of security (ibid.).

Conclusion

The primary goal of this chapter is to examine the unique processes shaping LGBT claims to the right to the city in Montreal over the past forty years. As I demonstrate, Montreal's LGBT activist history has been shaped not only by its unique situation as the primary urban centre of Quebec but also by broader processes at the national scale as well as by local urban politics. In this sense, many elements of Montreal's story indicate important departures from those of Toronto and Vancouver (for more details, see Chapters 9 and 10, respectively, this volume). At the same time, there is a more universally instructive component to this interpretation of LGBT claims to a right to the city in Montreal. The case studies detail a shift from a fight against police repression in the 1970s, through the development of LGBT territory and the mobilization of the gay vote in order to gain political representation in the 1980s, ending with a public-private partnership formed in recent years between the merchants

Julie Podmore

of Montreal's Gay Village and the city. This progression provides an example of LGBT activism that is far from the ideals of the right to the city expressed by Harvey (2003): while earlier claims on access to urban space focused on collective rights and social justice, these current claims highlight property and commercial interests (see also Floyd 2009). As more legal rights have been gained at other scales of citizenship, inclusion in municipal governance has also increased, resulting in increased access to and control over material space in the city. As a result of these inclusions, current LGBT claims to the right to the city have become increasingly normative and exclusionary, suggesting that urban governance – as at the federal and provincial scales – is in much need of critical analysis.

Notes

1 It should be noted that many francophone lesbians were active within the radical feminist movement in the early 1970s, especially in the activities at the Centre des femmes. On the centrality of feminist organizing for francophone lesbian activists in the 1970s, see Chamberland (2000) and Lamoureux (1998).

2 Before the conference, ACT UP worked with Toronto's AIDS ACTION NOW! to develop *The Montreal Manifesto*, a human rights declaration for people living with AIDS. Both groups joined with Montréal's Réaction SIDA to disrupt the plenary session of the conference and to present this declaration to the audience.

3 For example, as Namaste's (2000, 153) research suggests, the emphasis on the experiences of gay men and on the space of the gay village in the queer anti-violence movement in the early 1990s makes it clear that the concerns of trans activists were being sidelined by the mainstream movement. Anti-racist, anti-colonial, and ethnic identity groups also saw the need to create their own distinct movements during this period (see, for example, Chapter 2, this volume) often in relation to AIDS politics (Warner 2002, 255). Some lesbian activists also mobilized to create a separate movement after the 1993 commission, forming the Réseau des lesbiennes du Québec in 1996 (Demczuk and Remiggi 1998, 404).

4 As Kinsman and Gentile (2009, 310) argue, the campaign against gay and lesbian spaces and populations during preparations for the 1976 Olympics was part of a much larger policing campaign that was developed in response to an increase in gay activist organizing and the increased public visibility of gay populations, establishments, and organizations.

5 Despite the partial decriminalization brought by Bill C-150, the police continued to arrest men involved in homosexual relations using a variety of different charges, including "indecent actions," "indecent assault," and sodomy (see Corriveau 2011, 123–25). Even when these acts were consensual and conducted in private, the burden of proof remained with the defendant (124).

6 In 1986, local papers such as the *Montreal Gazette* claimed that Blain was the first openly gay person to be elected to public office in Canada. This is not entirely accurate. In 1979, Robert Douglas Cook of Vancouver was the first to seek public office as an openly gay candidate in the provincial election. He was followed in 1980 by George Hislop of Toronto

(see Chapter 9, this volume), who unsuccessfully campaigned for election to the Ontario provincial legislature. In fact, Jim Egan was the "first openly gay man living in an openly gay relationship to be elected to public office in Canada" when he was elected to the regional district of Comox-Strathcona in 1981 (Egan, quoted in Chapter 6, this volume, p. 142).

References

2B Magazine. 2011. "Homelessness in the Village: Turning the Lights on." 19 December. http://www.2bmag.com.

Armstrong, Elizabeth A., and Suzanna M. Crage. 2006. "Movements and Memory: The Making of the Stonewall Myth." *American Sociological Review* 71 (5): 724–51. http://dx.doi.org/10.1177/000312240607100502.

Bell, David, and Jon Binnie. 2000. *The Sexual Citizen: Queer Politics and Beyond.* Cambridge: Polity Press.

Berdache, Le. 1981. "Dossier anniversaire: 10 ans de militantisme gai." 20 May, 43–53.

Blain, Raymond. 1987a. "Des rapprochements significatifs entre la police et la communauté gaie montréalaise." *RG* 55 (April): 9.

–. 1987b. "Le RCM appuie la lutte contre le sida." *RG* 56 (May): 9.

Body Politic. 1976. "Olympic Crackdown." August, 1.

–. 1987. "Looking for Legitimacy: Montreal Voters Clean House, Elect First Openly Gay City Councillor." January, 11.

Burnett, Richard. 2009. "We Built This City." *Fugues* 26 (1): 166–68.

Castells, Manuel. 1983. *The City and the Grassroots: A Cross-Cultural Theory of Urban Social Movements.* London: Edward Arnold.

Chamberland, Line. 2000. "Québec." In Bonnie Zimmerman, ed., *Encyclopedia of Lesbian Histories and Cultures*, 627–29. New York: Garland.

Clough, Nathan, and Robert Vanderbeck. 2006. "Managing Politics and Consumption in Business Improvement Districts: The Geographies of Political Activism on Burlington, Vermont's Church Street Market Place." *Urban Studies* (Edinburgh, Scotland) 43 (12): 2261–84. http://dx.doi.org/10.1080/00420980600936517.

Collins, Alan. 2004. "Sexual Dissidence, Enterprise and Assimilation: Bedfellows in Urban Regeneration." *Urban Studies* (Edinburgh, Scotland) 41 (9): 1789–806. http://dx.doi.org/10.1080/0042098042000243156.

Commission des droits de la personne (CDPQ). 1994. *De l'illégalité à l'égalité: Rapport de la consultation publique sur la violence et la discrimination envers les gais et lesbiennes.* Québec/Montréal: La Commission, May.

Convercité. 2007. *Une monde, un village: La destination gaie.* Montréal: SDC du Village.

Corriveau, Patrice. 2011. *Judging Homosexuals: A History of Gay Persecution in Quebec and France.* Trans. Käthe Roth. Vancouver: UBC Press. Originally published as *La répression des homosexuels au Québec et en France: Du bûcher à la mairie* (Ville de Québec: Septentrion, 2006).

Côté, Isabel, and Jacques L. Boucher. 2008. "La mouvance sociale des personnes gaies, lesbiennes, bisexuelles, transexuelles et transgenres." *Bulletin d'Histoire Politique* 16 (3): 89–100.

Crawford, Jason B., and Karen Herland. 2014. "Sex Garage: Unspooling Narratives, Rethinking Collectivities." *Journal of Canadian Studies/Revue d'études canadiennes* 48 (1): 106–31.

de la Cuetra, Ines. 2011. "Village Residents Petition Mayor: 2000 Signatures Call For Heightened Security in the Borough." *McGill Daily* 101 (7): 7.

Demczuk, Irène, and Frank W. Remiggi. 1998. "Conclusion: À l'aube du prochain millénaire." In Irène Demczuk and Frank W. Remiggi, eds., *Sortir de l'ombre: Histoires des communautés lesbienne et gaie de Montréal*, 399–405. Montréal: VLB éditeur.

Faubert, Thérèse. 1976. "Les gais disent non au 'nettoyage Olympique.'" *Liberation* (Montreal), July.

Floyd, Kevin. 2009. *The Reification of Desire: Toward a Queer Marxism*. Minneapolis: University of Minnesota Press.

Fugues. 1986. "Entrevue: Raymond Blain, candidat gai." 3 (7): 42.

Guindon, Jocelyn M. 2001. "La contestation des espaces gais au centre-ville de Montréal depuis 1950." PhD diss., McGill University.

Hanhardt, Christina B. 2008. "Butterflies, Whistles and Fists: Gay Safe Streets Patrols and the New Gay Ghetto, 1976-1981." *Radical History Review* 100: 61–85. http://dx.doi.org/10.1215/01636545-2007-022.

Harvey, David. 2003. "The Right to the City." *International Journal of Urban and Regional Research* 27 (4): 939–41. http://dx.doi.org/10.1111/j.0309-1317.2003.00492.x.

Higgins, Ross. 1999. *De la clandestinité à l'affirmation: Pour une histoire de la communauté gaie montréalaise*. Montréal: Comeau and Nadeau.

–. 2011. "La régulation sociale de l'homosexualité." In Patrice Corriveau and Valérie Daoust, eds., *La régulation sociale des minorités sexuelles: L'inquiétude de la différence*, 82–120. Ville de Québec: Presses de l'Université du Québec.

Hildebran, Andrea. 1998. "Genèse d'une communauté lesbienne: Un récit des années 1970." In Irène Demczuk and Frank W. Remiggi, eds., *Sortir de l'ombre: Histoires des communautés lesbienne et gaie de Montréal*, 207–33. Montréal: VLB éditeur.

Hunt, Mia, and John Zacharias. 2008. "Marketing the Imaginary of Montréal's (Gay) Village." *Canadian Journal of Urban Research* 17 (1): 28–57.

Kinsman, Gary, and Patrizia Gentile. 2009. *The Canadian War on Queers: National Security and Sexual Regulation*. Vancouver: UBC Press.

Knopp, Lawrence. 1997. "Gentrification and Gay Neighbourhood Formation in New Orleans: A Case Study." In Amy Gluckman and Betsy Reed, eds., *Homo Economics: Capitalism, Community, and Lesbian and Gay Life*, 45–63. New York: Routledge.

Lafontaine, Yves. 2011. "Une pétition pour lutter contre le sentiment d'insécurité dans le Village." *Fugues en ligne*, 4 August. http://www.fugues.com.

Lamoureux, Diane. 1998. "La question lesbienne dans le féminisme montréalaise: Un chassé-croisé." In Irène Demczuk and Frank W. Remiggi, eds., *Sortir de l'ombre: Histoires des communautés lesbienne et gaie de Montréal*, 167–85. Montréal: VLB éditeur.

Lavoie, René. 1998. "Deux solitudes: Les organismes sida et la communauté gaie." In Irène Demczuk and Frank W. Remiggi, eds., *Sortir de l'ombre: Histoires des communautés lesbienne et gaie de Montréal*, 337–62. Montréal: VLB éditeur.

Leclerc, Roger. 1986. "Un conseiller municipal gai ou un gai conseiller municipal?" *Sortie* 42 (October): 28–29.

Lefebvre, Sarah-Maude. 2012. "Agressions dans le village gai: Le SPVM lance un formulaire de dénonciation." *24 Heures*, 20 June. http://24hmontreal.canoe.ca/24hmontreal/actualites/archives/2010/10/20101014-162629.html.

Léobon, Alain. 2006. "Champs de libertés et construction de territoires homo et bisexuels en France et au Québec." In Raymonde Séchet and Vincent Veschambre, eds., *Penser et faire la géographie sociale: Contributions à une épistémologie de la géographie sociale*, 277–94. Rennes: Presses Universitaires de Rennes.

Léveillée, Jacques, and Jean-François Léonard. 1987. "The Montreal Citizens' Movement Comes to Power." *International Journal of Urban and Regional Research* 11 (4): 567–80. http://dx.doi.org/10.1111/j.1468-2427.1987.tb00067.x.

Lewis, Nathaniel M. 2010. "Grappling with Governance: The Emergence of Business Improvement Districts in a National Capital." *Urban Affairs Review* 46 (2): 180–217. http://dx.doi.org/10.1177/1078087410378844.

Ley, David. 1996. *The New Middle Class and the Remaking of the Central City.* Oxford: Oxford University Press.

Lustiger-Thaler, Henri, and Eric Shragge. 1998. "The New Urban Left: Parties without Actors." *International Journal of Urban and Regional Research* 22 (2): 233–44. http://dx.doi.org/10.1111/1468-2427.00137.

MacKinnon, John. 1978. "Gays Want Drapeau Out, Police Restrained." *The Georgian*, 10 November.

Namaste, Viviane K. 2000. *Invisible Lives: The Erasure of Transsexual and Transgendered People.* Chicago: University of Chicago Press.

Nash, Catherine Jean. 2006. "Toronto's Gay Village, 1969–1982: Plotting the Politics of Gay Identity." *Canadian Geographer/Géographe canadien* 50 (1): 1–16. http://dx.doi.org/10.1111/j.0008-3658.2006.00123.x.

Passiour, André-Constantin. 2002. "Le Village vue par Bernard Rousseau." *Fugues* 19 (4): 46–48.

–. 2011. "Conseil d'arrondissement: L'itinérance et les incivilités au cœur des préoccupations." *Fugues* 28 (7): 20.

–. 2012a. "J'aime mon village!" *Fugues en ligne*, 17 February. http://www.fugues.com/main.cfm?l=fr&p=100_Article&article_id=20313&rubrique_ID=152.

–. 2012b. "Réduction des méfaits et sentiment de sécurité dans le Village: Un nouveau programme démarre!" *Fugues* 29 (4): 16–18.

Pieuvre. 2011. "Objectif: Se réapproprier le Village." *Pieuvre.ca*, 7 October. http://www.pieuvre.ca/2011/10/07/village-police/.

Pleau, Marcel. 1988. "L'administration RCM s'attaque au SIDA." *RG* 75 (December): 10–12.

–. 1990a. "Doré: Un maire à notre goût?" *RG* 97 (October):10–15.

–. 1990b. "Raymond Blain confiant de l'emporter." *RG* 98 (November): 10.

Podmore, Julie A. 2006. "Gone 'Underground'? Lesbian Visibility and the Consolidation of Queer Space in Montreal." *Social and Cultural Geography* 7 (4): 595–625. http://dx.doi.org/10.1080/14649360600825737.

Québec, Développement économique, Innovation et Exportation. 2009. *La société de développement commercial: Une force économique.* Ville de Québec: Gouvernement du Québec, Direction générale des communications et des services à la clientèle.

Ray, Brian. 2004. "A Diversity Paradox: Montreal's Gay Village." In Caroline Andrew, ed., *Our Diverse Cities*, 72–75. Ottawa: Canadian Federation of Municipalities. http://canada.metropolis.net/research-policy/cities/publication/diverse_cite_magazine_e.pdf.

Remiggi, Frank W. 2000. "Homosexualité et espace urbain." *Téoros: Revue de recherche en tourisme* 19 (2): 28–35.

Sivry, Jean-Michel. 1998. "Traces militantes éphémères: L'ADGQ et Le Berdache." In Irène Demczuk and Frank W. Remiggi, eds., *Sortir de l'ombre: Histoires des communautés lesbienne et gaie de Montréal*, 235–63. Montréal: VLB éditeur.

Smith, Miriam. 1998. "Nationalisme et politiques des mouvements sociaux: Les droits des gais et lesbiennes et l'incidence de la charte canadienne au Québec." *Politique et Sociétés* 17 (3): 113–40. http://dx.doi.org/10.7202/040131ar.

–. 1999. *Lesbian and Gay Rights in Canada: Social Movements and Equality-Seeking, 1971–1995.* Toronto: University of Toronto Press.

Sylvestre, Paul-François. 1979. *Les homosexuels s'organisent: Au Québec et ailleurs.* Montréal: Les Éditions Homeureux.

Temmerman, Thibaut. 2011. "Manifestation contre 'l'embourgeoisement' du Village et la répression policière." *Être en ligne,* 8 October. http://www.etre.net/manifestation-contre-la-gentrification-du-village-et-la-repression-policiere.

Ville de Montréal. 2005. *Montréal, Cultural Metropolis: Cultural Development Policy of the Ville de Montréal.* Montréal: Ville de Montréal.

Warner, Tom. 2002. *Never Going Back: A History of Queer Activism in Canada.* Toronto: University of Toronto Press.

Whelan, Robert K. 1991. "The Politics of Urban Redevelopment in Montreal: Regime Change from 'Drapeau to Doré.'" *Quebec Studies* 12: 155–69. http://dx.doi.org/10.3828/qs.12.1.155.

9

Gay and Lesbian Political Mobilization in Urban Spaces: Toronto

CATHERINE J. NASH

This chapter details the complex and often contradictory relationships between and among gay and lesbian organizations in Toronto and various levels
of state government from the 1970s to the present day.[1] I highlight how these
organizations, buffeted by changing political and social climates, both contributed to and were reconstituted by various substantive legislative and public
policy transformations largely arising from their political advocacy. These
transformations included reworked understandings of homosexual "identity,"
new understandings about the relationship between gays and lesbians and
mainstream society, and changing perspectives on Toronto's gay "Village," currently promoted as one of Toronto's major tourist attractions.

I begin with a necessarily brief overview of prominent gay and lesbian political organizations in Toronto over the last forty years, offering a summary of
their ideological approaches and their shifting perspectives on the emerging
gay village. While any attempt to offer a periodization for forms or "types" of
political activism is fraught with difficulty, given the unevenness and complexity of historical developments, the discussion here is meant as a rough overview of political activism in Toronto during this period. The next section
details three case studies exploring the intersections between local gay and
lesbian political organizing and their engagements with various levels of government. The final section offers some thoughts on the current state of political organizing in Toronto.

Historical Background

From the early 1970s to the present, gay and lesbian organizations in Toronto, as elsewhere, espoused varying and not necessarily compatible ideological perspectives underpinning their political agendas. These include the early 1970s "assimilationist" perspectives, the overlapping and more radical "liberationist" approach of the 1980s and 1990s, and an ethnic minority and/or neo-assimilationist approach from the 1990s onward (Nash 2005, 2006; for other ways of rendering the ideological diversities among queer activism see Chapters 7 and 10, this volume). Various organizations and their competing agendas often overlapped, and, although some might argue that a liberationist agenda disappeared by the mid-1980s, others argue that strains of a liberationist perspective continue to inform LGBT politics to the present day (Warner 2002, 5-6). What follows is an admittedly truncated account of the highly contested ideologies driving the gay and lesbian political agenda, but it provides the necessary conceptual framework for understanding the constitutive intersections between gay movement political engagements, governmental positions, and Toronto's gay and lesbian spaces (on queer activism in Ontario more generally, see Chapter 3, this volume).

The University of Toronto Homophile Association (UTHA), founded in October 1969, was the first homosexual organization in Toronto. A second, more broadly based community organization, Community Homophile Association of Toronto (CHAT), was founded in 1971. Both UTHA and CHAT were largely assimilationist in their activism, their main goal being to ensure the inclusion of homosexuals in all facets of mainstream society. CHAT's stated mission was "educating the community about homosexuality, working to combat discrimination against homosexuality and bringing a social and personal acceptance of homosexuality" (McLeod 1996, 46). CHAT worked to present homosexuals as "normal," recommending they adopt "a pattern of behaviour acceptable to society ... in the recognized institutions of home, church and state" and that they strive to reflect middle-class values and a conservative sensibility (Escoffier 1997, 42). CHAT worked with local social service agencies, provided guest speakers for radio and television interviews, and lecturers for public talks to teachers, nursing, and health organizations. CHAT also offered legal, medical, and psychiatric referrals and supported local research initiatives. Perhaps CHAT's most important contribution was the establishment of a community centre on Church Street in the 1970s, providing gays and lesbians with a place to socialize, digest the latest medical information on homosexuality, and learn about homosexual activism in the United

States and Europe. CHAT hoped this would help to engender political awareness and greater participation in local politics (Nash 2005, 2006).

Along with CHAT and UTHA, a more radical "liberationist" perspective surfaced in gay and lesbian politics with the formation of Toronto Gay Action (TGA) in July 1971 – an organization originally associated with CHAT but that was asked to leave. Rather than taking a conservative, assimilationist approach to the inclusion of homosexuals in everyday life, through education and quiet diplomacy, TGA was "devoted to peaceful confrontation with all elements of sexist oppression" (McLeod 1996, 71). TGA organized one of the first public protests on 28 August 1971 on Parliament Hill to mark the anniversary of the 1969 partial decriminalization of homosexuality through amendments to the Criminal Code and to continue to agitate against the amendment's shortcomings, including, for example, the age of consent being twenty-one years of age for homosexuals. The influential newspaper *Body Politic* was founded in 1971, and the Gay Alliance Towards Equality (GATE) replaced TGA in 1973. Both were largely liberationist, and the *Body Politic*, in its editorial stance, perceived itself as "a radical tabloid born of political conviction and a hunger for change" (Jackson and Persky 1982, 2).

Liberationists rejected assimilationist claims for the integration of gays and lesbians into mainstream society and pursued a more aggressive strategy of gender and sexual liberation for both heterosexuals and homosexuals. Taking a more historically nuanced and constructionist stance, liberationists argued that humans were born essentially polymorphous and bisexual, only to have that sexual fluidity rigorously constrained within a narrow and mutually reinforcing sex/gender system (Seidman 1997, 114). Liberationists argued against the assertion that there was some form of distinct homosexual identity as such a position worked against the goal of sexual liberation. CHAT, TGA, and the *Body Politic* co-existed uneasily in the early 1970s, espousing distinctly different views about the nature of same-sex desire; yet both liberationists and assimilationists agreed that the emerging "gay ghetto" was a form of forced segregation and discouraged gays and lesbians from frequenting homosexual establishments (Nash 2006).

By the late 1970s, both liberationist and assimilationist groups increasingly supported a human rights strategy designed to incorporate "sexual orientation" into provincial and federal human rights legislation. Scholars argue that the human rights agenda inadvertently worked against the liberationists' goal of emancipation from constructed sex/gender roles. This is because the

Catherine J. Nash

protection of sexual orientation required that "sexuality" and "gender" be presented as inherent and defining characteristics of an individual – a representation totally at odds with the liberationist conception of the homosexual subject as socially constructed and, therefore, as an entirely erasable category of identity (Smith 1999, 141–44). The human rights agenda engendered the representation of gays and lesbians as an "ethnic minority" group with a unique subculture that included literature, music, arts, social customs, and an identifiable territorial neighbourhood. Such a representation supported a politic that agitated for human rights protections, family recognition, military inclusion, and, ultimately, same-sex marriage.

From the 1980s to the present day, gay and lesbian activism in Toronto has largely focused on human rights and family status protections. The predominant focus was on obtaining the inclusion of "sexual orientation" as a protected class in provincial and federal legislation (Herman 1994, 5). The Toronto-based Coalition for Gay Rights Ontario (CGRO) battled against a vitriolic anti-gay religious conservative backlash to see the inclusion of human rights protection in the Ontario Bill of Rights in 1985. The Supreme Court of Canada (SCC) decision in *R. v. Egan* (1995) "read in" sexual orientation as a protected class under section 15 of the Charter of Rights and Freedoms (for more details on the *Egan* decision, see Chapter 6, this volume). A series of court decisions in the 1980s and 1990s ensured that gays and lesbians could serve openly in the military and in the Royal Canadian Mounted Police and that they had access to pension and health benefits and, finally, in 2005, to marriage (Rayside 2008, 119–20).

During the same period, a more radical liberationist agenda continued to surface on occasion (Warner 2002, 192). As Warner argues, the onslaught of HIV/AIDS in the early 1980s funnelled liberationist activist energies into protesting government inaction and lobbying for funding for support services, most of which were located in the gay village district downtown, thus contributing to its consolidation as the material core of gay and lesbian life (248; Nash 2006; on how HIV/AIDS encouraged queer activism, see Chapters 2 and 10, this volume). The AIDs Committee of Toronto (ACT), formed in June 1983, spearheaded much of the work for service provision, patient support, public education, and fundraising. At the same time, the diversity and complexity of the gay and lesbian community became clear with the formation of a wide-ranging set of community groups, including organizations for gays and lesbians with disabilities, gays and lesbians of colour, and gay Asians as well as an eclectic mix of interest groups, such as sports leagues, cycling and rowing clubs, and book clubs (Warner 2002, 163, 326).

Queer Activism Today

In the decades after the Second World War, Toronto developed a visibly concentrated homosexual population that circulated through various social and commercial networks in the downtown core, demarcated by quite porous boundaries to the east along Parliament, west to Spadina, south to Front Street, and north to Bloor Street West. Along with the establishment of groups such as CHAT and UTHA came the development of a number of gay- and lesbian-owned/operated businesses (including bathhouses, restaurants, bookstores, and newspapers) and the residential neighbourhood centred, today, around the Church Street and Yonge Street area. Gay men, in particular, were involved in the gentrification of housing stock in the surrounding residential districts (Nash 2006). Although lesbians certainly frequented these downtown areas from the 1970s onward, they have not developed a similar territorial visibility (Podmore 2006). In the 1950s and 1960s, working-class lesbians met in several downtown bars and taverns (Chenier 1995) and in places established through lesbian feminist activism in the 1970s (Ross 1995, 3–16). Today, lesbians and queer women continue to make use of gay village spaces, but they also frequent other areas, such as the Parkdale neighbourhood (Nash 2013a).

Gay activists did not universally greet the emergence of a so-called gay village or gay ghetto as a positive development for gays and lesbians. For assimilationists and early liberationists, the gay ghetto was understood as a location of exclusion and marginalization. By the late 1970s, however, many regarded the gay district as providing much needed political, social, and economic support, although tensions between gay activists and gay businesses surfaced often. As well, the existence of a territorial base legitimized gays and lesbians as a minority group. By the end of the 1990s, the Village was fully incorporated into Toronto's urban fabric, marked with rainbow flags and gay imagery and complete with its own municipally constituted Business Improvement Association (BIA) (in the same vein, see Chapter 8, this volume).

Queer Activism and Public Policy Changes: Case Studies

Three cases studies illustrate how engagement with multiple and overlapping forms of state regulation shaped the political activism that, in turn, helped to rework public policy on gays and lesbians across a variety of scales. The first case study considers gay activist George Hislop's candidacy for municipal office in 1980, illustrating an assimilationist model of gay and lesbian activism. The second case study examines the fallout around the laying of "obscenity"

Catherine J. Nash

charges against Toronto's Glad Day Bookshop for the sale of an issue of *Bad Attitude*, a lesbian magazine, and illustrates how local organizations can be caught up in larger debates about sexual identities and practices at both the provincial level and (as in this case) the federal level. The final case study examines the very recent battles around the inclusion (or not) of the group Queers against Israeli Apartheid (QuAIA) in Toronto's pride parade in 2010 and 2011. The political (and very public) divisions among community groups, including LGBT groups, over QuAIA pride participation illustrates the contemporary interweaving of political and social discourses across multiple scales, from the neighbourhood to the international/global.

Gay Power and Municipal Politics

In 1980, George Hislop, a prominent local activist and president of CHAT, became the first openly gay candidate to run for municipal office in Toronto (see Chapter 8, this volume, for a case study of Quebec's first openly gay political official, Raymond Blain; see also the discussion of BC's Jim Egan in Chapter 6 of this volume). Those spearheading Hislop's campaign argued that Ward 6's substantial lesbian and gay population would throw its support behind a gay candidate (Trow 1980). The Association of Gay Electors (AGE) argued that participation in local politics was necessary for the development of a "mature" gay and lesbian community and would help educate mainstream populations on issues of importance to gays and lesbians (AGE 1979, 1980). Many regarded Hislop's candidacy as an event that, "win or lose[,] would define for years to come the course of our relations with society around us" (Trow 1980). Not everyone supported Hislop, and liberationists in particular regarded him as too assimilationist and inclined towards accommodation and compromise. The Ward 6 Community Association, an established mainstream neighbourhood group, also endorsed Hislop, asserting he was well able to represent the district on a wide range of issues, not just those of importance to homosexuals (Laver 1980).

Hislop's campaign garnered little mainstream attention until receiving a public endorsement by the incumbent mayor, John Sewell, in September 1980, although the response to Sewell's endorsement was largely negative. Mayoralty candidate Art Eggleton warned that Toronto risked becoming a "San Francisco North" if the homosexual population actually had any political clout. Eggleton also argued that Hislop's candidacy was evidence of a wider and more insidious "homosexual agenda" operating beyond Toronto and Canada itself, and he claimed that "homosexual people from SF are coming here" to help Hislop (McCann 1980a; see also Donato 1980). A *Toronto Sun* editorial speculated that the 300,000 homosexuals in Toronto constituted a new "in" minority, making Toronto the "San Francisco of Canada as a Mecca for homosexuals." *Sun* columnist Claire Hoy (1980a) condemned Sewell for his alliance with Hislop, calling it "disgusting" that Sewell "ha[d] decided to jump into bed ... with homosexual activist George Hislop." Some pundits intimated that Sewell himself might be a homosexual (*Toronto Star* 1980c).

Warner (2002, 138) argues that the references to so-called gay power politics drew on a CBS documentary aired in Toronto, 26 April 1980, entitled "Gay Power, Gay Politics," which examined the influence of the gay population on San Francisco politics (see also Lynch 1980). The broadcast argued that the homosexual agenda endangered children and youth and that homosexuals were taking over public parks and infiltrating the school system with gay propaganda. Kinsman (1996, 334) argues that the show influenced the Canadian media in their portrayal of Toronto's gay community as being made up of a "gay elite" consisting of "white male businessmen, religious figures, professionals and politicians" that had the power and financial clout to influence local politics.

Anti-homosexual opposition was also well-organized, targeting both Sewell and Hislop. Ken Campbell, an anti-gay evangelical Christian, vowed to use "sophisticated straights" to get rid of the "radical homosexual fringe" in municipal elections (Hoy 1980b). A rally against the "deadly game of gay power politics" was held in Nathan Philips Square in October 1980 and was attended by some 250 people, including members of the Salvation Army, Campbell's Renaissance Ontario, and a group called Positive Parents (ibid.). The goal, according to organizers, was to defeat Sewell and Hislop on the grounds that gay involvement in politics was designed to "legalize pedophilia and pervert children" (Hluchy 1980). Many who had received anti-homosexual campaign literature from these various groups described it as "hateful" and "vicious" and dismissed opponents as right-wing religious "fanatics" (Stein 1980).

As the election campaign unfolded, many in the mainstream press developed a more nuanced approach, and debates emerged over whether there was a sufficiently cohesive "gay vote" to sway the election. Some claimed that with some ten to twelve thousand homosexuals living in Ward 6, a Hislop victory was all but assured (McCann 1980b), while others asserted it was not clear what influence homosexuals might have on city politics (Horsford 1980). The *Sun,* in its examination of gay voting "power," argued that calling homosexuals a "legitimate minority group like blacks" was ludicrous (*Toronto Sun* 1980a). The *Sun*'s Claire Hoy (1980b) argued that homosexuals' claim of minority

Catherine J. Nash

group status equal to "blacks, East Indians, the elderly and women ... [was] an insult to legitimate minority groups." While mainstream commentators seemed prepared to entertain the idea that gays and lesbians constituted some sort of social group, they remained divided over the exact characterization and legitimacy of such a group.

Both Hislop and Sewell were narrowly defeated in the 10 November elections, and post-election analysis focused on the role, if any, of the so-called gay vote. The *Globe and Mail* argued that the gay issue was central to Sewell's defeat, particularly his "alignment with the city's first openly homosexual aldermanic candidate" (Horsford and Jefferson 1980). The *Sun* argued that Sewell was defeated, in part, because of his "grabbing onto the coattails of the homosexuals" and because "decent people with a sense of propriety voted against him" (Sabia 1980). The dual loss also suggested that "gay voting muscle" simply did not exist (Downing 1980).

Hislop himself argued the loss was a result of poor voter turnout and the success of the anti-gay message, although he was not prepared to conclude categorically that Torontonians were anti-homosexual ("Losing and Learning" 1980, 21; Chapman 1980). The winner in Ward 6, Dan Chong, denied that anti-gay sentiments were at work and suggested that Hislop's strong ties with Alan Sparrow, the previous alderman, contributed to his defeat (Chapman 1980). Gay commentators argued the local gay and lesbian population was largely apolitical and too complacent (Jackson 1980–81). Nevertheless, the experience was regarded as a "right of passage," helping gays and lesbians to develop a collective sense of identity and a politicized community (ibid.).

Hislop's candidacy and his ultimate defeat illustrates the broad range of perceptions about gays and lesbians, both individually and collectively, and the fears about the territoriality of a gay and lesbian "community." His candidacy was grounded in an assimilationist sensibility that argued that homosexuals should be fully integrated, as homosexuals, into mainstream society. Concerns that Toronto might become a "San Francisco North" reflected a growing mainstream awareness that gay and lesbian political activism coupled with a territorial base might legitimately influence local politics. Gay commentary represented gays and lesbians as constituting a cohesive group and as a distinctive yet integrated minority with a territorial presence (e.g., Bearchell and Jackson 1980, 24). Taken together, by the early 1980s, the general perception was that gays and lesbians were a legitimate minority ably engaged in local political and economic ventures as a recognized, albeit contested, community.

Glad Day Bookshop and the Lesbian Magazine *Bad Attitude*

This case study examines the circumstances surrounding the 1992 trial of Toronto's Glad Day Bookshop on obscenity charges for the sale of the lesbian magazine *Bad Attitude*. First, this case study illustrates the ways in which Canada Customs, a federal agency, sought to limit or eradicate certain forms of lesbian literature available at the local community level. Second, it illustrates the internal disagreements between anti-pornography and anti-censorship feminists and how the ideological perspectives of anti-pornography feminists shaped Canadian law with unexpected outcomes. Finally, it also highlights the growing conflicts between so-called respectable gays advocating for equality rights and those activists pursuing a more radical agenda that supported less genteel sexual imagery and practices (Warner 2002, 269–70).

Glad Day Bookshop, a local Toronto bookstore, was charged with obscenity for selling an issue of *Bad Attitude* that included a fictional fantasy narrative with images of consensual lesbian s/m sex. The judge, in rendering a conviction, applied the Supreme Court of Canada's (SCC) reasoning in *R. v. Butler* (1992), a case many had already argued would be problematically applied to gay and lesbian materials (Cossman and Bell 1997, 3). The *Butler* decision and its application in the *Bad Attitude* case highlights disagreements between lesbian and feminist activists about the nature of lesbian sexual imagery and the meaning and effect of "pornography."

Prior to *Butler*, "any publication a dominant character of which is the undue exploitation of sex, or of sex and any one or more of the following subjects, namely, crime, horror, cruelty and violence, are deemed to be obscene" (Canada, Criminal Code, section 163). The 1963 SCC decision in *R. v. Brody* argues that, in making a finding of "obscenity," attention needs to be paid to determining prevailing "community standards" and protecting public morals. The shifting nature of state perspectives on the nature of obscenity and the wider question of pornography needs to be understood within the broader arguments made by the feminist anti-pornography movement in the 1970s. The feminist anti-pornography movement explicitly argued that violent and degrading images of women were inextricably linked to the ongoing subordination of women, including the prevalence of violence related to pornographic images (Cossman and Bell 1997, 7–8). As such, material found to be pornographic constituted a "social harm" in that it directly undermined women's right to equality. Interventions by anti-pornography feminists in forums such as the Special Committee on Pornography and Prostitution (Fraser Commission) and in court decisions, including *Towne Cinema* (1985)

Catherine J. Nash

and *Butler* (1992), resulted in the incorporation of feminist-based anti-pornography language regarding both pornography and prostitution (20).

The application of these ideas in *R. v. Butler* (1992) marks a watershed decision in terms of obscenity in the Canadian context, shifting concerns about obscenity from the preservation of public morals to the prevention of social harm, mainly to women and children. While some argue that the *Butler* decision constitutes a victory for feminists as it removes questions of morality and moral regulation in favour of a test concerning harm, others argue that state intervention often imposes forms of regulation that arguably conflict with how those groups themselves envision and constitute themselves – an argument vigorously presented in the *Bad Attitude* trial as the anti-censorship feminist argument (Cossman and Bell 1997, 18; Ross 1997). Anti-censorship feminists argued that, in working with the state, one could find oneself inadvertently working against the best interests of the gay and lesbian community and, in this case, lesbians. For example, Cossman and Bell (1997, 8) argue that the application of *Butler* in the *Bad Attitude* case "illustrate[s] the perils of feminist support for state censorship."

During the trial, both the Crown and the defence called witnesses to attest to the purported harm that might be caused by the fantasy s/m narrative and imagery in the *Bad Attitude* magazine. The Crown's expert witness asserted that there were causal links between s/m images and the violence and degradation of women. In opposition, the defence called Becki Ross, a sociologist and activist involved in censorship issues, to support the contention that lesbian sexual imagery articulates "particular social meanings and is received by intended lesbian audiences and performers in very specific ways" that are distinctive from heterosexual s/m narratives (Ross 1997, 158). In other words, it was argued that, in determining the nature of "community standards," the court should focus its attention on the "standards" of the gay and lesbian community.

Rather simplistically, both the Crown's expert witness and the court concluded that the lesbian images would be considered violent and degrading if one of the participants was envisioned as a man and the scene understood as heterosexual bondage. As Ross (1997) argues, applying a heterosexual template drained the narrative and related imagery of the lesbian content. Further, there was no evidence to support the notion of harm resulting from viewing the images, nor was there anything to suggest that the "community" would not tolerate these images. Nevertheless, the judge found a need to protect "the general public from lesbian material that would 'predispose individuals to anti-social behaviour'" (153).

The case highlights the ongoing split in the feminist community over what constitutes pornography and its purported impact or harm. The anti-pornography argument is supported in the academic literature, which argues that s/m is particularly problematic for women (e.g., Lewis and Adler 1994; Scales 1994). Canadian organizations such as Legal Education and Action Fund (LEAF), functioning as interveners in court cases and other venues, worked with or through the state to affirm lesbian identities but were arguably not prepared to see s/m activities as a legitimate aspect of lesbian identity. Conversely, anti-censorship feminists such as Ross (1997, 187) argue that the *Bad Attitude* case makes clear that strategies for creating lesbian community and culture "cannot be achieved through the law, police and courts," given the state's long history of regulating women's and lesbian sexualities. In this case, matters of interest at the local level were caught up in Canada-wide (in fact, North America-wide) debates about the nature of lesbian identity and sexuality.

Public Protest and Pride Toronto

Over the last decade, gay and lesbian activism has gone global, witnessed, for example, by US Secretary of State Hillary Clinton's call on 6 December 2011 for global gay and lesbian rights protections as a matter of US foreign policy. Canada's former foreign affairs minister, John Baird, was also an outspoken critic of anti-gay legislative initiatives in both Uganda and Russia (Blanchfield 2013; Chase 2013; Ling 2012). This case study examines how a local Toronto group, Queers against Israeli Apartheid, became embroiled in a political battle that included other local LGBT groups, Toronto's city council and Canadian and international Jewish groups; it illustrates how local LGBT activism engages with globalized debates about sexuality and human rights.

Recent scholarship argues that claims for tolerance for sexual diversity and human rights protections for LGBT people are often positioned as "Western" values of modern civility and liberal democratic ideals (Ahmed 2011; Hockberg 2010; Kirchick 2009; Puar 2011; Schulman 2012). This constitutes a form of homonationalism in which states that are "gay friendly" are regarded as "modern, cosmopolitan, developed, first-world ... and democratic" while those states that are painted as homophobic or anti-gay are regarded as pre-modern, uncivilized, and backward (Puar 2011, 138; see also Hockberg 2010). Scholars argue that Israel is undertaking a form of "pinkwashing" in its drive to rebrand itself as "an oasis of liberal tolerance in a reactionary religious backwater" for LGBT people in the Middle East (Kirchick 2009) and that this works to deflect attention away from what many see as Israel's violent degradation and

Catherine J. Nash

containment of Palestinians. While some support the perspective that LGBT people need to defend Israel, given Palestinian hostility to gays and lesbians (e.g., Kirchick 2009; StandWithUs 2010), others contest that this deployment of gay and lesbian rights discourses serves to deflect attention away from oppressive policies and regimes (Ahmed 2011; Puar 2011).

Toronto's QuAIA was formed in 2008 to work "in solidarity with queers in Palestine" (QuAIA 2012). QuAIA argues that Israel's recent attempts to present itself as a gay friendly state surrounded by nations overtly hostile to gays and lesbians attempts to present Israel in a more positive light in the world community and that this is a "queer" issue because "queer rights are not safe until people's rights are safe" (QuAIA 2012; see also Letson 2011).

QuAIA's visible participation in Toronto's 2009 pride parade ignited debate about LGBT activism, politics, and the contemporary and historical purpose of Pride. Indeed, QuAIA's 2009 public appearance in Pride caught the attention of a number of organizations and individuals, including the Canadian Jewish Congress (now the Centre for Jewish Affairs) (Brean 2009) and B'nai Brith Canada (2009). The *Jewish Tribune,* a Canadian-based newspaper, portrayed QuAIA's participation as a "microcosm of the anti-Semitism happening globally" (Beck 2009). Local lawyer Martin Gladstone lobbied to have QuAIA banned from Pride and to have Pride funding cut at all levels of government as well as corporate sponsorships. Conversely, some Jewish groups, such as Independent Jewish Voices, and many queer and non-queer activists supported QuAIA.

QuAIA's anticipated participation in 2010 Pride caused its detractors to put increasing pressure on the Pride organizing committee to ban its participation and on city council to withhold Pride funding. In a February 2010 letter, city councillor Kyle Rae argued that QuAIA participation in Pride was not in keeping with "the spirit and values of Pride Toronto" ("Councillor Kyle Rae ..." 2011). As the public rhetoric escalated, Pride attempted to defuse matters by announcing that all "messages and signage" would have to be pre-approved by a Pride Toronto ethics committee. The community response to the new rule was so negative that Pride rescinded it shortly thereafter. In May 2010, the Pride Committee voted four to three to ban the term "Israeli Apartheid," claiming the phrase was in breach of the city's anti-discrimination policy (Levy-Ajzenkopf 2011). Many regarded Pride's responses as reflecting its desire to avoid a confrontation that might jeopardize its "corporate sponsorship, tourism dollars and ... hard won public approval" (Cole 2010). In an attempt to resolve matters in time for the 2010 parade, Pride revised its position yet again, proposing that all participants sign an agreement to abide by the city's anti-discrimination policy and allowing QuAIA to march in Pride 2010. Nevertheless, the presence of visible supporters of QuAIA (sporting signs and tee-shirts) continued to outrage some city councillors who worked to ensure that city council approved a motion to withhold 2011 funding until after Pride and to commission an investigation into whether the presence of QuAIA and its supporters was not in violation of the city's anti-discrimination policy. Further, some councillors argued that if QuAIA's participation in the 2010 parade was found to be a violation of that policy, Pride should be made to reimburse the city for the 2010 expenses.

In response, Pride Toronto struck an advisory panel chaired by Reverend Brent Hawkes to make recommendations on how to deal with such controversies. The advisory panel report, released on 17 February 2011, did not make specific recommendations about QuAIA but did recommend that all participants sign an enforceable undertaking "not to portray messages or images that condone or promote violence, hatred or negative stereotypes against any group" (Levy-Ajzenkopf 2011). As well, the panel recommended the implementation of a comprehensive dispute resolution process to deal with complaints.

Such an approach did not please everyone. The local Jewish group Kilanu argued that Pride "is about the celebration of gay rights. It's not a platform from which to spew hatred and intolerance … QuAIA's message is clearly discriminatory, divisive and inflammatory" (Levy-Ajzenkopf 2011, 14). In a *Sun* editorial, Sue-Ann Levy (2011) accused Reverend Hawkes and the "lefty mouth piece, *Xtra*" of working to ensure that QuAIA could participate in the 2011 pride parade, at which point, she claimed, city funding should be withheld. Reverend Brent Hawkes warned against defunding Pride, arguing that if Pride went bankrupt, the situation might be worse as "more radical elements in the community [would] take control" of Pride (Levy-Ajzenkopf 2011, 14).

The Toronto city manager's report to council on April 2011 argued that, while QuAIA's message might be offensive to some, the specific words themselves were not in violation of city policy, the Canadian Criminal Code, or the Ontario Human Rights Code (Nickle 2011). Not satisfied, Mayor Ford and several members of council continued to insist that Pride funding should be withheld if QuAIA participated in the 2011 pride parade. Given these threats to Pride, QuAIA withdrew, although it did defiantly unfurl a QuAIA banner along the parade route (Alcoba 2012). Finally, while B'nai Brith did file a complaint with the Dispute Resolution Panel about QuAIA participation in 2012 Pride, the panel ruled in favour of QuAIA (Church and Grant 2012). In June 2012, city council condemned the term "Israeli Apartheid" while continuing

Catherine J. Nash

funding for the pride parade, recognizing it as a "significant cultural event that strongly promotes the ideas of tolerance and diversity" (Peat 2012). With that, QuAIA marched in the 27 June pride parade. Controversy continues to plague QuAIA participation in Pride Toronto, morphing into what Barbara Kay (2013) argues is an "annual controversy, where gay rights, free speech, the role of government in funding civic events and, of course, Middle Eastern geopolitics" foment into a "noxious summertime brew." In 2013, after considerable debate about whether the city would fund Pride (along with other cultural events), funding was granted, although the city's mayor Rob Ford and two members of council voted against the funding package, which included the Toronto International Film Festival and the Art Gallery of Ontario (Dale 2013).

The debates about QuAIA highlight how locally based political activism is increasingly caught up in global discourses on sexual diversity and LGBT rights. Mainstream LGBT organizations such as Pride are positioned as moderate, and Pride itself is often portrayed as an apolitical and celebratory event. Nevertheless, groups such as QuAIA reinscribe a political sensibility into local LGBT politics – albeit a politics that is increasingly positioned within complex globalized discourses circulating within the local political arena (Puar 2011).

Conclusion

Toronto's gay and lesbian political organizations have a long history of engagement in local, provincial, and federal government issues, from defence of the bathhouses in the early 1980s to pressuring for human rights protections and gay marriage in the 1990s and 2000s. Having a territorial or neighbourhood base from which to operate remains pivotal to the political, economic, and social successes of these various organizations. As the case studies reflect, notions of "place" figure prominently. For George Hislop and his failed electoral bid, the potential existence of a gay and lesbian neighbourhood lent credence to his campaign and ammunition to his opponents, who feared "gay power politics" based on territorial control. The very existence of gay bookstores and the circulation of gay-and-lesbian-themed materials (and ideas) across international borders gave rise to vigorous censorship on the part of state authorities such as Canada Customs. Provincial and federal funding for social service provision and support such as HIV/AIDS and queer youth shelters still operate on the premise that service delivery is focused on the downtown core. As various gay and lesbian rights discourses increasingly operate internationally, local gay and lesbian organizations find themselves embroiled in globally circulating resistances to gay and lesbian human rights claims from powerful religious and secular organizations. Yet, events such as Pride, locally funded and supported, reinforce the importance of local visibility and political strength even in the face of globalizing activism and resistance.

Forty years of place-based activism reinforces arguments about the importance of territorial concentrations for successful political, economic, and social engagement. Nevertheless, such locations have been astutely critiqued with regard to concerns about the neoliberal commodification of gay life and the racialized, gendered, and classed nature of such locations (e.g., Nast 2002). Further, recent scholarship suggests that we are seeing the "degaying" of the gay village in places as diverse as Manchester (Binnie and Skeggs 2004), Sydney (Ruting 2008), Bloemfontein in South Africa (Visser 2008), and Toronto (Nash 2013a, 2013b) as a new generation, beneficiaries of gay rights successes and new social media, no longer find the Village either socially or politically necessary. One might argue that place-based gay and lesbian activism is increasingly anachronistic as new information technologies and the globalized nature of contemporary political advocacy require organizations to operate across and between multiple scales. Nevertheless, places such as Toronto's gay village remain, at least for now, central to political activism and a territorially imagined gay and lesbian community.

Note

1 The terms "homosexual," "lesbian," "gay," "bisexual," "queer," and "trans" are employed here in their historical context. Nascent gay and lesbian political and social organizations in the 1970s and early 1980s used the terms "homosexual," "gay," and "lesbian" unproblematically and in a largely essentialist understanding that considered these to be fixed and stable identities (Nash 2006). By the mid-1980s, many gay and lesbian organizations had begun to include bisexuals in their mandate and, more recently, to acknowledge trans people, renaming their organizations some variation of "LGBT" or "LGBTQ." "Trans" is most often utilized to reflect a shifting understanding of gender and embodiment with varying degrees of stability and/or multiplicity (Nash 2011). The term "queer" is an emerging term, which, while often used in common parlance, is not often found in the names of gay and lesbian political organizations. "Queer" is often deployed as a term that rejects a fixed gendered, embodied, or sexual identity, although, despite its fluidity, its usage often results in some sense of fixity (Nash 2013a).

References

Ahmed, Sara. 2011. "Problematic Proximities; or, Why Critiques of Gay Imperialism Matter." *Feminist Legal Studies* 19 (2): 119–32. http://dx.doi.org/10.1007/s10691-011-9180-7.

Alcoba, Nancy. 2012. "Pride Toronto Gets Grant Despite Controversy." *National Post,* 8 June. http://news.nationalpost.com/2012/06/08.

Association of Gay Electors. 1979. *Constitution of the Association of Gay Electors.* Toronto: Canadian Lesbian and Gay Archives.

–. 1980. *Gay Issues: How Metro Votes: A Report by Association of Gay Electors.* 29 November. Toronto: Canadian Lesbian and Gay Archives.

Bearchell, Chris, and Ed Jackson. 1980. "Window on Sewell." *Body Politic* 60 (February): 23–25.

Beck, Atara. 2009. "Pride Parade Microcosm of Anti-Semitism Happening Globally." *Jewish Tribune,* 28 May.

Binnie, Jon, and Beverly Skeggs. 2004. "Cosmopolitan Knowledge and the Production and Consumption of Sexualized Space: Manchester's Gay Village." *Sociological Review* 52 (1): 39–61. http://dx.doi.org/10.1111/j.1467-954X.2004.00441.x.

Blanchfield, Mike. 2013. "John Baird Blasts Russia's 'Hateful' Anti-Gay Law after Pushing Privately for Change." *Globe and Mail,* 1 August. http://news.nationalpost.com/2013/08/01/john-baird-blasts-russias-hateful-anti-gay-law-after-pushing-privately-for-change/.

B'nai Brith Canada. 2009. "B'nai Brith Canada urges LGBT community not to allow their agenda to be hijacked by anti-Israel agitators." Press Release. 20 May.

Brean, Joseph. 2009. "Anti-Zionists Banned from Pride Parade: Protests Prohibited." *National Post,* 28 May.

Chapman, Dick. 1980. "Loser Hislop 'Campaign of Hate.'" *Toronto Sun,* 11 November.

Chase, Steven. 2013. "Baird Belies Conservative Image through Defence of Gay Rights Abroad." *Globe and Mail,* 8 August. http://www.theglobeandmail.com/news/politics/baird-belies-conservative-image-through-defence-of-gay-rights-abroad/article13680375/.

Chenier, Elise. 1995. "Rethinking Class in Lesbian Bar Culture: Living 'the Gay Life' in Toronto, 1955–1965." *Left History* 9 (2): 85–118. Reprinted in Adele Perry and Mona Gleason, eds., *Rethinking Canada: The Promise of Women's History,* 5th ed., 301–22. Toronto: Oxford University Press, 2006.

Church, Elizabeth, and Kelly Grant. 2012. "Toronto Council Funds Pride Week Despite Participation of Controversial Group." *Globe and Mail,* 8 June. http://www.theglobeandmail.com/news/toronto/article4241126.

Cole, Desmond. 2010. "They're Here, They're Queer: They're More Than Tassels and Beer." *Torontoist,* 8 June. http://torontoist.com/2010/06.

Cossman, Brenda, and Shannon Bell. 1997. "Introduction." In Brenda Cossman, Shannon Bell, Lise Gotell, and Becki L. Ross, *Bad Attitude/s on Trial: Pornography, Feminism, and the Butler Decision,* 3–47. Toronto: University of Toronto Press.

"Councillor Kyle Rae Pressured Pride Toronto to Oust QuAIA." 2011. *Xtra! Canada's Gay and Lesbian News,* 30 March. http://www.xtra.ca/public/National/Councillor_Kyle_Rae_pressured_Pride_Toronto_to_oust_QuAIA-8442.aspx.

Dale, Daniel. 2013. "Mayor Rob Ford Votes against Funding Pride, TIFF, Symphony." *Toronto Star,* 13 June. http://www.thestar.com/news/city_hall/2013/06/13/mayor_rob_ford_votes_against_funding_pride_tiff_symphony.html.

Donato, Tony. 1980. "I Know They Represent a Large Part of the Vote John ..." *Toronto Sun*, 28 September.

Downing, John. 1980. "Metro Voters Stand Pat Except in Sewell Upset." *Toronto Sun*, 11 November.

Escoffier, Jeffrey. 1997. "Political Economy of the Closet: Notes Toward an Economic History of Gay and Lesbian Life before Stonewall." In Amy Gluckman and Betsy Reed, eds., *Homo Economics: Capitalism, Community, and Lesbian and Gay Life*, 123–34. New York: Routledge.

Herman, Didi. 1994. *Rights of Passage: Struggles for Lesbian and Gay Legal Equality.* Toronto: University of Toronto Press.

Hluchy, Patricia. 1980. "250 Protest Homosexual 'Power Politics.'" *Toronto Star*, 20 October.

Hockberg, Gil Z. 2010. "Introduction: Israelis, Palestinians, Queers: Points of Departure." *GLQ: A Journal of Lesbian and Gay Studies* 16 (4): 493–516.

Horsford, Patricia. 1980. "Hislop Bid Triggers Debate on Homosexual Vote." *Globe and Mail*, 24 October.

Horsford, Patricia, and James Jefferson. 1980. "Both Camps Running Scared." *Globe and Mail*, 11 November.

Hoy, Claire. 1980a. "Gay Power Boosted by Sewell." *Toronto Sun*, 3 September.

–. 1980b. "Gay Issue Out of the Closet." *Toronto Sun*, 26 November.

Jackson, Ed. 1980-81. "Close, But Not Close Enough." *Body Politic* 69 (December-January): 9–10, 12.

Jackson, Ed, and Stan Persky. 1982. *Flaunting It! A Decade of Gay Journalism from the Body Politic.* Vancouver/Toronto: New Star Books/Pink Triangle Press.

Kay, Barbara. 2013. "Hey QuAIA, Heard about Russia?" *National Post*, 6 June. http://fullcomment.nationalpost.com/2013/06/24/barbara-kay-hey-quaia-heard-about-russia/.

Kinsman, Gary. 1996. *The Regulation of Desire: Homo and Hetero Sexualities.* Montreal: Black Rose.

Kirchick, James. 2009. "Queers for Palestine?" *Advocate* (Boston, MA) 28 (January). http://www.advocate.com/exclusive_detail_ektid71884.

Laver, Ross. 1980. "Homosexual Activist Declares Candidacy." *Globe and Mail*, 12 February.

Letson, Robyn. 2011. "Coming Out against Apartheid: A Roundtable about Queer Solidarity with Palestine." *Upping the Anti* 13: 137–51. http://uppingtheanti.org/journal/article/13-coming-out-against-aparheid/.

Levy, Sue-Ann. 2011. "Paying Price for Pride" (editorial). *Toronto Sun*, 19 March. http://www.torontosun.com/comment/columnists/sueann_levy/2011/03/18/17673631.html.

Levy-Ajzenkopf, Andy. 2011. "Mayor Lays Down Pride Parade Law: No Funding of Anti-Israel Group Included." *Canadian Jewish News*, 10 March, 3, 14.

Lewis, Reina, and Karen Adler. 1994. "Come to Me, Baby; or, What's Wrong with Lesbian S/M." *Women's Studies International Forum* 17 (4): 433–41. http://dx.doi.org/10.1016/S0277-5395(05)80050-0.

"Losing and Learning." 1980. *Body Politic* 69 (December): 7.

Ling, Justin. 2012. "Baird Battles Ugandan Politician over Gay Rights." *Xtra*, 25 October. http://dailyxtra.com/canada/news/baird-battles-ugandan-politician-gay-rights?market=210.

Lynch, Michael. 1980. "CBS Power, CBC Politics." *Body Politic* 64 (June-July): 28.

McCann, Sean. 1980a. "Art Fears Gay Alternatives." *Toronto Sun*, 5 November.

−. 1980b. "Gays May Swing It." *Toronto Star*, 20 October.

McLeod, Donald W. 1996. *Lesbian and Gay Liberation in Canada: A Selected Annotated Chronology, 1964–1975*. Toronto: ECW Press/Homewood Books.

Nash, Catherine Jean. 2005. "Contesting Identity: Politics of Gays and Lesbians in Toronto in the 1970s." *Gender, Place and Culture* 12 (1): 113–35. http://dx.doi.org/10.1080/09663690500083115.

−. 2006. "Toronto's Gay Village, 1969–1982: Plotting the Politics of Gay Identity." *Canadian Geographer/Géographe canadien* 50 (1): 1–16. http://dx.doi.org/10.1111/j.0008-3658.2006.00123.x.

−. 2011. "Trans Experiences in Lesbian and Queer Space." *Canadian Geographer/Géographe canadien* 55 (2): 192–207. http://dx.doi.org/10.1111/j.1541-0064.2010.00337.x.

−. 2013a. "Queering Neighbourhoods: Politics and Practice in Toronto." *ACME: An International E-Journal for Critical Geographies* 12 (2): 193–213.

−. 2013b. "The Age of the 'Post-Mo'? Toronto's Gay Village and a New Generation." *Geoforum* 49: 243–52. http://dx.doi.org/10.1016/j.geoforum.2012.11.023.

Nast, Heidi. 2002. "Queer Patriarchies, Queer Racisms, International." *Antipode* 34 (5): 874–909. http://dx.doi.org/10.1111/1467-8330.00281.

Nickle, David. 2011. "Mayor, Councillor to Fight against Group in Pride Parade." *Inside Toronto*, 14 April. http://www.zuza.com/news-story/62946-mayor-councillor-to-fight-against-group-in-pride-parade/.

"Our Task." 1974. *Body Politic* 13 (March–April): 2, 6.

Peat, Don. 2012. "Council Votes to Condemn Use of Term 'Israeli Apartheid.'" *Toronto Sun*, 7 June. http://www.torontosun.com/2012/06/07/council-votes-to-condemn-use-of-term-israeli-apartheid.

Podmore, Julie. 2006. "'Gone Underground'? Lesbian Visibility and the Consolidation of Queer Space in Montreal." *Social and Cultural Geography* 7 (4): 595–625. http://dx.doi.org/10.1080/14649360600825737.

Puar, Jasbir. 2011. "Citation and Censorship: The Politics of Talking about the Sexual Politics of Israel." *Feminist Legal Studies* 19 (2): 133–42. http://dx.doi.org/10.1007/s10691-011-9176-3.

QuAIA (Queers Against Israeli Apartheid). 2012. *Who We Are*. Toronto: Queers Against Israeli Apartheid. http://www.queersagainstapartheid.org.

Rayside, David. 2008. *Queer Inclusions, Continental Divisions: Public Recognition of Sexual Diversity in Canada and the United States*. Toronto: University of Toronto Press.

Ross, Becki L. 1995. *The House That Jill Built: A Lesbian Nation in Formation*. Toronto: University of Toronto Press.

−. 1997. "'It's Merely Designed for Sexual Arousal': Interrogating the Indefensibility of Lesbian Smut." In Brenda Cossman, Shannon Bell, Lise Gotell, and Becki L. Ross, *Bad Attitude/s on Trial: Pornography, Feminism, and the Butler Decision*, 152–98. Toronto: University of Toronto Press.

Ruting, Brad. 2008. "Economic Transformations of Gay Urban Spaces: Revisiting Collins' Evolutionary Gay District Model." *Australian Geographer* 39 (3): 259–69. http://dx.doi.org/10.1080/00049180802270465.

Sabia. Laura. 1980. "Politics and Sexuality Make Wrong Bedfellows." *Toronto Sun*, 14 November.

Scales, Ann. 1994. "Avoiding Constitutional Depression: Bad Attitudes and the Fate of Butler." *Canadian Journal of Women and the Law* 7 (2): 349–92.

Schulman, Sarah. 2012. *Israel/Palestine and the Queer International*. Durham, NC: Duke University Press. http://dx.doi.org/10.1215/9780822396536.

Seidman, Steven. 1997. *Difference Troubles: Queering Social Theory and Sexual Politics*. Cambridge: Cambridge University Press. http://dx.doi.org/10.1017/CBO9780511557910.

Smith, Miriam. 1999. *Lesbian and Gay Rights in Canada: Social Movements and Equality-Seeking, 1971-1995*. Toronto: University of Toronto Press.

StandWithUs. 2010. *LGBT Rights under the Palestinian Authority: Know the Facts*. Los Angeles: StandWithUs. http://www.standwithus.com/.

Stein, David Lewis. 1980. "The Issue Is Now Tolerance." *Toronto Star*, 2 November.

Toronto Star. 1980. "Are You a Homosexual? Sewell Asked." 22 October.

–. 1980a. "Gay Power?" 7 September.

–. 1980b. "Sewell, Gay Candidate 'on Same Wave Length.'" 4 September.

–. 1980c. "Gays and John." 9 November.

Trow, Robert. 1980. "First Open Gay at City Hall, Hislop Plans Ward 6 Campaign." *Body Politic* 60:13.

Visser, Gustav. 2008. "The Homonormalisation of White Heterosexual Leisure Spaces in Bloemfontein, South Africa." *Geoforum* 39 (3): 1347–61. http://dx.doi.org/10.1016/j.geoforum.2007.11.004.

Warner, Tom. 2002. *Never Going Back: A History of Queer Activism in Canada*. Toronto: University of Toronto Press.

Legal Cases
Egan v. Canada [1995] 2 S.C.R. 513.

R. v. Brody [1962] S.C.R. 681.

R. v. Butler [1992] 1 S.C.R. 452.

R. v. Towne Cinema [1985] 1 S.C.R. 494.

10

Building Queer Infrastructure: Trajectories of Activism and Organizational Development in Decolonizing Vancouver

GORDON BRENT BROCHU-INGRAM

Six decades of LGBT activism in Canada have transformed laws, decision-making frameworks, and a range of institutional practices at all levels of government leading to today's queer-friendlier metropolitan political economies. But with these obvious gains, local activist strategies have garnered few additional resources for service programs. Today, LGBT politics overlays increasingly volatile configurations of pressure for better social spaces and service programs. A focus on services and spaces as "queer infrastructure" provides an alternative lens for understanding local LGBT politics only partially centred on narratives of expanding rights and protections (which remain incomplete for trans communities).[1] Today, LGBT and queer coalition politics in Canadian cities is less and less focused on correcting remaining legal inequities and increasingly preoccupied with appropriating resources for diversifying social spaces, support programs, and strategic facilities upon which more vulnerable demographics remain dependent (see also Chapters 8, 9, and 11, this volume).

This chapter explores the queer organizational politics of Canada's third largest metropolitan region, Vancouver, and its suburbs in British Columbia's Lower Mainland, and it poses questions about the adequacy of theoretical and strategic capabilities for maintaining and developing organizations, service programs, and facilities. Metropolitan Vancouver is undergoing a shift in conversations around sexual minority vulnerability, needs, and entitlements from earlier activist challenges to inequities (and subsequent constructions of rights and protections) to building expanded and truly inclusive social spaces, entertainment establishments, service programs, and facilities. This emerging politics of service provision and "space-taking," while at times confrontational, is less defined by the half century of strategies of constructed visibility and appropriating public "spectacle" (Debord [1967] 1994). The resulting shift in electoral narratives reflects demographic and cultural changes across the Lower Mainland, with huge implications for LGBT stakeholders, organizational formations, and political actors.

The growing concerns for infrastructure in contemporary LGBT politics parallels the emergence of sexual minority populations that have not been dependent upon the historic central Vancouver neighbourhoods that were crucial to initial gay and lesbian feminist rights activism. Centres of queer metropolitan political economies throughout North American cities are shifting from historic inner-city enclaves, such as Vancouver's West End (Ingram 2010; Ross and Sullivan 2012) and Commercial Drive (Bouthillette 1997; Lo and Healy 2000), to outer neighbourhoods and municipalities with more affordable housing and rapid growth in jobs – communities that still have few services for LGBT populations. This urban migration, in large part a response to intensified gentrification in central Vancouver, represents a reversal of a century of sexual minority concentration in pedestrian-oriented urban cores and has been possible only because of the institutionalization of a raft of rights and protections.

This chapter theorizes queer infrastructure as the sum total of protections, organizations, social spaces, and service programs for overcoming homophobia and transphobia, along with intersecting inequities rooted in misogyny, racism, neocolonialism, cultural chauvinism, and anti-migrant xenophobia. I consider methods to identify pressures for new forms of community development and respective programs, which are often articulated within older conversations about rights and protections. I sketch historical factors that formed cultures of sexual minority resistance and reflect upon a half century of LGBT activism. I then describe three incomplete LGBT "community development projects" and follow this with an inventory of the diversifying models of agency, organizing, and service provision that have been initiated.

Historical Background

Urbanization of Indigenous populations in much of British Columbia, and the cultural crossroads around Vancouver and Victoria in particular, were intrinsic to colonial expansion and concentration of settler populations. Indigenous com-

Gordon Brent Brochu-Ingram

munities were often highly mobile, making cultural adaptations and trade links and engaging with an array of colonial actors. Diverse, multiple-gender Indigenous networks provided a poorly policed alternative to the onslaught of the late Victorian heteronormative project. On the West Coast, Indigenous populations were present at all phases of the formation of urbanizing LGBT communities, although "Indian" groups remained cordoned and marginal until the 1990s.

Indigenous bodies and sexual minorities soon became targets of the new state apparatus. First enabled through section 3, first written in the Indian Act, 1884, federal policing of Indigenous networks that neither conformed to neocolonial gender expectations nor suppressed homosexuality became conflated with the suppression of potlatch gatherings, along with virtually all traditional ceremonies, religious observance, and material culture. One of the more substantial records of alternative gender expression, homosexuality, and lethal repression in the late nineteenth century is contained in the biography of Chief Charles James Nowell of the Kwakwaka'wakw of northern Vancouver Island, a community whose members were increasingly working in, trading with, and depending on services provided in Vancouver (Ford 1941, 34, 38, 69, 130–32). The mass incarceration of Indigenous children in residential schools was preceded by decades of assaults on extended tribal families, especially of sexual minorities. By the turn of the century, one of the few places where Indigenous sexual minorities could partially escape detection, policing, and incarceration were the larger towns, most notably Vancouver.

For over a half century after Vancouver's incorporation in 1886, diverse populations were cordoned by language, origin, and citizenship (Ingram 2000, 2003). In large parts of the Lower Mainland, native English speakers and populations primarily of northwestern European heritages barely formed majorities. After extensive repression during the Second World War, the social spaces that prefigured LGBT activism coalesced soon after civil rights, most importantly enfranchisement, were restored to East Asians and South Asians in the years 1947 to 1949. Early organizing and organizations in British Columbia were exclusive, along neocolonial and language lines, whereby privileged white groups defined "gay" and "lesbian" as well as the notions of social equity upon which subsequent rights struggles were based.

In the 1960s, the tiered neocolonial social services delivery system, which ensured that First Nations and Asian immigrants often faced exclusion and substandard support, was effectively readapted for sexual minorities. People of colour had limited access to or control over LGBT-related services. This effectively racialized and dual character, embodied in the queer infrastructure of the Lower Mainland, hobbled activism and obstructed services, institutionalizing inequities that continued into the following health crises. Even after subsequent challenges to racism, and under the rhetoric of early multiculturalism in LGBT activism, an effectively dual system of program development persisted, along with unequal articulation, leadership, and service access.

The first homophile organization in Canada, the Association for Social Knowledge, was formed in Vancouver in April 1964 after a year of intensifying police harassment in the city's gay bars (Kinsman 1996, 230–48). "ASK supported law reform and sponsored public lectures and discussion groups, coffee parties (Gab'N'Java), social events and outings, a lending library, and, eventually, a drop-in and community centre" (McLeod 1996, 7–10) By mid-1966, three years before the partial decriminalization of homosexuality, Canada had its first queer metropolitan infrastructure thanks to one small organization, barely a collective, that coordinated a score of initiatives and service programs. The majority of the nascent leadership consisted of males, while well over half of the organizational work was carried out by women.[2] In a city in which perhaps more than one-third of the population was struggling with English literacy, ASK members were all English speakers from a demographic that was largely unilingual. Even so, some understanding of disparities within LGBT populations and some nascent knowledge of trans experiences and identifications did appear in early ASK discussions.[3] However, it would take another generation to articulate ideals of feminism, decolonization, and anti-racism that today are central to contemporary notions of functional organizations and effective service provision. It would take another generation to envision the support needs for the range of trans experiences. As Canada's first homophile organization, ASK's history has been neglected because it was primarily a *service* organization, more concerned with self-education and care-giving than with advocacy. ASK disbanded during 1969 and the partial decriminalization of homosexuality, but police repression of public intimacies (including kissing) continued to intensify. New, more visible and combative organizations, more squarely challenging homophobia in public space, were forming by and for a wider set of LGBT demographics.

In 1970, lesbians and gay men formed the short-lived Gay Action Committee (Q.Q. aka Kevin McKeown 1970). In November 1970, over a year after the Stonewall Riots in New York City, the Vancouver Gay Liberation Front (GLF) formed around a drop-in centre (shared with Yippies [Youth International Party]) on Carroll Street near Pender Street in Chinatown, and, in 1971, the small collective operated a switchboard (Georgia Straight 1970, 1971; Q.Q. aka Kevin McKeown 1971). However, the Vancouver GLF did not find a support base in the emerging gay male ghetto in the city's West End and was defunct

Gordon Brent Brochu-Ingram

within a year. The GLF was succeeded by the centrist Canadian Gay Activist Alliance and the specifically socialist Gay Alliance Towards Equality (GATE). Linked to activism in Toronto, GATE developed local strategies for challenging inequities and violence, coordinating the 1971 We Demand demonstration, the first act of constructed LGBT visibility on the West Coast. GATE was the first LGBT organization in Vancouver to engage in a wide range of tactics around demonstrations, publicity, and the appropriation of public space. The first local gay pride rally, in commemoration of the Stonewall Riots, was organized by GATE in June 1972 at Ceperly Park, a historic cruising area (Hill 1987a) on the edge of Stanley Park.

GATE challenged the state at all levels of government while confronting conservative business interests associated with the growing number of gay bars. Municipal politicians on both the left and the right were unapologetically homophobic. Not coincidentally, the conservative Non-Partisan Association, with direct ties to real estate speculation, was already exploring the role of white gay males in gentrification. GATE's first demonstration in front of the provincial legislature in Victoria was on 9 November 1973 (McLeod 1996, 142), little more than a year after the election of British Columbia's first New Democratic Party government.[4] The protections advocated by GATE that day were not achieved until the second social democratic provincial government was elected two decades later. The GATE campaign with the most national impact involved the legal action against the *Vancouver Sun,* which, in 1973, refused to print a GATE advertisement. The subsequent campaign, though unsuccessful in the short term, was eventually taken to the Supreme Court of Canada (Smith 1999, 301–3) and influenced a decade of Canadian legal interpretations around sexual orientation protections. Struggling due to a lack of participation from women and men whose ethnic heritages were not rooted in northwestern Europe, GATE dissolved in late 1979.

Lesbian feminism in British Columbia begins in the Women's Caucus in 1969 and 1970. New Morning, calling itself "a gay women's collective," played an important organizing role in the 1971 Indochinese Women's Conference.[5] Vancouver's first resource centre exclusively for lesbians opened in 1972. By 1973, lesbian feminism emerged as a political movement consciously divergent from male-oriented gay rights activism. Lesbians began organizing within a broader feminist coalition known as the British Columbia Federation of Women (BCFW). At its founding convention in 1974, the BCFW established a lesbian subcommittee with a lesbian caucus specifically comprised of self-identified lesbians. The organization soon developed policy related to lesbians around education, civil rights, age of consent, custody, health, and immigration.

That caucus existed for a decade and, throughout the period, was a central source of education and theory on sexuality and homophobia and intersections with gender inequities.

Lesbian separatist communes, camps, and retreats came to be seen as manifestations not only of a political movement but also of a cultural movement. There was a lesbian workshop at the 1975 British Columbia Women's Festival. In 1981, the first National Lesbian Conference supported numerous workshops, including one on rural organizing and bisexuality. Two years later, a regional follow-up conference featured, for the first time, workshops on sadomasochism and violence between women. In 1984, a series of annual provincial gay and lesbian conferences was initiated, and it laid the basis for the institutionalization of more inclusive public policy along with new service organizations and programs.

The 1970s saw the articulation of, and constructed visibility for, culturally specific lesbian and gay networks. In Vancouver, the recovery of the experiences and queer histories of Aboriginals, Chinese Canadians, South Asians, and African Canadians began to be publicly articulated (Ingram 2000). In the early 1980s, lesbians of colour began to organize caucuses. Indigenous LGBT organizing in Vancouver began in 1977 (Hill 1987b). Much of the focus was on providing peer support and creating networks for better health, ensuring protection from violence, and challenging racism. A decade later, Healing Our Spirit, the British Columbia First Nations with AIDS Society, initially focused on gay male experiences, and the Greater Vancouver Native Cultural Society nurtured a wider range of social spaces outside of the bars.

Since 1991, the use of the term "Two-Spirits" in British Columbia has had some currency for self-identified individuals reconnecting to older, localized gender and sexuality traditions.[6] But the majority of the comparatively large Indigenous demographic in British Columbia, and in Vancouver in particular, experiences two or more different heritages, with one often being settler. For these individuals, the Two-Spirits label represents another, though not always a dominant, aspect of self-healing and another concern in cultural recovery. In the 1990s, the Vancouver Gay and Lesbian Centre began providing space for a Two-Spirited youth drop-in meeting (for more details on Two-Spirits activism, see Chapter 2, this volume).[7]

Vancouver's first trans organization, Transsexual and Transvestite Info, formed early in the 1970s and was initially focused on male-to-female individuals. Throughout much of the 1970s and 1980s, female-to-male individuals tended to seek support in lesbian spaces. In the 1990s, the Foundation for the Advancement of Trans-Gender Equality (FATE) was founded as a monthly meeting. Vancouver saw its first demonstration for transgendered human

Gordon Brent Brochu-Ingram

rights protections in June 1998, with 150 people marching along Davie Street (Efron 1998). The Transgender Health Program was established by the local health authority, Vancouver Coastal Health, in 2003.

The first public LGBT Jewish observance in Vancouver occurred during the High Holidays in 1973. In subsequent years, gay networks defined by Chinese, Italian, and Asian cultures emerged, though networks stayed relatively private. The Lotus Root Conference for gay, lesbian, and bisexual East Asians was organized in 1996. In early 1998, a separate space for queer East Asian youth was established (Yueng 1998). In the following decade, a host of new organizations and support networks, for a wider range of ethnic and language groups, has coalesced. Vancouver's Trikone chapter, for South Asians, began meeting in 2005. Since the early 1980s, workplaces and collective bargaining have been arenas for discussion of sexual orientation and related equity and protections.

Throughout the proliferation of LGBT activist groups and service organizations, history, heritage, and contemporary culture have played central roles in articulating a wider range of experiences and unmet needs. The British Columbia Gay and Lesbian Archives was founded in 1976 and began collecting newsletters, newspaper articles, and documentation.[8] Video Inn, Western Front, and the Grunt Gallery were established in the Mount Pleasant neighbourhood in 1970, 1973, and 1984, respectively.[9] These alternative spaces were crucial for LGBT cultural groups in Vancouver, such as artists of Asian and Aboriginal heritages, historically designated as "outsiders."[10] In 1983, one of the early figures in Vancouver video, Paul Wong, saw his installation and nine hours of programming on bisexuality, *Confused: Sexual Views,* removed from the Vancouver Art Gallery (on censorship, see also Chapter 9, this volume). The subsequent court battles around censorship went on for years and generated a heightened awareness of institutionalized homophobia, the importance of queer culture, continued erasures, and the need for LGBT acrtivism to focus on developing new cultural institutions.

While the needs of LGBT populations have expanded beyond that for erotic expression, Vancouver has had, and continues to have, a perennial shortage of sex-positive spaces. The brutal murder of Aaron Webster by a homophobic gang of adolescent males in a well-known public sex area in Stanley Park in November 2001 galvanized LGBT groups around violence. Since the turn of the century, several suicides and countless abusive episodes in schools have ushered in the movement against bullying. But while homophobic violence has been challenged publicly for several decades (see also Chapter 6, this volume), there has been a lack of resolve and solidarity around the defence of sex-positive spaces, both public and commercial. This after half a century of nearly continuous police harassment and amid a marked decline of sex-positive commercial establishments (in the face of inflated rents). The solution for many gay men has been digital, involving a shift to geo-social networking applications such as Grindr and Scruff.

Queer Activism Today

Today, Metropolitan Vancouver's LGBT politics is dominated by an understated dialectic that consists of defending achievements (still incomplete) in the area of rights and protections, on the one hand, and of defending and expanding service provision (including for social contact and entertainment) and the necessary spaces for this, on the other. However, in contrast to the half century of rights victories, a cooperative politics of queer organizational development has been slower to develop in Vancouver than in other large Canadian cities. In recent years, the economic downturn combined with inflated rents has contributed to negligible growth in LGBT infrastructure. The discussion below highlights just one recent example of the difficulty involved in shifting from a local LGBT politics focused on rights and protections to one focused on providing infrastructure to better support vulnerable LGBT populations and on making service organizations and program offerings (upon which these thousands of individuals depend) more effective, inclusive, and fiscally sustainable.

On the cover of the 29 November 2012 issue of Vancouver's *Xtra! West* is the headline, "QMUNITY SHAKEUP: Four Staff Gone in Six Months." The article, by Natasha Barsotti (2012), describes the organizational implosion of the largest and longest functioning LGBT service organization in British Columbia, Qmunity, whose origins go back to a tactical alliance with Trudeau-era federal Liberals in 1976. In this article, readers are informed of a recently appointed director, conflicted labour conditions, and the invocation of a collective bargaining agreement. What is less clear to readers is that this director has succeeded more than a score of others over the last three decades of "the Centre," which the organization had operated under a number of names. Only at the end of the article does Barsotti mention that the new director is under considerable pressure from her board to "find[] a new location" for the organization, which is currently based in Vancouver's rapidly gentrifying West End, and to ensure Qmunity's "financial stability" in a time of wavering government funding and foundational support. The Barsotti article highlights deficiencies in community vocabulary and activist theory pertaining to

Gordon Brent Brochu-Ingram

organizational development. British Columbia's LGBT communities may have rights and protections, but resources allocated to services organizations are well below the basic needs of populations at risk, particularly populations facing factors compounding those related to identity and sexuality.

Queer Activism and Public Policy Changes: Case Studies

Today's deficiencies in Vancouver, particularly the lack of popular engagement in imagining more effective service organizations and extending their operations to suburban communities, are rooted in the legacies of only partially achieved decolonization along with a host of social and political projects initiated in the 1970s. Three incomplete LGBT projects in Vancouver have relevance to other Canadian regions: (1) the building of alliances with state actors, including agencies and sources of support outside of partisan patronage; (2) the expansion of service allocation during historic crises, such as the AIDS pandemic; and (3) diversifying policy goals for serving populations outside of central Vancouver.

LGBT Organizations Building Alliances with Overlapping State Actors

On the West Coast, the first political alliances between LGBT service-oriented organizations and the state were funded through federal governments led by the Liberal Party. The centrist partisan nature of this alliance was only partially transformed in the mid-1990s with a series of NDP provincial governments. The federal Liberal Party's dominance over the first two decades of funding and provision of services to LGBT populations, in contrast to equality and rights advocacy (which, in British Columbia, was nearly always allied with provincial New Democrats), was effectively a reiteration of the neocolonial social division on the West Coast. Sexual minority populations with a strong command of English and a northwestern European heritage articulated goals for middle-class rights and protections, and directed service allocation that, more often than not, identified with federal Liberalism. The other half of LGBT populations received those services but had little agency with regard to their allocation – except through engagement with the BC NDP. Given the different funds dispersed by federal and provincial agencies, partisan changes in government generated peaks and dips in funding over generational cycles. The province of British Columbia never accepted a public mandate for the needs of specifically LGBT communities, except for health and sometimes (as with recent work against bullying) education.

Vancouver's pioneering LGBT organizations were driven to alliances with the federal Liberal Party because, until the early 1990s, the two other levels of government, provincial and municipal, would rarely engage with them. For a number of reasons, virtually no public funds went to the early gay and lesbian organizations from British Columbia's 1972–75 NDP government. GATE embarrassed that government as it struggled to fashion itself as the most socially equalitarian and progressive in Canada history.[11] Just before his fall, homophobic premier David Barrett travelled to China during the Cultural Revolution, and congratulated local politicians on their supposedly successful suppression of "homosexualism" (*Body Politic* 1975; *Province* 1974). As well as more centrist government ministers being at odds with the new lesbian and gay groups, a split emerged within the provincial caucus, where MLAs representing Vancouver, notably pioneering black feminist Rosemary Brown, squarely allied with lesbian feminist and gay rights groups, who were major supporters and electorates in urban ridings (on allies, see also Chapter 4, this volume). A second reason for the lack of funding from the first NDP provincial government is more complex. At that time, most of the gay and lesbian organizations in Vancouver were not oriented towards receiving high levels of service or ongoing budgets. These groups would not have qualified to administer government funding as they were operated as collectives, were not transparent, and were not legal societies. While more often preoccupied with political developments in Quebec and Ontario, Pierre Trudeau's cabinet in Ottawa viewed the leftward shift in Victoria and Vancouver with a mixed sense of concern and opportunity.[12] Small amounts of federal funding generated considerable political currency for that central Vancouver riding. Federal Liberal support for programs for LGBT populations, while ungenerous, was well-calculated.

Throughout the 1970s and into the 1980s, funding for initiatives for social programs, crucial to the LGBT demographics most at risk, nearly all involved the approval of the office of Vancouver Centre MP Ron Basford, who represented the area from 1963 to 1979. More than any other individual in Vancouver's LGBT history, Basford, as the major advocate for this urban core neighbourhood in the Trudeau cabinet, laid the basis for the strengths and weaknesses of the region's current LGBT infrastructure. Basford began his work in the Trudeau cabinet as the minister of state for urban affairs from 1972 to 1974. He went on to be minister of justice and attorney general of Canada (1975–78), in which capacity he was responsible for the obstruction of the first proposal for federal protections for sexual orientation (Lamb 1977; Thompson 1977). Ron Basford's bisexuality was well-known in the Liberal cabinet, and the

Gordon Brent Brochu-Ingram

Liberal Party effectively assigned him the task of denying federal human rights protections to sexual minorities. Not coincidentally, it was in that same year, 1976, that federal funding for services to LGBT populations at risk commenced in Basford's riding. This was the first federal funding for LGBT services on the West Coast, and only Vancouver Centre saw that money.

The Basford funding of Vancouver's LGBT organizations was not entirely opportunistic. It was in keeping with a critique of the preoccupation of gay liberationists, lesbian feminists, social democrats, and some socialists with gaining rights and government protections without improvements in economic conditions and access to social services. Rooted in a century of Canadian nationalist ideology that advocated ministering to (and maintaining neocolonial relationships with) vulnerable and abject populations, socially progressive centrists were compelled to provide programs and benefits to increasingly visible populations often scarred and under-served by the homophobic and transphobic state. And, at the same time, marginalized populations were often more organized around obtaining basic services for survival, especially for sexual health and social contact, than around obtaining legal rights and protections. For many impoverished members of Vancouver's LGBT communities in the 1970s, the human rights and workplace protections proposed for federal civil servants were not especially relevant because few of them expected to obtain such middle-class jobs and benefits.

The initial conduit for federal government support for sexual minorities was SEARCH. Organized in late 1974, the Society for Education, Action, Research and Counselling on Homosexuality was a response to city police efforts to close several gay bars. In 1975, SEARCH was one of the first of the new LGBT groups to incorporate as a society. A significant portion of SEARCH's early clients were male sex workers.[13] In subsequent years, the organization allied with, and eventually was absorbed by, the Vancouver Gay Community Centre (VGCC). In the mid-1970s, SEARCH established the West Coast's first gay switchboard, which provided information and peer counselling. The downtown SEARCH office soon housed a gay resources library and bulletin boards for employment and housing. SEARCH operated and staffed a clinic for sexually transmitted diseases and another for counselling. It responded to and was organized around providing services for the most marginalized, and, compared to more confrontational organizations such as GATE, it was "much more focused on the bars and helping street people, hustlers, etc."[14] By 1986, SEARCH was fully absorbed into VGCC, and the entire organization was renamed "Qmunity" in 2009. It continues to be the province's major LGBT service organization.[15]

Basford's legacy remains enigmatic with regard to the formation of Canadian LGBT politics and the development of services programs. The political calculus in Vancouver Centre was focused on a trade-off between little expansion of rights in the 1970s and minimal levels of funding for portions of a fractured voting group that was coping with the worst impacts of homophobia and transphobia, along with the marginalization of youth. The small amount of federal funding for LGBT organizations in Vancouver clearly excluded the involvement of NDP-allied advocacy groups such as GATE. If there is a single reason for the two decades of political longevity of Vancouver-Centre MP Hedy Fry, briefly the minister of state for women in the Chretien cabinet, it is the four decades of tying the bulk of federal funding of LGBT social programs to accommodations with, and benefits from, government agencies led by the federal Liberal Party.

AIDS Activism: Organizing and Providing Services during a Crisis

With the AIDS pandemic, much of LGBT activism in Vancouver began to bridge struggles for equal treatment and protections, the rights of vulnerable groups to urgently needed resources (including nutrition and housing), and the need for public health policy to extend to access to medicines and treatments. The region's first AIDS services organization, AIDS Vancouver, was formed in 1984. As AIDS infections on the West Coast soared (Rayside and Lindquist 1993, 55–57), there was inertia in Mulroney's federal Progressive Conservative cabinet and hostility from the provincial government. These were the last years of the nearly continuous four-decade rule of British Columbia's ultra-conservative Social Credit Party. To avoid being seen by fundamentalist Christian groups as engaging with and supporting LGBT groups, provincial agencies moved modest amounts of federal funding, ear-marked for medical care, through organizations such as AIDS Vancouver. But this collaborationist strategy could not keep pace with needs for basic services.

The southeast edge of Vancouver's Downtown, on the edge of gentrifying Yaletown, the early gay entertainment area from the 1960s and the major historic location of most of the region's gay bathhouses, became British Columbia's major site for the first AIDS service programs. The neighbourhood became an interzone for provision of care, with government funding a step removed from the malevolent state. Not coincidentally, the neighbourhood's bathhouses stayed open and became major testing-grounds for providing sex-positive information on HIV prevention (Bolan 1987).

Gordon Brent Brochu-Ingram

The limits to collaborating with a hostile provincial government became clear with the passage of the Health Statutes Amendment Act. Bill 34 was intended to provide the basis for putting individuals with HIV into quarantine. The bill conflated sexually active gay men with HIV transmission and saw them as threats to public health. Social Credit Party politicians not-so-privately called for "a special ghetto" in Vancouver and the use of a former leper colony for quarantine (Baldrey 1994). The legislation was first tabled in 1987 and met with tremendous resistance. There was additional concern that health status and treatment information would be made available throughout and beyond the provincial government (Baldrey 1987; Canadian Press 1987). Resistance to enactment of the legislation became the focus of the early August lesbian and gay pride march as well as demonstrations on 26 September 1987 (Pollak 1987) and 2 December 1987 (Flather 1987). The civil disobedience before and as the bill was passed in December 1987 prefigured the tactics of ACT UP Vancouver by two years. For five years, the provincial government effectively blocked new housing for people with AIDS as shortages intensified (Monk 1990; Myers 1986). Finally, in 1991, the government supported Helmcken House in Vancouver's Downtown South, which provided only thirty-two units.

ACT UP Vancouver formed in response to the failure of the collaborations and the provincial government's refusal to fund expensive anti-retroviral medications such as AZT (Persky 1989, 181). ACT UP Vancouver was the first LGBT coalition in British Columbia *not* dominated by white middle-class males, and it was in marked contrast to the early leadership of the AIDS service groups that obtained provincial funds (Buttle 1990). The participation of women in ACT UP Vancouver expanded from caregivers, as had been the case in previous AIDS service organizations, to leadership, especially as female groups were increasingly afflicted by HIV (Marin 1992). On 11 July 1990, the first meeting of ACT UP Vancouver was announced in a full-page article in the *Vancouver Sun* (Shariff 1990). On 23 August 1990, ACT UP Vancouver held a demonstration in front of a fundraiser for the Social Credit Party of British Columbia (Buttle 1990) as that party was struggling to prepare for the upcoming provincial elections, which it would lose – a public repudiation that would be that party's death knell. Fifty activists confronted the homophobic premier of British Columbia, Bill Vander Zalm, at an opening performance of Hugo's *Les Misérables*. The event became legendary because of accusations that several activists, notably John Kozachenko, spat on the premier (McIntyre 1990).

The *Les Misérables* episode marked the coalescence of queer nationalism in the weeks after the Gay Games in Vancouver (a series of events that transformed public spaces in the city) and just before Queer Nation's skirmishes around the ejection of two women kissing each other at Joe's Café on Commercial Drive. Later in 1990, there were demonstrations at the constituency offices of the provincial minister of health (Vancouver Sun 1990). There were several more actions, less publicized, in 1991, but ACT UP Vancouver soon saw most of its demands met. In the autumn of 1991, Michael Harcourt's NDP provincial government was elected and quickly fulfilled campaign promises for increased levels of funding for HIV education, health care, and social welfare benefits for people living with AIDS. This new support for people with AIDS and HIV did not make ACT UP Vancouver entirely redundant. But most of the activists involved soon had other preoccupations as the new options for treatment took more and more of their time. The last ACT UP Vancouver demonstration was on 1 December 1991, International AIDS Day, and it "protested mandatory testing of health care workers and the lack of access to new drugs to battle HIV"(West Ender 1991).

Diversification, Diffusion, and Institutionalization of LGBT Activism and Public Policy

After the first decades of LGBT organizations, businesses, and cultural institutions, most of the earlier "strategic sites" (Ingram 1997) and spaces in central Vancouver, so important for surviving the criminalization and early decriminalization periods, were gone. Those early establishments and services transformed communities, giving rise to pressures and opportunities for new constellations of entertainment and social spots, along with better meeting places and facilities. As more rights and protections came into place, governments were effectively required, by public pressure and laws, to provide and manage additional and better services. These developments made some early programs offered by LGBT organizations less important and, eventually, redundant. Similarly, the strategic roles of the neighbourhoods of the 1950s and 1960s – Vancouver's Downtown South (with its early gay bars) and the butch/femme spaces along Main Street's Skid Road – were usurped in the 1970s and 1980s by the West End and Commercial Drive, respectively. And today, the roles and relative importance of these enclaves are shifting again.

Few of the older LGBT organizational models, going back to ASK, have disappeared – especially for suburban communities and outlying cities. The building of the AIDS organizations signalled a further institutionalization of LGBT non-governmental organizations, extending to life support, with

Gordon Brent Brochu-Ingram

increasing compromises with government actors. But many personal and collective projects, involving just a few individuals or small memberships, continue and proliferate. A raft of services for youth, elders, families, and, most recently, to educate about and to counter bullying have reiterated those early service models pioneered by ASK and SEARCH.

Social networking has changed the organizational calculus for both small and large organizations. Two examples of new organizations with primary operations grounded in digital transmission and interactions are Our City of Colours and Cancer's Margins. Our City of Colours presents imagery of "different linguistic and cultural communities" providing information and imagery across digital appliances.[16] Similarly, Cancer's Margins: LGBT Community and Arts Project provides information and support across a diversifying set of venues.[17] Both organizations operate as much, perhaps more so, in the suburbs than in central Vancouver.

How can we imagine new policy goals, programs, and spaces based on and increasingly diverging from a half century of organizational models and modes of redistribution of social resources? How can badly needed LGBT infrastructure for suburban communities be envisioned and established in a time when sexual minorities have new opportunities and fewer constraints? The recent discussion around Qmunity (see above) highlights local difficulties in shifting from a politics preoccupied with rights and protection advocacy to a politics more linked to service provision for an increasingly diverse but fragmentary array of LGBT populations. To envision functional organizational models for the future, we can revisit the modes of organizational and spatial development that successfully confronted homophobia/transphobia (and its intersections with misogyny, neocolonialism, racism, cultural chauvinism, and xenophobia) but that have been less effective at appropriating badly needed funding.

1 **Small projects** involving one or a few individuals, such as the BC Lesbian and Gay Archives,[18] are centred on public conversations, such as the need to safeguard historical material and to make it available. Policy goals are operational, such as secure storage, adequate cataloguing, and a secure facility. Funding for this organizational model is limited, personalized, and based on volunteer work and private funding. There is no formal governance and accountability. Spatial allocation is limited to homes and temporary meeting rooms.

2 **Political collectives** are in their fifth decade of providing crucial supports to LGBT populations on the West Coast because their mode of operation is

cheap and flexible. One of the longest surviving collectives was that behind Vancouver's monthly LGBT newspaper *Angles*, which operated from the 1980s to the 1990s. Policy goals are simple and often partisan. Much of the work is carried out by volunteers, and funding is often obtained through memberships and sales. Growth and service provision is often constrained by the difficulty of obtaining non-profit society status, which would qualify groups for foundation and government funding. Modes of governance are more often informal, with modest documentation and little accountability other than to memberships.

3 **Service organizations with memberships,** such as ASK, have been based around high-profile public conversations responding to problems and unmet needs. Largely member-funded, some of these organizations have stabilized and become legally recognized societies with boards administering grants from government agencies and foundations. Much of the work is still undertaken by volunteers with some paid staff. Modes of governance range from well-documented collective decision making to elected boards with appointed officers. Accountability ranges from legal frameworks, such as under the British Columbia Society Act, to ethics, and individual ambitions are linked to generating prestige for board members and officers. Spaces and facilities are rented and are rarely permanent or purpose-built.

4 **Small businesses,** such as Little Sister's Book and Art Emporium (for more details on Little Sister's, see Chapter 10, this volume), provide goods and services to LGBT populations while trying to stay in business. In the case of Little Sister's, this business weathered several terrorist bombings in the 1980s. One of the overriding objectives is to pay staff and bills while building some owner equity. Staff members often agree to be underpaid and to forego benefits. Some businesses have been activist and exceptionally altruistic (e.g., Little Sister's challenge to Customs Canada policy in cooperation with the BC Civil Liberties Union).

5 **Grassroots advocacy organizations,** like ACT UP Vancouver, challenged institutional obstacles through policy solutions (e.g., providing antiretroviral medications). Modes of governance are simple but responsive to immediate issues through regular meetings, combined telephone trees, and, more often, social media. Largely accountable through the laws governing the use of public space, ACT UP Vancouver, which focused on public challenges, was not actually involved with unlawful acts and was never charged with criminality.

6 **Service organizations with linked programs,** such as Vancouver's monthly *Xtra! West,* often function to provide information and to generate public

conversations. Policy goals centre on generating interest through information and discussion to, in turn, maintain readership and advertisers as part of ensuring fiscal viability. Funding strategies can be complex, as with *Xtra! West,* which depends on a corporate entity, Pink Triangle Press, which generates additional income in other parts of Canada. Staff members often work for more standard remuneration packages but with limited prospects for long-term employment and promotions. The mode of governance is complex, with a local editorial group under a mandate from Pink Triangle Press in Toronto. Accountability is through advertiser and reader feedback and the parent organization in central Canada.

7 **Service organizations with numerous programs,** such as Qmunity, reflect multiple convergences of public conversations focused on underserved LGBT populations, especially for mental health,[19] and project-specific collaborations with politicians, agencies, and foundations. The policy goals of such larger organizations are complex, shifting, and linked directly to partisan political and related funding climates. The overall budget is derived from support from multiple sources, involving asymmetrical "collaborations and partnerships."[20] Core funding from more dependable partners is still tenuous. Staff members often expect relatively standard remuneration packages, and Qmunity has collective bargaining agreements. As well as paid stuff, volunteers remain crucial (e.g., the centre's Gay and Lesbian Legal Clinic in the 1990s, which relied on pro bono lawyers).[21] With multiple sources of funds, the modes of organizational governance and accountability are complex. A single board relies on advisory groups, staff, and consultants. Accountability mechanisms are complex, spanning formal program evaluations and audits as well as less public feedback from politicians, government administrators, board members, and clients.

8 **Collaborative government programs with limited accountability to LGBT stakeholders,** such as Vancouver's succession of community liaison programs with law enforcement agencies, have been infrequent and volatile in the Lower Mainland. Such largely politicized initiatives are based on high-profile public conversations, such as those around homophobic and transphobic violence. Typically, government agencies are motivated by a desire to garner more public trust and electoral favour. Policy goals have been linked, in no small part, to media coverage. A range of shifting actors includes government agencies, politicians, political parties, and non-governmental organizations. Funding comes from municipal, provincial, and federal agencies. Modes of governance are complex and only partially

transparent. Accommodation with public agencies on the part of LGBT organizations can be problematic in that it provides increased credibility to public agencies while generating limited results for vulnerable populations. Accountability can span various advisory boards, administrators, and politicians.

Over a half century, the modes of organizational development described above have been combined and reconfigured in scores of ways supporting hundreds of social spaces and service provision teams. But new models and configurations are necessary in order to overcome chronic service gaps. Barriers to program development and funding persist. Consider, for example, the comments of Jennifer Breakspear, the director of Qmunity from 2008 to 2012:

> An issue that demanded a lot of my time was homophobic and transphobic violence and I lobbied hard for funding from the Province for a queer community victim services worker. While the notion received considerable attention in the media and support from at least two Solicitors General (who were both shuffled out of that role before their support could result in funds) it failed to get traction within the provincial government overall.[22]

After decades of public education on homophobia and transphobic violence, the province of British Columbia still insists that its general victim services, staffed by professionals who are not particularly focused on responding to LGBT experiences and needs, remains sufficient.

Conclusion

LGBT sexualities, subcultures, identities, and communities are not simply defined by desires and aspirations for full rights but also by networks of vulnerability, need, and mutual support. Queer organizational and spatial politics remains an under-investigated and poorly theorized field in Canada. As this discussion of BC's Lower Mainland makes evident, a framework for allocating social services and space to LGBT populations has been insufficiently expanded and only partially queered and decolonized.

This chapter examines the development of the organizations, spaces, and facilities for metropolitan Vancouver's LGBT populations as a kind of infrastructure. The myriad decisions around the development of organizations,

Gordon Brent Brochu-Ingram

businesses, service development, and spaces in metropolitan regions have too often relied on poorly nuanced understandings of the synergies between political economies, activism, service allocation, and community development. LGBT activism increasingly operates within an expanding range of policy arenas at federal, provincial, metropolitan, and municipal levels, along with non-governmental organizations and commercial interests. Within this broad set of actors, there continue to be disparities between political and organizational rhetoric, operational goals, written agreements, budgets, and implementation, on the one hand, and funding and administrative support for services to LGBT populations, on the other.

In this chapter, I sketch a framework within which it is possible to inventory synergies, spaces, and benefits spanning activism, policy making, program development, and implementation often conceived through grassroots activism but with subsequent support, funding, and accountability spread across several levels of government, other civil society institutions, and economic actors. Vancouver's LGBT infrastructure gestated under criminalization-era heroism, through ASK, and was then co-opted through the quasi-Keynesianism of the cabinets of Pierre Trudeau's Liberal governments. With globalization and the consequent increasing disparities of wealth in Canadian cities, especially as related to housing costs, some West Coast sexual minorities are again experiencing greater vulnerability (Ingram 2012, 67–76). Over the past decade of neoliberal policies, Vancouver's early modes of garnering social resources for LGBT populations have been eroded and have become increasingly inadequate for dealing with persistent violence and poverty (along with new vulnerabilities). While the extent of the impacts of a range of neoliberal policies on sexual minorities over the last decade and a half is a topic for additional research, what remains most lacking is a "queered" notion of gap analysis vis-à-vis current social programs and the collective imagination to conceive of and to organize new initiatives. These historical and contemporary experiences of numerous LGBT populations, especially those marked by minority race and language status, in not having access to basic social infrastructure, related to being sexual minorities, have barely been acknowledged and may well warrant new expressions of anger and subsequent reconciliation. As LGBT communities diversify and diffuse throughout the metropolitan region, new initiatives to serve the most marginal and vulnerable will require more careful and innovative research, project design, and advocacy, along with a second half century of grassroots activism.

Epilogue

In December 2013, Qmunity – British Columbia's major centre for LGBT services – was allocated a $7 million payment from developers, brokered by the City of Vancouver, in order to finally develop a purpose-built centre. The nature and amount of that funding, triggered by the approval of two huge towers that will transform and largely destroy the old "gay village," differed profoundly from the tiny grants of the past four decades. Not coincidentally, a new LGBT community politics has swiftly emerged, centred on issues of locale, space, facilities design, and service delivery.

Notes

The research for this chapter was supported by grants from the Canada Council for the Arts and the Chicago-based Graham Foundation for Advanced Studies in the Arts.

1 "The trans community is still in dire need of attention, resources, and services." Personal communication with Jennifer Breakspear, 30 November 2012.
2 Personal communication with Cornelia Wyngaarden (an early member of ASK) in 1998 and 2013.
3 I have read every ASK Newsletter published.
4 Don Hann (a GATE member from 1973 to 1979 and present at the 1973 demonstration in Victoria), personal communication in 1999 and 2013.
5 Personal communication with Dorothy-Jean O'Donnell, 17 February 2013.
6 The scant written record of early Two-Spirit activism in Vancouver, often involving small networks, includes an announcement in the late 1991 issue of the local lesbian journal, *Diversity*, for the upcoming 1992 Native Gay and Lesbian Spiritual Gathering hosted by the Vancouver Two-Spirited Society and a 1995 handout for a "Two Spirited Group" meeting weekly at the Gathering Place on Helmcken Street. Personal communication with Ron Dutton, British Columbia Gay and Lesbian Archives, Vancouver, 18 October 2013 (email message on file).
7 Personal communication with Jennifer Breakspear, 30 November 2012.
8 Personal communication with Ron Dutton, 25 September 2012.
9 Personal communication with Michael Morris (co-founder of the Western Front), 18 January 2013.
10 Personal communication with Laiwan, 19 October 2012.
11 During the second and third year (1974 and 1975) of the short-lived Barrett government, I was a teenage university student research intern for the New Democratic Party Caucus in the BC legislature.
12 Celebrated Vancouver and Berlin-based artist Michael Morris, an "out" co-founder of the Western Front artist centre in the 1970s, has noted that the early artist-run cultural organizations in British Columbia, including those that pioneered in being LGBT-friendly, were formed through crucial seed funding from Local Initiatives Projects (LIP) grants (all of which had some scrutiny by federal Liberal politicians and appointees) "because the federal Liberals were terrified of revolution spreading from Quebec." Personal communication with Michael Morris, 18 January 2013.

Gordon Brent Brochu-Ingram

13 "Vancouver [in the 1970s] had a very large hustling scene compared to [Montreal and Toronto, the] other cities I knew ... a widely indulged scene of gay commercial sex workers." Personal communication with Cass (Frank) Brayton, 8 November 2012.

14 Ibid.

15 Personal communication with Jennifer Breakspear, 30 November 2012.

16 Our City of Colours was founded in March 2011 with a Facebook page, https://www.facebook.com/ourcityofcolours/info.

17 Cancer's Margins was formed in 2012 with the leadership of University of British Columbia Faculty of Education professor Mary Bryson. http://www.lgbtcancer.ca/ and https://www.facebook.com/CancersMargins?ref=ts&fref=ts.

18 Personal communication with Ron Dutton, 25 September 2012.

19 Personal communication with Jennifer Breakspear, 30 November 2012.

20 Ibid.

21 Personal communication with Dorothy-Jean O'Donnell, 27 November 2012.

22 Personal communication with Jennifer Breakspear, 30 November 2012.

References

Baldrey, Keith. 1987. "New Quarantine Power Called Frightening to AIDS Sufferers." *Vancouver Sun*, 8 July.

–. 1994. "Advocate of AIDS Colony Remains Mystery." *Vancouver Sun*, 30 March.

Barsotti, Natasha. 2012. "Staff Shakeup at Qmunity." *Xtra! West*, 29 November. http://dailyxtra.com/vancouver/news/staff-shakeup-at-qmunity-3376.

Body Politic. 1975. "Vancouver Gays Hit Barrett Slanders." 17: 6.

Bolan, Kim. 1987. "Safer Sex Campaign Focuses on Gay Clubs, Bathhouses." *Vancouver Sun*, 12 June.

Bouthillette, Anne-Marie. 1997. "Queer and Gendered Housing: A Tale of Two Neighbourhoods in Vancouver." In Anne-Marie Bouthillette, Gordon Brent Ingram, and Yolanda Retter, eds., *Queers in Space: Communities/Public Places/Sites of Resistance*, 213–32. Seattle: Bay Press.

Buttle, Jeff. 1990. "AIDS Activists Won't Stop Confrontations, Protests." *Vancouver Sun*, 13 September.

Canadian Press. 1987. "Prospect of Quarantine Spreads Fear among Gays." *Times-Colonist*, 18 July.

Debord, Guy. (1967) 1994. *The Society of the Spectacle*. Trans. Donald Nicholson-Smith. New York: Zone Books.

Efron, Sarah. 1998. "Dancing in the Streets: Transgendered Hold First-Ever Demo and March." *Xtra! West*, 25 June.

Flather, Patti. 1987. "AIDS Law Protesters Jeer Socred Fundraiser." *Vancouver Sun*, 3 December.

Ford, Clellan S. 1941. *Smoke from Their Fires: The Life of a Kwakiutl Chief*. New Haven, CT: Yale University Press.

Georgia Straight. 1970. "We Are the People Our Parents Warned Us About." *Georgia Straight*, 2–9 December, 9.

–. 1971. "YIP and GLF Space-In." *Georgia Straight*, 3–10 March, 4.

Hill, Harry. 1987a. "Happy Trails." *Angles* (March): 7.

–. 1987b. "Alternative Lifestyles." *Angles* (July): 3, 14–15.

Ingram, Gordon Brent. 1997. "'Open' Space as Strategic Queer Sites." In Anne-Marie Bouthillette, Gordon Brent Ingram, and Yolanda Retter, eds., *Queers in Space: Communities/Public Places/Sites of Resistance*, 95–125. Seattle: Bay Press.

–. 2000. "Mapping Decolonisation of Male Homoerotic Space in Pacific Canada." In Richard Phillips, Diane Watt, and David Shuttleton, eds., *De-Centring Sexualities: Representation and Politics beyond the Metropolis*, 213–34. London: Routledge.

–. 2003. "Returning to the Scene of the Crime: Uses of Trial Narratives of Consensual Male Homosexuality for Urban Research, with Examples from Twentieth-Century British Columbia." *GLQ: A Journal of Lesbian and Gay Studies* 10 (1): 77–110.

–. 2010. "Fragments, Edges, and Matrices: Retheorizing the Formation of a So-called 'Gay Ghetto' through Queering Landscape Ecology." In Catriona Mortimer-Sandilands and Bruce Erickson, eds., *Queer Ecologies: Sex, Nature, Politics, Desire*, 254–82. Bloomington: Indiana University Press.

–. 2012. "From Queer Spaces to Queerer Ecologies: Recasting Gregory Bateson's *Steps to an Ecology of Mind* to Further Mobilise and Anticipate Historically Marginal Stakeholders in Environmental Planning for Community Development." *European Journal of Ecopsychology* 3:53–80.

Kinsman, Gary. 1996. *The Regulation of Desire: Homo and Hetero Sexualities*. Montreal: Black Rose Books.

Lamb, Jamie. 1977. "Basford Denies Rumour." *Vancouver Sun*, 30 April.

Lo, Jenny, and Theresa Healy. 2000. "Flagrantly Flaunting It? Contesting Perceptions of Locational Identity among Urban Vancouver Lesbians." *Journal of Lesbian Studies* 4 (1): 29–44. http://dx.doi.org/10.1300/J155v04n01_03.

Marin, Nikola. 1992. "Talking about AIDS." *Kinesis* (May): 10–11.

McIntyre, Greg. 1990. "ACT UP Faces Five Possible Police Charges." *Vancouver Province*, 26 August.

McLeod, Donald W. 1996. *Lesbian and Gay Liberation in Canada: A Selected Annotated Chronology, 1964–1975*. Toronto: ECW Press/Homewood Books.

Monk, Katherine. 1990. "Wanted: Four Walls." *Vancouver Sun*, 21 September.

Myers, David. 1986. "Hospice Funding Denied." *Angles*, November.

Persky, Stan. 1989. *Fantasy Government: Bill Vander Zalm and the Future of the Social Credit*. Vancouver: New Star Books.

Pollak, Nancy. 1987. "Photograph and Caption." *Kinesis* (October): 3.

Q.Q. aka Kevin McKeown. 1970. "Page 69 Column." *Georgia Straight*, 19–26 August, 21.

–. 1971. "Out of the Closets and into the Street." *Georgia Straight*, 20–27 January, 18.

Rayside, David M., and Evert A. Lindquist. 1993. "AIDS Activism and the State in Canada." *Studies in Political Economy* 39 (Autumn): 37–76.

Ross, Beckie, and Rachael Sullivan. 2012. "Tracing Lines of Horizontal Hostility: How Sex Workers and Gay Activists Battled for Space, Voice, and Belonging in Vancouver, 1975–1985." *Sexualities* 15 (5–6): 604–21. http://dx.doi.org/10.1177/1363460712446121.

Shariff, Shaffin. 1990. "Anger Alone Isn't Enough: ACT UP's Antics Get Attention – But More Constructive Action Now Is Needed." *Vancouver Sun*, 11 July.

Smith, Miriam. 1999. *Lesbian and Gay Rights in Canada: Social Movements and Equality-Seeking, 1971–1995*. Toronto: University of Toronto Press.

Thompson, Joey. 1977. "Making the 'Right' Promises." *Province*, 2 May.

Province. 1974. "Chinese Oilfield Villages Blow Barrett's Mind." 26 November.

Vancouver Sun. 1990. "Seven AIDS Protesters Arrested: Occupied John Jansen's Office." 1 December.

West Ender. 1991. "Group Acts Up." *West Ender* 5 (December): 1.

Yueng, Tom. 1998. "Asian Youth to Gab Together." *Xtra West*, 8 January.

11

"Punch[ing] More Than Its Weight": LGBT Organizing in Halifax, Nova Scotia

NATHANIEL M. LEWIS

Halifax, the capital of Nova Scotia (estimated population of 130,000 in the city proper, 390,000 in the regional municipality), has never been associated strongly with lesbian, gay, bisexual, and transgender (LGBT) movements in Canada. The lack of association is perhaps due, in part, to Halifax's location in a province often characterized as conservative, resistant to change, and governed by old-money elites (Tomblin 1995, 75–78). These generalizations, however, belie diverse political movements that have spawned some of the most notable advances in Canadian LGBT politics. The broad brush of conservatism may be due more to long-term economic and social inequalities than to recent political events: Halifax once anchored a key region in the Canadian staples economy and, more recently, is a "have-not" province recovering from the closure of mines, fisheries, and lumber mills in the 1980s and 1990s. While the agrarian and industrial past of the region established arguably more traditional gender and sexual norms, its current economic downturn has further limited health and social programming for marginalized and "non-mainstream" groups (Bulman 2005). Halifax also lies within a contradictory geography, where distances between communities are long, but the social linkages within and among them – often forged through the long-standing networks of intergenerational families – are dense and tight. Some might consider this a difficult environment for LGBT people, one where big-city opportunities for social anonymity and coming out are limited. Yet, even within a milieu that appears initially discordant with LGBT empowerment, Halifax is home to a large community with a historically strong commitment to political organizing.

Haligonians (residents of Halifax) and other Nova Scotians have frequently led Canada in striking out against homophobia. Residents of the rural Central Nova parliamentary riding protested publicly in 1994 when MP Roseanne Skoke proclaimed that gays and lesbians were a deviant and immoral group with an agenda to seek "special" treatment. The public uproar over her comments was called "Skokewall" to commemorate of the twenty-fifth anniversary of the Stonewall Riots in New York City. Similarly, it was a Haligonian who filed the complaint to the Canadian Broadcast Standards Council in 2000 that required conservative pundit Dr. Laura Schlesinger's radio show to be edited for "abusively discriminatory" comments (Hartlieb 2000). Both events showed that Nova Scotia's communities – even those well outside the city of Halifax – regularly upend conservative stereotypes of the province (Parker 2009).

The history of Halifax's LGBT community, however, has been explored only rarely (see, for example, Plumb 2005). There has long been a tendency in studies of Canadian social and cultural life, particularly those concerned with innovative, progressive, or radical movements, to focus on the "MTV" cities of Montreal, Toronto, and Vancouver (Lewis and Donald 2010). This is especially true of research on LGBT movements, where much of the work suggests that LGBT identities, social movements, and political organizing typically develop in the largest cities and then diffuse outwards to the rest of the country (Knopp and Brown 2003; Parker 2009). It has also been suggested, however, that politics can "jump scale" when movements in neighbourhoods, towns, and municipalities – sometimes in distinctly out-of-centre locations – influence decisions at higher (i.e., provincial and federal) levels of government (Smith 1992). The LGBT community in Halifax has often *appeared* to be on the periphery of queer cultural diffusions in Canada (see Chapter 7, this volume, for a similar argument), yet at particular times has mobilized and jumped scale to promote meaningful changes in provincial and federal policy making.

While the term "LGBT" best approximates the multiplicity of identity-focused rights-seeking movements taken up in Halifax during the past several decades, there has been little simultaneity in these mobilizations (transgender issues have only come to the forefront in the past few years) and perhaps only a limited sense of collective queer mobilization characterized by fuzzier identity categories (Sullivan 2003). Early movements focused on simply outlining gay and lesbian counterpart identities amid the agrarian, rural heteronormativity of the Maritime provinces of Nova Scotia, New Brunswick, and Prince Edward Island (Bulman 2005). As this chapter shows, the divisions between gay and lesbian interests have often been reinforced in the context of a relatively small "pond" of activism where support and resources for LGBT issues are perceived as limited.

Amid these unusual circumstances Halifax has, according to one local HIV/AIDS activist, always "punched more than its weight" in LGBT politics. This chapter demonstrates that the smallness and density of communities has also allowed LGBT Nova Scotians to mobilize quickly and effectively – sometimes resulting in policy changes that have outpaced those in larger provinces. After outlining some of the historical tensions (and resultant pessimism) over LGBT organizing in Halifax in the 1980s and 1990s, I turn to the transitions and events that have shaped LGBT activism here today. The shift is highlighted by three case studies: (1) mobilizations to protect LGBT individuals in Nova Scotia schools, (2) the advent of provincial pension and partnership rights for same-sex couples, and (3) ongoing HIV/AIDS education and prevention efforts in the province.

Historical Background

Historic experiences of fragmentation and competition within Halifax's LGBT community reflect the unique challenges of LGBT organizing in a small city in which a few leaders and institutions have often performed the bulk of the work at any given time. Although archival history prior to the early 1980s is spotty, the earliest organizing in Halifax took the form of the Gay Alliance for Equality, or GAE (1972–88), a liberationist organization housed in *and* funded by a membership-based bar and social club called the Turret, located in downtown Halifax on Barrington Street (Murphy 1995). GAE focused largely on making the community more cohesive and visible. The organization sponsored a "Gayline," a telephone hotline on which GAE members answered questions about upcoming events or how to join GAE. GAE published the city's first gay periodical, the *Gaezette,* during the 1970s and 1980s, as well as several pamphlets about coming out, such as *I Think I Might Be Gay, What Do I Do?* and – for parents and families – *Now That I Know, What Do I Do?* (Nova Scotia Archives, GALA Fonds, 1972–95). For a brief period between 1981 and 1982, GAE also published *Making Waves,* Atlantic Canada's only gay and lesbian quarterly. The publication featured 50 percent lesbian content at a time when gay male identities had begun to dominate the LGBT media of other cities (Murphy 1995; Nash 2005).

By the mid-1980s, however, the management of the Turret bar became both the focus of GAE and a source of tension within the gay and lesbian community. Although other LGBT advocacy organizations in Canada have

　　　　　　　　　　　　　　　　　　Nathaniel M. Lewis

had bars or bar nights – Gays of Ottawa (GO), for example, ran the GO Bar at its organizational headquarters in the 1980s – they were often small, low-profit venues that offered alternatives to larger commercial gay establishments (Smith 2009). In Halifax, funding local LGBT advocacy primarily *through* the management of the community's only bar, one that made $500,000 per year in revenue, was an unusual and ultimately contentious strategy (Murphy 1995).

GAE's successor, the Gay and Lesbian Association of Nova Scotia (GALA NS, or simply GALA), formed in 1988 and had a members-and-guests bar of its own called Rumours. Much like the Turret, Rumours earned annual revenue of $300,000 to $550,000 between 1983 and 1992 (Nova Scotia Archives, GALA Fonds, *GALA News*, 1992, nos. 1–2). By the early 1990s, some began to question whether a commercialized, bar-based mode of organizing served to advance the community or, indeed, if it constituted activism at all. As the main gay (and, to a lesser extent, lesbian) social venue in Halifax *and* the fundraising device for GALA, Rumours muddled the political and financial interests of existing GALA members and foreclosed the participation of potential members who were supporting more specific causes (e.g., HIV/AIDS) or who did not want to organize from the home base of a bar. A 1993 issue of *GALA News*, a newsletter for the organization, said that GALA's agenda of political activism and education was being ignored in order to simply keep Rumours in business. In addition, the patrons of the bar and the dwindling membership of the board were becoming almost exclusively male, white, and able-bodied (Nova Scotia Archives, GALA Fonds, *GALA News*, 1993, nos. 1–2). The tension heightened the next year when a lesbian who had a mobility impairment filed a formal complaint against GALA, citing the lack of disabled access to Rumours. The incident further angered members of both the lesbian and disabled communities and created a rift between local gay men and the rest of Halifax's LGBT community (Nova Scotia Archives, GALA Fonds, *GALA News*, 1994, May–June).

Later that year, female patrons of Rumours insisted that they should be allowed to dance shirtless like the male patrons, an act prohibited by the bar because of its incompatibility with municipal bylaws for alcohol-serving establishments (Feldman 2011). The resultant "Shirtless Wars," which involved widespread boycotts of Rumours by lesbians and other disaffected community members, were less about attire than representation. Many had begun to feel that a bar should neither act as the most visible face of the community nor distract from GALA's broader mission of advocacy. With a dwindling patron base, by 1994 Rumours was no longer clearing a profit. The lack of funds, combined with multiple resignations from the GALA board, rendered the organization non-functional (Boutilier 1995; Vance and Boutilier 1996). In early 1995, GALA declared bankruptcy, Rumours was sold (money from the sale went to the trust company rather than the community), and the organization was dissolved.

By the mid-1990s, a more pessimistic attitude towards LGBT organizing had replaced the buoyancy of the 1970s and 1980s. While a trio of new bars had opened (Paddock 1995), and the still-existing Nova Scotia Rainbow Action Project (NSRAP) took the place of GALA, some community members mourned the loss of Rumours and resented GALA chair Jane Kansas for dissolving the organization during a poorly attended final board meeting (Boutilier 1995). Commentaries in *Wayves,* the new gay and lesbian monthly that replaced *GALA News,* suggested that Halifax's still-fledgling community had been left stranded. Citing low attendance at the new bars and other gay and lesbian events, one commentary claimed that losing Rumours was like losing the community's "central nervous system" (Kozak 1996). Referring to Halifax as a bastion of "conservative absurdities and bewildering beauty," another commentator mused, "I'm still searching for a glimmer of hope for a truly gay, positive, and comfortable social scene in this lovely, semi-old conservative city. Evidence of a gay community would be even better" (Paddock 1997).

Queer Activism Today

A geographically dispersed mode of activism characterizes the LGBT community in Halifax today. This is reflected in both the absence of a recognizable gay neighbourhood in Halifax and the provincially (rather than locally) focused mandates of most of the city's LGBT organizations. Unlike Canada's larger cities, Halifax never experienced the more territorialized forms of organizing built around gay entrepreneurialism and the formation of neighbourhoods such as Church-Wellesley in Toronto, Le Village Gai in Montreal, and Davie Street in Vancouver (Miller 2005; Nash 2005; Podmore 2006). While at least two or three gay and lesbian businesses are (and typically have) clustered around the southern end of Gottingen Street in Halifax's North End, LGBT Haligonians have never had anything resembling a gay village. The absence of a village, however, has not necessarily been seen as a deficiency. In 2001, *Wayves* asked the owner of a new gay bar why he had opened his venue in the middle of downtown Halifax rather than in the North End. By opening the bar in a safer neighbourhood (where many gay men and lesbians already went to straight bars) and offering free entry after lesbian dances, he reasoned, the new bar would draw patrons already going out downtown, offer a space that was accessible to women, and facilitate the type of gay-straight interaction that was unique to Halifax (MacEachern 2001).

Due in part to the lack of a territorial neighbourhood focal point, and perhaps in part to the sense of inter-community kinship that cut across Nova Scotia, LGBT organizing in Halifax has become more of a provincial and regional affair. NSRAP, headquartered in Halifax and comprising fifteen board members from Halifax and nearby towns, lobbies policymakers on several issues (e.g., adding gender identity and gender expression to the Nova Scotia Human Rights Act), organizes local events such as the International Day against Homophobia and Transphobia (IDAHT), and represents the LGBT community in local and national media. Other advocacy organizations focus on LGBT health. The AIDS Coalition of Nova Scotia (ACNS) facilitates care for people who have HIV/AIDS (PHAs) and does HIV prevention outreach at local bars and in public schools across the province. The Lesbian, Gay, and Bisexual Youth Project (informally known as "the Youth Project"), perhaps one of the most visible LGBT organizations in Halifax, offers youth support meetings at its downtown office and organizes anti-homophobia workshops at schools across the province.

Some institutions connect the entire Atlantic Region. *Wayves,* for example, has always included stories on LGBT venues, events, and initiatives beyond the city limits and into New Brunswick, Prince Edward Island, and Newfoundland and Labrador. Halifax Pride, an event that began inauspiciously in 1988 when bystanders heckled the parade marchers – many of whom wore bags over their heads to conceal their identity – now garners thousands of dollars in yearly federal funding and has grown to become the fourth largest pride festival in Canada (Canadian Heritage 2012; Legge 2012; Willick 2012; see also http://halifaxpride.com/about/history/ for a history of Halifax Pride). LGBT advocacy in Halifax is now not only more diffuse geographically and organizationally than it was in the 1980s and 1990s, it is also more diverse. Although Halifax's LGBT community never became a market phenomenon like those in Toronto and Montreal, its tight-knit social connectivity and far-reaching mandate has allowed advocates to make inroads into a wide range of public policy domains.

Queer Activism and Public Policy Changes: Case Studies

Three case studies offer insight into both the challenges experienced by Halifax's LGBT community in the 1990s and the advances grounding the community today: (1) the battle for LGBT rights in Nova Scotia's public schools, (2) securing same-sex pension benefits and partnership in Nova Scotia, and

(3) the history of the HIV/AIDS movement in Halifax. To investigate the three cases, I use a mixed-method approach. Archival sources, especially *Wayves* magazine and the GALA Fonds (located in the Nova Scotia Archives), provided historical context and analysis of these events. I also interviewed eight long-term LGBT activists in order to provide additional insights.

Barometers and Battlegrounds: Transformation in Nova Scotia's Public Schools

Nova Scotia's public schools have frequently acted as barometers for anti-gay stigma and as flashpoints for some of the most contested LGBT equality debates. The case of Eric Smith, a Shelburne County (Southwestern Nova Scotia) schoolteacher whose tenure was terminated because of his HIV-positive status in 1987, is one of the first highly public cases of anti-gay and anti-HIV discrimination in the province. After leaving the Shelburne County School District, Smith was appointed to the province's first HIV/AIDS Task Force, an organization created in response to his termination. He was the only gay-identified and HIV-positive member of the group (CBC News 2011). Although he was uncomfortable with his new position at first, Smith pledged to have both sexual orientation and HIV status added to the Nova Scotia Human Rights Act as grounds for protection from discrimination.

Over the next three years, Smith joined Lesbian and Gay Rights Nova Scotia (LGRNS) and held several meetings with the Nova Scotia Department of Education, while his own case against the Shelburne County School District was fought by the Nova Scotia Teachers Union. Smith achieved his goal of amending the Human Rights Act in 1991, though perhaps not in the way he would have imagined. In May 1991, the provincial government offered him a trade-off: if he would willingly go on disability leave without being reinstated in his teaching position, the province would make the requested changes to the Human Rights Act. In a press release dating from 8 May 1991, Smith indicated that he would not return to his position because "strongly held beliefs within the community ... would make the stress of [his] return very difficult to bear" (Nova Scotia Teachers Union 1991). In contrast, the Shelburne County School Board was dismissive, declaring in its own press release that, while there were "no winners" in the situation, the students would benefit from going to school in a less "emotionally charged" environment (Stoddard 1991). AIDS Nova Scotia and GALA countered with their own releases, stating, respectively, that the case had "created a precedent where individuals, communities, and groups can establish their own set of human rights creating inconsistent rights

Nathaniel M. Lewis

throughout the province" and that it was exemplary of "the sorry state of so-called human rights in Nova Scotia" (AIDS Nova Scotia 1991; GALA 1991).

In 1991, a motion introduced in the Nova Scotia Legislative Assembly by the member for Sackville, John Holm, moved for an amended Human Rights Act protecting Nova Scotians from discrimination on the basis of sexual orientation, something that the provincial government had "promised" in 1989 but never granted (New Democrat Caucus 1991). Smith's battle for an amended Human Rights Act not only lent visibility to LGBT equality in Nova Scotia but also revealed to the rest of Canada that Nova Scotians themselves were more progressive than what Smith's termination had demonstrated (for a similar discussion on progressiveness, see Chapter 7, this volume). A province-wide poll in 1991 found that the vast majority of Nova Scotians did *not* agree that sexual orientation or HIV status constituted grounds for teacher dismissal (GALA 1991). In addition, residents of many parts of the province – even the "little old ladies who had seen him on TV" – approached Smith to express their support and make clear that what was happening in Shelburne County did not represent their views (CBC News 2011).

The Smith case shed light on the challenges of living as both gay and HIV-positive in the context of Nova Scotia's small communities. The fact that Smith's sexual orientation and HIV status became public knowledge so quickly reflects the ongoing difficulties with keeping one's sexuality or HIV status private in places where – as one health care provider put it – "the six degrees of separation are more like two." She continued: "Nova Scotia has big, old families ... in Halifax, and outside of Halifax ... and there's, you know, that whole ... you don't want the Joneses to know. We don't want them to know we have a gay son ... there's that fear that, uh, the family's going to be, uh, somehow implicated, or, you know, treated negatively" (forty-something female health care worker). The Smith case also revealed the highly variegated experiences of LGBT inclusion and exclusion in the province's schools and the ongoing interplay between advocacy in Halifax and events occurring outside the city limits. Smith's emergence as a "reluctant activist" cooperating with Halifax-based lawyers and organizations such as GALA (CBC News 2010) reflects the fact that much of LGBT activism in Halifax has emerged in response to events in other parts of the province rather than to local ones as in Montreal and Toronto.

Despite the lasting effect of the Eric Smith case, Nova Scotia schools have remained flashpoints in debates over LGBT inclusion. In 2000, Lindsay Willow, a Halifax West high school physical education teacher, was accused of inappropriate conduct with a female student because she was seen leaving a locker room with the student and was *believed* to be a lesbian. When the Halifax

Regional Police interviewed Willow and the student and found no basis to proceed with the investigation, Willow filed a complaint with the Nova Scotia Human Rights Commission, stating that she had been forced to come out at work and that her career had been damaged irreparably (CHLN 2006; Hinchliffe 2006; McKinnon 2006). Although Willow ultimately won the case and was awarded $27,000, the compensation was insufficient to cover the $70,000 she had accrued in legal fees (Van Berkel 2006).

In the 2000s, the focus of LGBT movements in Nova Scotia schools shifted to the protection of students rather than teachers. During the decade, many public high schools in Nova Scotia formed student-based gay-straight alliances (GSAs) to support LGBT students and to educate their respective student bodies about sexual difference. Yet, as of 2011, individual schools could still decide whether to permit the formation of a GSA, and at least one high school in the Halifax area had blocked students from creating a GSA. Halifax's Youth Project reacted swiftly. In November 2011, the group organized the Making Waves Conference, an event that brought high school students from across the province to Halifax to learn how to create GSAs (Hinchliffe 2012). Following the conference, the Youth Project began cataloguing and coordinating GSAs in Nova Scotia through a portal on its website.

The next year, representatives of the Youth Project met with Nova Scotia minister of education Ramona Jennex to discuss the dangers of leaving GSA authorization up to individual schools. In June 2012, the minister mandated that no school in Nova Scotia could prohibit the formation of a GSA (Elliott 2012; Youth Project 2012). The new policy spawned GSAs in several schools, including many in rural Nova Scotia (Hinchliffe 2012; NSDE 2012). Tellingly, the change was made almost simultaneously with the passage of Ontario's Accepting Schools Act, 2012 (see Chapter 3, this volume), showing that Nova Scotia was unwilling to be a casual follower in protecting LGBT students (CBC News 2012). According to one activist, the transformation in Nova Scotia schools was also significant given the long-standing culture of silence surrounding LGBT issues:

> I think it's much better now than it was then, simply because I think the educational system has changed. We now have gay and straight alliances in most of the schools, there are support mechanisms now in place for young, gay students, and you know they can actually, it's almost cool to have a gay friend. It might have been cool years ago, but nobody dared to talk about it. (Sixty-something male HIV/AIDS activist)

Nathaniel M. Lewis

LGBT protections in Nova Scotia's schools advanced significantly from the time of the Eric Smith case (1991) to the advent of a provincial GSA policy in 2012. Where LGBT teachers and students were once highly vulnerable to discrimination in an education system that ignored anti-LGBT stigma, universal protections are now firmly entrenched thanks to the mobilizations of Halifax union members, lawyers, and youth.

From Pensions to Partners: Nova Scotians Leading the Canadian LGBT Rights Battle

By the mid-1990s, Canada had taken its first tentative steps towards enshrining equality rights for LGBT citizens. In the *Egan v. Canada* (1995) case, a same-sex spousal benefits case, the Supreme Court of Canada found that sexual orientation was analogous to the other grounds (race, national or ethnic origin, colour, religion, sex, age or mental or physical disability) on which equal rights could not be denied, but it did *not* change laws regarding marriage, adoption, or same-sex partner benefits (Vance 2001). Haligonians, however, quickly initiated a bottom-up drive to translate the *Egan v. Canada* ruling into well-defined same-sex partner rights. In 1995, Wilson Hodder and Paul Boulais, two surviving partners of same-sex couples, immediately began working with Halifax lawyers to gain access to the pensions their partners had earned. They filed complaints with the Nova Scotia Human Rights Commission and built the corresponding cases (*Nova Scotia v. Hodder* and *Nova Scotia v. Boulais*) against their spouses' respective employers, the Nova Scotia Teachers Union and the Nova Scotia Department of Education Pension Plan.

In June 1998, the Canada Pension Plan Appeals Board in Halifax determined that Hodder and Boulais would both receive benefits. They were the first two members of same-sex couples in Canada to receive Canada Pension Plan benefits. Notably, the decision went beyond what had just been mandated by the Ontario Court of Appeal in the 1998 *Rosenberg v. Canada* case. *Rosenberg* ruled only that Revenue Canada could not withhold special tax status from public-sector employers who *opted* to provide pensions to same-sex couple survivors but did not *mandate* that they provide them. The Nova Scotia decision went a step further to suggest that public-sector employers should, in the first place, consider same-sex couples as equal to opposite-sex couples in terms of pension provision (Boutilier 1998). The response to the decision showed that the provincial government was primed to accept same-sex couples as equal: unlike the government of Alberta, which had just appealed (unsuccessfully) a Supreme Court of Canada ruling against using sexual orientation as grounds for employment discrimination (*Vriend v. Alberta* 1998), the Nova Scotia government consented to the Pension Plan Appeals Board's decision immediately.

The Nova Scotia pension ruling, while significant, was a partial victory at best. The decision did not apply to private-sector employees (Morris 1999) and, more important, it did not fundamentally change the laws governing custody, shared property, pensions, and benefits for same-sex couples. It was not until the case of Halifax resident James Bigney, another surviving same-sex partner, that Nova Scotia was forced to consider the legality of the definition of spouse in the Canada Pension Plan Act (Wile 1999). Citing the *Vriend* and *Rosenberg* cases, Bigney and his lawyers applied for and received funding from the now defunct Federal Court Challenges Program to pursue the case in the Nova Scotia Supreme Court in 1999. It was uncertain, however, which level of government – federal or provincial – would provide a solution first. The federal government introduced Bill C-23, the Benefits and Obligations Modernization Act, in 1999 (Vance 2000). C-23 proposed that same-sex common-law couples should have the same pension and benefits rights as opposite-sex common law couples. C-23 passed in 2000, with 75 percent of Atlantic Canadian MPs voting in support of the bill (Vance 2000).

Later in 2000, however, the Nova Scotia government again went a step further than its federal counterpart by introducing the concept of domestic partnership in Canada. The move was a response to mobilizations generated by the *Bigney* case. During a meeting with Bob Fougere from NSRAP, Nova Scotia minister of justice Michael Baker expressed that the province wanted to respond to the community's demands with a more "comprehensive" change in legislation. Nova Scotia's Bill No. 75, tabled on 6 November 2000, not only changed the definition of "common-law" itself to include same-sex couples but also allowed same-sex couples to *purposefully* register as domestic partners under the Vital Statistics Act. This bill meant that same-sex couples in Nova Scotia could actively *acquire* the full battery of benefits afforded to registered opposite-sex couples, as opposed to simply having the right to be *classified* as common-law after a year of co-habitation. Nova Scotia's Domestic Partnership Act, the first in Canada, passed with almost no public opposition (Vance 2001). A year later, in 2001, Nova Scotia also amended the Provincial Adoption Act to allow same-sex couples to adopt children jointly. Drawing from the support of the LGBT community in Halifax, a female couple seeking to jointly adopt one partner's child hired attorney Lara Morris and used funds raised at

Nathaniel M. Lewis

community dances to cover the costs of a swiftly adjudicated provincial case (Donovan 2001). The province became the fourth – after British Columbia, Ontario, and Alberta – to permit same-sex joint adoption.

The Nova Scotia government rendered its decisions on same-sex pensions, partnerships, and adoptions during a time when similar changes were underway at the federal level and in some other provinces (as discussed in this volume). Notably, however, Nova Scotia has often made the choice to actively change the status of its LGBT residents, while other provinces have waited for the results of court cases or top-down decisions from the federal government. Nova Scotia's avant-gardist approach to LGBT policy in the 1990s and early 2000s (i.e., making swift and substantial changes rather than incremental ones), while triggered by mobilizations in Halifax, is perhaps also representative of how Nova Scotians view themselves in the context of the Canadian state. While many value Nova Scotia's small communities, collectivist culture, and rural agricultural traditions as traits to be defended, they are also wary of the possibility that other Canadians might associate them with conservatism or backwardness. Consequently, policymakers and leaders in Nova Scotia, and particularly in Halifax, have also taken pains to position the province as a distinctive yet forward-thinking place with its own identity and its own approaches to Canadian politics (Marontate 2002).

Beyond the Epicentres: Halifax as an Unlikely Site of HIV/AIDS Organizing

In other Canadian cities, the HIV/AIDS epidemic has provided a central point of mobilization for LGBT communities. Much like the movements in New York, San Francisco, and elsewhere in the United States, the beginnings of HIV/AIDS advocacy in cities like Vancouver occurred against the backdrop of neighbourhoods such as Yaletown and the West End, where hundreds of victims were neglected by a health care system that could not (or would not) care for them (see Brown 1997, 31–56; see also Chapter 10, this volume). In Halifax, the epidemic has been less dramatic. Only 361 cases of AIDS have ever been registered and reported in Nova Scotia and Prince Edward Island combined (PHAC 2010). Consequently, Halifax has frequently been overlooked in national-level policy and planning discussions related to HIV/AIDS. In 1997, for example, Halifax was bypassed in Health Canada consultations regarding the National Strategy on HIV/AIDS, despite experiencing an outbreak that was still significant relative to its population (Wile 1997). As the Eric

Smith case suggests, HIV/AIDS has also been a more contentious LGBT issue in Nova Scotia than have pension or partnership rights. Due to public apathy, scepticism towards the epidemic, and a lack of government funding, along with poor condom use rates and significant anti-HIV stigma within the gay community itself, HIV/AIDS work in Nova Scotia has "always been an uphill battle" (Leyte 1995). According to one activist:

> Politicians are always concerned about how things are going to play to the public at large, and so if they do [fund HIV/AIDS work], if they are seen as being too supportive of druggies and fags, so there's always been that dynamic ... When [HIV/AIDS task force reports] came out, you know, in the late '80s, the provincial government funding did start to respond ... [T]hey came out with the report and all the recommendations that actually had some meat attached to them were taken out ... [I]t's a have-not province; there's never been extra money in the budget to throw around. (Fifty-something male HIV/AIDS outreach worker)

As in other sectors of LGBT advocacy in Halifax, the HIV/AIDS movement has also endured several internal conflicts. In 1988, several board members of the Metro Area AIDS Coalition (MacAIDS) observed that the organization, while focused on preserving "public health," seemed to care little about the needs of the gay-identified men who had contracted HIV/AIDS or were most likely to contract it. In response, the dissenting members formed the Nova Scotia Coalition of People with AIDS (NSCPWA) and adopted a mission of targeted education with an emphasis on outreach in vulnerable communities. In 1995, however, funding cuts forced NSCPWA to join up with AIDS Nova Scotia (the new iteration of MacAIDS) to become the AIDS Coalition of Nova Scotia (ACNS) (Boutilier 1996). This time, the group members were divided by their views on race rather than by their views on sexual difference. While the new ACNS president (from NSCPWA) had begun a Black Outreach Program, the vice-president (from AIDS Nova Scotia) believed that the new agency should move "toward the mainstream" by focusing on very general public health concerns. In 1996, the vice-president urged the ACNS board to fire the president because of his supposed failure to address alleged acts of fiscal impropriety on the part of two of the board members – a claim that was eventually dropped. Even under siege, the Black Outreach Program was one of the first programs in Canada to recognize the marginalization of gay black men in Halifax and the distinct HIV-related risks they faced, including poverty, lack of education, and prejudices from within African Canadian communities (Boutilier 1996).

Despite conflicts, HIV/AIDS advocates in Halifax have continued to target underserved populations in innovative ways. The Nova Scotia Men's Project, initiated in 1991, was the first group in Nova Scotia to conduct outreach with rural communities and marginalized groups such as male sex workers (Leyte 1995). In 1997, the Men's Project created the *Community Development Handbook for Gay and Bisexual Men,* a tool to educate gay and bisexual men and the agencies serving them (Connors 1998). ACNS was also one of the first AIDS organizations in Canada to have a rural residing chair and to attempt training health care workers in rural communities (McNutt 2000). In addition, several smaller AIDS organizations, such as the (Annapolis) Valley AIDS Concern Group, the Pictou County AIDS Coalition, and the AIDS Coalition of Cape Breton, operated in rural areas from the early 1990s onward. The partnership between the ACNS and the provincial government, augmented by earlier groundwork among these regional organizations, resulted in the first *provincial* strategy on HIV/AIDS in Canada (2003), as opposed to the localized (and usually urban) interventions levied in other provinces. As of 2012, the Nova Scotia strategy is one of two in Canada, along with Saskatchewan's.

Some local activists say, however, that the creation of a strategy document cannot overcome a funding regimen that remains constrained by the province's economy and bureaucracy and persistent beliefs among policymakers that HIV is not an important issue in Nova Scotia. One of the key gaps is the lack of anonymous HIV testing (AHT) sites. There are only two in Nova Scotia, compared with seven in New Brunswick and over fifty each in British Columbia and Ontario, respectively. One outreach worker explained why many Nova Scotians are still unlikely to be tested for HIV unless it can be done anonymously:

> Well, the one thing I guess I had noticed [in online educational outreach to gay men] was concern about the amount of discretion of getting STD tests, or STI tests, in their local community, and this very much was a concern outside of Halifax, in smaller communities where, you know, as one person put it quite literally, "The person who works, who does the tests in the lab knows me, if they see my name, they're going to know who's having the test done." (Fifty-something male HIV/AIDS outreach worker)

Another pointed out the challenges of HIV/AIDS education in an aging province where teachers, often from an older generation, are uncomfortable with teaching the topic (see also Langille et al. 2001): "We all know that HIV is in the curriculum from Grade 3 up. However, the teachers ... don't have the capacity, they don't have the knowledge and [HIV should be] taught by a teacher who cares and [who works] in a [health-related field]" (sixty-something male HIV/AIDS advocate). A third activist explained that the anti-HIV stigma in Nova Scotia is not confined just to institutions such as schools but, rather, is dispersed through the community itself. She described the response to an HIV prevention messaging program initiated in the mid-2000s:

> We developed a campaign called "Are you Negative About Positives" ... and we actually had local volunteers who wanted to participate in the pictures for the campaign which was great ... but the stigma, the harassment that the volunteers received, we had to pull the campaign, it was that bad ... they had past lovers calling saying: "You're positive, I'm going to get tested, I'll see you in court" ... they had parents, family members crying, people yelling at them in bars, it was bad. (Forty-something female HIV/AIDS organization director)

Although Nova Scotia is currently a province with relatively low HIV prevalence, the scenario of a still-reluctant education system, increasing accessibility of sex (e.g., online and in the media), and out-migration (and return migration) of men who have sex with men and resource-economy workers could significantly create a "powder keg" situation with regard to HIV incidence in a province still poorly equipped to manage the disease (forty-something female HIV/AIDS policy specialist). Despite long-terms efforts among Halifax activists and advocates to address the needs of those with HIV/AIDS, it appears that they will also need top-down support to ramp up prevention and education in the province.

Conclusion

Even with the significant legislative victories gained by LGBT Nova Scotians in the 1990s and 2000s, the day-to-day inclusion of LGBT Nova Scotians has not always seemed so secure. In 2007, the town council of Truro – the fourth largest community in the province – voted against flying the pride flag during the August pride celebrations in Halifax and nearby Pictou County. The mayor cited the Bible and his Christian duty as the reasons for standing by the decision (CBC News 2007; Malloy 2007). As in the past, activists from Halifax, Truro, and other towns responded, organizing a rally of more than one hundred in front of Truro Town Hall just two days later (Tanner 2007). The man who led the rally explained that it was a significant event in a town in which LGBT identities had previously been invisible: "I mean most gay men in rural Nova Scotia are so, to some degree, so closeted ... they don't want everybody to know they're

Nathaniel M. Lewis

gay ... [M]y mayor refused to fly the Pride flag and then compared us to pedophiles and, uh, quoted scripture to me" (thirty-something male activist).

Occasionally, the local media has also employed the tropes of the irresponsible gay male and the besieged LGBT community to sensationalize moments of tragedy. In the second week of May 2007, two murders of gay men – one at Spectacle Lake in the Halifax area and another in the town of Lunenburg about sixty-five kilometres (forty miles) southwest of Halifax – set off a series of articles that linked "gay cruising" and "serial killers," some of which indicated that the LGBT community was in a "state of panic" (Flinn 2007; McKinnon 2007). On the one hand, the response universalized and pathologized the behaviours of gay men; on the other hand, it also furnished an opportunity for bridge-building between the Halifax Regional Police and the community. For the first time, an unofficial liaison, Debbie Carleton, addressed the gay community directly, urging men to avoid areas like Spectacle Lake as a safety precaution, rather than simply "cracking down" on cruising activity that had reportedly been the source of complaints for the past several years (McKinnon 2007; NSRAP 2004). While the policing of sexual activity in the name of "safety" can still be read as an oppressive form of regulation, the 2007 events also marked the first time that the local police acknowledged LGBT people as a community with distinct protection concerns.

More recently, on 17 April 2012, well-known Halifax activist Raymond Taavel was murdered outside Menz Bar on Gottingen Street in Halifax's North End. Since the perpetrator was heard uttering the word "faggot" while beating Taavel, it was quickly labelled a hate crime. An investigation revealed, however, that the perpetrator was an Aboriginal man on leave from a nearby psychiatric facility. Some mused that the media's efforts to link the terms "gay activist" and "murder" was yet another ploy to paint the LGBT community as one beset by tragedy (Mombourquette 2012). Again, however, the event lent an opportunity for visibility and cooperation. In under twenty-four hours community members planned and led a vigil on Gottingen Street that was attended by over three hundred people (Shiers and Jeffrey 2012; Stephenson 2012). Within the next several months, the Youth Project had planned a fundraiser in Taavel's memory, business owners had created a "Gaybourhood Watch" program for lower Gottingen Street, and the health authority began investigating the protocols for patient leave at psychiatric care facilities (Fraser 2012; Ross 2012).

Finally, the power of the closet is still considerable in educational institutions and rural communities, two places that, incidentally, have been central in the province's LGBT rights-seeking movement. In a recent commentary in the

Halifax *Chronicle Herald,* columnist Angela Mombourquette (2011) said: "Here's what I know: a lot of teachers and school administrators in Halifax Regional Municipality are homosexual – and most of them are not even close to being out at school." While protected from the type of discrimination encountered by Eric Smith, LGBT teachers are still harassed in the workplace by students, parents, and other teachers. Other professionals may continue to closet themselves due to the perception of a "pink ceiling" that will limit their career advancement after coming out. For those outside the city of Halifax, the struggle for any kind of routinized visibility of LGBT identities is perhaps more dire. One activist described the challenges of LGBT livelihoods in central Nova Scotia as follows:

> When you come to a smaller community ... there are none of those festivals around, none of those events. You know there may be the odd dance, but you know the odd dance turns into a hidden fiasco ... [T]hey still want to have it on a street where there's no street lights ... so nobody actually sees who's coming and going ... The Pride groups in Pictou County and Cumberland County and Colchester County have all gone belly up because nobody wants to sort of stick their head out to be the leader. (Sixty-something male HIV/AIDS activist)

These narratives reveal that the swift, sometimes surprising, legal progress of the 1990s and early 2000s has ushered in an era of improved but still incomplete and geographically variable inclusion of LGBT visibilities and identities in Nova Scotia.

Perhaps the important lesson in this chapter is that LGBT mobilizations in Halifax have not always followed the linear, evolutionary trajectory of public protest, territorialization (e.g., gay village creation), and "mainstreaming" described in much of the work on gay neighbourhoods (Collins 2004) or LGBT advances more generally (Seidman 2002, 61–96; Weeks 2007, 23–56). Consequently, these cases call into question whether linear progress narratives hold significant explanatory power beyond the places (e.g., large metropolitan areas) where liberal social milieus, gay liberation movements, and favourable economic trends (e.g., urban growth and redevelopment) have aligned more neatly. In contrast, the LGBT community in Halifax has been more focused on defending the rights of LGBT people *across* the province and animating provincial politics rather than developing an urban LGBT community in Halifax.

Due to Nova Scotia's contradictory geography, however, the outcomes of this broad-based approach are as diverse as is Nova Scotia. The smallness and

Nathaniel M. Lewis

connectivity of Halifax's LGBT community and the province itself have allowed for swift organizational mobilizations and the quick diffusion of legislative change through the various levels of government. At the same time, this small-ness and connectivity in the province's smaller and more remote communities – or even within segments of Halifax's population – can create inertia and resistance to those changes, resulting in a highly variegated landscape of day-to-day inclusion for LGBT Nova Scotians. Funding for some work (e.g., HIV/AIDS outreach) remains limited, instances of discrimination continue, and access to services is still a problem for LGBT Nova Scotians living outside of Halifax. The spectre of a more intolerant past, however, continues to be whit-tled down as Halifax's LGBT community continues to engage in its own unique mode of politics. Its location may be peripheral to Canada's larger centres, but its politics – as the previous cases show – is anything but.

References

AIDS Nova Scotia. 1991. Press Release. 8 May. Nova Scotia Archives, GALA Fonds.

Boutilier, Ross. 1995. "Rumours of My Death Are Not Exaggerated." *Wayves*, February, 4.

–. 1996. "Perspectives: AIDS, Homophobia, and Other Stories." *Wayves*, December/January, 4.

–. 1998. "Nova Scotia Leads the Way." *Wayves*, June, 1.

Brown, Michael P. 1997. *RePlacing Citizenship: AIDS Activism and Radical Democracy*. New York: Guilford Press.

Bulman, Diane. 2005. "A Constructivist Approach to HIV/AIDS Education for Women within the Maritime Provinces of Canada." *International Journal of Lifelong Education* 24 (6): 475–87. http://dx.doi.org/10.1080/02601370500280165.

Canadian Heritage. 2012. *Harper Government Invests in Arts and Culture in Nova Scotia*. Ottawa Department of Canadian Heritage. 18 July. http://pch.gc.ca/eng/1342612211921.

Canadian, HIV/AIDS Legal Network (CHLN). 2006. *Gay and Lesbian Legal Issues and HIV/AIDS: Final Report. Law 2*. Toronto: Canadian HIV/AIDS Legal Network. http://www.aidslaw.ca/Maincontent/issues/gaylesbian/finalreports/gllilaw2.htm.

CBC News. 2007. "Truro in Gay Flag Flap." 3 August. Toronto: Canadian Broadcasting Corporation. http://www.cbc.ca/news/canada/nova-scotia/story/2007/08/03/truro-gay.html.

–. 2010. "AIDS Activist Lauded for Perseverance." 23 October. Toronto: Canadian Broadcasting Corporation. http://www.cbc.ca/news/canada/nova-scotia/aids-activist-lauded-for-perseverance-1.971608

–. 2011. "At the Table (Episode with Eric Smith)." 10 February. Toronto: Canadian Broadcasting Corporation. http://www.cbc.ca/atthetable/2011/02/eric-smith.html.

–. 2012. "'Gay-Straight Alliances' Get Green Light under Ontario Bill." 25 May. Toronto: Canadian Broadcasting Corporation. http://www.cbc.ca/news/canada/toronto/story/2012/05/25/gay-straight-alliances-ontario297.html.

Collins, Alan. 2004. "Sexual Dissidence, Enterprise and Assimilation: Bedfellows in Urban Regeneration." *Urban Studies* (Edinburgh) 41 (9): 1789–806. http://dx.doi.org/10.1080/0042098042000243156.

Connors, L. 1998. "Men's Sex Project Update." *Wayves*, December/January, 6.

Donovan, M. 2001. "We Are a Family … and It's Legal." *Wayves*, October, 8.

Elliott, Wendy. 2012. "Elliott Column." *Kings County Register/Kings County Advertiser*, 15 May. http://www.kingscountynews.ca/Opinion/Columns/2012-05-15/article-2983707/Elliott-column/1.

Feldman, Jake. 2011. "The Shirtless Debates: The Beginning of the End of Halifax Liberationist Activism from 1989–1995." Paper delivered at "We Demand": History/Sex/Activism in Canada / "Nous demandons": Histoire/Sexe/Activisme au Canada. Vancouver, 25 August. http://ocs.sfu.ca/history/index.php/wedemand/2011/schedConf/program.

Flinn, Sean. 2007. "Fair Warning: How the Cops Managed to Turn Cruising into a Public Safety Issue without Pissing off the Gay Community." *Coast*, 17 July. http://www.thecoast.ca/halifax/fair-warning/Content?oid=961039.

Fraser, Laura. 2012. "Gaybourhood Watch Launched in Halifax." *Chronicle Herald*, 17 August. http://thechronicleherald.ca/metro/127339-gaybourhood-watch-launched-in-halifax.

Gay and Lesbian Association of Nova Scotia (GALA). 1991. *Gay and Lesbian Association Calls for New Human Rights Bill*. Press Release. 9 May. Nova Scotia Archives, GALA Fonds.

Hartlieb, Renee. 2000. "Cleaning up the Airwaves: Halifax Man Takes on American Giant." *Wayves*, June, 1.

Hinchliffe, Aethne. 2012. "Gay/Straight Alliance Group to Promote Awareness." *Advance*, 13 March. http://www.theadvance.ca/Living/2012-03-13/article-2925386/Gay-straight-alliance-group-to-promote-awareness/1.

–. 2006. "Human Rights Commission Hearing to Examine Complaint Based on Perceived Sexual Orientation." *Wayves*, January/February, 11. http://wayves.ca/online/Wayves_2006_01.pdf.

Knopp, Larry, and Michael Brown. 2003. "Queer Diffusions." *Environment and Planning D: Society and Space* 21 (4): 409–24. http://dx.doi.org/10.1068/d360.

Kozak, Ben. 1996. "Commentary." *Wayves*, December/January, 1.

Langille, Donald, David MacKinnon, Emily Marshall, and Janice Graham. 2001. "So Many Bricks in the Wall: Young Women in Nova Scotia Speak about Barriers to School-Based Sexual Health Education." *Sex Education: Sexuality, Society and Learning* 1 (3): 245–57. http://dx.doi.org/10.1080/14681810120080640.

Legge, Lois. 2012. "Remembering When It Wasn't OK to Be Gay." *Chronicle Herald*, 28 July. http://thechronicleherald.ca/metro/121618-remembering-when-it-wasn-t-ok-to-be-gay.

Lewis, Nathaniel, and Betsy Donald. 2010. "A New Rubric for 'Creative City' Potential in Canada's Smaller Cities." *Urban Studies* (Edinburgh) 47 (1): 29–54. http://dx.doi.org/10.1177/0042098009346867.

Leyte, D. 1995. "What Is the Men's Project?" *Wayves*, May, 4.

MacEachern, Brenley. 2001. "Eagle Owner Spreading His Wings." *Wayves*, April, 8.

Malloy, Jason. 2007. "Town Won't Be Flying Gay Pride Flag." *Truro Daily*, 3 August. http://www.trurodaily.com/Living/Faith/2007-08-03/article-353883/TOWN-WONT-BE-FLYING-GAY-PRIDE-FLAG.

Marontate, Jan. 2002. "Les rapports d'appartenance aux lieux de création et l'art contemporain en région périphérique: Le cas de la Nouvelle-Écosse, 1992–2002." *Sociologie et Sociétés* 34 (2): 139–61. http://dx.doi.org/10.7202/008136ar.

McKinnon, Bill. 2006. "HRM School Board Wants to Know." *Wayves*, March, 4.

–. 2007. "Double Homicide Shock in Nova Scotia." *Wayves*, June, 1.

McNutt, Al. 2000. "ACNS General Meeting: Report from the Chair." *Wayves*, July/August, 2.

Miller, Vincent. 2005. "Intertextuality, the Referential Illusion and the Production of a Gay Ghetto." *Social and Cultural Geography* 6 (1): 61–79. http://dx.doi.org/10.1080/1464936052000335973.

Mombourquette, Angela. 2011. "For Gay Teachers, Coming Out Is a Lot Harder Than It Sounds." *Chronicle Herald*, 14 November. http://thechronicleherald.ca/hcw/32713-gay-teachers-coming-out-lot-harder-it-sounds.

–. 2012. "Inappropriate to Label City in Wake of Taavel's Killing." *Chronicle Herald*, 23 April. http://thechronicleherald.ca/hcw/89428-inappropriate-to-label-city-in-wake-of-taavel-s-killing.

Morris, L. 1999. "That's Nice for Ontario But What about the Maritimes?" *Wayves*, June, 4.

Murphy, Lynn. 1995. "Making Waves." *Wayves*, February, 3.

Nash, Catherine Jean. 2005. "Contesting Identity: Politics of Gays and Lesbians In Toronto in the 1970s." *Gender, Place and Culture* 12 (1): 113–35. http://dx.doi.org/10.1080/09663690500083115.

New Democrat Caucus. 1991. Notice of Motion. 10 May. Nova Scotia Archives, GALA Fonds.

Nova Scotia Department of Education. 2012. "Students Honoured for Making Positive Difference in Schools, Communities." 6 June. Halifax: Department of Education. http://novascotia.ca/news/release/?id=20120606008 (accessed 23 September 2012).

Nova Scotia Rainbow Action Project (NSRAP). 2004. "A Public Spectacle at Dartmouth's Spectacle Lake?" *Wayves*, October. http://www.nsrap.ca/docs/wayves_10_04.pdf.

Nova Scotia Teachers Union. 1991. Press Statement, 8 May. Nova Scotia Archives, GALA Fonds.

Paddock, Norm. 1995. "GALA: Ask Not for Whom the Bell Tolls." *Wayves*, March, 4.

–. 1997. "Commentary." *Wayves*, February.

Parker, David. 2009. "Queer Country: Mapping Queer Liberation in Rural Nova Scotia." *Dominion*, 23 November. http://www.dominionpaper.ca/articles/3023.

Plumb, Donovan. 2005. "Grassroots Response to HIV/AIDS in Nova Scotia." *New Directions for Adult and Continuing Education* 10 (105): 65–73. http://dx.doi.org/10.1002/ace.170.

Podmore, Julie A. 2006. "Gone 'Underground'? Lesbian Visibility and the Consolidation of Queer Space in Montreal." *Social and Cultural Geography* 7 (4): 595–625. http://dx.doi.org/10.1080/14649360600825737.

Public Health Agency of Canada (PHAC). 2010. *HIV/AIDS Epi Update 2 (July 2010): Undiagnosed HIV Infections in Canada*. Ottawa: Public Health Agency of Canada. http://www.phac-aspc.gc.ca/aids-sida/publication/epi/2010/2-eng.php.

Ross, Selena. 2012. "Gay Youth to Benefit from Taavel Fundraiser." *Chronicle Herald*, 16 May. http://thechronicleherald.ca/metro/96808-gay-youth-to-benefit-from-taavel-fundraiser.

Seidman, Steven. 2002. *Beyond the Closet: The Transformation of Gay and Lesbian Life*. New York: Routledge.

Shiers, Kelly, and Davene Jeffrey. 2012. "Gay Activist Beaten to Death." *Chronicle Herald*, 19 April. http://thechronicleherald.ca/metro/87595-gay-activist-beaten-to-death.

Smith, Dale. 2009. "25 Years of Pink Triangle Services." *Capital Xtra*, 25 March. http://www.xtra.ca/public/Ottawa/25_years_of_Pink_Triangle_Services-6485.aspx.

Smith, Neil. 1992. "Contours of a Spatialized Politics: Homeless Vehicles and the Production of Geographical Scale." *Social Text* 33 (33): 54–81. http://dx.doi.org/10.2307/466434.

Stephenson, Marilla. 2012. "Death of Gay Activist Demands Investigation of System." *Chronicle Herald*, 19 April. http://thechronicleherald.ca/opinion/88177-stephenson-death-of-gay-activist-demands-investigation-of-system.

Stoddard, M. 1991. Press Statement from Shelburne County School Board. 8 May. Nova Scotia Archives, GALA Fonds.

Sullivan, Nikki. 2003. *A Critical Introduction to Queer Theory*. New York: New York University Press.

Tanner, Kim. 2007. "More Than 100 Gather in Truro, NS, for Gay Pride Rally Amid Flag Flap." *Guardian*, 6 August http://www.theguardian.pe.ca/Faith/2007-08-06/article-1282961/More-than-100-gather-in-Truro-N.S.-for-gay-pride-rally-amid-flag-flap.

Tomblin, Stephen. 1995. *Ottawa and the Outer Provinces: The Challenge of Regional Integration in Canada*. Toronto: James Lorimer and Company.

Van Berkel, Lis. 2006. "The Destruction, Rebuilding, Vindication, and Progression of Lindsay Willow." *Coast*, 20 July. http://www.thecoast.ca/halifax/the-destruction-rebuilding-vindication-and-progression-of-lindsay-willow/Content?oid=959377.

Vance, Kimberley. 2000. "It's About Time." *Wayves*, March, 8.

–. 2001. "Domestic Bliss? Nova Scotia Introduces Registered Domestic Partnership Legislation." *Wayves*, December/January, 1.

Vance, Kim, and Ross Boutilier. 1996. "Our Invitation to the Bench." *Wayves* (December/January): 2.

Weeks, Jeffrey. 2007. *The World We Have Won*. London: Routledge.

Wile, Michael. 1997. "AIDS Conference Opens before National Strategy Finalized." *Wayves*, November, 5.

–. 1999. "Jim Bigney's Pension Pursuit." *Wayves*, May, 1.

Willick, Frances. 2012. "Turning 25 with Halifax Pride." *Chronicle Herald*, 29 July. http://thechronicleherald.ca/metro/121950-turning-25-with-halifax-pride.

Youth Project. 2012. "Go GSAs!!!" 6 June. Halifax. http://www.youthproject.ns.ca/news.php.

Conclusion

MANON TREMBLAY

The image of a state hounding and repressing lesbian, gay, bisexual, transsexual, transgender, and queer (LGBTQ) people is certainly not unfounded in Canadian history. In effect, the "fruit machine" symbolizes the fantasy of being able to detect and to identify homosexuals, and proposals made in some provinces to put people suspected of testing positive for HIV into quarantine cast a shadow on the constitutional state. In reality, the repression of queer people has resulted from a mode of hegemony – that is, "a power formation of the modern state that is grounded in civil society" (Ludwig 2011, 50) – and operates through private groups such as neighbourhood communities, social organizations, schools, and religious groups. In this regard, as Julie Depelteau and Dalie Giroux explain in Chapter 2 (this volume), residential schools constituted machines for crushing the multiple-gender systems of Aboriginal youth: "The residential schools policy effectively created spaces for the clergy to, with state authority, permanently settle Aboriginal bodies in two genitally based categories. Two body types were established within this non-mixed normative and disciplinary set-up, with two sexes corresponding to two genders – boy/girl, man/woman" (see p. 72). These two images – open repression and subtle performative heteronormative hegemony – in a way define the vast arena in which, since the partial decriminalization of homosexuality in 1969, queer activism has confronted Canadian governments and public policy. It is this vast arena upon which the authors in *Queer Mobilizations: Social Movement Activism and Canadian Public Policy* have tried to shed light by exploring how LGBTQ movements and Canadian governments have been interacting since the 1970s.

In this book, queer activism has been apprehended, analyzed, and assessed in the light of governments in Canada and their public policies. These protagonists – the LGBTQ movement and Canadian governments – interact in the context of a political regime that, as a general rule, has worked favourably for queer activism. This general conclusion concurs with Miriam Smith's (2008) well-developed analysis, which brings to light the influence on queer activism of the legacies of both past public policies and the political regime. As she explains:

> [Political] institutions provide the strategic context for political actors, structuring the play of social forces in the policy process. Differences in core political institutions (federalism, separation of powers, and the role of the courts) combined with differences in constitutional rules and practices between [Canada and the United States], have played a major role in facilitating very rapid policy change in Canada over the last decade while blocking policy change in the US. While courts have played a central role in policy changes in the US and Canada, the impact of courts can only be assessed in relation to the larger political institutional structure of which they are a part. In Canada, since the entrenchment of a constitutional bill of rights (the Charter) in 1982, courts are uniquely powerful in part because they are not as hemmed in by institutional limits, as US courts. (Smith 2008, 3)

The centralization (or "federalization") of the protection of human rights since the Canadian Charter was adopted, the concentration of state power within the cabinet (or in the hands of first ministers), whose omnipotence is assured by a disciplined parliamentary caucus, and the lack of means available to the opposition both inside and outside of Parliament to counteract the government's plans were all factors that contributed to advances in LGBTQ activism in Canada (see Smith 2010, 2011). Simply put, political institutions matter. In this conclusion I provide several examples to support the *first observation* emerging from these chapters: as a general rule, the Canadian political regime has offered favourable institutional opportunities to queer activism. There are several possible reasons for this: the federal structure of the Canadian state, the Charter and the interpretations of it made by the courts, governments resolved to act in favour of LGBTQ rights, and forces hostile to queer activism having little influence on the political decision-making process.

Although federalism no doubt provides the most obvious of these opportunities, it cannot be understood in isolation as it interacts with other aspects of the Canadian political regime to mould the environment in which the queer movement takes collective action. Thus, although the political regime generally results in positive institutional opportunities for queer activism, the contrary

Manon Tremblay

has also occurred. For instance, as illustrated in chapters in this book, negative outcomes occurred under governments led by political parties with ideologies unfavourable to LGBTQ movements. More generally, such outcomes occurred because the state (including its civil service) is rife with contradiction: it is not a rational actor pursuing a single objective but, rather, is diversified, fragmented by several and contesting voices, and fraught with conflict and tension. The state may confer rights and services with one hand and repress with the other (one example is the censorship exercised by Canada Customs in its attempt to limit the availability of, if not ban outright, certain lesbian magazines). The state may also respond to the demands of some segments of the queer community but ignore claims made by other segments (such as those put forward by trans people). Hence, a question for future researchers is: For which forms of queer activism and for which groups of queers does the Canadian political regime offer favourable institutional opportunities? For instance, section 15 of the Charter of Rights and Freedoms was the key to recognition of the equality of LGBTQ people before the law; however, it has also helped to reshape queer activism towards greater professionalization. This is no doubt beneficial to LGBTQ people who are willing to play the mainstreaming and homonormalization game, but it marginalizes other LGBTQ people, giving them a less enviable status and stripping them of resources with which to interact with governments. In this sense, relations between LGBTQ activism and governments in Canada fully embody power relations modelled by gender, ethnicity and race, social class (including schooling and wealth), and a plethora of other variables. In *Queer Mobilizations*, we lift the veil slightly on this dimension, but a more detailed analysis remains to be done. Thus, although political institutions matter, they are not decisive; their effects also vary depending on the profiles and resources of LGBTQ people.

Below, I identify and analyze some of the observations made by the authors in this book and suggest several avenues for future research. As the analysis shows, LGBTQ activism has benefited from the institutional architecture of the Canadian political regime.

A *second observation* that emerges from *Queer Mobilizations* is that queer activism in Canada is in the image of Canada itself: both united and diversified. In fact, the coexistence of these two features should not be surprising because the function of federalism is to unite what is diversified. Speaking of Ontario, David Rayside (Chapter 3, see p. 85, this volume) explains:

> The waves of advocacy in this province, as well as their successes and limitations, display a central contradiction in the story of Canadian LGBT politics. On the one hand, this is a profoundly local and regional story ... The modern

movement began with local groups, and today the majority of work that is done to address inequity and marginalization is effected at the local level. Canada is also a highly "regionalized" country, with significant jurisdictional decentralization in areas of most concern to equity advocates, and a strong sense of regional distinctiveness in places like British Columbia, Alberta, parts of Atlantic Canada, and, of course, Quebec. On the other hand, there are strong similarities in the LGBT political narrative across the country, more so, certainly, than in the United States, and in some ways more so than in countries like Brazil, Spain, and Australia.

LGBTQ people have expressed similar demands – for example, for human rights laws to protect them against arbitrary discrimination – notwithstanding where they live in Canada. The existence of several national organizations (such as the Canadian Lesbian and Gay Rights Coalition, and Equality for Gays and Lesbians Everywhere [EGALE]) also feeds into the idea of a national queer movement – even though they may be very different kinds of groups. In fact, the LGBTQ movement in Canada is not at all "federalized" – that is, its organization does not reflect the federal structure of the Canadian political regime in which there are a central (i.e., federal) organization and satellite organizations in the provinces and territories (or regions). That said, the federalist framework should not be abandoned out of hand as it is useful for analyzing the queer movement in Canada. The case of EGALE is telling in this regard. Although EGALE has invested much energy in dossiers falling within the federal government's purview (such as same-sex marriage), more recently it has become involved in the issue of youth and safer schools, a field of provincial jurisdiction. This interest is particularly challenging from a federalist framework, for two reasons. The first leads us to suppose that federalism may be deployed not only from the top down but also from the bottom up – from grassroots organizing and mobilizing. "Despite provincial jurisdiction over education, EGALE was pressured by activists from across Canada to develop a strong pan-Canadian network that could build on local and provincial efforts," notes Miriam Smith (Chapter 1, see p. 55, this volume). The second reason reinforces what attentive observation of Canadian politics clearly illustrates: separation of powers between the federal government and the provinces is, in reality, theoretical, since, as Miriam Smith notes, "[Queer] political mobilization crosses the jurisdictional boundaries of federalism, with urban LGBTQ groups intervening in federal policy issues and federally organized groups intervening in provincial matters" (see p. 55). It is worth quoting this long excerpt from Julie Podmore (Chapter 8, see pp. 198–99, this volume), as it illustrates the fluidity of queer issues or, seen otherwise, how these issues make a mockery of the division of powers among the governments:

> While two of the primary concerns of his gay constituency (the AIDS crisis and the application of the rights guaranteed in the Charter) were concerns to be addressed at the provincial and federal levels, he [Raymond Blain] did find innovative ways to work on both of these issues at City Hall. He lobbied the municipal government to extend insurance benefits to employees in same-sex relationships. He also worked to develop a non-disclosure policy for city employees living with HIV, enabling workers to declare their status without fear of exposure and prejudice ... He worked with AIDS Community Care Montréal (C-SAM) to lobby the provincial government for funding and initiated a campaign that would see safe-sex information posted in all municipal buildings.

Here lies the genius of federalism: to provide several places where public decisions are made. This can certainly make interactions with the state more complex and sometimes pits local, regional, and provincial organizations against each other with regard to objectives to pursue, strategies to enact, and limited resources to share, but it also offers a number of points of access to the political decision-making process: if one door is locked, there are a number of others that may be unlocked. That said, federalism can also be a thorn in the side of LGBTQ activism, for example by multiplying the sites of struggle for a queer movement with few resources or feeding into confusion about the appropriate target (e.g., a municipal regulation, a provincial program, or a federal statute) for attaining an objective, thus shunting LGBTQ activists from one location to another within a bureaucratic maze. Simply put, how federalism and queer activism interact – and, more precisely, how the LGBTQ movement is able to profit from federalism – constitutes a promising and fruitful research field for the coming years.

As the chapters in *Queer Mobilizations* eloquently show, however, it is difficult to think of LGBTQ activism in Canada in terms of a unified movement as it is carved up into a checkerboard of territories, ideologies, organizations, and constituencies. In fact, queer activism in Canada may be seen as a collection of regional and local stories, in the sense that claims advocated coast to coast to coast are framed by specific socio-political contexts that, in turn, affect their outcomes. For instance, although lesbians and gays throughout Canada demanded protection against discrimination, it took more than a quarter of a century, from 1977 to 2002, for all fourteen federal, provincial, and territorial human rights laws in Canada to be amended to include sexual orientation as a prohibited ground for discrimination. The relevance of particular socio-political contexts is also felt at the local level – in smaller cities, such as Halifax, and large urban centres, such as Montreal, Toronto, and Vancouver, which have constituted particularly fertile ground for the birth of queer activism. However, the large cities also have their specificities, as Julie Podmore (Chapter 8, see p. 187, this volume) explains: "There are a number of local factors that distinguish Montreal's history of LGBT activism within Canada, including the postcolonial nationalist movement, the constitutional status of Quebec, language politics, local history, and forms of municipal governance."

LGBTQ activism in Canada is also divided by ideological and organizational considerations. As Alexa DeGagne (Chapter 7, this volume) writes: "Mainstream/liberal LGB organizations [that] tend to focus on attaining liberal rights and equality through formal political avenues" (see p. 169) can be differentiated from "grassroots/community-based organizations [that] tend to have less structured governance models (they may reject hierarchical models), fluctuating and ever-changing members, revolving leaders (if they have leaders at all), and few, if any, sources of funding and/or resources" (see p. 168). Several contributions in this book underline ideological complexities that have characterized queer activism in Canada since the 1970s. It is also likely that nationalism – English-Canadian nationalism versus Québécois nationalism – has constituted another aspect in the fracturing of LGBTQ activism in Canada. That said, although the LGBTQ movement in Canada cannot in any way be thought of as ideologically homogeneous, what DeGagne labels "mainstream/liberal LGB organizations" surely dominate its public (and media) faces.

Furthermore, the Canadian LGBTQ movement is internally diverse, as evidenced by the letters composing its initialism – "L" for lesbians, "G" for gays, "B" for bisexuals, "T" for transsexuals and transgenders, to which Two-Spirited people must be added, and "Q" for queer. Historical sections of chapters in this book show that queer activism in Canada has been largely dominated by white, anglophone, middle-class, urban gay men. In fact, it is a bit naïve to think that the "L," "B," "T," and "Q" have had the same influence and power within queer activism as has the "G." As David Rayside (Chapter 3, see p. 101, this volume) observes:

> Across the issue spectrum, the willingness to fully accept transgenderism or bisexuality is significantly more limited than is the preparedness to respond favourably to "straight-forward" homosexuality. And across all issue areas, there is no question that invidious distinctions are created between those lesbians and gays who appear "respectable," or who have other middle-class credentials, and those whose demeanour or social background deviates more drastically from what is thought normal or safe.

Resistance manifested by the Senate to Bill C-279, which would add gender identity to the Canadian Human Rights Act, is a recent example of the very limited acceptance of trans* claims (King 2015).

Commenting in her chapter on the 1992 trial of Glad Day Bookshop in Toronto on obscenity charges for selling the lesbian magazine *Bad Attitude*, Catherine Nash (Chapter 9, see p. 216, this volume) also notes this gap "between so-called respectable gays advocating for equality rights and those activists pursuing a more radical agenda that supported less genteel sexual imagery and practices." Racism and colonialism are additional – but in fact transversal and intersectional – factors that segment LGBTQ activism in Canada, as Julie Depelteau and Dalie Giroux (Chapter 2, see p. 68, this volume) argue: "The LGBTQ movement ... can be seen as a colonial institution that contributes to the continued erasure of Indigenous Two-Spirited persons." It is likely that other issues that smack of colonialism and racism also favour conflicts, divisions, and exclusions, as illustrated by the controversy generated by the participation of Queers against Israeli Apartheid in the Toronto pride parade in 2010 and 2011. As Miriam Smith (Chapter 1, see p. 59, this volume) puts it: "The multiple diversities of a multinational and multiethnic state create structural obstacles to movement coherence."

That being said, this fragmentation has not precluded the expression of queer activism in Canada since the very early 1970s (and even before that, with the creation of the University of Toronto Homophile Association in October of 1969). This raises the following questions: What happened in the late 1960s and early 1970s to bring queer activism into the public theatre? How did it evolve? What have been its main resources? What outcomes has it achieved? Each of these questions generates findings.

Why did queer activism – and especially gay liberationism – emerge in the late 1960s and early 1970s?[1] This question may lead us to turn to resource-mobilization and political-process theories and, notably, the concept of opportunity structure (Goodwin and Jasper 1999; McAdam, McCarthy, and Zald 1988). A *third observation* that emerges from this collection, and that may seem to be a truism, is that the very existence of the LGBTQ movement as a political actor – its ability to express itself quite freely and safely in the public square – is intrinsically linked to the state's positions (criminalization, tolerance, permissiveness) towards homosexuality. Of course, the existence of a queer movement is not strictly dependent on the state, although queer activism certainly developed in relation to queer oppression. In Canada, criminal law is a federal power (although the provinces are responsible for the administration of justice on their territories, including criminal justice); the rapidity of the process of the partial decriminalization of homosexuality in 1969 is explained, at least in part, by the fact that a single government made the decision (Smith forthcoming). It must also be considered that the government led by P.E. Trudeau was determined to move ahead with partial decriminalization (for details, see the Introduction). Otherwise, serious obstacles to the progress of queer activism might have been thrown up, as is illustrated by the case of Alberta under the governments of Ralph Klein: "The Klein government handled same-sex marriage much the same way as it did the *Vriend* decision: by choosing not to make a decision" (DeGagne, Chapter 7, see p. 166, this volume).

A very short time after Trudeau's Liberal government decriminalized buggery and gross indecency in private between consenting adults, the LGBTQ movement emerged from the underground and made a political place for itself in the public space. The historical sections in the chapters in this book identify a plethora of groups that mushroomed across Canada in the years following the partial decriminalization of homosexuality. Thus, it appears that the LGBTQ movement emerged in the 1970s in part because an important mechanism in the repression of homosexuality – its criminalization – had been removed (although decriminalization was followed by accentuated policing of queer sexualities in public spaces, which had become more visible in the 1970s; see Kinsman and Gentile 2010, 221–335). In this respect, the fact that, under certain conditions, buggery and gross indecency were no longer criminal offences provided LGBTQ people with what can be interpreted as a "negative political opportunity" – that is, the opportunity not to be a criminal due to one's sexual practices. This new opportunity to enjoy life in the public space falls, to a certain extent, within a vaster organizational undertaking consisting of accumulating various resources to form a movement. I return to this below. But there is more: the rather limited scope of the 1969 reform of the Criminal Code, linked to the inspiring example of the Stonewall Riots and the ensuing gay liberationist organizing and to the accentuated sexual policing in the 1970s, stimulated LGBTQ activism, as is evidenced, among other examples, by the We Demand demonstration held on 28 August 1971 on Parliament Hill in Ottawa.

For the moment, it suffices to mention here that the history of queer activism in Canada has not been extensively documented. Of course, Canada followed in Great Britain's footsteps in decriminalizing homosexuality, at least partially, in 1969, but the Canadian government might also have followed the United States' hard line without too much trouble – at least, until the adoption of the Canadian Charter. In fact, the American model of sexual regulation

Manon Tremblay

exerted an influence in Canada in the 1950s and 1960s via national security campaigns and the development of "criminal sexual psychopaths" and "dangerous sexual offenders" legislation (Kinsman 1996, 169–87; Kinsman and Gentile 2010, 72–75). That said, although one of the effects of the adoption of Bill C-150 was to decriminalize buggery and gross indecency when engaged in by two consenting adults in private, it was not the result of pressure exerted by the gay liberation movement (Corriveau 2011, 123). Pressure by homophile groups in the 1960s did have an influence on the 1969 reform (such as the Association for Social Knowledge; Kinsman 1996, 230–73), but its extent remains to be established. It would also be interesting to try to better understand the motivations of the Trudeau government in this regard, especially the motivations of Pierre Elliott Trudeau himself.[2] One of his basic political projects was to construct a Canadian identity that, in many regards, was different from that of the United States. Was partial decriminalization of homosexuality one plank in his nation-building enterprise? This would be a stimulating question for future research.

Why did queer activism emerge in the 1970s? One part of the answer suggested by the authors in this book is that partial decriminalization of homosexuality offered LGBTQ people a "negative political opportunity" – that of no longer being labelled criminals because of their sexual practices. The lifting of this criminalization mechanism contributed to the public emergence of the LGBTQ movement, its (limited) access to the polity, and its organization to mobilize as a broader constituency – if not a mass movement. This raises the question: How did queer activism evolve?

A *fourth observation* is that, on the ideological level, queer activism transitioned from a radical and revolutionary perspective in the 1970s to a liberal and assimilationist perspective in the 2000s. At least, this is how Catherine Nash (Chapter 9, see p. 209, this volume) interprets it: "the early 1970s 'assimilationist' perspectives, the overlapping and more radical 'liberationist' approach of the 1980s and 1990s, and an ethnic minority and/or neo-assimilationist approach from the 1990s onward." In Chapter 10 (see pp. 227–28, this volume), Gordon Brent Brochu-Ingram also points out that, in recent years, queer activism has been displaced in the ideological space by a reconfiguration of issues affecting sexual minorities: "Metropolitan Vancouver is undergoing a shift in conversations around sexual minority vulnerability, needs, and entitlements from earlier activist challenges to inequities (and subsequent constructions of rights and protections) to building expanded and truly inclusive social spaces, entertainment establishments, service programs, and facilities." It is as if – although one could argue that the narrative is actually more complex than this – the liberationist approach had been only a parenthesis, or an exceptional moment, in the ideological trajectory of queer activism in Canada, an approach marginalized by "the advent of HIV/AIDS and the impact of the constitutional entrenchment of the Charter of Rights and Freedoms in 1982 and ... the coming into effect of the equality rights section (section 15) in 1985," as Miriam Smith (Chapter 1, see p. 48, this volume) suggests. The opening of civil marriage to same-sex couples also fed into this interpretation of a return of LGBTQ activism to an assimilationist perspective – which some people prefer to frame in equality language. And yet, it is possible that this interpretation does not take into account the complexity of queer activism, which has woven together different currents and forms of organizing. In this perspective, in *Never Going Back* Tom Warner (2002) demonstrates that both currents – what he calls equality-seeking assimilationism and liberationism – have coexisted, and still coexist, within the Canadian LGBTQ movement. Indeed, events reveal these tensions: for example, although the HIV/AIDS pandemic contributed to some institutionalization and mainstreaming of the LGBTQ movement, it also afforded an opportunity to remember that liberationist organizing remained alive and well within queer activism in Canada.

Is it possible to think that a more radical and critical reading of LGBTQ activism could re-emerge in coming years, or even that it will become predominant in queer organizing, in response to the social conservatism that seems to have recently gained ground in Canada?[3] The answer to this question depends in part on the longevity of the Conservative Party currently at the helm of the Canadian state and Stephen Harper's capacity to contain the ardour of the conservative social fringe within his party. If the Conservative Party were to consolidate its majority in the federal elections of 2015, social conservative activists in the Conservative Party might no longer agree to act in the shadows but, rather, demand more visibility, especially if the ideological centre of gravity of Canadians were to continue to move slowly but surely to the right. However, the arrival of Justin Trudeau at the head of the Liberal Party may turn this scenario on its head; as of early 2015, it seems that the Conservative Party is trying to reposition itself in the centre-right portion of the federal political checkerboard, as though in an attempt to counter Trudeau's progressive image. This interpretation is buttressed by the fact that, in recent months, Stephen Harper has pronounced himself in favour of human rights for LGBTQ people – though it must be said that the LGBTQ people he was talking about are in other countries – following the lead of his minister of foreign affairs, John Baird. In any case, how the LGBTQ and the social conservative movements will interact in the foreseeable future constitutes, no doubt, an exciting research issue yet to be explored.

In fact, the saga of same-sex marriage clearly unleashed the social conservative movement (Farney 2012, 119–28; Haskell 2011; Malloy 2011), to the point – and this is a *fifth observation* – that it has imposed itself as the perfect counter-movement to LGBTQ activism in Canada (Farney 2012, 22).[4] Its political impact, however, is ambiguous. As Smith (2008, 3) maintains, the nature of the Canadian political system – notably federalism, separation of powers, and the role of the courts in the political decision-making process – offers the social conservative movement limited institutional opportunities. Evidence of this is the movement's inability to block adoption of the Civil Marriage Act (Bill C-38), which had the effect of opening civil marriage to same-sex couples. As Smith (2010, 108) posits: "[Paul Martin's Liberal] government faced very little opposition as the opponents of same-sex marriage were not able to pressure the government to use the notwithstanding clause, they did not have the votes in the House of Commons to defeat the bill, and they were not able to undertake ballot initiatives or constitutional amendments [as in the United States] to forestall the passage of the legislation."

Nevertheless, social conservatism has clearly raised obstacles to progressivist perspectives advanced by queer activism. This is particularly true for themes involving youth, such as age of consent and expression of sexual diversity in the school environment, as illustrated by the resistance to the establishment of gay-straight alliances in a number of provinces and to the use of schoolbooks positively portraying families with same-sex parents. Despite these obstacles, not only has social conservatism not kept queer activism from making its presence felt in parts of the country supposedly unsympathetic to it (such as Alberta and Atlantic Canada) but also, in acting as a foil for the LGBTQ movement, social conservatism seems in fact to have contributed to its emergence and development. This is the analysis advanced by Nathaniel M. Lewis (Chapter 11, see p. 261, this volume):

> Nova Scotia has often made the choice to actively change the status of its LGBT residents, while other provinces have waited for the results of court cases or top-down decisions from the federal government. Nova Scotia's avant-gardist approach to LGBT policy in the 1990s and early 2000s (i.e., making swift and substantial changes rather than incremental ones), while triggered by mobilizations in Halifax, is perhaps also representative of how Nova Scotians view themselves in the context of the Canadian state. While many value Nova Scotia's small communities, collectivist culture, and rural agricultural traditions as traits to be defended, they are also wary of the possibility that other Canadians might associate them with conservatism or

backwardness. Consequently, policymakers and leaders in Nova Scotia, and particularly in Halifax, have also taken pains to position the province as a distinctive yet forward-thinking place with its own identity and its own approaches to Canadian politics.

In short, although social conservatism is an adversary that queer activism cannot ignore, the effect of its backward-looking vision and its influence on the LGBTQ movement and on Canadian public policy remains to be seen. Certainly, it is an avenue for future research. Indeed, that it is not possible to think of social conservatism as a steamroller crushing everything LGBTQ in its path is explained, at least in part, by the nature of the Canadian political system and by the fact that the queer movement is not without resources – quite the contrary.

What have been the main resources of LGBTQ activism in Canada? Suzanne Staggenborg (2012, 193) defines resources as "the tangible and intangible assets available to social movement organizations and other actors." In John D. McCarthy and Mayer N. Zald's (1987, 45) view, resources are located at both a meso level, thus encompassing "money, materials, people and technology," and a macro level, referring to "the set of roles and facilities that are generally available to people in a society or social segment." Bob Edwards and John D. McCarthy (2004) distinguish five types of resources available to social movements: (1) moral (including the legitimacy of the cause promoted by a movement in public opinion), (2) cultural (such as strategies and tactical repertoires), (3) social-organizational (such as infrastructure and groups associated with a movement and its networks), (4) human (the activists, their know-how and experiences), and (5) material (including office space, money, and technology). Resources that a social movement may mobilize depend at least in part on the nature of the political regime. For instance, if there is no bill of rights in a given country, queer activism will have to draw for its rights claims on international human rights law and institutions (Australia offers an excellent example of this; see Johnson, Maddison, and Partridge 2011). It is clear – and this is a *sixth observation* that emerges from *Queer Mobilizations* – that queer activism in Canada was able to develop and prosper thanks to a wide range of resources available to it, including a political regime architecture (e.g., federalism, separation of powers, the Canadian Charter and court decisions, and governments willing to act favourably on LGBTQ rights) that has offered institutional opportunities to the queer movement. Of course, it is possible for these resources to be judged insufficient or poorly adapted; this is the case, for example, with regard to the HIV/AIDS fight and homophobia, and especially transphobia. It

Manon Tremblay

is even more possible that these resources were not simply "gifts" from Canadian governments but, rather, a mixture of political regime opportunities and queer movement organizing from below. In any event, resources exist and the LGBTQ movement has been able to put them to use for its causes.

Thus, as Joanna Everitt (Chapter 5, see p. 139, this volume) writes: "There can be little doubt that attitudes have changed [and that p]ublic support and sympathy for LGBT individuals is much stronger now than it has been in the past." And this is an important moral resource. In support of this argument, J. Scott Matthews (2005) shows how rulings made by the Supreme Court of Canada regarding the recognition of lesbian and gay couples, decisions made by governments in response to these rulings, and the framing of recognition of same-sex unions in terms of equal rights have led Canadian public opinion to support the opening of civil marriage to same-sex couples (see also Langstaff 2011; Snow 2014). In other words, institutional framing by the Canadian political regime has been an asset to queer activism.

Authors in this book bring to light a wide range of cultural resources mobilized by queer activism, notably with regard to tactical repertoires. This notion refers to the set of protest actions developed and used by a social movement during a given time and in a specific space. In the view of Verta Taylor and Nella Van Dyke (2004, 69), tactical repertoires have three characteristics. The first characteristic is contestation – that is, "tactical repertoires in all their variants are interactions that embody contestation between groups with different and competing interests." Thus, tactical repertoires adopt several variants that Staggenborg (2012, 4) summarizes as being of two types, each of which has been employed in some way in Canada. The first type is institutionalized tactics: lobbying an elected official or a public servant, demanding human rights protection against discrimination based on sexual orientation and gender identity, testifying in a parliamentary commission, taking recourse to the courts, and intervening directly on the electoral scene as candidates or, as Brian Burtch, Aynsley Pescitelli, and Rebecca Haskell suggest (Chapter 6, see p. 144, this volume), by questioning "every candidate, asking for their position on various forms of legislation." The other type is direct-action tactics; examples discussed in this book include ACT UP Vancouver's (theatrical) confrontation with Premier Bill Vander Zalm in 1990, the rally held in the town of Truro to protest the refusal of the mayor and city council to fly the pride flag in 2007, and the CRACS satirical video entitled *Smaller Classes, Smaller Minds*, contesting the passage of Bill 44 by the Alberta government in 2009. The second characteristic of tactical repertoires, according to Taylor and Van Dyke (2004, 269), is intentionality – that is, "strategic decision-making [regarding] collective claims-making." Here again, the authors in *Queer Mobilizations* leave little doubt with regard to the intention of queer activism to change the heterosexist and heteronormative social order so that a wider range of sexualities may accede to legitimacy, or even respectability. The third characteristic is collective identity – that is, "the development of solidarity and an oppositional consciousness that allows a challenging group to identify common injustices, to oppose those injustices, and to define a shared interest in opposing the dominant group or resisting the system of authority responsible for those injustices" (Taylor and Van Dyke 2004, 270). Queer activism, and notably the lesbian and gay movement, is without a doubt the identity movement par excellence – that is, the one that has efficiently framed and deployed identity "as a form of strategic collective action" (Bernstein 1997, 531), even though the lesbian and gay movement cannot be reduced to identity-based activism alone. In addition to gay pride parades, which are events that strongly express queer identities, these identities are constructed through various tactics discussed by the authors in this book, including not only rights claiming but also institution building and the claiming of space, as Gordon Brent Brochu-Ingram and Julie Podmore eloquently demonstrate in their respective chapters on Vancouver and Montreal. More important, the mix of claiming space and institution building has contributed to the success of queer activism in Canada. As Catherine Nash (Chapter 9, see p. 221, this volume) states: "Having a territorial or neighbourhood base from which to operate remains pivotal to the political, economic, and social successes of these various organizations." It may be argued that successes, in turn, fortify LGBTQ identities.

To grasp the richness of the tactical repertoires deployed by queer activism in Canada, it is important to broaden the notion of "space" beyond its strictly geographic meaning and extend it to Canadian political institutions. Thus, aside from urban space, the LGBTQ movement has deployed its tactical repertoires within the federal, provincial, and municipal governments, before the courts and human rights commissions, with political parties, in the parliamentary and electoral arenas, in the corridors of executive power and public administrations, and before the media. This diversity of tactics, and of the spaces in which they are deployed, becomes meaningful in the light of the hostility manifested by certain governments towards LGBTQ people, as Alexa DeGagne (Chapter 7, see p. 171, this volume) explains:

LGBT2Q activists largely abandoned provincial lobbying efforts and engagement with provincial parties and politicians. Instead, LGBT2Q activism continued along two main tracks: (1) equality seekers depended on lawyers and the Charter to challenge discriminatory laws, and (2) queer activists formed grassroots responses to social and political heteronormativity through alternative systems of care, and community building and organizing ... By 2009, Alberta's LGBT2Q communities and activist organizations had grown, diversified, and were ready to respond to Premier Stelmach's changes to the IRPA [Individual Rights Protection Act].

Regarding the social-organizational resources available to queer activism in Canada, the "Historical Background" and "Queer Activism Today" sections of the chapters in this book bring to light the wide array of social movement organizations that have composed, and continue to compose, the Canadian LGBTQ movement "industry," to use McCarthy and Zald's (1977) term. Another one of these resources is allies. As defined in my chapter on Quebec, allies are "actors outside the lesbian and gay communities that share these communities' values, objectives, strategies, and struggles: these include interest groups, political parties, media outlets, and political and intellectual elites" (see p. 111). Alliances between queer activists and other civil society groups are not always easy to establish, at least in Vancouver, as Gordon Brent Brochu-Ingram (Chapter 10, this volume) underlines. And yet, these alliances are important because, as Alexa DeGagne (Chapter 7, see p. 169, this volume) notes, queer "issues are intersectional in nature: they concern not only sexuality but also race, gender, class/employment, and religion. As such, organizations that are focused solely or predominantly on sexuality could not and did not fully represent every facet of each issue." This is a very important observation: queer experiences are inscribed in, modelled by, and model in their turn a broader context of social relations based on gender, race and ethnicity, social class, age, ability, and other factors that shape LGBTQ citizenship. For instance, it is a likely bet that a white, well-educated professional lesbian living in an urban area will have a life path less hindered by various sorts of oppression and violence than will her Aboriginal counterpart with little education, no job, and living on a reserve. If one ignores the fact that queer experiences are mediated by such factors, one ends up studying privileged queers and constructing and promoting a false universal queer identity and experiences. An intersectional reading is crucial for a better understanding of queer activism in Canada; as of now, this remains to be done.

That said, the authors in *Queer Mobilizations* have identified different alliances and allies upon which the LGBTQ movement has been able to count. These allies have included straight and queer persons, such as public servants, politicians sympathetic to LGBTQ activism (e.g., Rosemary Brown in Vancouver and Louise Harel in Quebec), and, of course, openly lesbian and gay politicians (e.g., Raymond Blain in Montreal, Jim Egan in British Columbia, and George Hislop in Toronto). Yet, LGBTQ elected officials do not want to, and in any case cannot, represent queer issues exclusively.[5] In this regard, Julie Podmore (Chapter 8, see p. 198, this volume) writes of Raymond Blain that "he wanted to be known as 'the councillor who is gay rather than the gay councillor.'" Although being LGBTQ no longer sounds the death knell for a political career, Brian Burtch, Aynsley Pescitelli, and Rebecca Haskell (Chapter 6, see p. 157, this volume) believe that care must be taken when evaluating the effects of the presence of LGBTQ politicians, notably in terms of acceptability among certain citizens: "Despite such LGBTQ federal and provincial politicians in BC and elsewhere in Canada, doubts remain about their general acceptability to citizens." Although, as mentioned above, public opinion has evolved with regard to queer people since the 1970s, it is likely that this transformation has not been uniform among all segments of the population and that some groups are still showing resistance to LGBTQ people. In this respect, Nathaniel M. Lewis (Chapter 11, this volume) notes that the "power of the closet" remains strong in rural Nova Scotia communities. As mentioned in the introduction, under the surface of normality, "homosexuality remains contentious" (Altman 2013, 164). What is certain is that research is needed on the role of LGBTQ people who are elected to legislatures with regard to the representation of queer issues and the electoral impacts of a queer constituency.[6]

These allies have also included institutions: human rights commissions have been incontestable allies (e.g., Barbara Hall, chief commissioner of the Ontario Human Rights Commission), of course, but so have the labour movement and certain political parties, such as the New Democratic Party, the Parti québécois, and, depending on the conjuncture, Liberal parties across Canada. The authors in this book discuss two other institutional allies: the church and the women's movement. Although the church is considered to be quite hostile to the LGBTQ movement, David Rayside's (Chapter 3, see p. 94, this volume) observations would indicate a more nuanced analysis: he underlines the important contribution of some "progressive religious leaders (Christian and Jewish)" to queer activism. Smith (2008, 1–2) notes the role of institutional ally assumed by certain churches, notably the Metropolitan Community Church of Toronto (MCCT). In January 2001, the MCCT married two same-sex couples who, following the rejection of their request for registration of their marriage, brought a lawsuit against the federal government claiming that their equality rights had been denied. Joining the lawsuit, the MCCT argued that its freedom of religion had been violated.

Manon Tremblay

The women's movement, unlike the church, has traditionally been perceived as an ally of queer activism. Yet here, too, nuances are needed. Speaking of the 1992 trial of Toronto's Glad Day Bookshop for obscenity for having sold the lesbian magazine *Bad Attitude,* Catherine Nash (Chapter 9, see p. 218, this volume) recounts,

> Canadian organizations such as Legal Education and Action Fund (LEAF), functioning as interveners in court cases and other venues, worked with or through the state to affirm lesbian identities but were arguably not prepared to see s/m [sado-masochism] activities as a legitimate aspect of lesbian identity.

Furthermore:

> Anti-censorship feminists argued that, in working with the state, one could find oneself inadvertently working against the best interests of the gay and lesbian community and, in this case, lesbians. (see p. 217)

The formation from the 1970s on across Canada (though mainly in large cities) of various autonomous groups of lesbians (feminist, radical, or separatist) also testifies to an alliance that did not always sit well not only between lesbians and heterosexual feminists but also between lesbians and gays. What is more, as the explanations of Brian Burtch, Aynsley Pescitelli, and Rebecca Haskell (Chapter 6, this volume) indicate, it is possible that the confrontation that took place in the early 2000s between the Vancouver Rape Relief and Women's Shelter and Kimberly Nixon (a post-operative male-to-female transsexual woman) is also evidence of how difficult it is for *some* feminists to cooperate with trans people.

Finally, when it comes to human and material resources, the authors in *Queer Mobilizations* describe a queer activism that is both fragile and rich on these two levels. On the one hand, the pool of activists is unreliable, not always politicized (a number of LGBTQ people are preoccupied with socio-cultural and personal activities), and is often artificially swollen by extraordinary events (such as two thousand people protesting against the police raid on the Montreal gay bar Truxx in 1977, and the large protest in Truro in 2007 following the refusal of the mayor and city council to declare Pride Week).[7] It is therefore unsurprising to learn from the authors in this book that the LGBTQ movement in Canada, yesterday as today, has struggled with a paucity of material resources. On the other hand, queer activism is not paralyzed by the shortage of human and material resources as it has a wide variety of means to overcome it. Gordon Brent Brochu-Ingram (Chapter 10, this volume) reveals that one of the assets of LGBTQ activism in Canada lies in its great ingenuity, as illustrated by its innovative and proactive modes of organizational and spatial development and the shift of activities to social media. However, more research is needed in order to gain a better idea of the roles of social media in queer activism today and to find out whether social media are contributing to new forms of empowerment or, on the contrary, to the marginalization of less-privileged LGBTQ people. In particular, there are things to be learned from research undertaken with Two-Spirited people, a group that is especially ostracized and marginalized in Canada. Studies reveal the relevance of an intersectional approach to studying groups discriminated against on a number of fronts: "Two-Spirited People's access to health care is uniquely problematized by the combination of homophobia, heterosexism, racism, cultural insensitivity, and a legacy of distrust towards health care professionals" (2-Spirited People of the 1st Nations [2004], quoted in Julie Depelteau and Dalie Giroux, Chapter 2, see p. 74, this volume).

To sum up, LGBTQ activism in Canada has been able to mobilize a broad palette of resources that have developed and flourished since the 1970s. Yet the latter term – "flourish" – raises the following question: What outcomes have LGBTQ activism achieved?

For a number of reasons, it is not easy to assess the outcomes of social movements. First, it is simply not possible to establish a cause-and-effect relationship between changes promoted by a given social movement and the development of a society. For instance, although homophile organizing in the 1960s is part of the broader background that led up to the 1969 reform of the Criminal Code (Kinsman 1996, 240–64), it is not possible to argue a cause-and-effect relationship between homophile activism and the 1969 reform; as mentioned above, although homophile organizing certainly helped to facilitate the law reform process, its role remains to be established. Second, the effects of a social movement are multifaceted and not easily definable in that they may be single or multiple, intentional or unintentional, marked by advances and setbacks, and manifest in the short, medium, or long term. This is so, for example, for the evolution in public opinion with regard to homosexuality in Canada. Third, a social movement rarely speaks with a single voice, as illustrated by the multiple currents within queer activism. What constitutes a success for some may be a failure for others; for instance, although same-sex marriage is a victory for certain mainstream/liberal lesbians and gays, it is a setback for a number of liberationists (for one example, see Mulé 2010). Fourth, a social movement does not hold exclusive rights on the claims that it makes, as these may also be promoted by other movements and groups. The

Manon Tremblay

feminist and human rights movements – and even labour unions – have inspired LGBTQ activism and how it has framed its rationales and claims.

Gamson (1990) is essential reading for anyone who wishes to understand the consequences of social movements – especially in the context of this book – because he is most interested in their state-oriented and legislative consequences. He defines two key social movement outcomes: (1) being accepted by the state and establishing that a social movement speaks legitimately for a constituency, and (2) acquiring new advantages for that constituency. A *seventh observation* that emerges from *Queer Mobilizations* is that, considered from this angle, there is no doubt that LGBTQ activism in Canada has been successful, although, as David Rayside (Chapter 3, see p. 86, this volume) notes, there "is great variation in success across these fields [policing, human rights, family rights, and education] – an analysis much in line with what we would find across the country."

As for acceptance, in my chapter in this book I maintain that today the Quebec government recognizes the legitimacy of LGBTQ groups in its formulation of public policy with regard to sexual diversity: "Resulting from the demands and struggles of Quebec LGBT communities, *De l'égalité juridique à l'égalité sociale* was the fruit of close collaboration between these communities and the Quebec government in the battle against homophobia" (see p. 116). EGALE also embodies this acceptance. Governments in Canada have endorsed its legitimacy as an advocate, as Miriam Smith maintains (Chapter 1, see p. 48, this volume), in several court cases "for the recognition of same-sex couples in federal law and policy, the right of LGBTQ individuals to seek redress against discrimination in federal and provincial human rights legislation, and ... for same-sex marriage," or regarding age of consent, or, more recently, fights against homophobia. Aside from governments, the social conservatism movement, the countermovement par excellence for queer activism, has also recognized its legitimacy in numerous confrontations, including the *Chamberlain v. Surrey School District* (2002) case, the same-sex marriage saga in 2005, the age of consent issue in 2006, and, more recently, the question of trans human rights protection, in which social conservatism's resistance to queer progressiveness regarding sexual diversity is clearly embodied by the Harper government.

In terms of Gamson's "new advantages" outcome, here, too, the LGBTQ movement in Canada made, through its struggles, numerous gains that are meaningful in light of the multi-layered structure of the Canadian political regime and its institutional opportunities for queer activism. Thus, provinces and municipalities have been spaces in which LGBTQ people have mobilized and gained new advantages. All of the human rights laws in Canada today forbid discrimination on the grounds of sexual orientation, and some add gender identity. A number of governments have formulated policies to fight homophobia and transphobia. Services have been put in place to respond to the needs of LGBTQ communities. As David Rayside (Chapter 3, see p. 100, this volume) explains, "advocacy for LGBT inclusivity directed to schools, school boards, and the provincial education ministry has borne fruit in the policies of several school boards, in the creation of many GSAs, and in the belated development of provincial equity and harassment policies." Regarding the federal level of government, Miriam Smith (Chapter 1, see p. 60, this volume) observes: "For issues that fall clearly under federal jurisdiction [such as the Criminal Code and the definition of civil marriage], federalism will continue to play an important role in shaping the terrain of political battle." The opening of civil marriage to same-sex couples in the summer of 2005 was symbolic of the equality advances made by lesbians and gays, who have made the transition from the status of criminals before 1969 to that of respectable citizens today – at least, those lesbians and gays who have agreed to play the game of hetero- and homonormalization.

Yet, although the "regime of normal" may be satisfactory to some lesbians and gay men, it generates several criticisms. First, it makes the heterosexual lifestyle (i.e., the monogamous couple, living together, united by a life-long project, sometimes with children, consumers, and so on) the gold standard. In itself, this is eminently heterosexist. Second, by stressing privacy, monogamy, respectability, domesticity, and consumption, it is an institution that serves liberalism and, above all, capitalism (after hetero- and homonormalization, should we also talk of homo-liberal-capitalism?). In fact, the model of the middle-class consumer (Marso 2010) that it proposes remains accessible to very few lesbians and gay men interested in such a lifestyle. Third – and following the previous point – it causes problems within LGBTQ communities by establishing a hierarchy between the "good" lesbians and gay men located at the top, who are respectable sexual citizens due to their apparent normality, and those located at the bottom, who refuse to comply.

That said, to return to the title of the report of the Commission des droits de la personne et des droits de la jeunesse du Québec, although lesbians and gays have acquired *judicial equality* on paper, they must still acquire *social equality* – or, I would add, *cultural equality,* which encompasses "the right to symbolic presence, dignifying representation, propagation of identity and maintenance of lifestyles" (Pakulski 1997, 73). Indeed, although formal rights and equality before the law are important, they do not challenge and dislodge heteronormative hegemony, which plays a major role in queer social and cultural inequality and oppression. As is revealed in a number of chapters in this book, LGBTQ people do not always attain equality in fact, as numerous types of discrimination, manifest and latent, compromise their daily lives and remind them that they are second-class citizens. The hegemony of heterosexuality (or heteronormativity) that straitjackets Canadian society is without doubt the most powerful mechanism for marginalizing LGBTQ people: heterosexuality is omnipresent, embodied in the heterosexual couple imbued with its privileges, of course, but also infiltrating social and cultural representations through a battery of ideological apparatuses in schools, advertising, the work world, the recreational world, and, more subtly, the arts (songs, poetry), clothing, food, spaces, interactions and appeals, and so on (see Tin 2008, 6). The full weight of heterosexual hegemony in Canadian society can be sensed in the following observation: whereas a heterosexual couple walking on the sidewalk holding hands and exchanging the occasional kiss will go unnoticed, the same behaviour by a lesbian or gay couple will not fail to generate disapproving looks, perhaps homophobic insults or even serious physical violence. Social and cultural equality for LGBTQ people is far from being achieved. In this perspective, a titanic research program remains to be undertaken to distinguish the perimeters of heterosexual hegemony in Canada and how it operates as a subtle, but terribly effective, form of subjugation of the cisnormative and cissexist order. In this regard, the notions of acceptance and new advantages must be expanded from the political to the socio-cultural space.

The evaluation of outcomes of queer activism in Canada cannot be limited to the political field alone, especially because the LGBTQ movement is eminently cultural. Thus, as Joanna Everitt mentions above: "There can be little doubt that attitudes have changed [and that p]ublic support and sympathy for LGBT individuals is much stronger now than it has been in the past." Alexa DeGagne (Chapter 7, see p. 176, this volume) also notes this transformation in public opinion regarding queer activism and pleads for the label of conservatism to be nuanced, notably with regard to the image of an Alberta openly and unanimously hostile towards LGBTQ people: "The perpetual tension between the province's Protestant and socially conservative roots, Red Tories, the ever-more moderate majority, and mainstream/liberal LGB and queer activists was starkly played out in [the 2012] election, ultimately showing that Albertan voters are moving to the centre and that the vast majority do not support social conservative and homophobic politics."

This change of opinion regarding queer activism has been reflected in the education field, even making breakthroughs in some homophobic fortresses. As Brian Burtch, Aynsley Pescitelli, and Rebecca Haskell (Chapter 6, see p. 153, this volume) observe: "Recently, the Surrey School Board unanimously supported the creation of a working group to review anti-discrimination policy, with a heavy focus on homophobia." The working group recommended, among other things, that queer issues be integrated into the curriculum and that gay-straight alliances be set up. Of course, this remains to move from talk to action. In this regard, the case of Nova Scotia is inspiring as it shows that, although social conservatism raises barriers to all public manifestations of a sexuality that is not heterosexual and devoted to reproduction, these obstacles are not insurmountable as they have not prevented the adoption of measures to combat homophobia in the school environment. Nathaniel M. Lewis (Chapter 11, see p. 258, this volume) observes that "many public high schools in Nova Scotia formed student-based gay-straight alliances (GSAs) to support LGBT students and to educate their respective student bodies about sexual difference." Joanna Everitt (Chapter 5, this volume) also notes the deployment of alliances among LGBTQ organizations, ministries of education, school officials, and individuals as well as initiatives to fight homophobia and intolerance, notably among young people (such as the Pink Shirt Anti-Bullying Campaign and the Safe Spaces Project). In spite of such initiatives, Nathaniel M. Lewis (Chapter 11, see p. 265, this volume) writes, "the power of the closet is still considerable in educational institutions." And yet, schools are a nerve centre for queer mobilization as they are an obligatory passageway to socialization and fertile ground, from a child's early age, for the deployment and imposition of various procedures that (re)produce heteronormative hegemony: sex and gender roles portrayed as opposed and mutually exclusive, performative mechanisms responsible for femininities and masculinities, the regime of compulsory heterosexuality and the heterosexual matrix, and others.

To end on cultural outcomes of the LGBTQ movement, Julie Depelteau and Dalie Giroux (Chapter 2, see p. 75, this volume) maintain that the HIV/AIDS pandemic led Two-Spirited people to affirm their identity based on multiple-gender traditions: "The epidemic was also an occasion for Two-Spirited people living on reserves to assert themselves as the bearers of multiple-gender traditions and to take on public and political roles in their communities as caretakers, healers, teachers, and activists educating people about HIV/AIDS." This quotation reveals that, aside from acceptance of the Other, the HIV/AIDS crises also provided impetus for Two-Spirited people living on reserves to

Manon Tremblay

accept not only themselves but also their multiple-gender traditions, and this brought new social and political advantages to their communities.

In sum, seven observations emerge from this analysis of queer activism in Canada. First, as a general rule, the Canadian political regime has offered favourable institutional opportunities to queer activism. Second, the LGBTQ movement is both united and diversified. Third, partial decriminalization of homosexuality has contributed to the public emergence of the LGBTQ movement, its (limited) access to the polity, and its organization to mobilize as a broader constituency. Fourth, on the ideological level, queer activism evolved from a radical and revolutionary perspective in the 1970s to a more liberal and assimilationist perspective in the 2000s. Fifth, social conservatism constitutes the countermovement par excellence for the LGBTQ movement. Sixth, queer activism has been able to develop and prosper thanks to a wide range of resources. Seventh, queer activism has been successful in that it has gained public acceptance as well as new political and socio-cultural benefits. Although these observations are encouraging, they in no way justify a pause in queer activism as much work remains to be done to make social and cultural equality for LGBTQ people in Canada a reality.

Notes

1 As discussed in the Introduction, queer activism in Canada began well before the end of the 1960s; indeed, as early as the 1930s there existed a lively working-class lesbian bar culture in some cities, the 1950s and 1960s saw nascent forms of gay cultures and communities, and the second half of the 1960s saw limited but significant homophile activities and organizing. However, this book focuses on queer activism from the very late 1960s onward.

2 On some of the motivations of the Liberal Party and the Trudeau government, see Chambers 2010; Kinsman 1996, 264–78.

3 Of course, moral conservative organizing against queer rights did not start with the election of Stephen Harper in 2006 but goes back to the 1970s (see Dickey Young 2012; Farney 2012, 82–129; Herman 1994; McDonald 2010; Warner 2002, 132–40; 2010, 102–45).

4 That is, a movement of resistance to proposals for social change promoted by a given social movement (see McCarthy and Zald 1977; Meyer and Staggenborg 1996; Mottl 1980).

5 Some transsexuals have been recently elected: Georgina Bayer to the New Zealand House of Representatives and Stacie Laughton to the New Hampshire House of Representatives. Canada has yet to elect a self-declared transsexual politician.

6 A recent paper by Perrella, Brown, and Kay (2012) examines voting behaviour among LGBT people, but this topic needs further consideration. In a recent study conducted among openly lesbian and gay Members of the National Assembly of Quebec, Duval (2014, 63 [my translation]) concludes, "Bills passed between 1977 and 2002 that resulted in legal equality for homosexual people no doubt benefited from the presence of elected homosexuals in the National Assembly." The recently founded ProudPolitics (2014) has the mission of helping "openly LGBT leaders realize their potential to serve and win

elections to all orders of government through candidate support, fundraising, networking, and outreach."

7 One might question the idea of an "artificially swollen" pool of activists and plead the need to investigate the dialectics of mass versus smaller-scale forms of activism and the social basis for the ebbs and flows of more mass-based struggles. Although valuable, this theoretical proposition necessitates a fairly substantial reflection based on social movement theories, which is clearly beyond the scope of this conclusion.

References

Altman, Dennis. 2013. *The End of the Homosexual*. St. Lucia: University of Queensland Press.

Bernstein, Mary. 1997. "Celebration and Suppression: The Strategic Uses of Identity by the Lesbian and Gay Movement." *American Journal of Sociology* 103 (3): 531–65. http://dx.doi.org/10.1086/231250.

Chambers, Stuart. 2010. "Pierre Elliott Trudeau and Bill C-150: A Rational Approach to Homosexual Acts, 1968–69." *Journal of Homosexuality* 57 (2): 249–66. http://dx.doi.org/10.1080/00918360903489085.

Corriveau, Patrice. 2011. *Judging Homosexuals. A History of Gay Persecution in Quebec and France*. Trans. Kathe Röth. Vancouver: UBC Press.

Dickey Young, Pamela. 2012. *Religion, Sex and Politics: Christian Churches and Same-Sex Marriage in Canada*. Halifax: Fernwood.

Duval, Alexandre. 2014. *Les députés homosexuels de l'Assemblée nationale de 1977 à 2002: Un facteur dans l'atteinte de l'égalité juridique des gais et des lesbiennes du Québec?* Québec: Assemblée nationale du Québec, Fondation Jean-Charles-Bonenfant. http://www.fondationbonenfant.qc.ca/stages/documents/ALEXANDRE.pdf.

Edwards, Bob, and John D. McCarthy. 2004. "Resources and Social Movement Mobilization." In David A. Snow, Sarah Anne Soule, and Hanspeter Kriesi, eds., *The Blackwell Companion to Social Movements*, 116–52. Oxford: Blackwell.

Farney, James. 2012. *Social Conservatives and Party Politics in Canada and the United States*. Toronto: University of Toronto Press.

Gamson, William A. 1990. *The Strategy of Social Protest*. 2nd ed. Belmont: Wadsworth.

Goodwin, Jeff, and James M. Jasper. 1999. "Caught in a Winding, Snarling Vine: The Structural Bias of Political Process Theory." *Sociological Forum* 14 (1): 27–54. http://dx.doi.org/10.1023/A:1021684610881.

Haskell, David M. 2011. "'What We Have Here Is a Failure to Communicate': Same-Sex Marriage, Evangelicals, and the Canadian News Media." *Journal of Religion and Popular Culture* 23 (3): 311–29. http://dx.doi.org/10.3138/jrpc.23.3.311.

Herman, Didi. 1994. "The Christian Right and the Politics of Morality in Canada." *Parliamentary Affairs* 47 (2): 268–79.

Johnson, Carol, Sarah Maddison, and Emma Partridge. 2011. "Australia: Parties, Federalism and Rights Agendas." In Manon Tremblay, David Paternotte, and Carol Johnson, eds., *The Lesbian and Gay Movement and the State: Comparative Insights into a Transformed Relationship*, 27–42. Farnham: Ashgate.

King, Robin Levinson. 2015. "Trans Rights Bill Amendment Would Bar Trans People from Public Washrooms." *Toronto Star*, 25 February. http://www.thestar.com/news/canada/2015/02/25/trans-rights-bill-amendment-would-bar-trans-people-from-public-washrooms.html#.

Kinsman, Gary. 1996. *The Regulation of Desire: Homo and Hetero Sexualities*. 2nd ed. Montreal: Black Rose Books.

Kinsman, Gary, and Patrizia Gentile. 2010. *The Canadian War on Queers: National Security as Sexual Regulation*. Vancouver: UBC Press.

Langstaff, Amy. 2011. "A Twenty-Year Survey of Canadian Attitudes towards Homosexuality and Gay Rights." In David Rayside and Clyde Wilcox, eds., *Faith Politics and Sexual Diversity*, 49–66. Vancouver: UBC Press.

Ludwig, Gundula. 2011. "From the 'Heterosexual Matrix' to a 'Heteronormative Hegemony': Initiating a Dialogue between Judith Butler and Antonio Gramsci about Queer Theory and Politics." In María do Mar Castro Varela, Nikita Dhawan, and Antke Engel, eds., *Hegemony and Heteronormativity: Revisiting 'The Political' in Queer Politics*, 43–61. Farnham: Ashgate.

Malloy, Jonathan. 2011. "Canadian Evangelicals and Same-Sex Marriage." In David Rayside and Clyde Wilcox, eds., *Faith Politics and Sexual Diversity in Canada and the United States*, 144–59. Vancouver: UBC Press.

Marso, Lori Jo. 2010. "Marriage and Bourgeois Respectability." *Politics and Gender* 6 (1): 145–53. http://dx.doi.org/10.1017/S1743923X09990572.

Matthews, J. Scott. 2005. "The Political Foundations of Support for Same-Sex Marriage in Canada." *Canadian Journal of Political Science* 38 (4): 841–66. http://dx.doi.org/10.1017/S0008423905040485.

McAdam, Doug, John D. McCarthy, and Mayer N. Zald. 1988. "Social Movements." In Neil J. Smelser, ed., *Handbook of Sociology*, 695–737. Newbury Park: Sage.

McCarthy, John D., and Mayer N. Zald. 1977. "Resource Mobilization and Social Movements: A Partial Theory." *American Journal of Sociology* 82 (6): 1212–41. http://dx.doi.org/10.1086/226464.

–. 1987. *Social Movements in an Organizational Society*. Oxford: Transaction Books.

McDonald, Marci. 2010. *The Armageddon Factor: The Rise of Christian Nationalism in Canada*. Toronto: Random House.

Meyer, David S., and Suzanne Staggenborg. 1996. "Movements, Countermovements, and the Structure of Political Opportunity." *American Journal of Sociology* 101 (6): 1628–60. http://dx.doi.org/10.1086/230869.

Mottl, Tahi L. 1980. "The Analysis of Countermovements." *Social Problems* 27 (5): 620–35. http://dx.doi.org/10.2307/800200.

Mulé, Nick J. 2010. "Same-Sex Marriage and Canadian Relationship Recognition – One Step Forward, Two Steps Back: A Critical Liberationist Perspective." *Journal of Gay and Lesbian Social Services* 22 (1–2): 74–90. http://dx.doi.org/10.1080/10538720903332354.

Pakulski, Jan. 1997. "Cultural Citizenship." *Citizenship Studies* 1 (1): 73–86. http://dx.doi.org/10.1080/13621029708420648.

Perrella, Andrea M.L., Steven D. Brown, and Barry J. Kay. 2012. "Voting Behaviour among the Gay, Lesbian, Bisexual and Transgendered Electorate." *Canadian Journal of Political Science* 45 (1): 89–117. http://dx.doi.org/10.1017/S000842391100093X.

ProudPolitics. 2014. *About Us: What Is ProudPolitics All About? Mission*. http://www.proudpolitics.org/about.

Smith, Miriam. 2008. *Political Institutions and Lesbian and Gay Rights in the United States and Canada*. New York: Routledge.

–. 2010. "Federalism and LGBT Rights in the US and Canada: A Comparative Analysis." In Melissa Haussman, Marian Sawer, and Jill Vickers, eds., *Federalism, Feminism and Multilevel Governance*, 97–109. Farnham: Ashgate.

–. 2011. "Canada: The Power of Institutions." In Manon Tremblay, David Paternotte, and Carol Johnson, eds., *The Lesbian and Gay Movement and the State: Comparative Insights into a Transformed Relationship*, 73–87. Farnham: Ashgate.

–. Forthcoming. "Political Institutions and LGBTQ Activism in Comparative Perspective." In *The Ashgate Research Companion to Lesbian and Gay Activism*, ed. David Paternotte and Manon Tremblay. Farnham: Ashgate.

Snow, Dave. 2014. "Reproductive Autonomy and the Evolving Family in the Supreme Court of Canada: Implications for Assisted Reproductive Technologies." *Journal of Canadian Studies/Revue d'études canadiennes* 48 (1): 153–89.

Staggenborg, Suzanne. 2012. *Social Movements*. 2nd ed. New York: Oxford University Press.

Taylor, Verta, and Nella Van Dyke. 2004. "'Get up, Stand up': Tactical Repertoires of Social Movements." In David A. Snow, Sarah Anne Soule, and Hanspeter Kriesi, eds., *The Blackwell Companion to Social Movements*, 262–93. Oxford: Blackwell.

Tin, Louis-Georges. 2008. *L'invention de la culture hétérosexuelle*. Paris: Éditions Autrement.

Warner, Tom. 2002. *Never Going Back: A History of Queer Activism in Canada*. Toronto: University of Toronto Press.

–. 2010. *Losing Control: Canada's Social Conservatives in the Age of Rights*. Toronto: Between the Lines.

Contributors

GORDON BRENT BROCHU-INGRAM grew up north of Victoria, in an activist Indigenous community, is Métis, and holds a PhD in Environmental Planning from the University of California, Berkeley. He researches land use planning, Indigenous legacies and contemporary stewardship, public space, and related social and ecological infrastructure. Recently an associate dean and associate professor at George Mason University, outside of Washington, DC, he currently works at KEXMIN field station on Salt Spring Island and Utopiana in Geneva.

BRIAN BURTCH is a professor in the School of Criminology and associate member in the Department of Gender, Sexuality and Women's Studies at Simon Fraser University. An LGBTQ ally, he coauthored *Get That Freak: Homophobia and Transphobia in High Schools* (Fernwood, 2010) with Rebecca Haskell.

ALEXA DEGAGNE is a PhD candidate in the Department of Political Science at the University of Alberta. Her dissertation, "Investigating Citizenship, Sexuality and the Same-Sex Marriage Fight in California's Proposition 8," examines why and how same-sex marriage has become a pivotal point in debates about larger ideological issues, including the regulation of sexualities, the criteria for political belonging, and the nature of social justice. She has previously published works on American and Canadian LGBTQ activism and political organizing.

JULIE DEPELTEAU is a PhD candidate in political science at the University of Ottawa. She completed her master's in political science with a minor in feminist studies at the Université du Québec à Montréal. Her master's thesis focused on the work of Gloria Anzaldúa.

JOANNA EVERITT is a professor of political science and dean of arts at the University of New Brunswick in Saint John. She specializes in Canadian political behaviour with a particular focus on the impact of gender and sexual orientation on political participation, media coverage, and political representation in Canadian elections.

DALIE GIROUX has been a professor of contemporary political theory in the School of Political Studies at the University of Ottawa since 2003. She recently published *Ceci n'est pas une idée politique: Réflexion sur les approches à l'étude des idées politiques* (PUL, 2013, co-edited with Dimitrios Karmis) and *Arts performatifs et spectaculaires des premières nations de l'est du Canada* (L'Harmattan, 2014, co-edited with Jérôme Dubois).

REBECCA HASKELL-THOMAS is an independent researcher with a master's in criminology from Simon Fraser University. Her recent research involves exploring people's experiences of, and system responses to, intersecting experiences of mental health, substance use, and violence. Rebecca also studies factors contributing to, and effective means of addressing, gender-based violence, including violence against women, homophobia, and transphobia.

NATHANIEL M. LEWIS is a lecturer (assistant professor) in the Geography and Environment unit at the University of Southampton (UK) and formerly a Canadian Institutes of Health Research postdoctoral fellow at Dalhousie University in Halifax. His current research focuses on the links between place, mobility, life course, and health among gay men, and his published work can be found in journals such as *Health and Place; Gender, Place and Culture;* and *Annals of the Association of American Geographers.*

CATHERINE J. NASH is a professor in the Department of Geography at Brock University, St. Catharines, Ontario. Her areas of research include LGBT, queer, and feminist geographies; national/international resistance to LGBT rights; and the internet, new media, and LGBT urban landscapes.

AYNSLEY PESCITELLI is a PhD student in the School of Criminology at Simon Fraser University. Her master's thesis focused on homophobic and transphobic cybervictimization of post-secondary students. Additional research interests include the media and crime, minorities and the criminal justice system, gender and crime, bullying, cyberbullying, cybercrime, and hate crime.

JULIE A. PODMORE is a college professor of geosciences at John Abbott College and an affiliate associate professor in geography, planning and environment at Concordia University in Montreal. A socio-cultural urban geographer with a sustained interest in gender and sexuality in urban space, her published research focuses on Montreal's lesbian geographies.

DAVID RAYSIDE is a professor emeritus of political science and has been long associated with the Bonham Centre for Sexual Diversity Studies at the University of Toronto. His writing includes *Queer Inclusions, Continental Divisions* (2008); *Faith, Politics, and Sexual Diversity in Canada and the United States* (edited with Clyde Wilcox, 2011); and *Conservatism in Canada* (edited with James Farney, 2013). In 2014 he was elected Fellow of the Royal Society of Canada.

MIRIAM SMITH is a professor in the Department of Social Science at York University. Her areas of interest are Canadian and comparative politics, public policy, social movements, and LGBTQ politics. Among other works, she is the author of *Lesbian and Gay Rights in Canada: Social Movements and Equality-Seeking, 1971–1995* (University of Toronto Press, 1999) and *Political Institutions and Lesbian and Gay Rights in the United States and Canada* (Routledge, 2008).

MANON TREMBLAY is a professor in the School of Political Studies at the University of Ottawa. Her research interests are LGBTQ politics and social activism, and gender/women in politics. Her most recent publications include *Stalled: The Representation of Women in Canadian Governments* (co-edited with L. Trimble and J. Arscott, UBC Press, 2013); and *The Lesbian and Gay Movement and the State: Comparative Insights into a Transformed Relationship* (co-edited with D. Paternotte and C. Johnson, Ashgate, 2011).

Index

AIDS Coalition to Unleash the Power (ACT UP), 191
AIDS Committee of Toronto, 88, 211
AIDS Community Care Montreal, 191, 198–99
AIDS NB, 126
AIDS Nova Scotia, 256–57, 262
Alberta and queer activism: adoption by same-sex couples (1990s), 21; "bastion of backwardness" re LGBTQ people, 31, 163; Bill 44 on parental rights re school curriculum, 163, 166–67, 172–76; Calgary, 19, 171, 178; Edmonton, 16, 171, 175, 178; gay liberation groups (1970s), 16; gender reassignment surgery, funding, 163, 167, 178; histories of LGBTQ activism, 25–26, 164–68; Individual Rights Protection Act (IRPA), 163, 165–67; LGBTQ groups allied with non-queer groups, 168–69; PC's promise to fight for LGBT Albertans, 176, 177, 178–79; public's changing attitudes, 163–64, 165–69, 176–78, 180n3, 291; same-sex marriage, 166, 278; sexual orientation in human rights law (1998), 20; social and religious conservatism, 164–65, 168, 180n3; Trans Equality Society of Alberta, 30; *Vriend* case re sexual orientation, 20, 163, 166, 170–71, 278; Wildrose Party, 164, 167–68, 176–78. *See also* Alberta Human Rights Commission; Progressive Conservative government (Alberta)
Alberta Civil Liberties Research Centre, 173
Alberta Human Rights Commission: complaints re defunding of SRS, 167; establishment (1972), 165; non-inclusion of sexual orientation in human rights code, 170; Wildrose Party's threat to dismantle, 168, 177, 178
Alberta School Boards Association, 173
Alberta School Councils' Association, 173
Alberta Teachers' Association, 172, 173
Altman, Dennis, 16

Anderson, Lance, 174
Anderson, Rob, 173, 175
Andrews, Karen, 95
Andrews v. Ontario, 95
Androgyny (Montreal bookstore), 189
Angles (newspaper), 242
ANKORS (AIDS Network Outreach and Support Society), 135
Are We 'Persons' Yet? Law and Sexuality in Canada (Lahey), 28
Armstrong, Elizabeth A., 12, 193–94
Arvay, Joseph, 152, 155
assimilationism: assimilationist groups (1970s) in Toronto, 209–10; conservative and assimilationist activism (1990s), 20, 91; gay districts and, 212; Hislop's candidacy for Toronto municipal office, 213–15; It Gets Better campaign, criticism, 54; one approach to queer activism, 12, 209–11; shift towards, from liberationism (1970s to 2000s), 279–80, 293
Association des commerçants et professionnels du Village (Montreal), 199
Association des gai(e)s du Québec, 17, 48
Association des mères lesbiennes du Québec, 114, 116
Association des transsexuels et transsexuelles du Québec, 30
Association for Social Knowledge (ASK) (Vancouver), 14–15, 143, 230, 241, 242
Association of Gay Electors (AGE), 213
Association of Village Business Owners, 199
Association pour les droits des gai(e)s du Québec (ADGQ), 108, 189, 190, 197
Atlantic Canada and queer activism: AIDS information, counselling, and support, 126–27; Atlantic Canada Gay Conference (1977), 127; attitudes of public, 127, 128–30, 129f, 135, 136–37, 139; birth certificates and same-sex parents, 134; Christian Right's resistance to LGBT gains, 129–30, 264–65; family and adoption rights (case study), 133–34; gay-straight

study), 154–56; Out in Schools group, 55, 151; political parties' support for LGBTQ persons, 144–45, 231; SRS funding, 57; trans activism in Vancouver (early to mid-1990s), 89–90, 232–33; Two-Spirited organizations, 158, 232. *See also* Vancouver and queer activism; Vancouver and queer infrastructure

British Columbia Civil Liberties Association, 147, 152

British Columbia Federation of Women, 17, 231–32

British Columbia First Nations with AIDS Society, 232

British Columbia Gay and Lesbian Archives, 233, 241

British Columbia Human Rights Code, 144, 145, 146, 231

British Columbia Human Rights Commission, 58, 145–47, 151–52

Brochu-Ingram, Gordon Brent: chapter on queer infrastructure in Vancouver, 227–49; on ingenuity of LGBTQ activism, 287–88; on LGBTQ community claiming space and institution building, 284; shift in issues affecting sexual minorities, 279. *See also* Ingram, Gordon Brent

Brody case (1963), 216–17

Brown, Michael P., 28

Brown, Rosemary, 236

Bunch, Charlotte, 7–8

Burtch, Brian: chapter on LGBTQ movement in Western Canada, 142–62; on impact of LGBTQ politicians, 286; on institutional tactics in queer activism, 283; on progress in attitudes in education sector, 292

Butler case (1992), 216–17

Calgary, Alberta, 19

Calgary Herald, 171, 178

Campbell, Gordon, 145

Campbell, Ken, 214

Campey, John, 99

Canada Customs: charges against Glad Day Bookshop, 88, 216–17; Little

Sister's challenge (2000) (case study), 147–50

Canada Pension Plan Appeals Board, 259

Canadian Aboriginal AIDS Network (CAAN), 68

Canadian AIDS Society, 52

Canadian Armed Forces, 20, 211

Canadian Association of Chiefs of Police, 53

Canadian Association of Lesbians and Gay Men, 18

Canadian Charter of Rights and Freedoms (1982): advantageous for equality rights of LGBTQ people, 21, 89; equality rights and (1985), 48–49; regulation/ repression of non-heteronormative sex and, 10–11; same-sex marriage, 21–22; sexual orientation (*Egan* case), 18–20, 96, 154–56, 211, 259

Canadian Civil Liberties Association, 173

Canadian Council on Religion and the Homosexual, 15, 86

Canadian Federation for Sexual Health, 52–53

Canadian Gay Activist Alliance (Vancouver), 231

Canadian Human Rights Act: efforts to prohibit discrimination re gender expression/identity, 46; gender identity and expression and, 58; sexual orientation amendment (1996), 20, 49; sexual orientation and, 95

Canadian Jewish Congress, 219

Canadian Lesbian and Gay Rights Coalition/Coalition canadienne pour les droits des lesbiennes et gais, 17, 47–48, 127

Canadian National Gay Election Coalition (NGEC), 47

Canadian Rainbow Health Coalition, 22

The Canadian War on Queers: National Security as Sexual Regulation (Kinsman and Gentile), 27–28

Canadians for Equal Marriage, 21

Cancer's Margins: LGBT Community and Arts Project (Vancouver), 241

Cannon, Martin, 69, 70

Capital Pride, 90

Carleton, Debbie, 265

Carter, Sarah, 69

case studies: age of consent, 51–53; alliances between LGBT organizations and political parties (Vancouver), 235–38; anti-homophobic initiatives in BC schools, 150–54; family and adoption rights (in Atlantic Canada), 133–34; family rights in Ontario, public recognition of, 95–97; fight against homophobia (in Atlantic Canada), 134–37; homophobia in education, 54–56; human rights provisions in Ontario re discrimination, 93–94; Indian Act and gender politics, 69–70; Little Sister's challenge against Canada Customs (2000), 147–50; Montreal's Gay Village designated a business improvement area, 199–202; municipal politics (Toronto) and gay power, 213–15; new filiation rules and same-sex parenting in Quebec, 113–15; Old Age Security, access for same-sex couples, 154–56; Olympics "clean-up" campaign (Montreal, 1976), 193–96, 203n4; pension benefits for same-sex spouses, 259–60; policing in Ontario, 91–93; political mobilizing of Gay Village vote (Montreal, 1986), 196–99; relationship recognition (in Atlantic Canada), 131–33; residential school and production of heterosexual bodies, 71–73; same-sex common-law unions recognized in Quebec, 111–13; same-sex rights recognition, 131–33, 259–61; sexual diversity, recognition in Ontario state-regulated schools, 97–100; struggles against homophobia in Quebec, 115–18; trans human rights protection, 56–59; Two-Spirited people, discrimination and HIV/AIDS mobilization, 73–76; *Vriend* decision (Alberta, 1998), 170–71

Castells, Manuel, 196

Catholic public officials: on gay-straight alliances in schools, 21, 54–55, 98, 281; on proposed expanded sex education in Ontario, 98–99; on same-sex couples at school proms, 54. *See also* social conservatism and religious right

Central Kings Rural High School (Nova Scotia), 136

Centre communautaire des gais et lesbiennes de Montréal, 191

Centre for Inquiry, 172

Centre humanitaire d'aide et de libération (Quebec City), 17

C'était du spectacle! (Namaste), 25

Challenging the Conspiracy of Silence: My Life as a Canadian Gay Activist (Egan), 25

Chamberlain, James, 152

Chamberlain v. Surrey School Board (2002), 54, 152–53, 157–58

Chamberland, Line, 25

Chambre de commerce gaie du Québec (Montreal), 199

Charlottetown, Prince Edward Island, 126

Chong, Dan, 215

Christian Right. *See* social conservatism and religious right

Chronicle Herald (Halifax), 266

cissexual, 33n8

Civil Marriage Act (Canada, 2005), 45, 49, 281

Clément, Dominique, 165

Coalition des familles homoparentales, 54–55

Coalition des organismes des minorités sexuelles du Montréal métropolitain, 191

Coalition des transsexuel(le)s et transsexué(e)s du Québec, 116

Coalition for Gay Rights in Ontario, 17, 93–94, 211

Coalition for Lesbian and Gay Rights in Ontario (CLGRO): assimilationist and liberationist, 12, 87; brief *The Homosexual Minority in Ontario* (1976), 93; lobbying re notions of "spouse" and "marital status," 20, 87; lobbying re sexual orientation in Ontario's Human Rights Code, 93–94; opposed to age of consent legislation, 52

Coalition for the Reduction of Alberta Class Sizes (CRACS), 175, 283

Coalition québécoise pour la reconnaissance des conjoints et conjointes de même sexe, 112–13, 114
collective behaviour theory, 11
College of Alberta School Superintendents, 173
colonialism: construction of Euro-Christian gender system, 65–66; destruction of Indigenous multiple-gender traditions, 64–66, 70, 78n3–4, 158, 229; Indian Act's nullification of diverse forms of marriage, 69–70; residential schools' production of heterosexual bodies, 71–73; role in development of Two-Spirit movement, 64–66; sexual division of labour, 70; Two-Spirit movement a decolonizing force, 76
Comité homosexuel anti-répression (CHAR), 108, 189, 195–96
Comité SIDA Aide Montréal, 191
Committee on Social Hygiene, 15
Community Development Handbook for Gay and Bisexual Men (Nova Scotia Men's Project), 263
Community Homophile Association of Newfoundland (CHAN), 127
Community Homophile Association of Toronto (CHAT), 86–87, 209–10
Confused: Sexual Views (video), 233
Conseil québécois des gais et lesbiennes, 116
Conservative government: inertia in face of AIDS epidemic, 238; positioning to counteract Liberals, 280; roots in social conservative and Christian evangelical movements, 45. *See also* government, federal; Harper government
Coop-Femmes, 189
Corren, Peter and Murray, 153–54
Corren Agreement (British Columbia), 153–54
Corriveau, Patrice, 26
Cory J., 156
Cossman, Brenda, 148–49, 150, 217
Court Challenges Program: funding and defunding, 159n1; pension benefits for same-sex spouses, 260; sexual orientation discrimination in section 15 of Charter (*Egan* case), 155–56, 211; sexual orientation in discrimination cases, 147

Crage, Suzanna M., 193–94
Crandall University (Moncton, NB), 130
Criminal Code of Canada: age of consent amendment, 119; amendment proposal re gender identity and expression, 58; decriminalization of homosexuality (1969), 12–13, 15–16, 45, 46, 293; efforts to include gender identity and expression, 58; homosexuality decriminalized but restricted to private realm, 46; impact of *Klippert* case, 15; *Little Sister's* case, obscene material vs erotica, 147–48; provisions allowing repression of homosexuality (1970s), 16; section 159, 16; section 210 on bawdy houses, 10, 12, 47, 53, 194
Cummins, John, 145

Davies, Libby, 143, 157
De l'égalité juridique à l'égalité sociale (report, 2007), 116–17, 193, 289
De l'illégalité à l'égalité (report, 1994), 109, 112–17, 120, 192
DeGagne, Alexa: chapter on LGBTQ activism in Alberta, 163–83; diversity of tactics used by LGBTQ movement, 284–85; on LGBT organizations' ideological differences, 276; on transformation in public opinion, 291
Demczuk, Irène, 26, 27
Depelteau, Julie: access to health care for Two-Spirited people, 288; chapter on Two-Spirit mobilization, 64–81; legacy of colonialism for Two-Spirited people, 158, 277
Des droits à reconnaître: Les lesbiennes face à la discrimination (Demczuk), 27
DiNovo, Cheri, 94
Domestic Partnership Act (Nova Scotia, 2000), 260
Doré, Jean, 197
Drapeau, Jean, 197

Fredericton, New Brunswick, 126, 127
"Free Space" (Aires Libres) project, 200–1
Friends of Lesbians and Gays (FLAG), 127
Front de libération homosexuel, 16, 107, 189
Fry, Hedy, 238
Fuller, S.D., 150

Gaezette (periodical, Halifax), 17, 252
GALA News, 253
Gamson, William A., 289
Gary, Mike, 172
Gay (magazine), 15, 86
Gay Action Committee (Vancouver), 230
Gay Alliance for Equality (Halifax), 16, 127, 252–53
Gay Alliance Towards Equality (Edmonton), 16, 17
Gay Alliance Towards Equality (GATE) (Ontario), 87, 93, 210
Gay Alliance Towards Equality (GATE) (Vancouver), 16, 143–44, 231, 236
Gay Alliance Towards Equality Saskatoon, 16
Gay and Lesbian Association of Nova Scotia·(GALA), 19, 253–54, 256
Gay and Lesbian Educators of British Columbia (GALE), 154
Gay Asians of Toronto, 19
Gay Friends of Fredericton, 127
Gay McGill, 189
Gay Montreal Association, 189
gay-straight alliances in schools: in Atlantic Canada, 23, 127, 135–37, 139, 258–59; combatting homophobia among youth, 54; in Ontario, 98, 281; opposition from social conservatives, 21, 54–55, 98, 281; website, 55–56
Gay Tide (newspaper, Vancouver), 17, 144
Gays and Lesbians of the First Nations, 68
Gays for Equality (Winnipeg), 16
Gays of Ottawa/Gays d'Ottawa, 16, 47–48, 87, 253
Gentile, Patrizia, 27–28
Gilley, Brian Joseph, 74
Giroux, Dalie: access to health care for Two-Spirited people, 288; chapter on

Two-Spirit mobilization, 64–81; legacy of colonialism for Two-Spirited people, 158, 277
Gladstone, Martin, 219
The Global Emergence of Gay and Lesbian Politics (Adam et al.), 25
The Globe and Mail, 215
Gonthier, J., 152
government, federal: ability to advance or to reverse LGBTQ rights, 51, 53; age of consent, non-equalization, 46, 51–53; benefits for same-sex partners of federal employees, 21; centralized legal framework, 49, 272; decriminalization of homosexuality (1969), 12–13, 15–16, 45, 46, 293; fight for trans human rights protection, 46, 56–59; homophobic bullying in schools, 46; Indian Act, 69–71; judicial appointment a federal power, 50; jurisdiction over criminal law, 46; parliamentary system produces governments with no opposition, 49–50, 53, 60, 272; political institutional architecture benefit to queer activism, 272–73, 282, 293; residential schools, 71–73, 78n10; rights of same-sex couples (*see* rights of LGBTQ individuals). *See also* Canadian Charter of Rights and Freedoms (1982); Conservative government; Criminal Code of Canada; Supreme Court of Canada
Government Action Plan against Homophobia, 2011–2016 (Quebec), 110, 117–18, 119
governments, provincial: benefits for same-sex couples, 21, 95, 131–32; human rights legislation and sexual orientation, 19, 130, 189, 190; policies re heterosexist school climates, 97; provincial human rights codes and bullying in schools, 54; SRS, funding and availability, 57, 102n4, 138, 163, 167, 178. *See also individual provinces*
Greater Vancouver Native Cultural Society, 232

Groupe de recherche et d'intervention sociale (GRIS), 54–55
Groupe de travail mixte contre l'homophobie, 116–17
Grunt Gallery (Vancouver), 233

Haig and Birch v. Canada (1992), 20, 95
Halifax, Nova Scotia: bar-based mode of organizing (Turret, Rumours), 252–54; Black Outreach Program, 262; Gay Alliance for Equality, 16, 127, 252–53; Gay and Lesbian Association of Nova Scotia (GALA), 19, 253–54, 256; gay liberation groups (1970s to 1990s), 16, 252–53, 256; gay publications, 252–53, 254–55; Halifax Pride, 128, 255; HIV/AIDS movement, history of (case study), 261–64; lack of gay district, 254–55; lack of studies on LGBT community, 251; largest urban centre in Atlantic Canada, 125; Lesbian, Gay and Bisexual Youth Project, 21, 127, 135, 255, 258, 265; LGBT community's commitment to political organizing, 250–52; LGBT organizing more provincial and regional, 255, 266; Nova Scotia Rainbow Action Project (NSRAP), 128, 138, 254, 255
Hall, Barbara, 94
Halpern case (2003), 48–49, 96–97
Hamilton, Ontario, 19, 95
Hancock, Dave, 175
Hanhardt, Christina B., 201
Hansman, Glen, 54
Harcourt, Kristy, 171
Harcourt, Michael, 240
Harel, Louise, 113
Haris, Jaye, 14
Harper government: antipathy to LGBTQ communities, 45; appointment of politically conservative judges, impact, 59, 60; differential age of consent for gay sex, 51; Harper in favour of human rights for LGBTQ people, 280; income splitting as protection of traditional heterosexual families, 119; LGBTQ rights removed from citizenship guide, 45; roots in social conservative and

Christian evangelical movements, 45. *See also* Conservative government
Harrison, Wayne, 127
Harvey, David, 187, 203
Haskell, Rebecca: on attitudes in education sector towards LGBTQ people, 292; chapter on LGBTQ movement in Western Canada, 142–62; on impact of LGBTQ politicians, 286; on institutional tactics used in queer activism, 283
Hawkes, Brent, 220
Hayes, Eldon, 127
Healing Our Spirit, 68, 232
health care: access limited for Two-Spirited people, 74–76, 288; homophobia, 29; LGBTQ-focused health organizations (1990s), 21
Healy, Theresa, 26
Helmcken House (Vancouver), 239
Herbert, Spencer Chandra, 157
Herman, Didi, 26
heteronormalization: *De l'illégalité à l'égalité,* 109; in health care, 29; same-sex civil marriage, criticism of, 22, 24, 120
heteronormative hegemony (heterosexism): heterosexual lifestyle the "gold standard," 7–8, 290; impact of Kinsey Report in 1950s, 13; impact of WWII, 13; mechanism to regulate/repress non-heteronormative sex, 3, 7–8, 10, 115, 271, 291; not challenged by LGBTQ rights and advances, 290–91; overvaluing of heterosexuality, 3; resistance by some LGBTQ to same-sex marriage, 22; social and cultural equality for LGBTQ people not yet attained, 291. *See also* regulation and repression of non-heteronormative sex
heterosexism, 8. *See also* heteronormative hegemony
heterosexuality: non-heterosexual individuals second-class citizens, 4, 5, 7, 291; overvalued in society, 3; seen as the norm, 5, 7, 8; values allegedly those of civil society, 8
Higgins, Ross, 10, 26, 107, 108
Hislop, George, 212, 213–15, 221

HIV/AIDS: access to health care limited for Two-Spirited people, 74–76; anonymous HIV testing, 263; criticism of government's handling of crisis, 89, 238; effects on gay and lesbian movement in Quebec, 108–9; Fifth International Conference on AIDS (Montreal, 1989), 19, 191; galvanizing of grassroots LGBTQ activism, 18–19; Helmcken House (Vancouver), 239; history of HIV/AIDS movement in Halifax, 261–64; homophobia and, 22; impact on gay liberation organizations, 48, 211; literature on crisis, 28; state funding of LGBTQ communities, impact, 28, 88; Two-Spirit groups formed in response to epidemic, 68, 73–76, 88, 292–93. *See also under individual provinces*

Hodder, Wilson, 259–60

Hogan v. Ontario (Health and Long-Term Care) (2005), 58

Holm, John, 257

Homophile Reform Society (HRS), 15

homophobia: in 1980s, 18–19; in 2000s, 22–23; among visible minorities, 157; backlash to *Vriend* case decision, 171; change in 1960s, 15–16; discrimination against Two-Spirited persons, 74; in education sector, 29–30, 54–55; government mobilization against, 29; in health care system, 29; HIV/AIDS and, 22; lack of protection in Charter, 18–19; LGBTQ fight against discrimination (2000s), 22–23; literature on struggle against, 28–30; violence in Vancouver, 233–34. *See also* regulation and repression of non-heteronormative sex; societal attitudes to LGBTQ people; transphobia

"Homosexual in Urban Society" (Leznoff), 14

Les homosexuels s'organisent au Québec et ailleurs (Sylvestre), 25–26

Horne, Fred, 178

The House That Jill Built: A Lesbian Nation in Formation (Ross), 25

Howard, Jennifer, 143

Hoy, Claire, 214–15

Hunsperger, Allan, 177

Hunt, Gerald, 89

Iacobucci J., 156

identity politics: challenge to politics and policy, 7; collective identity a tactical cultural resource, 284; defenders vs critics, 4; identity as radical political act, 5–7; LGBTQ movement as ultimate identity movement, 284; political perspective, 5–7; second-class citizenship for non-heterosexual persons, 4–5; socio-psychological perspective, 4–5, 7

Indian Act, 69–71, 229

Indigenous people. *See* Aboriginal peoples

Individual Rights Protection Act (IRPA) (Alberta), 163, 165, 166–67

Ingram, Gordon Brent, 26. *See also* Brochu-Ingram, Gordon Brent

International Conference on LGBT Community Human Rights (2006), 22, 193

International Day against Homophobia, 22

International Sex Equality Anonymous (ISEA), 15

Israel, 218–19

It Gets Better (IGB) campaign, 54, 151

Jackson, Ed, 25

Janoff, Doug, 93

Jennex, Ramona, 258

Jewish Tribute, 219

Jim Loves Jack (documentary), 155

Jubran case (responsibility re safe environment for students), 151–52

Judging Homosexuals: A History of Gay Persecution in Quebec and France (Corriveau), 26

Kansas, Jane, 254

Kay, Barbara, 221

Kelm, Mary-Ellen, 71–72

Kilanu, 220

Kinsey, Alfred, 13

Kinsey Reports (1948, 1953), 13

Kinsman, Gary: challenging heterosexual hegemony, 7; on "civilization" of

movement, 50. *See also* assimilationism; liberationism

LGBTQ Parenting Network, 90

LGBTQ youth: bullying and harassment of, 29, 46, 55, 136–37; combatting homophobia among youth, 135–37; Lesbian, Gay, Bi, Trans Youth Line (Ontario), 90; Lesbian, Gay and Bisexual Youth Project (Halifax), 21, 127, 135, 255, 258, 265; Main Street series (CBC), 138; OUTline (hotline for Nova Scotia youth), 127; Pink Shirt Anti-Bullying Campaign, 136, 139; "Safe Spaces" project (in Atlantic Canada), 135; Supporting Our Youth (Ontario group), 90. *See also* age of consent; gay-straight alliances in schools

L'Heureux-Dubé J., 156

Liberal government: ally of LGBTQ communities, 286; amendment to Human Rights Act to include sexual orientation (1996), 20, 49; decriminalization of homosexuality (1969), 12–13, 45, 46, 278; funding of LGBTQ social programs in Vancouver, 235–38; legalization of same-sex marriage in Civil Marriage Act (2005), 45, 49, 281. *See also* government, federal

liberationism: arguments by liberationists, 210–11; confrontational tactics, 88; gay districts and, 212; human rights agenda, disadvantage of, 210–11; liberationist groups (1970s), 86, 87, 189, 209, 252; literature on queer activism from liberationist perspective, 24–25; one approach to queer activism, 12, 210–11; shift in activism towards assimilationism (1970s to 2000s), 109, 209, 279–80, 293; view of civil same-sex marriage, 22, 288

Linden, Allen, 155

Lindquist, Evert, 28

Little Sister's Book and Art Emporium, 147–50, 242

Lloyd, Julie, 166, 170, 174

Lo, Jenny, 26

long-term facilities for aging LGBTQ community, 138, 156

Lotus Root Conference (1996), 21, 233

Lougheed, Peter, 165

M. v. H. (1999), 20–21, 48–49, 96

MacDougall, Bruce, 28

MacLeod, Cheri, 127

Main Street series (CBC), 138

Make It Better campaign, 151

Making Waves (quarterly, Halifax), 252

Making Waves conference (Halifax), 258

Manitoba, 16, 19, 95

March, James G., 9

Marcoux, Yvon, 116

Marois, Pauline, 113

marriage, civil, and same-sex unions: in Alberta, 166, 278; in Atlantic Canada, 132–33; Civil Marriage Act (2005), 45, 49, 281; EGALE's advocating for in legal cases, 48–49; literature on, 28–29; in Ontario, 96–97; possible due to equality rights in law, 21–22; in Quebec, 111–13, 113–15, 118, 192–93; rejection as "heteronormalizing," 22, 24, 120; social conservatism movement as reaction, 29, 281, 293; symbolic of equality advances, 290

Marsh, James, 165

Martin, Leonard, 155

Martin, Paul, 45, 49, 281

Mason, Gary, 157

Mattachine Society, 14

Matthews, J. Scott, 283

Mayencourt, Lorne, 143

McCarthy, John D., 282

McGuinty, Dalton, 55, 99

McLachlin, Beverley, 152, 156, 157–58

McLeod, Donald W., 14, 24, 107

M.D.R. v. Ontario (2006), 96

Mémoires lesbiennes (Chamberland), 25

Metro Area AIDS Coalition (MacAIDS), 262

Metropolitan Community Church, 87, 90, 286

Meyer-Cook, Fiona, 26

Milk, Harvey, 196

138; weak NDP representation affecting LGBTQ advances, 137–38. *See also* Atlantic Canada and queer activism

New Brunswick Human Rights Award (2009), 137

New Brunswick Rainbow Alliance (2001), 128

New Democratic Party: ally of LGBTQ communities, 286; funding fight against HIV/AIDS in Vancouver, 240; LGBTQ advances in Atlantic Canada and, 137–38; LGBTQ communities in Vancouver and, 235–36

New Morning collective (Vancouver), 231

new social movement theory, 11–12

Newfoundland and Labrador: AIDS group, 127; anti-bullying and LGBTQ training in schools, 56; birth certificates and same-sex parents, 134; Community Homophile Association of Newfoundland (CHAN), 127; family and adoption rights, 133–34; gay liberation groups (1990s), 21, 126–27; gay-straight alliances, 136; human rights legislation and sexual orientation, 130; Newfoundland Gays and Lesbians for Equality (NGALE), 126–28; recognition of same-sex rights, 131–32; Same-Sex Amendment Act, 132; same-sex marriage, 132–33. *See also* Atlantic Canada and queer activism

Newfoundland Gays and Lesbians for Equality (NGALE), 21, 126–28

Nichiwakan Native Gay and Lesbian Society, 19, 68

Nixon, Kimberley, 58, 145–47

Nixon v. Vancouver Rape Relief Society (2002), 145–46

Noël, Roger, 108

North Vancouver School District v. Jubran, 151–52

A Not So Gay World: Homosexuality in Canada (Foster and Murray), 24

Nova Scotia and queer activism: "avant-gardist" approach to LGBT policies, 250, 252, 257, 259–61; birth certificates and same-sex parents, 134; Christian Right's resistance (in Truro) to LGBT gains, 129–30, 264–65; commitment to political organizing, 250–52; Domestic Partnership Act (2000), 260; family and adoption rights, 133–34, 259–61; Gay Alliance for Equality, 16, 127, 252–53; Gay and Lesbian Association of Nova Scotia (GALA), 19, 253–54, 256; gay liberation groups (1970s), 16, 126; gay liberation groups (1980s and 1990s), 19, 21, 252–54; gay publications, 252–53, 254–55; Gayline (support line for LGBT communities), 126, 252; homophobia among youth, combatting, 135–37; Human Rights Act and sexual orientation, 130, 256–57; Lesbian, Gay and Bisexual Youth Project, 21, 127, 135, 255, 258, 265; LGBT seniors, study on long-term care facilities, 138, 156; NDP and LGBTQ advances, 137; Nova Scotia Human Rights Commission, 258, 259–60; Nova Scotia Rainbow Action Project (NSRAP), 128, 138, 254, 255; OUTline (hotline for NS youth), 127; pension benefits for same-sex spouses, 259–60; police recognition of LGBT people's protection concerns, 265; provincial and regional organizing, 255, 266; provincial HIV/AIDS strategy, 263; public and anti-HIV stigma, 264; public intolerance of homophobia, 251, 257, 292; reluctance of LGBT people to come out, 266–67; same-sex access to pension rights, 259–60; same-sex marriage, 132; same-sex rights recognition (case studies), 131–33, 259–61; trans activism re gender identity and gender expression, 138; violence against gays, public outrage at, 135. *See also* Atlantic Canada and queer activism; Nova Scotia and queer activism, education sector

Nova Scotia and queer activism, education sector: battle for LGBT rights in public schools (case study), 256–59; gay-straight alliances, 23, 127, 135–37, 258–59; harassment of LGBT teachers, 266; HIV/AIDS education challenging, 263–64; HIV-positive teacher dismissed, 256–57; teacher accused of inappropriate conduct, 257–58

Nova Scotia Coalition of People with AIDS (NSCPWA), 19, 262

Nova Scotia Department of Education Pension Plan, 259

Nova Scotia Men's Project, 21, 263

Nova Scotia Rainbow Action Project (NSRAP), 128, 138

Nova Scotia Teachers Union, 259

Nowell, James (chief of Kwakwaka'wakw), 229

Nunavut and delisting of SRS, 58

Olsen, Johan P., 9

Olympics "clean-up" campaign (Montreal, 1976), 189, 193–96, 203n4

Ontario Aboriginal HIV/AIDS Strategy (OAHAS), 68

Ontario and queer activism: adoption by same-sex couples (1990s), 21, 95–96; barriers to real inclusivity, 101; Canadian Council on Religion and the Homosexual, 15, 86; diversity of advocacy groups/constituencies, 90, 273–74; fight against HIV/AIDS, 88; Gay Alliance Towards Equality (GATE), 87, 93, 210; gender identity in human rights code (2012), 94; government's handling of HIV/AIDS crisis, 19, 89; LGBTQ family rights, public recognition of, 86, 89, 95–97; local level of activism, majority of work of queer movement, 85; Ottawa, 16–17, 92, 93, 95, 100; policing prejudicial and oppressive, 86, 87–89, 91–93; political organizing (late 1960s–early '70s), 16–18, 86–87, 100–1; public uneasy about recognition of sexual diversity, 100; same-sex marriage legalized, 21, 96–97; sexual orientation in Human Rights Code, 19, 93–94, 211; SRS funding, 57–58, 102n4; TEACH group and presentations on homophobia, 55; trans activism in Toronto (early to mid-1990s), 89–90; transgenderism and bisexuality less accepted, 101;

unions as allies, 89; weaknesses, lack of volunteers and complacency, 90–91; workplace benefits for same-sex couples, 95. *See also* Ontario and queer activism, education sector; Toronto, Ontario

Ontario and queer activism, education sector: Accepting Schools Act (2012), 23, 55, 98; bullying in schools and human rights code, 54; gay-straight alliances, controversy, 98, 281; Keep Our Kids Safe at School Act (2009), 98; LGBT resources for high schools, list, 90; policies on bullying and discrimination, 97–98; public concern over harassment and violence, 97, 99; Safe Schools Act (2001), 98; school boards and action re bullying, 99–100; sex education's new curriculum, 98–99, 100; sexual diversity recognized, 86; *Shaping a Culture of Respect*, 98; traditional gender norms reinforced in schools, 97, 100

Ontario Human Rights Code, 93–94

Ontario Human Rights Commission, 94

Organisation des êtres bispirituels du Québec, 117

Ottawa, Ontario: bathhouse raids by police (1975–84), 92; discrimination due to sexual orientation forbidden (1976), 93; gay liberation groups (1970s), 16–17; police more respectful of sexual minorities, 92; school board action re bullying, 100; workplace benefits for same-sex partners, 95

Our City of Colours (Vancouver), 241

Out in Schools group, 55, 151

Out Our Way: Gay and Lesbian Life in the Country (Riordon), 26

OUTline (hotline for Nova Scotia youth), 127

Padfield, Bethany, 174

Parents and Friends of Lesbians and Gays, 90, 127

Parti québécois, 17, 189, 190, 286

Peers, Daniel, 175

Persky, Stan, 25
Pescitelli, Aynsley: chapter on LGBTQ movement in Western Canada, 142–62; on impact of LGBTQ politicians, 286; on institutional tactics used in queer activism, 283; on progress in education sector's attitudes towards LGBTQ people, 292
Phair, Michael, 174
Picard, Ellen Chambers, 54
Pictou County AIDS Coalition, 263
Pink Shirt Anti-Bullying Campaign, 136, 139
Pink Triangle Press, 243
Plamondon, Vanida, 58
Planned Parenthood, 52
Podmore, Julie: chapter on LGBT activism in Montreal, 187–207; on fluidity of queer movement across provincial boundaries, 274–75; on queer activism in Montreal, 26, 276; on Raymond Blain's candidacy in Montreal, 286
policing: bathhouse raids (Toronto and Ottawa), 87–88, 91–92; few officers out as gay or lesbian, 93; Montreal repression pre-Olympics (1976), 194, 195; movement against police repression/brutality in Montreal (1990s), 191–92; prejudicial and oppressive actions in Ontario, 86, 87–89, 91–93; recognition of LGBT people's protection concerns in Nova Scotia, 265; regulation and repression of queer sexualities, 10–11, 16, 46–47; resistance strategies by LGBTQ people, 11; tempered by Charter of Rights and Freedoms, 10; tempered by police–queer community dialogue, 10–11
Political Institutions and Lesbian and Gay Rights in the United States and Canada (Smith), 27
political process theory, 11
PolitiQ Queers, 202
La politique québécoise de lutte contre l'homophobie (2010), 55
pornography: *Brody* decision (1963), 216; *Butler* decision (1992), 52, 216–17;

"community standards" for gay and lesbian materials, 216–17; feminist arguments for and against, 52, 217–18; Glad Day Bookshop case (1992), 88, 216–18, 221; *Little Sister's* case, 147–50, 242
Porter, Gordon, 137
pride parades: battle re participation of Queers against Israeli Apartheid (Toronto, 2010), 213, 218–21, 277; expressing queer identities, 284; in Halifax, 128, 255; Pride Toronto in LGBT resource list for schools, 90; in Toronto (1970s), 87; Truro's (NS) refusal to fly pride flag, 129–30, 264–65; in Vancouver, 231
Prince Edward Island and queer activism: Abegweit Rainbow Collective (ARCPEI), 128; birth certificates and same-sex parents, 134; Charlottetown AIDS group, 126; family and adoption rights, 134; human rights legislation and sexual orientation, 130; no gay-straight alliances, 136; outrage at attacks on gays, 135; same-sex marriage, 132–33; same-sex rights recognized, 131–32; weak NDP representation affecting LGBTQ advances, 137–38
Progressive Conservative government (Alberta): Bill 44 on parental rights re school curriculum, 163, 166–67, 172–76; funding of gender reassignment surgery, 163, 167, 178; parental rights re school curriculum (Bill 44), 163, 166–67; promise to fight for LGBT Albertans, 176, 177, 178–79; refusal to act on *Vriend* ruling re sexual orientation, 163, 166, 170–71; socially conservative and homophobic, 163–64
Proud of Alberta, 178
Provincial Adoption Act, amendment (Nova Scotia, 2001), 260–61
public policy, decision-making process: institutionalist perspective, 9–10; liberal pluralist approach, 8–10; method of overvaluing heterosexuality, 3, 8–10; postcolonialist approach, 8

Qmunity (Vancouver), 234, 237, 243, 244, 246

Quebec and queer activism: activist groups (1970s), 16–17, 106–8; ADGQ (Association pour les droits des gai(e)s du Québec), 108, 189, 190, 197; *An Act Instituting Civil Unions and Establishing New Rules of Filiation,* 113–15, 118; Association des transsexuels et transsexuelles du Québec, 30; birth certificates with same-sex parents, 111, 113; civil union rights, 111–13, 118, 192–93; *Government Action Plan against Homophobia, 2011–2016,* 110, 117–18, 119; government regulation of lesbian and gay movement, 110; government relations with LGBT movement, 106, 109–10; heteronormalizing of lesbians and gays, 109, 120; HIV/AIDS crisis and, 108–9; homophobia, government actions against (2009, 2011), 23, 115, 117–18; homophobia in schools, policy development, 54–55; insemination rights for same-sex couples, 113–14; lesbian and gay movement's influence on the state, 110–11; literature on discrimination against lesbians, 27; literature on LGBTQ activism, 25–26; negative, but not positive, rights obtained, 106; Quebec Charter of Human Rights and Freedoms, 17, 18, 189; *Québec Policy against Homophobia,* 110, 115–18; Quiet Revolution, impact of, 107; recognition of legitimacy of LGBTQ groups in forming policy, 289; resources widely diverse, 110; sex reassignment surgery, funding, 57; sexual orientation in Quebec Charter, 17, 18, 189; socially conservative climate recently, 119; trans activism in Montreal (1990s), 89–90; transphobia addressed in *Government Action Plan against Homophobia, 2011–2016,* 118; violence against lesbians and gays, public hearings on (1990s), 109. *See also* Montreal, Quebec; Quebec Human Rights Commission

Quebec Charter of Human Rights and Freedoms, 17, 18, 189

Quebec City, Quebec, 17

Quebec Human Rights Commission: *De l'égalité juridique à l'égalité sociale* (report, 2007), 116–17, 193, 289; *De l'illégalité à l'égalité* (report, 1994), 109, 112–17, 120, 192; public inquiry into violence against lesbians and gays, 109, 192

Québec Policy against Homophobia (Quebec), 110, 115–18

queer activism, overview: 1970s to 2000s, 16–23; activism both united and diversified, 273–77; assimilationist vs liberationist approaches, 12, 209–11; decriminalization of homosexuality, impact on gay liberation, 16, 293; grassroots activism, importance of, ix, 59–60; literature on, themes and general works, 24–25; literature on special issues, 25–30; political regime's institutional architecture and, 272–73; pre-1970s (setting the stage), 12–16; "setting the stage" for queer activism, 12–16; transition from revolutionary perspective (1970s to 2000s), 279–80, 293; US equal rights strategies, influence of, vii. *See also* rights of LGBTQ individuals; *entries beginning with* LGBTQ

Queer Allied Network (QAN), 174

Queer Inclusions, Continental Divisions (Rayside), 27

Queer Judgments: Homosexuality, Expression, and the Courts in Canada (MacDougall), 28

Queer McGill, 202

Queer Nation, 89, 191

Queer Nation Acts Up, 21

Queer Ontario, 55, 91

Queers against Israeli Apartheid QuAIA (Toronto, 2010), 213, 218–21, 277

racism: effect on methods of oppression, viii; racialized LGBTQ rights (marginalization of Aboriginals and non-Westerners), 49; against Two-Spirited persons off-reserve, 74

recognition of EGALE as legitimate voice of LGBTQ groups, 289; strengthened in recent years, 280

Social Credit Party (BC), 144, 238, 239

social media, 241, 288

social movement theory, approaches, 11–12, 110

societal attitudes to LGBTQ people: improvement, 283, 291, 292, ix; liberalization in 1960s, 15–16. *See also under individual provinces and regions*

Société de développement commercial du Village (SDC du Village) (Montreal), 199–202

Sparrow, Alan, 215

Staggenborg, Suzanne, 283

Stelmach, Ed, 163, 166–67, 172–75

Stevenson, Tim, 142

Stone, Sharon Dale, 25

Stonewall Riots (New York City, 1969), 16, 108, 193, 230–31, 251, 278

Sullivan, Rachael, 26

Supporting Our Youth (Ontario group), 90

Supreme Court of Canada: ban on LGBTQ-positive reading materials overturned (*Chamberlain* case), 54, 152–53; *Brody* case re obscene materials, 216; *Butler* case re obscene materials, 216–17; case re *Vancouver Sun*'s refusal to run gay ad, 144, 231; on consensual gay sex (*Klippert* case), 15, 33n6; declined to hear appeal of *Vancouver Rape Relief* case re trans discrimination, 58; on definition of "spouses," 21; *Little Sister's* case (2000), 149–50; recognition of same-sex relationships, 20; same-sex couples' legal status in Ontario (*M. v. H.* case), 20–21, 96; on same-sex partner benefits (*Mossop* case), 20, 95; sexual orientation in Alberta's human rights law (*Vriend* case), 20, 163, 166, 170–71; sexual orientation in Charter (*Egan* case), 20, 96, 155–56, 211, 259

Surrey School Board (BC), 54, 152–53, 157–58, 292

Surrey School Board, Chamberlain v. (2002), 54, 152–53, 157–58

Swann, David, 173

Sylvestre, Paul-François, 26

Taavel, Raymond, 135, 265

Table de concertation des lesbiennes et des gais du Québec, 109, 114

Tackling Violent Crime Act (Canada), 52

Taylor, Verta, 283–84

TEACH group, 55

Thompson, Charles, 130

Tobin, Brian, 130

Toronto, Ontario: assimilationist groups (1970s), 209–10; bathhouse raids by police (1981), 87–88, 91–92; Community Homophile Association of Toronto (CHAT), 86–87, 209–10; discrimination due to sexual orientation forbidden (1973), 18, 93; feminist groups, 87; gay liberation groups (1970s and 1980s), 16–17, 19–20, 87–89, 209–11; gay liberation groups (1990s), 21; *Gay* magazine, 15, 86; gay village and territorial visibility for gays, 212, 222; gay village's Business Improvement Association, 212; Glad Day Bookshop/*Bad Attitude* case, 87, 88, 90, 216–18, 221; Hislop's run for municipal office in 1980 (case study), 213–15, 221; homosexuals as a minority group, 213–14, 214–15; human rights strategy focus (1970s–80s), 210–11; liberationist groups (1970s), 209, 210–11; literature on history of LGBTQ activism, 25–26; police move towards reformism, 92; police prejudicial and oppressive, 87–89, 91–93; policy shifts by school boards, and amalgamation, 99–100; pride celebrations, 87; pride parade and Queers against Israeli Apartheid (2010), 213, 218–21, 277; Queers against Israeli Apartheid (QuAIA), 213, 218–21, 277; Right to Privacy Committee, 88; Toronto Gay Action (TGA), 16, 47, 210, 278; trans activism (early to mid-1990s), 89–90;

Two-Spirited identity: colonialism's suppression of Indigenous ceremonies and culture, 64–66, 70, 78n3–4, 158, 229; complexity of identities, 64, 75; definition and meaning, 66–67, 78n8; discrimination both on and off reserve, 67–68, 74–75; government's linking of "Two-Spirit" with illness, 76; Indian Act's nullification of diverse forms of marriage, 69–70; multiple-gender traditions, 65, 66, 77n1; multiple-gender traditions lost through colonialism, 65–66, 271, 277; residential schools' production of heterosexual bodies, 71–73; self-healing and cultural recovery aspect, 232; Two-Spirit identity distinct from LGBTQ identity, 68

Two-Spirited People of Manitoba, 19, 68

2-Spirited People of the 1st Nations, 20, 68, 88, 90

UN Geneva Convention on Genocide, 73

United States and queer activism: influence on queer activism in Canada, vii; legislation on "dangerous sexual offenders" and its influence on Canada, 279; LGBTQ rights policies in states' jurisdictions, 49; literature comparing Canada and US re LGBTQ activism, 27

University of Toronto Homophile Association (UTHA), 16–18, 86, 209

Urban Youth Native Association (BC), 158

Valley AIDS Concern Group, 263

Vallières, Pierre, viii

Van Dyke, Nella, 283–84

Vancouver and queer activism: ACT UP Vancouver, 239–40, 242, 283; alliances between LGBT organizations and political parties (case study), 235–38; ASK (Association for Social Knowledge), 14–15, 143, 230, 241, 242; culturally specific gay and lesbian networks, 232–33; Gay Alliance Towards Equality (GATE), 16, 143–44, 231, 236; gay liberation groups (1960s

and 1970s), 16–17, 143–45, 229–31; gay pride rally (first in 1972), 231; homophobic violence, 233–34, 245; Indigenous sexual minorities, suppression by state, 228–30; lesbian feminist groups and activities, 17, 231–32; literature on history of LGBTQ activism, 25–26; *Little Sister's* case (2000) (case study), 147–50; National Lesbian Conference (1981), 20; queer centres shifting from city centre to suburbs, 228, 240; Queerotica, 150; racialized LGBT communities and inequity of services, 229–30, 245; trans activism (early to mid-1990s), 89–90, 232–33; Transgender Health Program, 233; Two-Spirited organizations, 158, 232; *Vancouver Rape Relief* case re trans discrimination, 58, 145–47, 287; "We Demand" brief to government (1971), 17, 22–23, 231; "We Demand" conference (2011), 22–23; workplace benefits for same-sex couples, 95. *See also* British Columbia and queer activism; Vancouver and queer infrastructure

Vancouver and queer infrastructure: definition, 228; emerging politics of service provision and "space-taking," 228; grant to Qmunity for purpose-built centre, 245; Helmcken House for people with AIDS, 239; Liberals funding of service organizations, 235–38; modes of organizational/spatial development, 241–44, 244–45; need for better support, services and programs, 234–35, 245, 279–80; SEARCH (Vancouver), 237; shifting from city centre to suburbs, 228, 240; shortage of sex-positive spaces, 233–34; social networking organizations, 241

Vancouver Art Gallery, 233

Vancouver Gay and Lesbian Centre, 232

Vancouver Gay Community Centre (VGCC), 237

Vancouver Gay Liberation Front, 16, 144, 230–31

Vancouver Rape Relief and Women's
Shelter, 58, 145–47
Vancouver Rape Relief v. Nixon (2005), 58,
145–47, 287
Vancouver Sun, 144, 231, 239
Vancouver Two-Spirit, 19, 68
Vander Zalm, Bill, 239, 283
Video Inn (Vancouver), 233
Vriend v. Alberta (1998), 20, 48, 170–71

Waaldijk, Kees, 12, 27
Warner, Tom: on "gay power" references
in Toronto's 1980 election, 214; on
impact of HIV/AIDS on gay activism,
211; on LGBT movement in Montreal,
188; literature on queer activism, 24,
280; on two orientations of queer
activism, 12, 280
Wayne, Elsie, 125
Wayves (monthly, Halifax), 254–55
"We Demand" (brief presented to
government), 17, 22–23, 47, 278
Webster, Aaron, 233
Weil, Kathleen, 117
Wells, Kris, 177
Western Front (Vancouver), 233
Wilcox, Clyde, 27

Wildrose Party (Alberta), 164, 167–68,
176–78
Willow, Lindsay, 257–58
Wilson, Alexandria M., 67–68
Windsor, Ontario, 93
Winnipeg, Manitoba, 16, 19
Wittig, Monique, 8
Wolfenden Report (Britain, 1957),
12, 13, 15
women's movement and queer
activism, 287
Wong, Paul, 233
Woodside, Brad, 129–30
Woodstock High School, 137
World Outgames (Montreal, 2006), 193
World War II and same-sex
relationships, 13
Wynne, Kathleen, 3, 98, 143

Xtra! West (Vancouver), 234, 242–43
XY v. Ontario (2012), 58

Young, Pamela Dickey, 26
Yukon, 19, 95

Zald, Mayer N., 282
Zami (gay liberation group), 19

Printed and bound in Canada by Friesens
Set in Kozuka Gothic and Minion by Apex CoVantage, LLC
Copy editor: Joanne Richardson
Proofreader: Stephanie VanderMeulen
Indexer: Patricia Buchanan